*Oracle Press*™

# Oracle Backup & Recovery Handbook, 7.3 Edition

**International Information Technology Team**
24 Campus Plaza • Raritan Center
Edison, New Jersey 08837

Rama Velpuri

Osborne **McGraw-Hill**

Berkeley  New York  St. Louis  San Francisco
Auckland  Bogotá  Hamburg  London  Madrid
Mexico City  Milan  Montreal  New Delhi  Panama City
Paris  São Paulo  Singapore  Sydney  Tokyo  Toronto

Osborne **McGraw-Hill**
2600 Tenth Street
Berkeley, California 94710
U.S.A.

For information on translations or book distributors outside the U.S.A., or to arrange bulk purchase discounts for sales promotions, premiums, or fundraisers, please contact Osborne **McGraw-Hill** at the above address.

**Oracle Backup & Recovery Handbook, 7.3 Edition**

4567890 DOC 9987

ISBN 0-07-882323-4

**Publisher**
Brandon A. Nordin

**Editor in Chief**
Scott Rogers

**Project Editor**
Cynthia Douglas

**Proofreader**
Linda Medoff

**Computer Designer**
Peter Hancik

**Illustrator**
Rhys Elliott

**Series Design**
Jani Beckwith

**Quality Control Specialist**
Joe Scuderi

**Cover Design**
Ted Mader Associates

# About the Author

Rama Velpuri is the Director of the India Product Engineering Center (IPEC). Mr. Velpuri has been with Oracle for eight years. Before joining Product Division Operations, he worked in Oracle Worldwide Customer Support for seven years. He held various positions in Worldwide Support such as Manager of RDBMS and Languages Group, Manager of Escalation Center and Senior Manager of Premium Support group.

Over the years, Mr. Velpuri has helped hundreds of customers recover their databases. He has presented more than 15 technical papers on Disaster Recovery at various IOUW and other Oracle user conferences between 1988 and 1996. He designed an Oracle7 internals presentation in 1992 and has trained Oracle support personnel and customers in 15 different countries.

Mr. Velpuri has a Bachelor's degree in Electronics and Communications Engineering and a Master's degree in Electrical and Computer Engineering.

# Contents

# Foreword

**M**anaging a mission-critical operation amidst the pressures of globalization is a daunting task for any DBA or DBA team, and the growing complexity of software in an Open Systems environment only adds fuel to the fire. The Oracle7 server is no exception.

In order to provide users the option to compete in the global marketplace and take advantage of the Open Systems environment, Oracle has provided a highly flexible and tunable database engine. This flexibility comes at a price, however, because a DBA may not always know how to toggle all the switches and set all the dials properly for a particular configuration. More often than not, such tuning is geared toward performance and not toward backup and recovery issues. A proper and well tested backup strategy is a must for mission critical shops. This stategy, coupled with the knowledge of recovery mechanisms available through the Oracle7 Server software, makes for a well prepared DBA.

The author of this book has extensive experience in dealing with high-priority database recovery issues for some of Oracle's most demanding Fortune 500 customers. Together with a team of the "best and brightest" from Oracle Worldwide Support, Rama Velpuri has amassed a wealth of technical knowledge on the internals of Oracle7 backup and recovery issues. This day-to-day knowledge within Oracle Worldwide Support has never before been successfully compiled and documented, and this handbook will no doubt be useful not only for all Oracle

DBAs, but could also be a valuable training tool for new Oracle Worldwide Support technical analysts.

This book is a must for every Oracle DBA and system administrator, and will complement the existing Oracle7 Server Documentation.

Randy Baker
Senior Vice President
Worldwide Customer Support
Oracle Corporation

# Acknowledgments

**N**umerous people have helped me in many ways to make this book a reality. I would like to thank Tom Holmes, Vice President of Americas Support Operations, Randy Baker, Senior Vice President of Worldwide Support Operations, and Julie Gibbs, the editor of *ORACLE Magazine*, for encouraging me to write this book.

I would like to thank my family—Anuradha, Aruna, Raja, Ravi, Subrahmanyam, and Sudha, for all the support they have given me while writing this book. Thanks to my good friend Ramana Gogula for the inspiration he has given me in writing this book.

Thanks to the crew at Osborne/McGraw-Hill—Bob Myren, Project Editor, for the patience and support he showed me; Scott Rogers and Cindy Brown of the Acquisitions team, Jani Beckwith for production, proofreader Linda Medoff, and Scott Spanbauer for his developmental edit.

Thanks to Paul Nguyen for helping me write the Introduction, to Saar Maoz for writing and testing the VMS backup scripts, and to Susie Ehrsam and Sumant Chaudhari for providing me with the UNIX scripts for Chapter 4.

Thanks to Vinay Srihari for his input and technical review, and for testing some of the case studies for Chapter 7. Thanks to Andrea Borr for her technical review and input for Chapter 5. Thanks to Henry Ong for helping me with the outage analysis survey, done at various Oracle customer sites. And thanks also to Robert

Grant, Darryl Presley, and Anuradha Velpuri for their input. I would like to thank Lawrence To, Brian Quigley, and Basab Maulik for providing valuable information regarding standby databases.

The information in this book was culled from a number of sources. Technical bulletins written by Oracle Worldwide Support analysts were used. Some of the authors include Moe Fardoost, Ellen Tafeen, Walter Lindsay, Linda Fong, Tuomas Pystynen, Deepak Gupta, Sameer Patkar, Gita Gupta, Saleem Haque, Harmeet Bharara, Chitra Mitra, Ziad Dahbour, Darryl Presley, Roderick Manalac, Mark Ramacher, Vijay Oddiraju, Ramana Gourinani and, Lawrence To. E-mail messages sent by the staff of Server Technology were also used. Contributors include Jonathan Klein, Terry Hayes, Anurag Gupta, Bill Bridge, Greg Doherty, Greg Pongracz, Gary Hallmark, and Leng Leng Tan. Mary Moran's document on Backup and Recovery has provided the foundation for Chapter 3. "An Optimal Flexible Architecture for a growing Oracle database" by Oracle Core Technologies Services is used as a reference. Most of the Oracle7 Server documentation set was used, including the *Oracle7 Server Administrator's Guide, Oracle7 Server SQL Language Reference Manual, Oracle7 Server Concepts Manual, Oracle7 Server Utilites User's Guide* and the *Oracle7 Server Messages and Codes Manual.*

**This book is dedicated to my parents.**

# Introduction

The heartbeat of any company pulsates through its information system with a vital force that must be maintained for a healthy existence of the company. Much like the human body's health and resiliency to infections depend on the supply of oxygen carried through the blood stream, so does a company's success rely on its information system to supply critical data to all of its organizations for effective response to changing market conditions.

This comparison, though somewhat simplistic, nevertheless seems apt, as a company's success depends on the availability of its information system, and that this fact is often not realized until it is too late, and the information systems become unavailable—much like a person may ignore a potential health problem until it becomes a real problem to be dealt with. With this in mind, proper investment in planning and preparation must be made up front to deal with the inevitable systems failure whether by hardware, software, natural disasters, or otherwise.

If the information system is the vascular system providing life to a company, then the database engine—specifically, the Oracle Relational Database System—is the heart of the system. To properly maintain a healthy information system, certain measures must be taken to guard against systems failures affecting the Oracle RDBMS. These measures include backup planning and proper recovery procedures. The Oracle RDBMS is highly complex and configurable, and to make educated decisions in tailoring the backups to your business environment and information system, it is necessary to understand all the backup options available to you. Such decisions made up front will dictate or limit the options available for recovery if a crash occurs. This book gives details on how to tailor a backup plan and how to deal with systems failures affecting the Oracle RDBMS.

# Audience and Scope

Any Oracle user or any DBA who has installed an Oracle database will find this book useful. The discussions on backup and recovery procedures relate primarily to tools and environments built into Oracle that are available in any operating system. Taking backups in some special environments such as DSS (Decision Support System) and OLTP (OnLine Transaction Processing) is discussed as well. Operating system-specific topics relating to backup, and case studies of recovery will also be addressed. In addition to backup and recovery procedures, various diagnostic tools are also available. These tools, which help DBAs debug problems with the RDBMS, are also discussed in this book.

If you are a system administrator, and not an Oracle user or DBA, you can benefit as well from this book by reading the recommendations on how to plan for disaster recovery.

# How to Use This Book

This book focuses on Oracle background and specific operating system information that an Oracle DBA needs in order to plan a proper backup procedure. It also presents a short introduction to general Oracle concepts, pointing out the mechanisms built into Oracle that will be important for backup planning. General backup principles applicable to all operating systems are provided, with some discussions about the types of backups best suited for VLDB, DSS, OLTP, and OPS environments. You will also find operating system-specific details and issues relating to backups in VMS, MVS, UNIX, NetWare, OS/2, and WINDOWS NT, and recovery principles and hands-on strategies for failure analysis and Oracle recovery. Descriptions of available diagnostic facilities are provided, and lastly, you will find a number of case studies based on real-life backup and recovery situations.

The book is divided into 7 chapters and one appendix.

### Chapter 1: An Overview of Backup and Recovery
Chapter 1 gives an overview of Oracle backup and recovery procedures. It should prove to be helpful for any Oracle user or DBA.

## Chapter 2: The Oracle Architecture and Configuration

Chapter 2 gives an overview of the Oracle RDBMS from a backup and recovery perspective. The various database files that are installed on your system, database operation, and storage are discussed. In addition, this chapter discusses how to manage control files and online and archived redo log files. Experienced users may be able to skim this chapter or skip it altogether.

## Chapter 3: Backup Principles

Chapter 3 is organized into three sections. The first section describes physical and logical backups. The second section gives various backup commands and procedures in different operating systems. Some of the operating systems include: VMS, UNIX, MVS, NetWare, Windows NT and OS/2. The third section gives some tips on backups while running DSS and OLTP applications.

## Chapter 4: Backup Scripts in UNIX and VMS Environments

This chapter gives sample scripts to automate backup procedures in the VMS and UNIX environments. If you use Oracle in one if these environments, you should first go through the scripts to understand the logic, and then tailor them to suit your business needs (be sure to run them on a test machine). If you use Oracle on an operating system other than UNIX or VMS, you can still read the scripts to learn the logic and implement a similar scheme on your operating system.

## Chapter 5: Recovery Principles

This chapter describes the internal concepts and data structures related to recovery, and discusses various recovery methods. Some recommendations are also made that will help you plan for disaster recovery.

## Chapter 6: Diagnostic Facilities and Debugging the RDBMS

This chapter is primarily written to help DBAs understand the various diagnostic tools that Oracle provides. Reading this chapter will prepare you to diagnose all problems related to the RDBMS, such as data corruptions, memory corruptions, and performance issues.

## Chapter 7: Case Studies of Backup and Recovery

In this chapter, 15 case studies of backup and recovery are discussed. These case studies are based on different kinds of failures that have occurred in real life at customer sites, and recovery procedures that Oracle Worldwide Support has recommended. This chapter will give you an idea of the various failures that can occur at your site, and Oracle Worldwide Support's perspective on how to resolve such issues.

## Appendix A: New Features of Oracle7 Releases 7.1, 7.2, and 7.3

The appendix describes the new features that are introduced in Oracle7 releases 7.1, 7.2, and 7.3.

# CHAPTER 1

# An Overview of Backup and Recovery

In a last-gasp effort, an Oracle database administrator of a Fortune 500 financial firm escalates a call into Oracle Worldwide Support for a severity-one down database issue. The DBA had just spent several hours trying to recover a critical database amidst the turmoil of angry users, nervous managers, and frantic developers. "Help!" cries the DBA, "My database is down and I cannot restart it! People are on my back! Please help me bring the database back up!" Coming out of such systemic apoplexy depends on having an awareness of disaster recovery procedures.

# Why Plan Backups?

Planning and testing backup procedures for your Oracle database is the only insurance you have against failures of media, operating systems, software, and any other kind of failures that cause a serious crash resulting in loss of vital database files. The better a backup plan, the more choices available during recovery. Furthermore, a solid plan and rigorous testing will give you peace of mind and the tools to handle Oracle database recovery. Much like earthquake and fire drills, a proper backup and recovery procedure will require discipline and practice.

Backup planning is nothing new, but it has grown complicated due to constant adaptation to ever-changing technology. Client/server computing is rapidly becoming the computing environment of the 90's; but, for the information system organization, this change has complicated systems management tasks. Multiple customers call into Oracle Worldwide Support every day asking for help in bringing up their down production databases. The DBA's self-confidence in handling down production databases and the time it takes to bring the database back up—even with Oracle Worldwide Support's assistance—will depend on the types of backups that are available.

More often than not, a solid, well-tested backup strategy is *not* practiced at most Oracle sites. In a study conducted by the Core Technology Center within Oracle Worldwide Support, a majority of the severity-one recovery-related technical assistance requests result in incomplete recovery (based on the report, "Severity 1/Down System TAR Evaluation," by Core Technology Center, March, 1994). Recovering lost database files depends a great deal on the backup strategy employed, and backup strategies vary according to operating systems and application environments.

# What Causes Systems to Fail?

On large systems, managing a multi-gigabyte database in a complex client/server environment is a daunting task. Software and hardware components must cooperate with precise timing in order to provide information to an end-user. Consider, for example, a simple SQL query over SQL*NET. In a split second, the SQL command is parsed in SQL*PLUS, passed from the application to the operating system, where it is broken into packages by a network layer, and transmitted over ethernet to the server. At the server, the packages are recompiled and shipped from the host network layer to the host operating system, finally arriving at the server program. And this is just the transmission process. Once the database server receives the request, there are still many more processes that need to happen before data is finally ready for shipping back to the client machine. Add to that the millions of electronic switches flipping continuously within this split second. What can possibly go wrong?

According to IEEE, outages are classified into outage types and can be grouped into the following categories:

■ Physical

■ Design (software bug)

■ Operations

■ Environment

*Physical outages* are usually caused by hardware failures, such as media failure or a CPU failure. *Design outages* are caused by software failures, more commonly known as *software bugs*. Any software bug, whether in the operating system, database software, or application software, contributes to a design outage. *Operation outages*, on the other hand, are caused by human intervention. Some examples of operation outages are failures attributed to poor DBA skills, user errors, inappropriate system setup, or inadequate backup procedures. Finally, an *Environmental outage* is an outage due to external environmental concerns, such as earthquakes, power surges, and abnormal temperature conditions.

A DBA can exert the most control over operation outages. While a DBA may not be able to predict physical, design, or environment problems, he or she must be prepared for outages that they cause. The DBA should plan a solid backup procedure and periodically test the procedure for updating as the database grows. In addition, DBAs can also prepare for outages by practicing recovery methods through simulating outages on test systems.

To err is human, but many of our mistakes can be minimized if we plan for them by preparing appropriately. For example, consider the following operations problems and the steps a DBA can take to minimize outages.

| PROBLEM | LIKELY FIX |
| --- | --- |
| Poor DBA skills | Train and certify DBAs and improve documentation. |
| User errors | Increase database security, bulletproof software. |
| Inappropriate database setup | Plan upgrades, implement a test system, and control changes. |
| Inadequate backup procedures | Plan and test backup procedures. |

# Hardware Protection and Redundancy

Given the growing complexity of today's software—and Oracle is no exception—it is very important to consider protecting hardware and systems by building systems redundancy. Especially with high-availability or mission-critical systems, even a few minutes of down time can be very costly in terms of business lost. (Consider, for example, the millions of dollars lost when an airline booking system is down during high season.) Many corporations apply various, and sometimes drastic, measures to ensure high availability of systems. Some of these techniques are

- UPS, or uninterrupted power supply
- Disk mirroring, or RAID technology
- On-site spare parts
- Redundant switch-over systems or switch-over sites

Obviously, there will be cost and performance factors to consider before implementing one or more of these hardware protection methods. Each site will have to consider this issue and budget accordingly. Some of these techniques are described in Chapter 5.

# ARCHIVELOG Mode Versus NOARCHIVELOG Mode

One of the most important decisions that a DBA has to make is to decide whether to run the database in ARCHIVELOG mode or not. The archive log files contain the changes made to the database. There are advantages and disadvantages to running a database in ARCHIVELOG mode. The advantages are

- Since all changes made to the database are stored in the log files, if the database files are lost due to any kind of failure including media failures, you can use the physical backup (offline or online backup) and the archive log files to completely recover the database without losing any data. All committed transactions can be retrieved. In version 6, the one way that committed transactions could be lost was by losing the online log files. However, with Oracle7, multiplexing of online redo log files will resolve this problem.

- It is possible to take online (hot) backups. This will allow users to use the database while backup of the database is being performed.

- Tablespaces can be taken offline immediately.

- If all nodes of a distributed database system are running in ARCHIVELOG mode, it's possible to do distributed recovery.

The disadvantages are as follows:

- Additional disk space is required to store the archived log files.

- The DBA will have more administrative work to maintain the archive log destination and make sure that the archive log files are copied to tape. If enough disk space is not available in the archive log destination, the database will hang; and unless the online log files are archived, the database will not resume normal operation.

Chapter 2 gives details on managing online redo logs and ARCHIVELOG administration.

The following are the ramifications of running the database in NOARCHIVELOG mode:

- Due to loss of data files, if recovery is required, the DBA can restore only to the last offline backup. Any changes made to the database since then will be lost. Therefore, more frequent offline backups need to be performed.

- Since you cannot take online backups, the database is not available during offline backups.

- Tablespaces cannot be taken offline immediately.

- Less administrative work is required for DBAs.

# Diagnostic Facilities and Debugging the RDBMS

The Oracle RDBMS is a complicated piece of software engineering. Its stability depends not only on its internal programming, but on the environment in which it is running. When error conditions occur while running applications or in the RDBMS, the source of the error may require some investigation to uncover. Error messages printed to the users' terminals often give a good indication of what the problem is, but quite often these messages are cleared from the screen before being recorded by the user.

To allow better problem diagnosing, the Oracle system dumps information to *trace files*. These trace files contain many types of structured information dumps, as well as some standard messages that mark the occurrence of normal events. Errors are internally categorized according to severity. Fatal errors produce stack traces but some less severe errors might not. While diagnosing such problems, it might be necessary for Oracle Worldwide Support analysts to provide some diagnostic events that will capture diagnostic data during the next failure.

Oracle7 provides a wide variety of diagnostics events, SQL commands, SQL scripts, INIT.ORA parameters, and programs for data capture during failures. The DBA should be familiar with all diagnostic capabilities provided by the Oracle system. Chapter 6 discusses various types of information dumps and messages contained in trace files. Some helpful diagnostic utilities will also be discussed. Familiarity with the basic contents of the trace files and understanding when to use what diagnostic tool/command will allow the DBA to capture and provide complete diagnostic data before calling Oracle Worldwide Support.

# Overview of Backups

Taking backups of an Oracle database is similar to buying insurance on your car—you won't realize the importance of it unless you get into an accident, and the amount of coverage you have depends on the kind of insurance policy you have. Similarly, the type and frequency of your backups determine the speed and success of recovery. Various backup methods exist today; the DBA needs to determine what kind of backup procedures are required for his or her site. This section gives an overview of various backup types commonly used by Oracle DBAs.

Backups can be broadly categorized into physical backups and logical backups. A physical backup is a backup where the actual physical database files are copied from one location to the other (usually from disk to tape). Operating system backups, cold backups, and hot backups are examples of a physical backup. Logical backups are backups that extract the data using SQL from the database and store it in a binary file. This data can be imported back into the same database or a different database at a later time. The Export/Import utility provided by Oracle can be used to take logical backups of a database.

## Operating System Backups

This type of backup is the simplest to perform, but is also very time consuming and requires making the system unavailable. The procedure involves shutting down the database and logging all users off the system. Once all access is removed, the system is brought down and restarted in single-user (maintenance) mode, in which control is only available to the administrator at the system console. This step ensures that no user application software is running, which might modify data on the disks. Since the backup process is the only process reading data from the disk, you are assured that the data on the disk is consistent with the point in time when the system was taken down for backup. If this backup were to be used to restore a system, all changes to system configuration, user data, user files—essentially any modifications made to the disk since the last backup—would be lost.

This backup can be supplemented with other backups to build a more flexible backup strategy. For example, in an environment where the system files remain static and changes are made only to user files, a complete operating system backup can be augmented with more frequent backups of the user files. It is common practice for system managers to do operating system backups, and for DBAs to take backups of the Oracle database files.

A common strategy employs full operating system backups weekly, and daily backups of user files. The steps involved in this type of backup procedure are as follows:

1. Shut down everything.

   ■ Shut down all applications and then the Oracle RDBMS.

   ■ If in a multi-user environment, shut down the system and bring it back up in single-user mode.

2. Back up all files.

   ■ In single-user mode, back up all disks to tape using an OS utility.

3. Start up the system.

   ■ Bring the system up in multi-user mode.

   ■ Start up the Oracle database and the applications.

## Cold Database Backups

*Cold* database backups involve shutting down the Oracle database in normal mode and backing up all required Oracle database files. This kind of backup is also known as an *offline* backup. These two terms will be used interchangeably throughout this book. The offline backup procedure is similar to operating system backups, except only a subset of the disk files are backed up to tape—the Oracle-related files. Although users can still access the system at the OS level, access to the Oracle database is not allowed. It is also important to shut down any other in-house or third-party software that may be modifying Oracle files, before shutting the database. Once Oracle is unavailable, back up all Oracle files to tape and start up the Oracle database. In some cases, it might not be possible for DBAs to do a normal shutdown of the database before taking the cold backup. In such cases, the DBAs usually shut down the database using the IMMEDIATE option, then bring the database up in DBA mode, and finally shut it down gracefully.

The steps involved in this type of backup procedure are as follows:

1. Shut down Oracle.

   ■ Shut down all Oracle-related in-house or third-party software running on top of Oracle.

   ■ Shut down the Oracle RDBMS in normal mode.

2. Back up Oracle files.

   ■ Back up Oracle executables/code, configuration files, and control files.

   ■ Back up all Oracle data files and online redo log files.

3. Start up Oracle in normal mode.

## The HOT Backup

A *hot* backup is one taken while the Oracle database is open and operating in ARCHIVELOG mode. This kind of backup is also known as *online* backup. Although this allows users to access the database during the backup process, care must be taken to schedule this backup procedure during a time when the load on the Oracle database is low. For example, try not to take a backup of the database when a large update batch job is running, as it would generate more redo compared to the time when the data file is not in hot backup mode. Another option would be to schedule the batch job, if possible, after the backup procedure is complete.

The hot backup procedure consists of backing up all data files belonging to a particular tablespace or tablespaces, the archived redo logs, and the control file.

The steps involved in this type of backup procedure are as follows:

1. Perform an online backup of the tablespace.

2. Back up the archived redo logs.

3. Back up the control file.

**NOTE**
The above procedure must be performed for each tablespace in the database, and while the database is up and in ARCHIVELOG mode.

# The Logical Backup—Export

The *logical backup,* or *Export,* creates a logical copy of database objects and stores it in a binary file. Unlike physical backups, the Export utility actually reads the data in the objects using SQL and stores the data in the binary file. The Import utility uses this file to restore these particular database objects back into the database. So, the Export utility and the Import utility together allow DBAs to back up and recover particular database objects within the database and/or move an object from one database into another.

This backup mechanism does not provide point-in-time recovery and cannot be used with archived redo log files. There is no notion of importing a table and rolling it forward using redo log files. The archived redo log files are part of the physical online backups that record specific information about changes made to the data blocks on disk. The export file is essentially a file recording the SQL commands that the Import utility feeds to the Oracle SQL layer for processing. For example, an export of a table would create an export file which contains CREATE TABLE and INSERT statements. When the table is recovered using the Import utility, import would use the CREATE TABLE command to recreate the table and the INSERT statements to insert the rows back into the table using SQL.

If a particular database block is corrupted on disk for whatever reason, a physical backup would make a copy of the block, and the error would be propagated to the backup copy as well. One of the advantages of using a logical backup is that no such corruptions will be propagated to the backup due to the fact that a full table scan is performed while exporting a table. So in this case, such corruptions will be detected while exporting, and the export will fail. At that point, the DBA will need to take corrective action before making a backup again.

The steps involved in this type of backup procedure are as follows:

1. While the database is running, use the Export utility to export, for example, a table.

2. Once an export file is created, copy the export file off to tape.

**NOTE**
An export of a table will give a read-consistent view of the table at the time the export was initiated. Any changes made to the table during the export will not be incorporated into the export file.

# Automating Backups

Once backup procedures have been planned and well tested, it may be necessary to automate them—especially for hot backups of a large database. A hot backup of a database with many tablespaces will be tedious and error prone; therefore, automating the process using an OS script will make things more manageable. In Chapter 4, we discuss in detail how to write OS scripts to automate backups, but it is important to note a couple rules here.

### Flexibility
In order to avoid unnecessary maintenance, do not make the scripts dependent on the object names in the database. To accomplish this, use SQL queries against the database dictionary to dynamically generate backup scripts.

### Logging
It is also very important to tag each backup with a timestamp for proper identification during recovery, and to track the progress through logging. Timestamps for each step in the backup script should be logged into a backup script log file, which can be used by the administrator to verify that a backup procedure ran successfully.

# Overview of Recovery

Sometimes DBAs might feel that the number of recovery options provided by Oracle are overwhelming. It is true that there are a lot of ways recovery could be performed, even for a particular failure. However, every recovery option provided by Oracle is very important and has its own use, and it is crucial that DBAs understand how each recovery option works. Once the concepts of recovery are understood, then even though a lot of recovery options exist, it becomes quite clear to the DBAs what kind of recovery procedure to use during various kinds of failures.

## Types of Errors

A major responsibility of the database administrator is to maintain the up time of a database, and to prepare for the possibility of hardware, software, network, process, and system failure. In the event of a failure, the DBA should also be prepared to bring the database back to operation as quickly as possible, and with little or no data loss. If properly planned, recovery will be a smooth operation, thereby protecting the users and the database. Recovery processes vary, depending on the type of failure that has occurred, the structures that have been affected, and the type of recovery that is desired.

Some failures might cause the database to go down; some others might be trivial. Similarly, on the recovery side, some recovery procedures require DBA intervention, whereas some of the internal recovery mechanisms are transparent to the DBA. For example, if a process dies abnormally while modifying a block,

Oracle will do a block-level recovery, which is automatic and doesn't require human intervention. On the other hand, if a data file has been lost, recovery requires additional steps. Some of the common errors or failures include

- User error
- Statement failure
- Process failure
- Network failure
- Instance failure
- Media failure

## User Error

A user deleting a row or dropping a table are typical examples of user error. There are two issues to be considered here. The users and DBAs should be properly trained on administering the databases and developing applications. Furthermore, the DBAs should have proper backup and recovery procedures for recovering from user errors, which should be tested on test systems at regular intervals. In the above example, recovering a dropped table could be done in several ways; which procedure to choose depends on the amount of data you need to recover. The recovery procedure might be as simple as importing from a logical backup, or might involve a more complicated procedure such as doing point-in-time recovery from a physical backup on a test machine, exporting the table, and finally importing it into the production database. If the latter procedure needs to be performed, the DBA should have a physical backup of the database and all the archive log files.

## Statement Failures

A *statement failure* can be defined as the inability by Oracle to execute a SQL statement. While running a user program, a transaction might have multiple statements and one of the statements might fail due to various reasons. Typical examples are selecting from a table that doesn't exist, or trying to do an insert and having the statement fail due to unavailable space in the table. Such statement failures normally generate error codes by the application software or the operating system. Recovery from such failures is automatic. Upon detection, Oracle usually will roll back the statement, returning control to the user or user program. The user can simply re-execute the statement after correcting the problem conveyed by the error message.

## Process Failures

A *process failure* is an abnormal termination of a process. This could be caused either by Oracle itself, or by the user (such as when a user performs a ^C from

SQL*PLUS). If the process that is terminated is a user process, server process, or an application process, the Process Monitor (PMON) performs process recovery. PMON is responsible for cleaning up the cache and freeing resources that the process was using. Some of the work done by PMON includes resetting the status of the transaction table in the rollback segment for that transaction, releasing the locks or latches acquired by the terminated process, and removing the process ID from the list of active processes.

PMON doesn't clean up the processes that have been killed by Oracle. If a background process is terminated abnormally, Oracle must be shut down and restarted. During startup, crash recovery is automatically performed to do the roll forward and transaction recovery will roll back any uncommitted transactions.

## Network Failures

*Network failures* can occur while using a client-server configuration or a distributed database system where multiple database servers are connected by communication networks. Network failures such as communications software failures or aborted asynchronous (phone) connections will interrupt the normal operation of the database system. Sometimes, network failures will in turn cause process failures. In such cases PMON will roll back the uncommitted work of the process. If a distributed transaction is involved in a network failure, this would create an in-doubt transaction on one or more nodes. (A *distributed transaction* is a transaction that is executed in a distributed environment.) Once the connection is reestablished, the RECO background process resolves such conflicts automatically.

## Instance Failure

An *instance failure* can be caused by a physical (hardware) or a design (software) problem—for example, when one of the database background processes (DBWR) detects that there is a problem on the disk and can't write to it. In situations like this, an error message is written to a log file (and might also create a trace file, depending on the severity of the problem) and the background process terminates. In this case, you need to shut down the instance and restart it. Crash recovery or instance recovery is automatic.

Depending on the amount of work that is being done at the time of the failure, database instance failures might take a long time to recover. For example, suppose a transaction has updated a huge table and decided to roll back, but before the transaction finished rolling back, the instance fails. Crash recovery has to do roll forward and then transaction recovery has to roll the transaction back, which might take a long period of time.

## Media Failures

*Media failures* are the most dangerous failures. Not only is there potential to lose data if proper backup procedures are not followed, but it usually takes more time to recover than with other kinds of failures. In addition, the DBA's experience is a very important factor in determining the kind of media recovery procedure to use to bring the database up quickly, with little or no data loss. A typical example of a media failure is a disk controller failure or a disk head crash, which causes all Oracle database files residing on that disk (or disks) to be lost. Every DBA needs to plan appropriate backup procedures to protect against media failures. This is probably the most important responsibility of a DBA.

There are a lot of factors that determine recovery time, such as how fast data can be transferred from tape to disk, how often backups are taken, the size of the database, the kind of failure that occurred, and what kind of media recovery needs to be applied.

A detailed look at outage classes and specifically backup and recovery–related errors will be discussed in the "Failure Analysis" section of Chapter 5.

# Types of Recovery

There are three types of recovery mechanism that Oracle uses: block-level recovery, thread recovery, and media recovery.

*Block-level recovery* is the simplest type of recovery, and is automatically done by Oracle. It is done when a process dies just as it is changing a buffer. The online redo logs for the current thread are used to reconstruct the buffer and write it to disk.

*Thread recovery* is done automatically by Oracle when it discovers that an instance died leaving a thread open. Thread recovery is performed as part of either crash recovery or instance recovery. If the database has a single instance, then crash recovery is performed. This requires the DBA simply to start up the database and crash recovery is automatically performed by Oracle. If multiple instances are accessing the database and if one of the instances crashes, the second instance automatically performs instance recovery to recover the first thread. Either way, the goal of thread recovery is to restore the data block changes that were in the cache of the instance that died, and to close the thread that was left open. Thread recovery always uses the online redo log files of the thread it is recovering.

The third type of recovery is *media recovery*. It is only done in response to a recovery command. It is used to make backup data files become current, or to restore changes that were lost when a data file went offline without a checkpoint. During media recovery, archived logs—as well as online log files—can be applied.

Though all media recovery procedures use the same algorithm, choosing the right kind of recovery procedure can reduce the mean time to recover. Chapter 5 discusses in detail the fundamental concepts of recovery and describes various recovery strategies. In addition, Chapter 7 gives some real-life examples.

## Recovery with Physical Backups

If the database is operating in NOARCHIVELOG mode, recovery with physical backups involves restoring the data files and starting up the database. There is no roll forward involved. If the database is operating in ARCHIVELOG mode, recovery involves multiple steps. First, the lost data files need to be restored from tape to disk (or disk to disk). The next step is to apply the changes from redo log files to the data files. You can do this in one of three ways: *database recovery, tablespace recovery,* or *data file recovery*. There are special SQL commands for each of the above methods.

Which recovery method to use primarily depends on which files are lost as part of the media failure. For example, if you lose your online or archived log files, and you don't have a mirror copy, then you must do *incomplete recovery*, which means that some of the data will be lost. This will limit your choices since data file or tablespace recovery cannot be performed if doing incomplete recovery. This example shows that there are some restrictions in using each of the above methods. For example, if you decide to perform database recovery, then the database needs to be mounted but not open. However, if you decide to do data file recovery, you can take the data file in question offline, start up the database, and recover the data file. The advantage in doing this is that a portion of the database can be used by users while you perform recovery on a specific data file.

To summarize, two factors that influence the DBA in choosing one recovery method over the others are

- Can I do complete recovery, or do I have to do incomplete recovery?

- Do I want part of the database open while doing recovery or not?

Chapter 5 gives a detailed discussion of the various recovery methods and how to decide which method to choose.

## Recovery with Logical Backups

The Export/Import utility is very easy to use, and a lot of DBAs use this utility to back up and recover their databases. Some DBAs do weekly exports in addition to the physical backups that they normally perform. For customers with large databases or high availability requirements, the Export/Import utility for backup and recovery purposes might not be feasible due to the performance reasons. One should note that Export and Import (unlike the fast loader) use the SQL layer for data transfer. Chapter 3 discusses the feasibility of using logical backups.

Database Recovery ———> ⓪ Startup mount

Datafile Recovery ———> 1 take the datafile offline
[a portion of database         2 Startup database
can be used by users          3 Recover the datafile
while you perform
recovery on a datafile]        4 Bring the datafile online

# CHAPTER 2

# The Oracle Architecture and Configuration

**B**efore we discuss backup and recovery strategies, it is important to understand some basic concepts of Oracle and the Oracle system's architecture. This information is detailed in the *Oracle7 Server Concepts Manual*, but will be briefly presented here with a perspective on backup and recovery.

# Oracle Files on Your System

An understanding of the various Oracle files and their locations on the disk is necessary for backup planning. Various files are created on your system after an Oracle install, and you, the DBA, should take time to locate and note where these files reside. The most important files to note are the control files, data files, online redo log files, archive redo log files, the initialization parameter file, and the Oracle code. A full operating system backup will include all of these files; however, for partial backups, subsets of these files will be backed up in varying frequencies. Let's take a closer look at how each of these types of files fits into the big picture.

## The Oracle Code

When the Oracle software is installed on your system, various subdirectories and files are created. Installation procedures are operating system-dependent. For example, on the UNIX operating system, all the Oracle related subdirectories and files are created under the main directory ORACLE_HOME. The subdirectories include **dbs**, **bin**, **rdbms**, and so on. In addition, one subdirectory is created for each Oracle product installed as well. These subdirectories include files such as the Oracle executables and various SQL scripts, which are crucial for database operation and administration and are generally referred to as the *Oracle code*. The Oracle executables are the set of program files that make up the database engine and the various tools that work with the engine to provide a data access channel to the data in the database. These are the files that start up the Oracle processes, run applications such as SQL*DBA and SQL*PLUS, and numerous other tools that are included in the installation package. Since these files do not change, a one-time backup of these files should be adequate. Every time the software version of Oracle is upgraded, these executables are replaced by new ones. An initial full operating system backup or partial backup of just the executables taken after an install would be advisable. The backup strategy should also include taking backup of these files after every Oracle version upgrade.

## The Data Files

The *data files* make up the physical repository for all the data in the database. Oracle divides the data files into numerous logical entities with the smallest unit being an Oracle block. As part of the database creation, Oracle creates the SYSTEM data file, which contains system tables known as the *data dictionary*. As the database grows and more space is needed, the DBA needs to create and add more data files to the database. These files are a major concern for backup and space management. (Space management and data files are discussed later in this chapter.)

# The Redo Log Files

The *redo log files* are used by Oracle to record changes made to the database during normal operation. Since these files are open, or *online,* during normal operation of the database, they are commonly referred to as the *online redo log files.* These files are used by Oracle during recovery to reapply the changes made to the database in the event such changes were not permanently written to the data files on disk at the time of the failure. Oracle DBAs have a choice to run the database in the ARCHIVELOG mode or the NOARCHIVELOG mode. If the former is chosen, contents of the online redo log files are copied to an archive area by one of the Oracle background processes. These archive files are known as the *archived redo log files,* or simply, *archived redo.* These files are sometimes referred to as the *offline redo log files* since they are not open during normal operation of the database and are required only during media recovery. The redo log files (online and archived) are essential for database recovery since they contain information on all changes made to the database. If the database is chosen to operate in NOARCHIVELOG mode, *online backups* and database media recovery will not be possible. The backup strategy you design should include copying archived redo log files to tape periodically.

# The Control File

The control file is a very important piece of the database. This file contains the schema of the database. The names, location, status, and states of all the data files and online redo log files are recorded in the control file. Similar to the data files and online log files, the control file is essential for normal operation of the database. As part of the database startup procedure, Oracle reads the control file to locate the data files and online log files. If the control file is lost due to a media failure, a new control file can be created. This is discussed in detail in Chapter 5. This would cause some down time of the database, so it is suggested to maintain at least three copies of the control file, each on a separate disk drive mounted under different controllers. As part of the backup procedures, in addition to the data files and log files, the control file should be copied as well. There is a special SQL command available to back up the control file while taking online backups.

# The INIT.ORA File

As part of the software distribution, Oracle provides an *initialization parameter* file called INIT.ORA. This file contains the Oracle system parameters and should be used by the DBA to customize the RDBMS configuration at a specific site. Oracle reads this file during database startup to determine the size of the system global area (discussed later in this chapter) and to locate the control files, among other things. Since the control and INIT.ORA files are crucial for database startup, they should be backed up frequently. Since the size of these files is negligible, it is also advisable to keep online copies of these files. For a complete listing of the INIT.ORA parameters, refer to Appendix A of the *Oracle7 Server Administrator's Guide*. Among other things, the INIT.ORA parameters are used to do the following:

■ Tune the memory

■ Set diagnostic events to obtain trace files

■ Trace the SQL statements

■ Indicate the location of the control files and the trace files

■ Distribute the PCM locks if using the Parallel Server option

## The Oracle Trace Files

For purposes of problem diagnosis and application tuning, Oracle creates text files called *trace files*. Each Oracle background process can write to an associated trace file when appropriate. These files are commonly known as *background trace files*. The user processes can create trace files as well, and these files are called the *user trace files*. The location where the background and user trace files are created can be controlled by setting the appropriate INIT.ORA parameter. All the background trace files are created in a directory specified by the BACKGROUND_DUMP_DEST parameter. Similarly, the USER_DUMP_DEST parameter determines where the user trace files are created. Oracle automatically creates trace files when internal Oracle errors occur. In addition, a DBA can force Oracle to create trace files by setting various *diagnostic events* in the INIT.ORA file or by issuing the **alter session** statement while connected to the database, from SQL*DBA or SQL*PLUS. Note that if the INIT.ORA file is used to create trace files, tracing will be turned on at a database-wide level, whereas the **alter session** command will turn on tracing only at a session level. This behavior could change in the future releases of Oracle. Chapter 6 deals with setting diagnostic events and various other diagnostic tools that are available to the DBA for debugging the RDBMS.

One of the common INIT.ORA parameters used by application developers is SQL_TRACE. When this parameter is set to TRUE, every SQL statement that is executed in the database will be traced and the information is written to a trace file. Alternatively, SQL tracing can be turned on at a session level by typing the following command:

```
SQL> ALTER SESSION SET SQL_TRACE = TRUE;
```

The trace directory needs to be regularly examined every day to see if Oracle has created any important trace files. DBAs should delete the unwanted trace files and save the ones that are important. It is a good practice to archive the trace files to tape on a regular basis. Some DBAs automate these procedures.

For other important configuration files specific to your environment, refer to the *Installation and User's Guide* for your operating system.

Figure 2-1 gives the locations of all Oracle files in a typical OFA (Optimal Flexible Architecture) compliant structure (UNIX example).

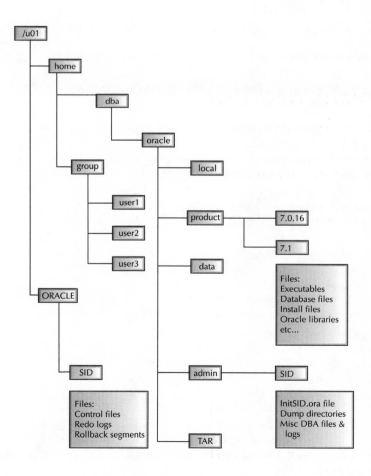

**FIGURE 2-1.** *Oracle files in the Optimal Flexible Architecture*

# Database Operation

It is important to understand the functions of the various Oracle processes and the different players involved during database operation. These processes, files, and shared memory areas make up the Oracle database server, and a basic understanding of the roles of each player will be vital in problem diagnostics during database recovery.

## The System Global Area

The *system global area* (or SGA) is a piece of memory allocated by Oracle. All the memory structures that reside in the system global area are shared by concurrent users connected to the instance. This is why the system global area is commonly referred to as the *shared global area*. When the database is started, information regarding the SGA is displayed by Oracle. The following example shows the output when the Oracle database is started.

```
SQL*DBA: Release 7.1.3.2.0 - Production on Wed Feb 22 15:06:42 1995

Copyright (c) Oracle Corporation 1979, 1992.  All rights reserved.

ORACLE7 Server Release 7.1.3.2.0 - Production Release
With the distributed, parallel query and Parallel Server options
PL/SQL Release 2.1.3.2.0 - Production

SQLDBA> Connect internal
Connected.
SQLDBA> Startup
ORACLE instance started.
Database mounted.
Database opened.
Total System Global Area      4817708 bytes
    Fixed Size                  28376 bytes
    Variable Size             3904536 bytes
    Database Buffers           819200 bytes
    Redo Buffers                65596 bytes
SQLDBA>
```

Alternatively, the DBA can issue a **show sga** command from SQL*DBA to examine the SGA size. For example,

```
SQLDBA> show sga
Total System Global Area       4817708 bytes
      Fixed Size                 28376 bytes
      Variable Size            3904536 bytes
      Database Buffers          819200 bytes
      Redo Buffers               65596 bytes
```

The INIT.ORA file is read as part of the database startup and the size of the SGA is determined. The SGA contains a *fixed size* portion and a *variable size* portion. The fixed size portion of the SGA contains the database- and instance-specific information that is needed by the background processes. This portion of the SGA is not tunable. The size of the fixed portion of the SGA might change between different versions of the database. This size could also vary between different UNIX platforms due to different *alignment procedures.* The *variable size* portion of the SGA consists of arrays of variables that are allocated based upon some INIT.ORA parameters. This variable size of the SGA is tunable, using the INIT.ORA parameters. The INIT.ORA parameters that most affect the SGA size are the following:

- DB_BLOCK_SIZE

- DB_BLOCK_BUFFERS

- LOG_BUFFERS

- SHARED_POOL_SIZE

The DB_BLOCK_SIZE is specified in bytes, and represents the size of an Oracle block. DB_BLOCK_BUFFERS is the total number of buffers in the SGA, each with a size of DB_BLOCK_SIZE. So DB_BLOCK_SIZE * DB_BLOCK_BUFFERS gives the total amount of space allocated in the SGA to cache data blocks. Since this portion of the SGA caches the database information, this area is also known as the *buffer cache.* Data blocks are usually read into the buffer cache for two reasons: either to read the buffer, or to modify the buffer. The modified buffers in the SGA are commonly referred to as the *dirty buffers.* There are various lists that Oracle maintains for the buffers in the buffer cache. The *dirty list* contains the list of all the dirty buffers that haven't yet been written back to the disk. All the dirty buffers will be flushed back to the disk at a later time and this event is called a *checkpoint.* There are various ways in which a checkpoint can be triggered. We will discuss this concept in greater detail in Chapter 5.

LOG_BUFFERS is specified in bytes, and represents the amount of space allocated for the redo log buffer. This is the area where any changes made to the data blocks are recorded before they are flushed to the redo log file on disk. The

SHARED_POOL_SIZE is specified in bytes as well, and this is the amount of space in the SGA allocated to shared SQL and PL/SQL statements.

The following INIT.ORA parameters minimally impact the size of the SGA. For a complete listing and explanation of the INIT.ORA parameters, refer to Appendix A of the *Oracle7 Server Administrator's Guide*

- DB_FILES
- DB_FILE_MULTIBLOCK_READ_COUNTS
- DML_LOCKS
- ENQUEUE_RESOURCES
- PROCESSES
- SEQUENCE_CACHE_ENTRIES
- SEQUENCE_CACHE_HASH_BUCKETS
- SESSIONS
- TRANSACTIONS
- TRANSACTIONS_PER_ROLLBACK_SEGMENT

## Oracle Processes

A *process* of an operating system is a thread of control that executes a piece of code. Every process has a private memory area in which it runs. Some operating systems support running multiple processes concurrently, and some don't. In a single process Oracle instance, the Oracle code is executed by a single process. This means only one user can access the database at any given point in time—multiple users cannot access the database concurrently. An example is the DOS operating system.

On the other hand, in a multi-process Oracle instance, several processes execute different parts of the Oracle code concurrently, and each process has a specific job to do. In this environment, the processes can be categorized into two groups: *user processes* and *Oracle processes*. A process that is created to run a user application or an Oracle tool is called a user process. Oracle processes can be further subdivided into two types: *Oracle server processes* and *Oracle background processes.* In some operating systems such as VMS (single-task environment), the user process and the server process are combined into a single process. On operating systems such as UNIX (two-task environment), for every user process, a server process exists. The Oracle background processes along with the SGA is generally called the *Oracle instance.* Let's take a closer look at the various tasks handled by the Oracle processes.

The server process (in a two-task environment) or user process (in a single-task environment) is responsible for parsing and executing the SQL statements issued by the application. Also, when the user issues a **select** statement, and if the blocks to be read are not in the SGA, the server/user process is responsible for reading those blocks from disk into the SGA. Once a SQL statement is parsed and executed, data is fetched from the block. The server/user process is responsible for returning this data back to the application.

In a multi-process Oracle instance (with the two-task environment), the DBA can configure the database to operate with a *dedicated server* or a *multi-threaded server.* In the former, every user process will have a dedicated server process to execute the Oracle code on its behalf. The dedicated server serves only one user process. In the latter, multiple user processes are serviced by a few *shared server processes.* All the user processes are connected to a special process known as the *dispatcher process.* The dispatcher process routes user process requests to the next available shared server process. The advantage of using the multi-threaded configuration is to reduce the overhead of running too many processes on the system. For example, if 50 user processes are running applications in a dedicated server configuration, 50 server processes need to be established to serve the user processes, taking the total number of processes running on the system to 100. If the database is configured to operate as a multi-threaded server with 10 shared servers, then the total number of processes running on the system will be 61 (50 user processes + 10 shared processes +1 dispatcher). We have assumed, in this example, that the user processes are running on the same machine as the server processes. Various INIT.ORA parameters are available to configure the multi-threaded server.

The Oracle background processes have different tasks and interact with different parts of the database. Note that all the Oracle background processes are not present in all environments. The number of Oracle background processes running on a server depends on the type of database configuration chosen by the DBA. The following is a complete list of all the Oracle background processes followed by a brief description of each process.

- Database writer (DBWR)
- Log writer (LGWR)
- Checkpoint (CKPT)
- System monitor (SMON)
- Process monitor (PMON)
- Archiver (ARCH)

■ Recoverer (RECO)

■ Lock (LCKn)

■ Dispatcher (Dnnn)

■ Server (Snnn)

The *database writer process* (DBWR) is responsible for writing data blocks from the database buffer cache to the data files on disk using an LRU (least recently used) algorithm. Committed transactions do not force DBWR to write blocks to disk; however, DBWR is optimized to minimize disk I/O by only writing to disk when needed due to demand on SGA memory by other transactions. While using the Parallel Server option (the Parallel Server option is discussed at the end of this chapter), it might be necessary for one instance's DBWR process to write a dirty buffer to disk because a user needs to modify the same buffer from another instance. This operation is known as *pinging*. Pinging is a major concern in designing applications on a database running with the Parallel Server option because pinging will keep the DBWR process very busy, thus degrading database performance. The DBWR process is essential for normal operation of the database and is automatically started when the instance is started.

The *log writer process* (LGWR) is responsible for writing redo log entries from the redo log buffer to the redo log files on disk. LGWR also updates the headers of control files and data files to reflect the latest *checkpoint* when the checkpoint process is not present. The LGWR process is required for normal operation of the database and is automatically started when the instance is started.

The *checkpoint process* (CKPT) sends a signal to the DBWR at checkpoint and updates the headers of control files and data files. Enabling this background process is optional and can be done by using the INIT.ORA parameter CHECKPOINT_PROCESS. If this process is not present, the LGWR process performs the tasks of the CKPT process. By default, this process is not enabled. It is recommended to enable this process where there are many data files.

The *system monitor* process (SMON) of an instance performs recovery when another instance belonging to this database (Parallel Server) has crashed or has terminated abnormally. The SMON process also cleans up *temporary segments* not in use, and recovers dead transactions skipped during crash/instance recovery. The concept of temporary segments is discussed later in this chapter, and Chapter 5 discusses in detail the concepts of crash and instance recovery. The SMON process is started automatically by Oracle and is required for normal operation of the database.

The *process monitor* (PMON) performs process recovery on failed user processes and frees up any resources the failed process was using. The PMON process also checks the *dispatcher* and *server* processes to restart them if necessary.

The PMON process is essential for normal operation of the database and is automatically started when an instance is started.

The *archiver process* (ARCH) is present if the database is operating with *automatic archiving* enabled. Automatic archiving can be enabled by using the INIT.ORA parameter LOG_ARCH_START or issuing the SQL*DBA command **archive log start**. Note that the database needs to be in ARHIVELOG mode to take advantage of the ARCH process (you can start the ARCH process even when the database is in NOARCHIVELOG mode, but this doesn't achieve anything). The ARCH process is responsible for copying the redo entries from the online redo log files to the archive area. If automatic archiving is not enabled, then the DBA needs to manually archive the redo log files when they become full. The INIT.ORA parameter LOG_ARCHIVE_START can be used to enable the ARCH process on database startup.

The *recoverer process* (RECO) is responsible for resolving failures involved in distributed transactions. In a distributed environment, Oracle may have multiple databases on multiple machines connected by a network. When a network or a node fails, some transactions will be put in an *in-doubt* state, depending on when the failure occurred. The RECO process attempts to establish communication with remote servers. When a connection between the database servers is reestablished, the RECO process automatically resolves all the in-doubt transactions. If an instance is not permitted to do distributed transactions, this process doesn't need to be enabled. The INIT.ORA parameter DISTRIBUTED_TRANSACTIONS is used to enable the RECO process.

As discussed earlier, the *dispatcher processes* (Dnnn) are present only if you are operating the database with a multi-threaded server configuration. The dispatcher processes manage requests to/from user processes and shared server processes. Multiple dispatcher processes can be started by the DBA. At least one dispatcher process is required for each network protocol being used by users to communicate with Oracle.

The *server processes* are responsible for communicating with user processes and interacting with Oracle to carry out tasks on behalf of the associated user processes. If you are operating the database with a multi-threaded server configuration, each server process will service multiple user processes, thereby minimizing system resources. If you are operating the database with a dedicated server configuration, every user process will have a dedicated server process.

The *lock processes* (LCKn) are used for inter-instance locking in an Oracle Parallel Server environment. The Parallel Server option is described at the end of this chapter. For more details on this background process, refer to *Oracle7 Parallel Server Administrator's Guide*.

# Database Startup and Shutdown

During the Oracle database startup and shutdown, a number of events occur that take the Oracle database through various stages. The *ORACLE7 Server Utilities*

*User's Guide* gives the complete syntax to start up and shut down the Oracle database. To access the Oracle database, the DBA needs to open the database. The following example shows how to open an Oracle database.

```
SQLDBA> Startup open [dbname]
ORACLE instance started.
Database mounted.
Database opened.
```

When the **startup open** command is issued, the database passes through three stages—*nomount, mount,* and *open*—before becoming available. The DBA can also manually start up the database to a particular stage using the SQLDBA **startup** command. This is necessary during particular operations. For example, if database recovery needs to be performed, the database has to be mounted and the **recover database** command issued. The following example shows how to set the database to *nomount* and *mount* stages, respectively:

```
SQLDBA> Startup nomount [dbname]
SQLDBA> Startup mount [dbname]
```

During the *nomount* stage, Oracle reads the INIT.ORA file, locates the control files, creates and initializes the SGA, and finally, starts all Oracle background processes. As mentioned earlier, the combination of the Oracle background processes and the SGA is referred to as an Oracle instance. As shown in the above example, when the database is at the nomount stage, Oracle displays a message saying that the instance has started. You need to set the database to the nomount state while creating the database for the first time or while re-creating a control file after losing the current control file. During the *mount* stage, Oracle opens the control files to identify the location of the data files and the online redo logs. However, no verification checks are performed on the data files and log files at this time. The instance mounts the database and gets an instance lock, and it verifies that no other instance has mounted this database. After this is done, Oracle displays a message to the user screen saying that the database is mounted. There are a number of reasons why you might want to set the database to a mounted state. In general, any SQL command that starts with the keywords **alter database** can be executed while the database is mounted (note that some of these commands can be executed while the database is open as well). Some of the database operations that can be performed while the database is mounted are

- Performing media recovery
- Taking a data file offline or online

■ Relocating data files and redo log files

■ Creating a new redo log group (or member) or deleting an existing redo log group (or member)

During the *open* stage, the instance opens the database, gets a lock on the data files, and opens all the online redo log files. (If it is the first instance to open the database, it gets a *startup* lock as well.) If the instance is opening the database after an abnormal termination or after a database crash, crash recovery will be performed automatically by Oracle using the online redo log files. After the database is opened, Oracle displays a message to the user screen saying that the database is open. Figure 2-2 gives a schematic diagram of the various stages that the Oracle database goes through during startup.

There are three options available to DBAs while shutting the database down: *normal, immediate,* and *abort.* The *normal* shutdown process stops all user access to the database, waits until all users complete their requests and disconnect from

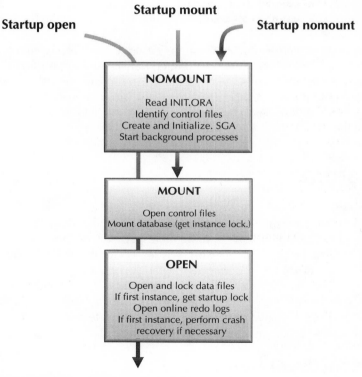

**FIGURE 2-2.**    *Three stages during database startup*

the server, purges data buffer and redo log caches and updates data files and online redo logs, drops file locks, completes ongoing transactions, updates file headers, closes thread, drops the database instance lock, and synchronizes control files and data files. In short, the shutdown *normal* option closes the database, dismounts the database, and shuts down the instance gracefully. The *normal* shutdown should be done before a cold database backup—it ensures complete consistency of the database and will not require crash recovery during next startup. The *normal* option is always recommended while shutting down the database.

In certain situations, it might be necessary for you to choose the *immediate* option while shutting the database down. For example, the DBA might decide to increase the SESSIONS parameter in the INIT.ORA file. If this needs to be done immediately, the DBA should use the *immediate* option. If this option is used to shut down the database, the current SQL statements that are being processed by Oracle are terminated immediately, any uncommitted transactions are rolled back, and the database is shut down. The only disadvantage of using this option is that Oracle doesn't wait for the current users to disconnect. However, the database will be consistent and no recovery is required during next startup.

Likewise, in emergency situations and when all else fails, a shutdown with the *abort* option can be used. An example would be when one of the background processes dies and you cannot shut down the database using the *normal* or *immediate* options. When the abort option is used, current SQL statements are immediately terminated and the uncommitted transactions are not rolled back. Shutdown with the *abort* option will require *crash recovery* on the next startup of the database, and this option should be used only when it is absolutely necessary. The stages of the shutdown and paths taken for normal, immediate, and abort are shown in Figure 2-3.

# Data Storage

The database's data is collectively stored in the tablespaces. A *tablespace* is a logical entity that corresponds to one or more physical data files on disk or disks. The database is divided into one or more tablespaces. Each tablespace can have one or more physical data files. The primary reason for this logical grouping of data is to increase the flexibility in performing database operations. In this section we look at some of the database administrative operations corresponding to tablespaces and data files that are necessary while doing backup and recovery. The *ORACLE7 Server Administrator's Guide* gives a complete description of managing the tablespaces and data files.

## Tablespaces and Data Files

A *tablespace* is used by DBAs to perform space management tasks, control the availability of data in the database, and perform partial backup and recovery of the

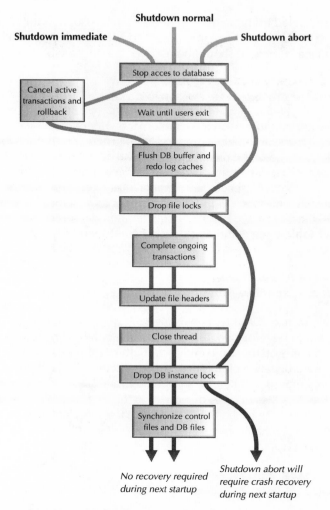

**Shutdown normal**

**Shutdown immediate**

**Shutdown abort**

Stop acces to database

Cancel active transactions and rollback

Wait until users exit

Flush DB buffer and redo log caches

Drop file locks

Complete ongoing transactions

Update file headers

Close thread

Drop DB instance lock

Synchronize control files and DB files

*No recovery required during next startup*

*Shutdown abort will require crash recovery during next startup*

**FIGURE 2-3.**    *The three options of shutting down the Oracle database*

database. The space management tasks include, among other things, controlling disk allocation and usage by users. The availability of the data can be controlled by taking a specific tablespace offline so that users cannot access the data. The first tablespace in the database is always the SYSTEM tablespace. This tablespace has to be available *all* the time for normal operation of the database because it contains the data dictionary information of the database. After initial creation of the database, it is recommended that additional tablespaces be created so that the user data can be separated from the data dictionary data. Also, if multiple applications are running on the database, you might want to keep the data separately. The **create tablespace** command should be used for creating a tablespace. For example,

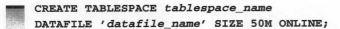

```
CREATE TABLESPACE tablespace_name
DATAFILE 'datafile_name' SIZE 50M ONLINE;
```

The above command will create a tablespace with one data file of size 50MB. The *tablespace_name* and *datafile_name* parameters represent the tablespace name and the full path name of the data file, respectively. Each tablespace has a default *storage* parameter that determines how much space should be allocated for each object created in that tablespace. Note that at least one physical data file should be created with each tablespace. If more space needs to be allocated to the tablespace after creation, the tablespace can be altered to add one or more physical data files to it. The **alter tablespace** command should be used for this purpose. For example, the command

```
ALTER TABLESPACE tablespace_name
ADD DATAFILE 'datafile_name' SIZE 20M;
```

adds a data file of size 20MB to an existing tablespace. If the data files of a tablespace need to be relocated, this can be done either with the **alter tablespace** command or the **alter database** command. If **alter tablespace** is used, the tablespace should be taken offline first. If **alter database** is used, the database needs to be in a mounted state but not open. Before issuing either of the above commands, the data files need to be copied to the destination. While relocating the data files that belong to the SYSTEM tablespace, **alter database** is the only way since the SYSTEM tablespace can never be taken offline. Consider the following examples:

```
ALTER TABLESPACE tablespace_name
RENAME DATAFILE 'old_filename' TO 'new_filename';

ALTER DATABASE RENAME FILE 'old_filename' TO 'new_filename';
```

**NOTE**
It is always a good practice to take a complete backup of the data files, log files, and control files before and after any schema changes to the database.

## Taking Tablespaces Offline

Taking a tablespace *offline* means making the data in the tablespace unavailable to users. When a tablespace is taken offline, Oracle will take all the associated data files offline as well. The SYSTEM tablespace can never be taken offline. Sometimes it is necessary to take a non-SYSTEM tablespace offline because Oracle signaled a *write error* on one of the data files of the tablespace. In other cases, the DBA might have to take the tablespace offline for regular maintenance. For example, if the DBA needs to relocate a data file that belongs to a tablespace called *users,* then the *users* tablespace needs to be taken offline. After the appropriate work is done, the DBA needs to make the tablespace available to the users again. This is known as bringing the tablespace *online.* While running a production database, you need to be very careful when taking tablespaces offline as it might impede the database user's work. Such operations should normally be done during scheduled database maintenance time.

There are three *modes* in which a tablespace can be taken offline: *normal, temporary,* and *immediate.* If no error conditions occur on any of the data files, it is always recommended to take a tablespace offline in the *normal* mode. In this mode, Oracle would do a checkpoint for the tablespace before taking it offline gracefully.

If a tablespace is taken offline with the *temporary* option, Oracle checkpoints all the data files that are available and then takes the tablespace offline. If one of the files has a corruption and you can't write to it, then the *normal* option will fail and the *temporary* option needs to be used. You should use the *temporary* option only when one of the data files has a write error and you can't write to it. For example, let's assume that tablespace T1 contains two data files, D1 and D2, and that file D1 was taken offline by Oracle due to a write error. If the *temporary* option is used to take tablespace T1 offline, then Oracle checkpoints data file D2 before taking T1 offline. After the problem is fixed, while bringing the tablespace online, Oracle will do recovery for data file D1.

The *immediate* option can be used only if the database is operating in ARCHIVELOG mode. If the tablespace is taken offline with this option, no checkpointing is done before taking the tablespace offline, and Oracle requests *media recovery* for this tablespace when it is brought online. You should use this option only when all the data files of a tablespace have a write error and you can't write to them. Chapter 5 gives details on media recovery. In the following example, tablespace *prod_tables* is taken offline with the *normal* option.

```
ALTER TABLESPACE prod_tables OFFLINE NORMAL;
```

## Taking Data Files Offline

It is not normal to take data files offline and online. If a specific data file is damaged, you need to take it offline, get it repaired, and bring it online again. If the file is lost and a backup file is restored, recovery needs to be done on the data file before bringing it online again. As mentioned earlier, The following example will illustrate why it might be necessary to take a non-SYSTEM data file offline.

Let's assume that a tablespace called *user_data* contains two data files: File1 (residing on Disk1) and File2 (residing on Disk2). Let's further assume that File1 contains users' tables and File2 contains the indexes for tables that are in File1. Let's say that Disk2 crashed making File2 unavailable. At this time, using the **alter database** command, File2 can be taken offline. The advantage of this is that the users can still access the tables in File1 but cannot use the indexes that reside in File2. Once disk D2 is restored and File2 is recovered, the data file can be brought online again. If an older copy of File2 is restored, you need to apply recovery to File2 by using the **recover datafile** command before bringing the file online. The **recover datafile** command is described in Chapter 5. In this example, we have assumed that the objects are not spanning data files but in a relational model it is very well possible for objects to span data files within a tablespace. The following is the syntax to take data files offline.

```
ALTER DATABASE DATAFILE 'DISK2:[DBS]FILE2.DBS' OFFLINE;
ALTER DATABASE DATAFILE 'DISK2:[DBS]FILE2.DBS' OFFLINE DROP;
```

The first command should be used only if you are operating the database in ARCHIVELOG mode. If operating in NOARCHIVELOG mode, you should use the second command. If you want to know if a specific data file is online or offline, select the STATUS column from the V$DATAFILE view. Appendix B gives a description of this view.

## Segments, Extents, and Blocks

The data in the database is stored in *Oracle blocks*. An Oracle block is the smallest unit of physical space, and is a multiple of operating system blocks. The Oracle block size is usually 2048 bytes, but can be set as high as 8K. The DB_BLOCK_SIZE parameter in the INIT.ORA file determines the size of the Oracle block. Keeping the Oracle block size high could result in better buffer cache hit ratio because an individual physical read gets more data, which increases the likelihood that the next read will find what it needs without going to disk, especially in OLTP (Online Transaction Processing) environments. Some DBAs find general read-throughput improvements by migrating from a 2K database block size to 4K database block size. However, with a bigger Oracle block size, it takes more space in SGA to have the same DB_BLOCK_BUFFERS. If memory is constrained, it is recommended to have more Oracle blocks of a smaller size than fewer Oracle blocks of a larger size.

A contiguous collection of Oracle blocks is called an *extent.* This is a logical unit of space. A collection of extents is called a *segment,* which is the next level of logical storage unit. There are different kinds of segments in the database. For example, the data of tables is stored in a *data segment.* Similarly, an *index segment* contains the data of an index. Other segments in the database are *temporary segments, rollback segments,* and *bootstrap segments.* When an object (such as a table, index, or rollback segment) is created, an extent is allocated to the object's segment. As the object grows, more space is required and extra extents are allocated to the segment. The first Oracle block of the first extent contains the *segment header.* For example, when table *emp* is created, the first Oracle block of the first extent of the emp table contains the data segment header. Among other things, the segment header contains information about freelists and also the *extent map.* The extent map contains information about the number of extents allocated to the segment and each extent's size. Note that while using the Parallel Server option, if the FREELIST GROUPS is set to a number greater than 1 while creating a table, the segment header doesn't contain the freelist information but another Oracle block is allocated to maintain the freelist information. We will discuss the Parallel Server option at the end of this chapter.

While designing a database, careful consideration should be given to sizing the database and anticipating growth of tables and data. Sizing is essential for implementing a production (or test/development) database that will be around for a long time. The space requirements for database objects should be carefully calculated and accounted for before the database goes into production.

Accurate sizing of the data dictionary, user tables, user indexes, rollback segments, and redo logs depends on accurate estimates of

- The number and size of rows stored (or to be stored) in user tables
- The transaction mix
- The sizes and performance characteristics of database objects

The next section gives some tips on space management issues for different database segments.

## Data Segments

Consideration should be made for the larger tables that will reside in the database, as well as for tables that will grow considerably over time. To size the transactions, you will need to ascertain the nature of your transactions. These can fall into three basic categories:

- Short update transactions affecting relatively small amounts of data
- Long-running *update* transactions that alter significant amounts of data before committing or rolling back
- Long-running *read-only* transactions that only query data but require that read-consistent snapshots of tables remain available until the last fetch of the query is completed

The transaction mix for different times should also be considered since it may vary throughout the day. For example, during the daytime work hours users might perform short update transactions, whereas in the evening you may execute longer running batch jobs doing updates or queries. Both cases should be investigated and planned for in the production system. This transaction mix may also change over time as the number of users increases or decreases and the amount of data to be processed changes. Once the row and transaction information is gathered from an analysis of the application, object sizes for the database can be estimated.

**Data Dictionary/SYSTEM Tablespace**    The data dictionary space should remain relatively constant, growing only as the database objects increase. Whenever the database is in operation, the Oracle RDBMS updates the data dictionary in response to every DDL statement, reflecting changes in database structures, auditing, grants, and data. The data dictionary generally requires only a small percentage of space when compared with application requirements. It is critical to allow enough room for the data dictionary to grow and for other objects such as *deferred rollback segments* to exist in the SYSTEM tablespace.

To ensure that space remains available for the data dictionary and other objects that must reside in the SYSTEM tablespace, place all other user tables, indexes, temporary segments, and rollback segments in other tablespaces. In addition, make the SYSTEM tablespace large enough so that it has at least 50 to 75 percent free space. Finally, ensure that your users do not have privileges on the SYSTEM tablespace for creating objects or temporary segments.

**Tables**    Table size increases proportionally with the number of rows in the table, assuming average row length remains constant. It is very important to know the types of transactions that will affect the data in the tables. This will help you size the storage clause parameters PCTFREE and PCTUSED accordingly when the table is initially created. A detailed description of the storage clause is given in the *ORACLE7 Server SQL Language Reference Manual*. For example, as the rows lengthen in a block, *row chaining* may result if PCTFREE is not set sufficiently high. (Row chaining is when pieces of a single row reside in multiple Oracle blocks.)

### Index Segments

Indexes are objects that are associated with tables and clusters, and are used to speed up the execution of a SQL statement. Dropping or creating indexes doesn't affect the associated tables. Indexes increase in size slightly faster than the corresponding table if the data in the table is modified frequently, so you should estimate the size of the index carefully.

Space management is more efficient if you maintain indexes for large tables in separate tablespaces—it decreases fragmentation and also makes managing the index growth easier if re-creating the index is necessary.

## Rollback Segments

A rollback segment is a segment in the database that stores the before image information of data when a transaction modifies a block. The information in the rollback segment is used for read consistency, transaction rollback, and during transaction recovery. For example, if a transaction modifies a block by changing the key value of a column from 10 to 20, then the old value of 10 needs to be stored in the rollback segment and the data block will have a new value of 20. If the transaction is rolled back, then the value 10 is copied from the rollback segment back to the data block.

**Contents of Rollback Segments**     It's important to understand what is stored in the rollback segment when a transaction modifies a block. The rollback segment does not store the whole data block—only the before image of the row or rows that were modified. Information in the rollback segment consists of several rollback entries called *undo*. For example, if a row is inserted into a table, the undo created by that transaction would include the rowid of that row, among other information. This is because the undo operation of an insert is a delete and all you need to delete a row is the rowid. If a delete operation is performed on a table, the complete row will be part of the undo. For update transactions, we store the old value of the updated columns. If the transaction modifies an index as well, then the old index keys will also be stored as part of the undo. Rollback segments guarantee that the undo information is kept for the life of a transaction.

Every rollback segment has a *transaction table*. When a transaction modifies a data block, it updates the data block header, which points to the rollback segment that has the undo information for that transaction. The transaction also inserts an entry into the transaction table of the rollback segment. Among other information, the transaction table entry gives the address of the data block that was modified, status of the transaction (commit or active), and the location within the rollback segment where the undo for that transaction is stored.

**Operation of Rollback Segments**     A rollback segment, like any other segment, consists of multiple extents. However, the main difference between a data segment and a rollback segment is that the rollback segment uses its extents in an ordered, circular fashion, moving from one extent to the next after the current extent is full. A transaction writes a record to the current location in the rollback segment and advances the current pointer by the size of the record. The current writing location of undo is called the *head* of the rollback segment. The location of the oldest active undo record is called the *tail* of the rollback segment. The undo generated by a transaction is guaranteed to remain in the rollback segment until the transaction commits or rolls back.

Some important rules in allocating space for rollback segments are as follows:

- A transaction can only use one rollback segment to store all of its undo records. In other words, a transaction cannot span rollback segments.

- Multiple transactions can write to the same extent of a rollback segment.

- Only one active transaction can be in a rollback segment block. This reduces contention on the rollback segment block.

- The head of the rollback segment never wraps into an extent currently occupied by the tail.

- Extents in the ring are never skipped over and used out of order as the head tries to advance.

- If the head cannot wrap into the next extent, it allocates a new extent and inserts it into the ring between the two original extents.

The following example illustrates the space allocation in rollback segments.

A transaction has started and is updating blocks in a table. The undo generated by the transaction is being written to the rollback segment. Let's assume the current *head* of the undo is in block 5 of extent 1 (which is the current extent) and needs to generate more undo records. If extent 1 has no more blocks, it will look at the next extent (either extent 2 or 0), say extent 2. If all the undo records in extent 2 belong to transactions that are already committed, then the transaction can use the first block of extent 2. A new transaction or continuing transaction that needs more space can then use the next available block in extent 2 without doing the same checks, because *extent 2* is now the head.

Now let's discuss the algorithm used in selecting a rollback segment. The following steps will make this algorithm clear:

**0.** If forced to use SYSTEM (for certain operation) go to step 5.

**1.** If using **set transaction use rollback segment** command, go to step 6.

**2.** Skip rollback segment SYSTEM to consider other rollback segments if present. Else go to step 5.

**3.** Skip a rollback segment if marked OFFLINE, NEEDS RECOVERY or PENDING OFFLINE.

**4.** Find and select the rollback segment with least number of active transactions. In case of a tie between multiple rollback segment, select the rollback segment after the one last used (round-robin) and go to step 6.

**5.** Select SYSTEM rollback segment.

**6.** Use the selected rollback segment if possible. If the rollback segment already has maximum number of active transactions, then wait and loop back to step 1.

Note that in Oracle7, in the rollback segment storage clause, the PCTINCREASE parameter has been replaced by a parameter called OPTIMAL. This specifies the optimal size of a rollback segment in bytes. It can also be specified in kilobytes or megabytes. The RDBMS tries to keep the segment at its specified optimal size. The size is rounded up to the extent boundary, which means that the RDBMS tries to have the fewest number of extents such that the total size is greater than or equal to the size specified as OPTIMAL. If additional space is needed beyond the optimal size, it will eventually deallocate extents to shrink back to this size. The process of deallocating extents is performed when the head moves from one extent (n) to the next (n+1). At the time, the segment size is checked and the RDBMS checks if the n+2th extent can be deallocated. The extent can only be deallocated if there are no active transactions in it. If necessary, the RDBMS will deallocate multiple extents at one time until the segment has shrunk back to its optimal size. The RDBMS always deallocates the oldest inactive extents as they are the least likely to be used for read consistency.

The optimal size can be set on the SYSTEM rollback segment as well. This is important because the SYSTEM rollback segment can grow like any other rollback segment but can never be dropped by the DBA since it belongs to the user SYS. There are two main reasons why SYSTEM rollback segments can grow: either there are no non-SYSTEM rollback segments created by the DBA, or the user has specifically requested Oracle to use the SYSTEM rollback segment by issuing the following command before executing the transaction:

```
SQLDBA> set transaction use rollback segment SYSTEM;
```

In either case, the SYSTEM rollback segment will grow and the only way to shrink it is to use the OPTIMAL parameter. However, it's very important to note that the OPTIMAL parameter should not be set too small for the SYSTEM rollback segment. The initial size of the SYSTEM rollback segment is 100K, and the OPTIMAL for it should not be smaller than that. If the OPTIMAL value is set less than the MINEXTENTS size, you will get an error. Setting the OPTIMAL parameter too small for the SYSTEM rollback segment (or any rollback segment) may degrade the system's performance because the rollback segment keeps shrinking too often, which is an expensive operation.

ORACLE7 allows *dynamic onlining* and *offlining* of rollback segments. What this means is that, unlike with version 6, the database doesn't need to be shut down and started up to change the status of a rollback segment. By default, whenever a rollback segment is created it is offline and must be acquired by the instance or brought online. If a rollback segment has to be brought online, the SQL command **alter rollback segment** with the *online* option can be used. To take a rollback segment offline, you can use the *offline* option. If a rollback segment is taken offline and the specified rollback segment does not have any active transactions, it is immediately taken offline. But if the specified rollback segment contains rollback data (undo) for active transactions, it is taken offline once all the active transactions are either committed or rolled back. No new transactions are written to a rollback segment that is either marked offline or is waiting for other transactions to complete so that it can be brought offline. To become available again, a rollback segment that is taken offline has to be explicitly brought back online or it has to be specified in the INIT.ORA file when the instance is started. This means that when a public rollback segment is taken offline it remains offline, even if the database is shut down and restarted.

### Configuration of Rollback Segments

What should the size of a rollback segment be? How many rollback segments should I have? These are two questions commonly asked by DBAs.

There are two issues that need to be considered when deciding the size of the rollback segment. First, you need to make sure that transactions will not cause the head to wrap around too fast and catch the tail. This causes the segment to extend in size. Second, if you have long-running queries that access frequently changing data, you want to make sure that the rollback segment doesn't wrap around and prevent the construction of a read-consistent view. In this case, the ORA-1555 error occurs.

The size needed for a rollback segment depends directly on the transaction activity in a database. DBAs should be concerned about the activity during normal processing of the database, not with rare or infrequent large transactions. These special cases will be discussed later in this section.

The number of rollback segments needed to prevent contention between processes can be determined by monitoring the rollback segments through the SQL*DBA *monitor* screen and with the use of the V$WAITSTAT view. The rollback monitor column *header waits/sec* gives an indication of the current transaction table contention. Waits are a definite indication of contention. The following V$WAITSTAT query will display the number of waits since instance startup:

```
SELECT * FROM V$WAITSTAT WHERE
OPERATION = 'buffer busy waits'   AND
CLASS = 'undo segment header';
```

To find out the size and number of rollback segments needed to handle normal processing on the database, DBAs need to do some testing. A good test is to start with small rollback segments and allow your application to force them to extend. Here are the steps to run such a test:

1. Create a rollback segment tablespace.

2. Select a number of rollback segments to test and create them in the tablespace.

3. Create the rollback segments so that all extents are of the same size. Choose an extent size that you suspect will need between 10 to 30 extents when the segments grow to full size.

4. Each rollback segment should start with two extents before the test is run. This is the minimum number of extents any rollback segment can have.

5. Activate only the rollback segments that you are testing by making the status ONLINE. The only other segment that should be ONLINE is the SYSTEM rollback segment.

6. Run transactions to simulate a typical load of the application.

7. Watch for rollback segment contention.

8. Watch for the maximum size a rollback extends to.

The maximum size any one of the rollback segments reaches during the test is the size you should use when configuring. We will call this size the *minimum coverage size*. If you see contention, adjust the number of segments and rerun the test. Also, if the largest size requires fewer than 10 extents or more than 30, it is a good idea to lower or raise the extent size, respectively, and rerun the test. Otherwise, you may be wasting space.

For sizing rollback segment extents, Oracle strongly recommends that each extent be of the same size. In fact, for all strategies listed below we assume that all rollback segments have extents of the same size and that the size of the rollback tablespace is some multiple of the common extent size. The number of extents for an individual segment should be between 10 and 30.

You now have some good base estimates for the size and number of rollback segments needed for normal data processing. After calculating the size and the number of rollback segments required, it is time to plan for the configuration of the rollback segment tablespace. To do this, you first need to understand the amount of undo that is being generated and the transaction pattern that is being executed.

You can estimate the amount of undo generated by a transaction with the help of the following script, UNDO.SQL. Note that this script should be run from SQL*Plus only.

```
REM: UNDO.SQL
set   feedback off
set termout   off
column name format A40
define undo_overhead = 54
DROP TABLE undo$begin;
DROP TABLE undo$end;
CREATE TABLE undo$begin ( writes number );
```

```
CREATE TABLE undo$end ( writes number );
INSERT INTO undo$begin
SELECT sum(writes) FROM v$rollstat;
set termout on
set feedback on
REM: The following statement runs a script called TEST.SQL, which
REM: contains the test transactions
@TEST.SQL
set termout off
set feedback off
INSERT INTO undo$end
SELECT sum(writes) FROM v$rollstat;
set termout on
set feedback on
SELECT  ( ( e.writes - b.writes) - &undo_overhead) "number of bytes
generated"
FROM undo$begin b, undo$end e;
set termout off
set feedback off
DROP TABLE undo$begin;
DROP TABLE undo$end;
```

The value reported by this script is the undo generated during the transaction. You need to make sure that this is the only running transaction in the database. The UNDO_OVERHEAD defined in the script is a constant that compensates for the unavoidable overhead of the **insert into undo$begin**... statement.

Now you need to examine the *transaction pattern* that you run on your database. There are primarily three different transaction patterns:

- A steady average transaction rate
- Frequent large transactions
- Infrequent large transactions

For databases with a *steady average transaction rate* (i.e., there are no abnormally large transactions), create a tablespace that will fit your calculated number of rollback segments with the minimum coverage size you have determined. Make all extents the same size. As a safety net, allocate some additional space in the tablespace to allow segments to grow if they need to. If you elect to do this, use the OPTIMAL feature to force all rollback segments to free up any additional space they allocate beyond their determined size requirement. You do not want to make OPTIMAL smaller than the minimum coverage size. Otherwise performance will suffer due to excessive segment resizing.

Databases with *frequent large transactions* are the hardest case to deal with. By *frequent,* we mean that the time between large transactions is less than the time needed to allow all rollback segments to shrink back to optimal size. A large transaction is one in which we don't have enough space to create all rollback segments of the size necessary to handle its rollback information. Since we can't depend on the segment shrinking in time to allow repeated large transactions, OPTIMAL is not really an option for this environment.

There are basically two options that you can choose from for your rollback segment tablespace. One is to reduce the number of segments so that all are large enough to hold the largest transactions. This option will introduce contention and will cause some degradation in performance. It is a reasonable choice if performance is not extremely critical. The second option is to build one or more large rollback segments and make sure that large transactions use these segments. The **set transaction use rollback segment** command is necessary to control the placement of these large transactions. This option is difficult to implement if large transactions are being run with ad hoc queries and there is no systematic control of large transactions. This option is recommended in an environment where the large transactions are issued from a controlled environment (i.e., an application that will set the transaction to the appropriate rollback segment).

For databases with *infrequent large transactions,* you can use the OPTIMAL feature to set up a flexible rollback segment scheme, one in which you are not concerned about which rollback segment the large transaction falls upon. The key is to leave enough free space in the rollback segment tablespace that the largest transaction's rollback information can fit entirely into it. To do this, create the rollback segement tablespace with the space needed for your calculated number of segments and their minimum coverage size plus this additional space. Then set the OPTIMAL for each segment equal to the minimum coverage size. What you will see is that the large transactions will randomly make one of the segments grow and eat up the free space, but the segment will release the space before the next large transaction comes along. Note that you are sacrificing some performance for this flexibility.

Finally, you need to remember two points from this discussion. First, though the use of the OPTIMAL clause is a very handy tool, beware that the extent allocation and deallocation are expensive operations with regard to performance. This means that an OPTIMAL setting may decrease performance if it is too low. The second point is that there is no guarantee when a rollback segment will shrink down to its optimal size, because a rollback segment only shrinks when a transaction attempts to move into another extent and sees that the extent meets the requirements for deallocation.

## Maintenance of Rollback Segments
As a DBA, you need to monitor the rollback segment activity from time to time in the database. This is necessary to

maintain the correct number of rollback segments and the correct OPTIMAL size for each rollback segment. Monitoring also helps you identify the long-running transactions and the users running these transactions. For example, the following SQL script identifies all users with active transactions and the rollback segment each transaction is using.

```
SELECT r.name "ROLLBACK SEGMENT NAME",
l.pid "ORACLE PID",
s.pid "SYSTEM PID",
NVL ( p.username , 'NO TRANSACTION'),
p.terminal
FROM v$lock l, v$process p, v$rollname r
WHERE   l.pid = p.pid(+)
AND TRUNC (l.idl(+)/65536) = r.usn
AND l.type(+) = 'TX'
AND l.lmode(+) = 6
ORDER BY r.name
```

Also, note that V$ROLLSTAT gives some valuable information regarding the rollback segments and amount of redo being generated.

The rollback segment *monitor* screen has been enhanced to help you determine how successfully you have chosen your OPTIMAL size. Some of the statistics give you information such as the highest number of extents that were allocated to the rollback segment, the OPTIMAL size, and the number of shrinks performed. Based on these statistics, you can analyze the OPTIMAL setting for a rollback segment. If the cumulative number of shrinks is low and the average size of shrinks is high, that's an indication that the OPTIMAL value is set appropriately. If the cumulative number of shrinks is high and the average size of shrinks is low, the OPTIMAL size needs to be increased. If the number of shrinks is very low, then you should decrease the OPTIMAL value.

## Temporary Segments

Oracle often requires temporary work space for intermediate stages of data processing. These areas are referred to as *temporary segments* and are allocated as needed during a user operation. A DBA may occasionally need to find additional database space on disk for temporary segments that are larger than normally anticipated. This section describes a procedure in which disk space currently allocated to the database can be managed or even *borrowed* to accommodate the creation of large temporary segments. Let's first examine when and how temporary segments are created.

The following SQL operations may require the use of a temporary segment:

- CREATE INDEX
- SELECT with DISTINCT, ORDER BY, GROUP BY, UNION, INTERSECT, and MINUS clauses
- Nonindexed JOINs
- Certain correlated subqueries

If the table/index can be sorted in memory, then the sorting method is called *internal*. If the table is very large, the sorting process is *external* to main memory and requires disk storage. The INIT.ORA parameter SORT_AREA_SIZE influences whether the sort is performed in memory or on disk. If the amount of data to be sorted is greater than the allocated sort area, the data is divided into smaller pieces. Each sort piece is then sorted individually and stored on disk in the form of a temporary segment. These temporary segments are merged among numerous sort passes and eventually merged into a final sorted result.

Increasing SORT_AREA_SIZE will reduce the creation of temporary segments on disk and therefore the amount of disk storage space needed. Some operating systems impose limits on the allocation of main memory. In these situations, the creation of large temporary segments on disk is inevitable. For example, creating a large index requires temporary segments. To satisfy the **create index** SQL statement, the RDBMS performs a sort operation to populate the index in the desired order. If resource constraints on main memory exist, the sort operation will result in the creation of one or more temporary segments on disk.

Temporary segments, like any other segments, can consist of multiple extents. If the sort requirements are great, temporary segments will grow by allocating additional extents. If there's insufficient contiguous space on the database to allocate the next extent, the following error will occur:

```
ORA-1652 Failed to allocate extent of size num for temporary segment
```

There are a number of ways to provide adequate temporary storage. One approach is to allocate another data file to the tablespace, thereby increasing the amount of contiguous free space in the tablespace. This space is now permanently allocated to the tablespace whether or not the space is normally needed. Another option is to use the **alter user** command to point the given user's temporary segments to another tablespace that contains more contiguous free space. However, space may not be adequate in the other tablespaces. Perhaps disk space outside the database can be temporarily borrowed by creating a new tablespace, altering the user's definition to point to this tablespace for the creation of temporary segments, and then subsequently dropping the tablespace after the operation completes. If the additional disk space is not available, a more complex form of the *tablespace shuffle* is required.

The *tablespace shuffle* is useful for creating indexes on large tables, especially in database environments that haven't been sized for exceptionally large temporary segments. First, identify a user tablespace that doesn't contain database objects relevant to the creation of a specific index. Specifically, the tablespace should not be SYSTEM, contain the target table, or contain any rollback segments that are IN USE. In addition, the DBA should approximate whether the elimination of this tablespace will free up enough storage. The tablespace is then taken offline. After the tablespace is taken offline, an operating system backup is performed on all associated data files. After verification, delete those data files at the operating system level.

Next, create a new tablespace that will be used exclusively to build temporary segments for your **create index** statement. The data file(s) specified should point to the same disk that contained the recently deleted data file(s). You may also want to access space from additional disks. Once the tablespace is created, alter the user's definition to point to this tablespace for the default creation of his temporary segments. During index creation, monitor temporary segment space requirements by issuing the following statement:

```
SELECT SEGMENT_NAME, BYTES, EXTENTS FROM SYS.DBA_SEGMENTS
WHERE SEGMENT_TYPE='TEMPORARY';
```

Determine how much free space remains in the tablespace by issuing the command:

```
SELECT MAX(BYTES) FROM SYS.DBA_FREE_SPACE
WHERE TABLESPACE_NAME= tablespace_name;
```

After the index is successfully created, modify the user definition to point back to that user's original temporary tablespace default and drop the recently created tablespace. Delete these data file(s) and restore the above backups. Bring the offline tablespace online and, if necessary, perform media recovery.

# Database Configuration

When configuring the database, three major areas of concern are control files, online redo log files, and archived redo log files. While designing the database layout, the DBA also needs to consider *disaster recovery,* and the *performance* of the database. For example, placing all the data files that contain indexes on one disk might be a good thing to do from a recovery point of view. If the disk crashes and you lose all the index datafiles, online recovery can be performed on the index tablespace, thereby minimizing the down time of the database. But from a performance point of view, this might not be pragmatic if all the applications heavily read and write to the index data files. This might create an I/O bottleneck since all data files reside on the same disk drive. So the database design and configuration primarily depends on the business requirements and resources available. Once the business requirements are known, the database needs to be designed right, and proper operational procedures should be put in place to meet the business needs.

# Managing Control Files

The control file contains the schema of the database. This is one of the most important and essential files for normal operation of the database. In this section, we will look at some of the guidelines for managing control files. Control file administration is probably the easiest and takes very little time. However, if the DBA doesn't do the initial setup right, losing the control file may cause a significant amount of database down time. This is a concern for customers running mission-critical applications with high availability requirements. This section discusses some of the basic operations, such as adding, renaming, relocating, and dropping control files.

The INIT.ORA parameter CONTROL_FILES lists the names of all the control files that are being used by the database. As mentioned earlier, when the database is started up, during instance start up, Oracle reads the INIT.ORA file to find out how many control files are being used with the database and where their locations are. During the mount stage, the control file is opened to read the schema of the database, so it's necessary for the DBA to include all the names of the control files in the CONTROL_FILES parameter separated by commas. Oracle will write to all the control files during normal operation of the database. However, only the first control file listed in INIT.ORA is read by Oracle.

To protect against media failures, it is suggested that at least two control files be maintained; it is a good practice to maintain three or four copies of the control file on different disks. Keeping multiple copies of the control file on the same disk drive defeats the purpose of mirroring control files. The idea of mirroring is to plan for media failures. If a disk crashes, you may lose all files on that disk. For this reason, maintaining copies of the control file on different disks is essential. Also, if multiple disk controllers are being used, it is a good idea to keep control files on different disks that are mounted under different disk controllers. This will protect control files against disk controller failures as well.

Oracle very strongly recommends mirroring of control files. There is a slight overhead in maintaining multiple copies of the control files. Every time the database checkpoints, or the schema of the database changes, all the control files are updated. This will take a little longer if more copies of the control file are maintained. Also, additional disk space is required if control files are mirrored (the size of the control file is determined by the parameters MAXDATAFILES,

MAXLOGFILES, MAXLOGMEMBERS, MAXLOGHISTORY, and MAXINSTANCES, which are specified during the creation of the database). However, the performance overhead is really insignificant and the size of the control file is negligible compared to the total database size.

At the current time, even if the control file is mirrored, if one of the control files becomes unavailable because of a disk failure, you need to shut the database down with the *abort* option. Once the database is shut down, the INIT.ORA file needs to be edited such that the unavailable control file is not specified in the CONTROL_FILES parameter. Then the database can be started up. Once the disk drive is repaired, shut down the database one more time, copy the current control file to the new disk, edit the INIT.ORA file to reflect this change, and finally start up. This is not very practical, yet necessary for shops running with high availability requirements. This is probably one of the areas where Oracle should consider changing the functionality in the future releases. If a control file were to become unavailable, it would be nice if Oracle notified the DBA that a specific control file is not available and continued to function normally, ignoring the bad control file.

## Creating, Adding, and Renaming Control Files

When a database is created, the initial control file is created as part of the database. Before creating the database, the INIT.ORA file can be edited to specify the names of the control files to be created. The file specification is operating system-dependent. This would create all the requested control files as part of the database creation. For a given database, if you want to add a new control file, or change the name or location of an existing control file, execute the following steps:

1. Shut down the database using the *normal* option. If the database had to be shut down with the *abort* option, restart the database in RESTRICT mode and shut it down cleanly using the *normal* option.

2. Exit SQL*DBA.

3. Using the appropriate operating system command, copy an existing control file to a different location. If the existing control file's name needs to be changed, rename the control file.

4. Edit the CONTROL_FILES parameter in the INIT.ORA file and add the new control file's name. If renaming an existing control file, change the name of the existing control file.

5. Log on to a SQL*DBA session.

6. Restart the database.

If all control files of the database are permanently damaged and no backups of the control file exist, then the **create controlfile** command can be used to create a new control file. Alternatively, if one of the database settings needs to be modified, this can be achieved by creating a new control file as well. The parameters, MAXLOGFILES, MAXLOGMEMBERS, MAXLOGHISTORY, MAXDATAFILES, and MAXINSTANCES, are specified when the database is originally created. To modify any of these values, you might assume that the database needs to be rebuilt. However, using the **create controlfile** command, the values of these parameters can be changed without rebuilding the database.

For example, let's assume that you have created the database with MAXDATAFILES =20. This means that you cannot have more than 20 data files in the database. At a later time, if you realize that this value is set too low, you might want to change this by setting a new value for this parameter while re-creating the control file using the **create controlfile** command (the **create controlfile** command is described in detail in Chapter 5).

### Dropping Control Files

There are a number of reasons why a DBA might decide to drop a particular control file. For example, there may be too many control files, or multiple control files may exist on the same disk drive. Or due to a system reconfiguration, a particular disk drive may no longer be available. In such cases, the DBA can drop the control file, but note that there should always be a minimum of two control files. The following example gives you the steps involved in dropping a control file from the database.

1. Shut down the database gracefully using the *normal* option.

2. Exit SQL*DBA.

3. Edit the CONTROL_FILES parameter in the INIT.ORA file to delete the old control file's name.

4. Restart SQL*DBA.

5. Restart the database.

6. Delete the control file at the operating system level by using the appropriate OS command.

# Managing Online Redo Log Files

A single point of failure in version 6 of Oracle was to lose the online log file. Oracle7 provides a *mirroring* mechanism known as *multiplexing online log files*. This is very similar to having multiple copies of your control file—the main difference is that the database will not become inoperable when one of the online log file members is damaged or inaccessible. Oracle very strongly suggests multiplexing the online redo log files. By multiplexing the redo log files you will eliminate the chance of a single point of online redo log failure.

### Normal Operation

Oracle needs a minimum of two log file *groups* for normal operation of the database. Each log file group needs a minimum of one log file *member* and can contain multiple log file members. Every member within a log file group is identical and contains exactly the same information. When mirrored, since the LGWR process needs to write to multiple members of a log group, performance will be affected. However, this can be mitigated or almost eliminated by setting up the mirrors across disk controllers. The LGWR process does parallel writes to members of a log group. If members are on the same device, the writes would actually be serial. The LGWR process waits until the write completes—log blocks are always synchronously written. If the *parallel write* call returns an error, LGWR checks the status of each open log member to see which file gave the error. Also, the LGWR process keeps a counter of errors on each log file member. When an error occurs it marks the log member as STALE in the control file and you should see the ORA-346 error in the LGWR trace file. The STALE status indicates that the contents of the file are incomplete. If the LGWR process encounters more than four errors on a file, it simply closes the file and does not write to it anymore. A message is written in the trace file with the ORA-345 error. It is possible to write to a STALE file until the error count hits four. If the LGWR process can't write to any one of the members, then it kills itself with the ORA-340 error. After this error is encountered, you need to shut the database down with the *abort* option. After the cause for write errors is investigated and the problem rectified, the database needs to be started up again.

### Configuring the Online Redo Log Files

It is very important to choose the right size for an online log file. If the proper log file size is not chosen, then the LGWR process has to switch log files too often, which will affect the performance. On the other hand, if the log file size is too big, then during recovery Oracle needs to recover a lot of transactions and will take a longer time. Though Oracle allows the DBA to maintain different file sizes for different groups, there is no advantage in doing so. For most Oracle shops, the default log file size is sufficient; the default size is operating system-dependent. Even if the wrong file size is chosen for an online log file, it can be dropped and re-created at a later time. When you drop log files, Oracle will make sure that you have a minimum of two groups at any given time.

Choosing the number of online log groups is also very important. Having too few log groups could become a serious problem while using the database in ARCHIVELOG mode in some shops with a high transaction rate. Consider the case where there are two log groups. When the LGWR process fills up the log file in group 1 (say logA ), it switches to the log file in group 2 (say logB). At this time, the ARCH process starts copying the redo from logA to an archived log file. If the LGWR process finishes filling up logB, it cannot switch to logA until the ARCH process finishes archiving logA. In the meantime, the database will hang because logA cannot be written to until it is archived. In this case, adding additional groups would help. For most shops, keeping the number of online log files between 2 and 10 is sufficient. The total number of log groups cannot exceed MAXLOGFILES. Similarly, the total number of members per group cannot exceed MAXLOGMEMBERS. These parameters are specified in the **create database** command and can be changed later by either rebuilding the database or re-creating the control file.

### Creating and Relocating Online Redo Log Files

The **alter database** command can be used to add log groups or add a member to an existing group. Consider the following example:

```
ALTER DATABASE ADD LOGFILE GROUP 3 ('DISK$3:[LOGDIR]LOG3A.LOG',
'DISK$4:[LOGDIR]LOG3B.LOG') SIZE 500K;
ALTER DATABASE ADD LOGFILE MEMBER 'DISK$5:[LOGDIR]LOG3C.LOG' TO GROUP 3;
```

In this example, the first statement would create a group with two online log file members, one on each disk. The second statement would add a third member to that group on another disk.

Similar to the control files, the online log files need to be relocated for various reasons. Files need to be relocated for load balancing or due to removal of existing disk drives. To relocate the online log files, the following steps need to be taken:

1. Shut down the database gracefully, using the *normal* option.

2. Take a complete backup of the database including the log files, data files, and control files.

3. Copy the online log files to the new location using the appropriate OS command.

4. Start up SQL*DBA and mount the database.

5. Rename the online redo log members.

6. Open the database for normal operation using the **alter database** command.

7. Back up the control file since the schema of the database has changed now.

### Dropping Online Redo Log Groups and Members

You might want to drop a redo log group for various reasons. For example, the application's transaction rate might change, thereby generating less redo. This is a dangerous operation and should be executed cautiously. If the online redo log group is the *active* log group (which means the LGWR process is currently writing to this group), it cannot be dropped. Also, as mentioned earlier, there has to be a minimum of two redo log groups at any given time for database operation. The above restrictions apply while dropping a member of a redo log group as well. In addition, note that there has to be at least one member for each group available to the database. Consider the following example:

```
ALTER DATABASE DROP LOGFILE MEMBER 'DISK$5:[LOGDIR]LOG3C.LOG';
ALTER DATABASE DROP LOGFILE GROUP 3;
```

Here, the first statement drops a log file member from the log file group. The second statement drops the entire redo log group 3.

There are three views that help the DBA administer the online log files: V$LOG, V$LOGFILE, and V$THREAD. The STATUS column in the V$LOGFILE view gives the status of the log file member. As discussed earlier, status STALE shows that the log member is not complete. Status INCOMPLETE indicates that the file is not accessible by Oracle. If there is no status for the online log file, this indicates that the file is in use.

# Managing Archive Redo Log Files

*Archiving* is the process of copying a filled online redo log file to a different disk drive or a tape drive by the ARCH process. As discussed earlier, the DBA can configure the database to operate in ARCHIVELOG mode or NOARCHIVELOG mode. Oracle writes to the online redo log files regardless of the mode the database is operating in. If the database is configured to run in ARCHIVELOG mode, the online redo log files are saved (archived) before being overwritten by the LGWR process. In NOARCHIVELOG mode, the redo log files are overwritten each time a redo log file is filled and a log switch occurs. In other words, the past changes made to the database are not available in the log files.

This section discusses some of the advantages of running the database in ARCHIVELOG mode, as well as the costs involved. A procedure to turn on *manual archiving* and *automatic archiving* is also described.

### Normal Operation

The ARCH process has been made robust in Oracle7. In version 6, Oracle just did a straight copy of blocks from the online redo log file to the archive log file. In Oracle7, every block of the online log file is verified before copying. This ensures that if a block is bad in the online redo log file, the ARCH process signals an error *before* copying, and the DBA would know of it immediately instead of realizing it during recovery. Oracle doesn't check the contents of the online redo log data blocks. The algorithm for archiving begins by attempting to open all log members. If none can be opened, an error is signaled. Otherwise, Oracle opens as many members of the log group as possible. Next, the headers of the log file members are read and validated. Oracle keeps switching between members, reading a range of blocks from each member at a time. If the read is successful, Oracle remembers that log as an anchor point so that if a read fails on a range of blocks later for some other member, it can switch to any good member. This round robin reading procedure helps to distribute the disk I/O.

## Archive Destination

The INIT.ORA parameter LOG_ARCHIVE_DEST can be set to point to the destination where the archive log files need to be created. Archiving to disk and tape is supported on some operating systems (e.g., UNIX). Archiving to tape is not supported on all operating systems, but it is the only way supported on IBM VM (after Oracle7 release 7.1, VM will support archiving to disk). Operating systems such as VMS, Macintosh, NETWARE, OS/2, Windows, and DOS do not support archiving to tape directly, unless it looks like a normal volume (i.e., you can do a directory listing command on the tape drive). Oracle supports only local tape archiving on some operating systems such as UNIX System V, and on others (UNIX BSD, for example), remote archiving to tape is supported. Table 2-1 gives a listing of some of the major operating systems and their supported archive destinations.

| OPERATING SYSTEM | ARCHIVING TO DISK | ARCHIVING TO TAPE |
| --- | --- | --- |
| UNIX | Yes | Yes |
| VMS | Yes | No |
| DOS and Windows | Yes | Not normally |
| MAC | Yes | No |
| OS/2 | Yes | Not normally |
| NETWARE | Yes | Not normally |
| VM | Not until 7.1 | Yes |
| MVS | Yes | Yes |

**TABLE 2-1.**  *Supported Archive Destinations on Various Operating Systems*

**Archiving to Disk**   If you are archiving the redo log files to disk, here are some recommendations:

- ■ Archive the redo logs to a dedicated disk with sufficient disk space.
- ■ Copy the archived redo log files to tape at least once per day.
- ■ Once on tape, archived redo log files may be removed from disk.

**Archiving to Tape on UNIX**   On UNIX System V, only the UNIX pipe driver is supported with archiving to tape, so the archive monitor process (known as *archmon*) can only monitor archiving of database instances local to its machine. On UNIX BSD-based systems, the pipe and TCP/IP drivers are supported. To start archmon, type one of the following commands:

```
$ archmon @p:sid
$ archmon @t:host:SID
```

The archmon process displays a confirmation that it has connected to the archiving process. When the tape volume is full, the ARCH process suspends operation, signals archmon to prompt for a new tape, waits for a user response, and then resumes log archiving. You must run archmon either in a dedicated window or on a dedicated terminal. You can interrupt or kill the archmon process; however, the database will hang when all redo logs are filled until you re-invoke archmon to automatically archive them or until you manually archive them. You can stop archmon by doing a shut down or by stopping log archiving.

### Enabling Manual Archiving

The ARCHIVELOG mode can be set upon database creation or by using the **alter database archivelog** command. To issue this command, the database needs to be mounted but not open. Once ARCHIVELOG mode is set it remains in effect until you explicitly set the database to run in NOARCHIVELOG mode. Redo log files will be archived, by default, to the destination specified by the INIT.ORA parameter LOG_ARCHIVE_DEST. Once the database is operating in the ARCHIVELOG mode, there are two ways in which online redo log files can be archived: *manual* or *automatic*. Manual archiving allows you to choose and control at what time archiving is done. You must issue a SQLDBA command each time you want to archive a redo log file. All or specific redo log files can be archived manually with the **archive** command. The **archive log all**  command archives all the online redo log files that haven't been archived yet.

Assuming that the database is running in NOARCHIVELOG mode, executing the following series of commands in the specified order will put the database in ARCHIVELOG mode with the *manual archiving* option:

```
SQLDBA> shutdown
SQLDBA> startup mount [dbname]
SQLDBA> alter database [dbname] archivelog;
SQLDBA> alter database [dbname] open;
SQLDBA> archive log all
```

When the database is operating in the ARCHIVELOG mode with the manual archiving option, the SQL*DBA command **archive log list** should show the *database log mode* as ARCHIVELOG and *automatic archival* as DISABLED. For example,

```
SQLDBA> archive log list
Database log mode              ARCHIVELOG
Automatic archival             DISABLED
Archive destination            /dsk2/Oracle/arch
Oldest online log sequence     75
Next log sequence to archive   76
Current log sequence           76      ──➤ How far it goes ?
```

## Enabling Automatic Archiving

Alternatively to the manual archiving option, you can choose to run with the *automatic archiving* option. Enabling automatic archiving starts the ARCH process. The ARCH process archives the  online log files automatically every time the LGWR process switches log files. Automatic archiving can be enabled in either of two ways: by using the INIT.ORA parameter LOG_ARCHIVE_START (it should be set to *true*) or by using the SQL*DBA command **log archive start**. If the database is operational with manual archiving, and if you decide to enable automatic archiving using the INIT.ORA parameter,  note that the database has to be shut down and re-started again. While running the database with automatic archiving enabled, the SQL*DBA command **archive log list** should show *automatic archival* as ENABLED, as shown here:

```
SQLDBA> archive log list
Database log mode              ARCHIVELOG
Automatic archival             ENABLED
Archive destination            /dsk2/Oracle/arch
Oldest online log sequence     75
Next log sequence              78
Current log sequence           78
```

## Advantages and Costs of Archiving

Configuring the database to operate in ARCHIVELOG mode allows you to do complete and point-in-time recovery from media failures using offline or online backups. For customers running mission-critical applications where loss of data is not acceptable, this is the mode of operation recommended by Oracle. Shops that don't configure their database to run in ARCHIVELOG mode can restore the database from a backup in case of failure, but cannot roll forward from that point. For example, let's assume that you take a cold backup of the database every Sunday night and run the database in NOARCHIVELOG mode. Let's further assume that a media failure occurred on Friday and all the database files were lost. The only option you have is to restore the database from Sunday night's backup and restart the database. All the data entered or transactions done between Sunday and Friday are lost. Had you operated the database in ARCHIVELOG mode, you could have restored the database and then applied all the changes made to the database, thus not losing any data. In summary, operating the database in ARCHIVELOG mode allows you to recover the database completely.

Operating the database in ARCHIVELOG mode requires extra disk space (if archiving to disk) and adequate tape facilities. The DBA will have additional administrative work to do, such as space management and log file tracking.

# Configuring the Oracle Parallel Server Option

The majority of Oracle installations today are *single instance* configurations, i.e., one instance on one system provides access to one Oracle database for all users of that database. The *Parallel Server* option, using *shared disk access* and a *lock manager*, allows two or more Oracle instances, running on independent systems, to share coordinated access to one shared database, thus allowing users connected to different systems to submit transactions that will be executed by the system to which the user is connected against the shared database. The *shared disk access* is a capability provided by some platform vendors to allow multiple systems to share concurrent physical access to the same set of disk drives. A *lock manager* is a component, also provided by platform vendors, that is used by the Parallel Server option to coordinate Oracle activities globally across multiple systems. The implications of such a capability are that more computing resources (the aggregate CPU and memory structures of all systems sharing the database) can be provided to access the same physical database, enabling increased capacity, increased performance, more users supported, and more available database service since the failure of one system affects other systems only for a brief period without interrupting user transactions on surviving systems. The Parallel Server option is available on platforms that provide both shared disk access and a lock manager. Some of the platforms that currently support the Parallel Server option are DEC Open VMS, Sequent, Pyramid, NCR, nCUBE, Parsys, Meiko, KSR, Encore, and IBM. Support is expected to be forthcoming from other vendors as well.

In order to realize the benefits of using the Parallel Server, database and application designers and DBAs need to take into account various attributes of the Parallel Server option, such as deciding which applications are appropriate for the Parallel Server option (and which are not), partitioning of data access, space management, understanding and managing global locks used by the Parallel Server Option, measuring and alleviating contention, and configuring a Parallel Server for high availability. The *Oracle7 Parallel Server Administrator's Guide* gives details on all of these issues.

Each instance in a Parallel Server has its own *thread* of redo log files. Each thread will have a minimum of two log groups. Some concepts—such as *thread switching* and *instance recovery*—are unique to databases operating with the Parallel Server option and are discussed in detail in Chapter 5.

# CHAPTER 3

# Backup Principles

**A** valid backup is, quite simply and generally, a copy of the necessary information in a database that can be used to rebuild the database should the database reach an unusable state. The loss of a disk device, or the accidental removal of a database file or table are ways a database could be brought to an unusable state. Naturally, if the backup scheme relies upon image backups of the database and archiving of the log files, copies must be maintained of the data files, control files, online redo log files, and archived redo log files. If you lose one of the archived redo log files, you can say that there is a *hole* in the sequence of files. A hole in the archived log files invalidates a backup, but does allow the database to be rolled forward up to the beginning of the hole. For example, if you have 25 archived redo log files to roll forward and archived redo log file 15 is missing, then you can roll forward only until log 14.

A robust backup scheme is the method used to ensure that valid backups occur. Fundamental to a robust backup scheme is an understanding of the physical location of database files, the order of events during the backup process, and the handling of certain errors that occur during backups. A robust backup scheme is one which is resilient in the face of media, programmatic, and operator failures.

The Oracle database, and the operating system where Oracle runs, together offer a rich set of features that allow a wide range of robust backup schemes. This chapter gives an overview of the backup procedures that Oracle provides and the backup commands that you can use with various operating systems. *Physical* and *logical* backups are generally the two types of backups that are used by DBAs. A physical backup involves copying the physical database files to a backup destination, whereas a logical backup uses an Oracle utility (Export) to read the data in the database using SQL and stores the data and definitions in a binary file at the OS level. In this chapter, we will take a closer look at these types of backups. In addition, some of the design considerations while planning backup procedures are discussed for DSS (Decision Support Systems) and OLTP (OnLine Transaction Processing) shops using Very Large Databases (VLDB).

# Database Design and Basic Backup Rules

Before we can discuss online and offline backup procedures, it is very important to understand certain rules about placing the database files and other design considerations, which greatly affect the backup scheme. Following are some simple rules that will make a backup scheme robust in case of a disk or tape drive failure and will decrease the length of time needed for recovery.

1. It's recommended to archive the log files to disk (i.e., set the archive destination such that the archived redo log files are created on disk) and later copy them to tape. However, the archived log destination should not reside on the same physical disk device as any database file or online redo log file. If a database file or the currently active redo log file is lost, the archived log files will be needed for recovery. If the archived redo log file or an online redo log file that is not currently active is lost, the current database should be backed up using an online or offline backup procedure that copies the database files to a backup device (disk or tape). Operations can then safely continue. When creating the database using the **create database** command, setting the MAXLOGFILES parameter to a value greater than 2 will simplify recovery from the loss of an inactive but online redo log file. We will discuss the recovery procedures in greater detail in Chapter 5.

2. If database files are being backed up to disk, a database file residing on the same physical device as its backup copy is not adequately backed up. You should have a separate disk or disks to maintain the backup copy of the

database files. Backing up database files to disk can speed recovery, since the file need not be restored from tape. Also, backing up to disk often allows recovery to run in a shorter amount of time.

**3.** You should maintain multiple copies of the control file; a copy of the control file should be placed on several different disk devices mounted under different disk controllers. A control file can be added to the database by shutting down the database, copying the control file, altering the INIT.ORA parameter CONTROL_FILES, and restarting the database. For details refer to Chapter 2.

**4.** Online log files should be multiplexed and a minimum of two members for each group should be maintained. Two members of a log group should not reside on the same physical device, as it defeats the purpose of multiplexing log files.

**5.** Many systems may benefit from keeping a *hot spare* disk. A hot spare is an unused empty disk sitting in the disk cabinet that can be brought online should any other disk fail.

**6.** Maintaining multiple copies of archived redo log files will in many cases allow recovery from multiple media failures. For example, if the log files are archived to disk, periodically copied to tape, and then removed from disk, data loss could result if the tape and a database file are both lost. It is recommended to maintain a backup copy on disk, as well as on tape.

**7.** The procedure of rolling forward a database or database file from a backup can in many cases be simplified and made faster by keeping on disk all archived redo log files needed to roll forward the least recently backed up database file of a database. For many systems, much of the time necessary for recovery is spent restoring archived redo log files from tape.

**8.** Whenever the database structure is changed by adding, renaming, or dropping a log file or a data file (you can drop a data file only by dropping the tablespace that the data file belongs to), the control file should be backed up since the control file stores the schema of the database. In addition, any data file that is added should be backed up as well. The control file can be backed up while the database is open using the following command:

```
SQLDBA> alter database backup controlfile to 'filespec';
```

Keeping the above rules in mind, following is an example of a typical backup strategy:

**1.** Operate the database in ARCHIVELOG mode.

2. Perform offline backups at least once a week if you don't need to operate your database 24 hours a day, 7 days a week (24x7). However, if your shop is operational 24x7, take daily online backups.

3. Back up all archived redo log files at least once every four hours. The number of archived log files to back up depends on the log file size and the amount of redo generated. The amount of redo generated is dependent on the transaction rate.

4. Perform a weekly full database export (or incremental, cumulative, table-level export for large databases) in RESTRICT mode. For shops with 24x7 requirements, perform full exports when no database access or reduced database access is expected.

# Physical Backups

A physical backup is a backup where the actual physical blocks of the database files are copied from one location to the other. You can copy the database files from disk to tape or from disk to disk depending on the type of backup procedure you use. Oracle gives you two options while using physical backups to back up your database.

The first option is to back up the database files after the database is shut down clean with the **shutdown normal** command. This is known as an *offline* or *cold* backup since the database is offline (shutdown) while the backup is being performed. Some DBAs perform an offline backup of the Oracle database as part of the operating system backup. This means that when the system manager takes a backup of the entire system, the Oracle files get backed up as part of it. The DBA just needs to make sure that the database is shut down before the system manager takes the OS backup.

The second option is to take a physical backup of your database while the database is open and operational. This is the preferred backup procedure if, due to high availability requirements, you can't shut the database down. This kind of physical backup is called an *online* or *hot* backup due to the fact that the database is online while the backup is being performed. There are some special steps that you need to take while performing online backups.

## Offline (Cold) Backups

The first step in taking an offline backup is to shut down the database with the *normal* option. If you shut the database down with the *abort* or *immediate* option, you should restart the database in RESTRICT mode and shut it down again with the *normal* option before copying the database files. Then use the OS backup utility to copy all the online redo log files, database files, and control files. Any archived log files that haven't yet been backed up must be copied as well. In future releases, Oracle will recommend not to back up the online log files because you really don't need them to recover your database. In general, it is recommended to take an offline backup of your database at least once a week. However, the frequency of your backups should really be determined from your business needs.

Some DBAs tend to take backups manually instead of automating the backup procedures. There are some problems with this approach. First, after shutting down the database, you may not remember how many files exist in this database or where they are located. Next, if you have added a new data file recently, you might not remember to take a backup of that file. In situations like this, some DBAs dump the control file to obtain the information of the data files and the log files (i.e., $ strings *controlfile* for UNIX; $dump *controlfile* for VMS). Instead, in such cases, the best thing to do is to open the database and get the information you need. The data dictionary views, DBA_DATA_FILES or V$DATAFILE, V$LOGFILE, and V$CONTROLFILE will list, respectively, all the data files, redo log files, and control files associated with the database. (You don't need to open the database to select from these V$ views; you can mount the database and select the information.) Automating the backup procedures alleviates the administrative work for you and minimizes human errors. Note that automating the backup procedures requires writing backup scripts. Some example scripts are given in Chapter 4.

While taking offline backups (or online backups), since blocks are physically copied from the source to the destination, some data block corruptions might go undetected while copying the data files. In other words, the corruptions will be propagated to the backup copy of the data file. The only time you will realize this is when you restore the data files and try to recover the database. For this reason, testing your database backups is very important—the procedure to do so includes restoring the database files from a backup and rolling forward. You can also simulate a failure before doing recovery. Chapter 7 gives you a lot of examples on how to perform such tests. It is recommended that you test your backups at least once every three months or as frequently as your business allows you to.

## Offline Backup Procedure

Following are the steps required to take an offline backup of the database.

1. Prepare for the backup.

   a. Create a text file at the OS level that marks the start of the backup.

   b. Disable logon to the application.

   c. Provide warning messages that the database will be unavailable.

   d. Shutdown the database with the **shutdown normal** or **shutdown immediate** command.

**2.** Perform the backup.

   **a.** Remove the day-old archived redo logs from the day-old disk area. (The term "day-old" presumes you are doing daily backups.)

   **b.** Move the current day's archived logs to the day-old area.

   **c.** Perform the image copy of the data files, control files, and online log files to their backup disk locations.

**3.** Finishing the procedure.

   **a.** Start the database.

   **b.** Enable login to the applications.

   **c.** Copy the database image (data, control, online log, and archived log files) to tape.

   **d.** Finish the backup by removing the file that indicated the backup was started.

Step 1a can be used to ensure that the backup procedure is not inadvertently run twice at the same time for a database. Steps 2a and 2b keep the archived redo log files on disk until they are no longer needed for online recovery, but do not provide for keeping multiple copies on disk. Multiple copies could be kept on disk by copying the "day-old" logs to a "two-day-old" disk area, and copying the "two-day-old" disk area to tape during step 3c.

In an OFA (Optimal Flexible Architecture) compliant database, all database files can be manipulated with a single command. The operating system backup procedures and the commands used to back up the operating system files are given in Table 3-1. Some of these commands will be discussed later in this chapter.

# Online (Hot) Backups

If your business requires you to operate the database 24 hours a day, 7 days a week, you should take online or hot backups. To use online backups, you should operate the database in ARCHIVELOG mode. Otherwise, Oracle will give you an error and will not allow you to use the online backup procedure. The online backup procedure is very similar to taking offline backups. There are two additional steps involved. You should issue a **begin backup** command before you start the backup and an **end backup** command after the backup is completed. For example,

```
SQLDBA> alter tablespace users begin backup;
SQLDBA> alter tablespace users end backup;
```

These commands are issued, respectively, before and after the hot backup of tablespace *users* is taken.

Unlike offline backups, which back up the entire database, the unit of an online backup is a tablespace, and any or all tablespaces can be backed up as needed. The online backup includes a backup of the data files (for one or more tablespaces), the current control file, and all archived redo log files created during the period of the backup. All archived redo log files generated after the online backup are also required for complete recovery. Though the unit of backup for online backups is a tablespace, all tablespaces need to be backed up eventually and this is very important. The following example should make this point clear.

Let's assume that you have 3 tablespaces T1, T2, and T3 in your database, and you take partial online backups of your database every night. That means you take an online backup of T1 on Monday, T2 on Tuesday, and T3 on Wednesday. You repeat this procedure by taking an online backup of T1 again on Thursday, T2 on Friday, and so on. That means that at the end of every 3 days (on Wednesday and Saturday, in this example), you will have a complete backup of the database, though not all tablespaces are backed up at the same point in time, as in the case of offline backups. In this example, if you have a media failure on Friday after the online backups are done, and lose all your database files, you need to restore your

| OPERATING SYSTEM | OS PROCEDURE | COMMANDS |
| --- | --- | --- |
| UNIX | Cron job | obackup, cpio, tar, dd, fbackup,... |
| VMS | Batch job | backup |
| Windows NT | Interactive | Backup Manager or OCOPY utility |
| MAC | Interactive | GUI Finder to copy to disk, third-party software |
| OS/2 | Interactive | Standard DOS/OS2 copy commands |
| NetWare | Interactive | NetWare NBACKUP utility, third-party software |
| MVS | JCL submit | DFDSS or IDCAMS using EXPORT (not REPRO) |

**TABLE 3-1.** *Backup Procedures and Commands in Various Operating Systems*

entire database from backups. Since you have only two tablespaces (T1 and T2 from Thursday and Friday, respectively) and T3 has not been backed up yet, you need to restore T3 from the Wednesday night's backup. That means you also need to restore all the archived redo log files starting from Wednesday night's backup.

From the above example, you can see that recovery using partial backups (data files backed up at different times) begins with the oldest database file being restored. Therefore, you must preserve archived redo log files dating back to the time of the least recently backed up database file. Also, you need to make sure that full database backups should periodically be performed to ensure that a backup of all the database files is available.

The advantages of using online backups compared to offline backups are as follows:

- The database is completely accessible to users while backups are being made, including access to tablespaces that are being backed up.

- All data files do not have to be backed up at the same time—partial backups can be obtained. Redo logs can be applied to partially backed up tablespaces to perform full database recovery

## Sample Online Backup Procedure

The following are the steps involved in taking an online backup:

**1.** The database should be in ARCHIVELOG mode. If not, mount the database and issue the following commands:

```
SQLDBA> alter database archivelog;
SQLDBA> archive log start
SQLDBA> alter database open;
```

The first command sets the database to ARCHIVELOG mode. The second command enables automatic archiving (creates ARCH process), and the third command opens the database.

**2.** The next step is to obtain the oldest online log sequence number by issuing the following command:

```
SQLDBA> archive log list
Database log mode            ARCHIVELOG
Automatic archival           ENABLED
Archive destination          /home/orahome/product/7.2.1/dbs/arch
Oldest online log sequence   59
Next log sequence to archive 61  60
Current log sequence         61  60
```

You need to keep all the archived log files starting from sequence number 59 as part of the online backup. Though recovery will start from the SCN where backup has started (which will be in log sequence number 61), as a precautionary measure you should keep all the archived log files starting from the *oldest online log sequence* number. (SCN is discussed in Chapter 5.)

**3.** Set the tablespace you want to back up to *hot backup* mode as follows:

```
SQLDBA> ALTER TABLESPACE tablespace_name BEGIN BACKUP;
```

**4.** Back up all database files associated with the tablespace using an operating system command.

**5.** Set the tablespace back to *no hot backup* mode by using the following command:

```
SQLDBA> ALTER TABLESPACE tablespace_name END BACKUP;
```

Repeat steps 3 to 5 for each tablespace that you want to back up.

**6.** Execute the **archive log list** command again to obtain the *current log*  sequence number. This is the last redo log file you must keep as part of the online backup. Force a log switch so that Oracle will create an archived log file using the following command:

```
SQLDBA> ALTER SYSTEM SWITCH LOGFILE;
```

*NOTE*
While recovering a database using online backups, you need to apply a minimum of all the archived log files that were created between the **begin backup** command and the **end backup** command, so it's very important to back up all the archived log files. If complete recovery is required, all archived redo log files are required.

**7.** Back up all the archived log files (determined from steps 2 and 6) using an OS command. You should never take an online backup of the online redo log files, as the online log file has the *end of backup* marker and would cause corruptions if used during recovery.

**8.** Back up the control file using the following command:

```
SQLDBA> ALTER DATABASE BACKUP CONTROLFILE TO 'filespec';
```

*NOTE*
Control files should be backed up after a log file or data file is added, removed, or renamed in the database. New database files should be backed up immediately after they are added.

## Internal Operation of Hot Backups

It is important to understand some of the internal mechanisms of hot backups. When an **alter tablespace begin backup** command is issued, the data files that belong to the tablespace get flagged as *hot-backup-in-progress*. Taking the backup before issuing the **alter tablespace begin backup** command would make the backup data files useless. This command would checkpoint all the data files that are in hot backup mode. This means that any dirty buffers that belong to the data files in hot backup mode are flushed to disk. The file header's *checkpoint SCN* (checkpoint SCN is discussed in Chapter 5) is advanced to the SCN captured when the **begin backup** command is issued. This is important because the checkpoint SCN in the backup files must be the same as when the backup started, and Oracle cannot guarantee that the file header is the first block that the OS backup utility would copy. Now, after the initial checkpoint, succeeding checkpoints will cease to update the file headers when in hot backup mode.

The **alter tablespace begin backup** command will begin logging entire block images on the first change to the block if the INIT.ORA parameter _LOG_BLOCKS_DURING_BACKUP is set to TRUE (which is the default value). Why? Because, it might be necessary to have a copy of the whole block while applying recovery. To explain this, you need to understand a phenomenon called *split blocks.* If the Oracle block size is a multiple of OS blocks, then depending on how the OS copies blocks, it is possible for a hot backup to contain an inconsistent version of a given data block. For example, if a block is updated on disk between the reads, the copy in the backup file could be useless since the front and back halves of a block may be written at different times. By logging the before image of a data block to the redo log file before the first change, it can be used later to reconstruct a fractured block during recovery.

The checkpoint done during the execution of the **alter tablespace begin backup** command ensures that only blocks that are changed during the hot backups are written to the redo log file. This explains why excessive redo would be generated for data files in hot backup mode. Note that if a block remains in cache for a long period of time, it will be logged only once; but if it is flushed to disk and read into cache again while still in hot backup mode, the before image of the block is logged again.

To verify the consistency of the block before recovery, the version number at the beginning of the block is compared to the version number at the end of the block to determine whether the block has been split during a hot backup. If the version of the block at the beginning and end are the same, then the block is consistent. If not, a consistent version of the block is required and the before image of the block in the redo is copied to disk before applying redo changes.

What this means is that if more DML (i.e., insert, update, or delete operations) is performed on the data files during hot backup, more redo will be generated during this period. This is why Oracle Worldwide Support recommends that you take hot backups when there is less DML activity in the database. This also suggests that you should end the hot backup of a tablespace by issuing the **alter tablespace end backup** command before you take a hot backup of the next tablespace. For example, if two tablespaces need to be backed up, it is recommended that you issue a **begin backup** command for the first tablespace, take the backup at the operating system level, then issue the **end backup** command before taking the backup of the second tablespace—rather than issuing a batch of **begin backup** commands, followed by a batch of backups, and finishing with a batch of **end backup** commands. In summary, you should keep the tablespaces open in hot backup mode for as little time as possible under the lightest usage conditions.

The file copy during hot backups is done by utilities that are not part of Oracle. The presumption is that the manufacturer of the hardware will have backup facilities that are superior to any portable facility that Oracle would develop. It is the responsibility of the DBA to ensure that copies are only taken between the **begin backup** and **end backup** commands.

The **alter tablespace end backup** command creates a redo record containing the begin backup checkpoint SCN. The SCN is also in the header of the hot backup data files. This is how Oracle knows when all the redo generated during the backup has been applied to the data files. In other words, while using hot backups, during recovery, the DBA needs to apply *at least* the redo generated between the **begin backup** and **end backup** commands to make the backup data files consistent. If you stop the recovery before applying the redo and try to open the database, an error will be signaled. Also, when the **end backup** command is issued, logging of block images is stopped and the data file checkpoints are advanced to the database checkpoint. Chapter 5 discusses checkpoints in detail.

While taking a hot backup, Oracle will not allow you to shut the database down using the *normal* or *immediate* options. Also, you cannot take a tablespace that is in hot backup mode offline with the *normal* or *temporary* option. A message is displayed to the DBA indicating that the files are in hot backup mode and thus the DBA cannot shut the database down or take the tablespace offline. This is to ensure that an end backup marker is generated and to remind the DBAs to issue the **end backup** command. Chapter 7 describes a *case study* on how to deal with situations when the database crashes while you are taking a hot backup of the database.

# Logical Backups

The logical backup is defined as a backup that copies the data in the database and does not record the location of the data. The *Export* utility offered by Oracle can be used to take logical backups of the database. The export utility copies the data and database *definitions* and saves them in a binary operating system file in Oracle internal format. In order to use the Export utility, the database must be open. Since a snapshot of the table is taken before exporting, read consistency for individual tables is guaranteed, but inter-table consistency is not. So if you want a snapshot of all the tables in the entire database, then no changes should be made to the database while taking an export of the database. This can be achieved if you open the database in RESTRICT mode (so users cannot access the data) and export the database.

Export backup usually takes more time than a physical backup. If you are exporting to disk or if you have multiple tape drives and exporting to tape, you can run parallel export sessions to decrease the time to obtain a full export. You can export to tape or multiple export files can be copied across the network when there is not enough local disk space. The following are some of the advantages of taking a database export with the Export utility.

- One of the biggest advantages of using a logical backup is that data block corruptions can be detected while exporting and the export procedure will fail. Then you need to fix the corruption in the table before you can attempt to take a logical backup again.

- Export provides an extra level of protection from user errors or structural failures. For example, if a user accidentally drops a table, it is very easy to use the *Import* utility to restore the table compared to doing incomplete recovery with physical backups.

- Export offers a great deal of flexibility in choosing what data and definitions you want to export.

- You can take COMPLETE, INCREMENTAL, or CUMULATIVE exports.

- Export backups are portable and can be imported into any database on the current machine. The export file can also be transferred through the network (i.e., using ftp) to another machine, and data imported into another database on the remote machine.

One of the disadvantages of using Export to take logical backups is that it could be very slow if exporting large amounts of data. It is recommended that you take a full database export (in addition to your physical backups) at least once a month, if possible. This will help you maintain high database availability if object-level recovery is required. Depending on the kind of transaction rate and pattern, you can take INCREMENTAL, CUMULATIVE, or COMPLETE export backups. We will discuss some of the export parameters and export modes in the next two sections. For complete details, refer to the *Oracle7 Server Utilities User's Guide*.

To summarize, logical backups should be taken *in addition* to the physical backups that you take. Depending on the failure, sometimes it is quicker to use the physical backups to recover the database—for example, a data file loss. In other cases, you can recover quicker using an export backup. An example is when a user accidentally drops a table and point-in-time recovery needs to be performed on the database to recover the table.

# Export Parameters

Table 3-2 gives a list of parameters you can use to control an export. A brief description of each parameter is given.

# Export Modes

There are three modes in which you can export the data. The *full* export mode is the first one; it can be enabled by using the FULL=Yes option in the export command. The second mode is the *user* export mode. Using the OWNER parameter you can export tables owned by certain users in the database. The third mode is the *table* mode where you can use the TABLES parameter to export selected tables in the database. The following table shows the objects exported for the three export modes:

| TABLE MODE | USER MODE | FULL DATABASE MODE |
|---|---|---|
| table definitions | *Table Mode +* | *User Mode +* |
| table data | clusters | roles |
| owner's grants | database links | all synonyms |
| owner's indexes | views | system privileges |
| table constraints | private synonyms | tablespace definitions |
| table triggers | sequences | tablespace quotas |
| | snapshots | rollback segment definitions |
| | snapshot logs | system audit options |
| | stored procedures | all triggers |
| | | profiles |

These exports can be run in parallel to speed up the process of obtaining an export of the entire database or when there is not enough time to obtain a full export.

### Full Database Export
The full database export mode can be further divided into *COMPLETE, CUMULATIVE,* and *INCREMENTAL* exports. CUMULATIVE and INCREMENTAL

| PARAMETER | DEFAULT VALUE | DESCRIPTION |
|---|---|---|
| USERID | Undefined | The username/password of the user performing the export. |
| BUFFER | OS dependent | The size in bytes of the buffer used to fetch data rows. If zero is specified, or if the table contains LONG data, only one row at a time is fetched. |
| FILE | expdat.dmp | The name of the binary output file created by export at the OS level. |
| GRANTS | Yes | A flag to indicate whether to export grants. |
| INDEXES | Yes | A flag to indicate whether to export indexes. |
| ROWS | Yes | A flag to indicate whether to export rows in the tables. If set to NO, only table definitions are exported without data. |
| CONSTRAINTS | Yes | A flag to indicate whether to export constraints. |
| COMPRESS | Yes | A flag to indicate whether to compress table data into one extent upon import. |
| FULL | No | A flag to indicate whether to export data in the entire database. |
| OWNER | Current user | A list of usernames whose objects are exported. Specify OWNER=(*userlist*) to export in user mode. |
| TABLES | Undefined | A list of table names to export. Specify TABLES=(*tablelist*) to export in table mode. |
| RECORDLENGTH | OS dependent | The length in bytes of the file record. |
| INCTYPE | Undefined | The type of incremental export. Valid values are COMPLETE, CUMULATIVE, and INCREMENTAL. |
| RECORD | Yes | A flag to indicate whether to record an incremental export in database tables, SYS.INCVID, and SYS.INCEXP. |
| PARFILE | Undefined | The name of a parameter file that contains one or more export parameters. |

**TABLE 3-2.** *Description of Export Parameters*

exports take less time than COMPLETE exports and allow you to get an export of just the changed data and definitions. Which type of export to use depends on how the data is modified in your tables. For example, if your applications modify only one table or a small set of tables you can back up only those tables using the INCREMENTAL export. All three modes should be used in a robust backup scheme. Let's take a closer look at these different export options.

**COMPLETE**   A COMPLETE export should be done as part of an incremental database export backup scheme. In a typical incremental backup scheme, instead of taking a full database export every day, you will start with a COMPLETE backup on day one (say, Sunday), and take INCREMENTAL exports for the rest of the week. This way, only the tables in the database that are modified are exported from Monday through Saturday, thereby saving export time. A COMPLETE export performs an export of all the tables in the database and resets the INCREMENTAL export information for each table. In other words, this type of export is the same as a full database export, but it also updates some bookkeeping information regarding exports. To perform this kind of export you should set the parameter INCTYPE=COMPLETE in the export command. If the INCTYPE parameter is specified, information is written to tables SYS.INCVID (reset to 1 if INCTYPE=COMPLETE), SYS.INCFIL, and SYS.INCEXP. After each COMPLETE export, both the preceding CUMULATIVE and INCREMENTAL export files are no longer required. For example,

```
$ exp userid=system/manager full=Y inctype=complete constraints=Y
file=full_export_filename
```

**CUMULATIVE**   The CUMULATIVE database export exports only tables that have been modified or created since the most recent CUMULATIVE or COMPLETE export, and records the export details for each table exported. To perform this kind of export you should set the parameter INCTYPE=CUMULATIVE in the export command. After each CUMULATIVE export, any preceding INCREMENTAL export files are no longer required and may be archived/deleted. For example,

```
$ exp userid=system/manager full=Y inctype=cumulative constraints=Y
file=cumulative_export_filename
```

**INCREMENTAL**   The INCREMENTAL database export exports all tables modified or created since the most recent INCREMENTAL, CUMULATIVE, or COMPLETE export, and records the export details for each table exported. To perform this kind of export you should set the parameter INCTYPE=INCREMENTAL in the export command. Incremental exports are beneficial in environments where users are able to create their own tables. In this case, many tables will remain static for periods of time, while others will be updated and need to be backed up. Also, INCREMENTAL exports allow a table that has been accidentally dropped or modified to be quickly restored. For example,

```
$ exp userid=system/manager full=Y inctype=incremental constraints=Y
file=incremental_export_filename
```

You may use any of the following export combinations:

COMPLETE alone
COMPLETE with CUMULATIVE
COMPLETE with INCREMENTAL
COMPLETE with CUMULATIVE and INCREMENTAL

**NOTE**
A COMPLETE export is needed in order to do INCREMENTAL or CUMULATIVE exports. The FULL=Y export parameter, in addition to the INCTYPE parameter, should be specified when performing COMPLETE, CUMULATIVE, or INCREMENTAL exports.

# Sample Export Procedure

The following export procedure assumes that you don't want any changes made to the database while taking a full database export. So the database will be shut down and started in RESTRICT mode before taking the full database export. The steps are as follows:

1. Shut down any applications or third-party tools running on top of Oracle, and then shut down the database using the command

   ```
   SQLDBA> shutdown immediate
   ```

2. So that users can't access the data, start up the database with the *restrict* option by using the command:

   ```
   SQLDBA> startup restrict open
   ```

3. Obtain the export with the following export command:

   ```
   $ exp username/password full=y file=full_exp.dat constraints=Y
   ```

4. Use the following command to give the users access to the database again:

   ```
   SQLDBA> alter system disable restricted session;
   ```

# Backup Commands in Various Operating Systems

This section focuses on various operating system-specific commands that are used to back up and restore the database files during an offline or online backup. In some operating systems, such as IBM MVS, some of the basic concepts (such as archiving redo log files) are different compared to other operating systems. Such mechanisms are described in this section.

## Backup/Restore in VMS Environment

The data files in the VMS environment have a *dbs* extension. The control files have a *con* extension, and the archived and online redo logs have an *rdo* extension. **backup** and **copy** are the two commands used in VMS to back up and restore database files. Wildcards can be used while backing up with the **backup** and **copy** commands. If the database layout is OFA compliant, all the data files can be backed up with one command using wildcards (i.e., wildcards can be used for the disk, part of the file path, and for the filename without the extension). Refer to Chapter 2 for an OFA-compliant database layout.

**NOTE**
The **backup** command does some file verification, whereas, the **copy** command does not.

The following examples show how to back up the data files, log files and control files, respectively, from disk to disk.

```
$ backup/log/ignore=(interlock, nobackup) -
DiskA:[dir_path]*.dbs DiskB:[backup_dir_path]*.dbs

$ backup/log/ignore=interlock DiskA:[dir_path]*.rdo -
DiskB:[backup_dir_path]*.rdo

$ backup/log/ignore=interlock DiskA:[dir_path]*.con -
DiskB:[backup_dir_path]*.con
```

The following commands should be used if backing up from disk to tape.

```
$ mount/foreign tape_device:
$ backup/log/ignore=interlock DiskA:[dir-path]*.dbs -
tape_device:db_test.bck/sav
```

The **copy** command does not do any verification or ignore lock contentions to access files-11 copy to tape. The **copy** command is given below to copy to tape.

```
$ mount/over=id tape_device:
$ copy  DiskA:[backup_dir_path]*.dbs  tape_device:
```

The **backup** or the **copy** command can be used to restore the database files from tape to disk as well. Again, wildcards can be used. The **backup** command must be used if the tape is mounted with the *foreign* option. The **copy** command is used if the tape is mounted files-11. The following example shows how to use the **backup** command to restore files from tape to disk:

```
$ mount/foreign tape_device:
$ backup/rewind/list tape_device:*/sav
```

To retrieve a file from tape the following command should be issued:

```
$ backup/rewind tape_device:db_test.bck/sav/select=(test.dbs,..) -
disk:[dir_path]file/new_version/owner=parent/log
```

The following command shows how to use the **copy** command to restore files from tape to disk:

```
$ mount  tape_device:  volume_label    !OR you can use the following command:
$ mount/over=id tape_device:
$ dir tape_device:                           ! To list all the files on tape
$ copy tape_device:file  disk:[dir_path]file  ! To retrieve a file from tape
```

# Backup/Restore in UNIX Environment

In this section, we will describe some of the commands that are used in UNIX to take physical backups of the database files.

### cpio
The **cpio** is a standard utility on UNIX System V Platforms. It's a nonstandard utility on UNIX BSD platforms, but many BSD vendors include it. This command is used to copy files and directory structures in and out of archive files and to copy directory structures from one location to another. To generate a required single

column list of path names, use the **cat**, **ls**, or **find** commands. The **cpio** command can back up files describing devices (special files), as well as data files.

There are basically three **cpio** modes:

**1.** *Copy out* mode, which creates an archive file, as in

**cpio -o** [aABcLvV ] [ -C size ] [ -H hdr ] [ -O file ] [-M msg ]

**2.** *Copy in* mode, which allows you to retrieve a previously archived file, as in

**cpio -i** [ 6bBcdfkmrsStuvV ] [ -C size] [ -E file ] [ -H hdr ] [ -O file ] [ -I file ] [ -M msg ] [ -R ID ] [ patterns ]

**3.** Pass mode, which passes a copy of a directory structure from the source to a new destination. It works like copy out, except the files are copied to a new *directory tree.* For example,

**cpio -p** [adlmruvV ] [ -R ID] *directory*

Please refer to the **man** pages in UNIX for explanation of the various options used with **cpio**.

The following three examples show how to copy a directory tree from the source location to a new directory location on disk. The first command is used to back up all files in the same directory path, the second example is used to back up all data files and control files, and the last example is used to back up the redo log files.

```
$ ls /dsk*/ORACLE/prod/*.*   |   cpio -pdk new-dir

$ ls /dsk*/ORACLE/prod/*.dbf   |   cpio -pdk new-dir

$ ls /dsk*/ORACLE/prod/*.rdo   |   cpio -pdk new-dir
```

To restore files from an archive file ( arch010194 ) on disk use the following command:

```
$ cpio -ic < /bck/arch010194
```

or

```
$ cat /bck/arch010194 | cpio -ic
```

On *some* platforms the -r option (not used with -p) can be used to interactively rename files. To restore and rename files from an archive file ( arch010194 ) on disk, use the following command:

```
$ cpio -icr < /bck/arch010194
```

While copying from disk to tape, if **cpio** reaches the end of the tape it will prompt you for the device name, allowing you to insert a new tape to continue or press RETURN to exit. To copy files in the directories to tape, use the following command:

```
$ ls /dsk*/ORACLE/*.* | cpio -ocBv  >  tape_device
```

To copy the current directory and all subdirectories (directory trees) to tape, use the following command:

```
$ find . -depth -print | cpio -ocBv  >  tape_device
```

While restoring from tape, first identify the tape that contains the files needed by issuing the following command:

```
$ cpio -itBv < tape_device
```

Then copy the file or directory tree of files from tape to disk using the command

```
$ cpio -icBv file  < tape_device
$ cpio -icdBv file < tape_device
```

### tar

The **tar** command is a standard utility on System V and BSD UNIX. This command is used to archive files from disk to tape or used to retrieve archived files from tape. It can also be used to copy directory structures from one directory to a new directory. Some BSD systems do not support a hyphen preceding the options to the **tar** command. If the device is a hyphen (-), **tar** writes to the standard output or reads from the standard input. For a detailed description of the options for the **tar** command, refer to the **man** pages in UNIX.

The following is an example of using the **tar** command to back up one directory structure to a new directory location on disk:

```
$ tar cf - . | ( cd to_dir; tar xf - )
```

In the above example, the **tar** command is used to create a tar file to the standard output (the device argument is a hyphen). The output is piped to a subshell that changes directories (**cd**) to the directory you want to copy the files to. The second **tar** command extracts the files back out into a hierarchical structure.

The following example shows how to back up files from one directory to tape:

```
$ tar -cvf  /dev/rmt0h  /dsk*/ORACLE/*.*
```

where **rmt0h** is the tape device.

Similarly, to list the contents of an archive tape and restore files from the tape device, use the following commands, respectively:

```
$ tar -tvf tape_device
```

```
$ tar -xvf tape_device
```

### tar versus cpio

The advantages of using the **tar** command are

■ It has relatively simple syntax.

■ It allows you to replace archived files with different versions and append new files to the end of an archive without having to rewrite the file from the beginning.

The advantages of using the **cpio** command are

■ It can back up files describing devices (special files), as well as data files.

■ It writes data in a stream format, saving space and time when creating a tape backup; **cpio** tends to be faster than **tar** and stores data more efficiently than **tar**.

■ **cpio**, unlike **tar**, will attempt to read a tape several times if it encounters problems.

■ **cpio** will skip a bad area on tape.

### cp

**cp** is a System V and BSD UNIX command to copy files or directory structures from one location on disk to another. The syntax is as follows:

**cp** [-ip] *source_file destination_file*
**cp** [-ipr] *source_file_list destination_directory*
**cp** -r [-ip] *source_directory destination_directory*

where option **-i** is used if interactive confirmation is required. You are prompted if the copy will overwrite an existing file. If you answer *yes* to the prompt, the copy is done. Option **-p** is used to preserve the characteristics of the source file. The contents, modification times, and permission modes of the source file are copied to the destination file. Option **-r** recursively copies any source directories. If a directory is given as the source file, then all of its files and subdirectories are copied. The destination must be a directory.

The following examples show how to back up a file and a directory structure to another location on disk, respectively.

```
$ cp datafile  /bck/datafile
```

```
$ cp -r data_file_dir    bck_dir
```

## volcopy

This is a System V command that makes a literal copy of the file system using block size matched to the device. The syntax is

$ **volcopy** *[option] fsname srcdevice volname1 destdevice volname2*

where *option* can be **-a** or **-s**. If you use the option **-a**, it invokes a verification sequence requiring a positive operator response instead of the standard 10-second delay before the copy is made. The **-s** is the default option that aborts the operation if a wrong verification sequence occurs. The program requests length and density information if not given on the command line or not recorded on an input tape label. *fsname* represents the mounted name (i.e., root) of the file system being copied. *srcdevice* and *volname1* represent the device and physical volume name from which the file system copy is extracted. *destdevice* and *volname2* represent the target device and volume.

## dump and restor

**dump** and **restor** are standard BSD UNIX commands. The **dump** command copies all files changed after a certain date from a specified file system to a file, a pipe, magnetic tape, or disks. This utility supports EOF handling, which allows the use of multiple media. The utility prompts for the next volume when the current one is filled. The syntax is as follows:

$ **/etc/dump** *[key [argument ...] file_system ]*

where the *key* specifies the date and other options about the dump; some keys require an *argument*. The various options for the *key* are

[0123456789aBdFfnsSuWw]

where 0 through 9 is the dump level. Level 0 means dump the entire system. Level 1 dumps only those files modified since the last level 0 dump. Level 2 dumps only those files modified since the last level 0 or 1 dump, and so on. Refer to the **man** pages in UNIX for detailed descriptions of all the options (i.e., **man** dump).

The following example dumps the entire file system (/bck/db_files) to the device (/dev/rra2a) with a size of 400 blocks and each block of 1024 bytes:

```
$ dump 0Bf 400 /dev/rra2a  /bck/db_files
```

The following example dumps the entire file system (/bck/db_files) to a 6250-bpi tape on a TU78 tape drive:

```
$ dump 0undf /dev/rmt0h /bck/db_files
```

The **restor** command performs an incremental file system restore for BSD UNIX. The **restor** obtains files from a file, magnetic tape, or disk that was saved by a *previous* dump. You can restore all or part of a corrupted file system, or retrieve individual files overwritten by users. Only a *super* user may restore a file system containing special files. You must be in stand-alone mode to restore the root file system and the **restor** command does not accept any arguments; the **-r** argument is implicit. The syntax is as follows:

$ **restor** *key [ argument ] [ file-system ]*

The following command creates an empty file system on the disk device, destroying the existing file system, and then restores a complete dump to the same device. The device cannot contain the root device, since after the **mkfs** command the root file system wouldn't exist.

```
$ restor r device          (This assumes the default device)
$ restor r /dev/da0        (The file system is restored on disk, da0.)
```

To restore a file from the previous dump, use the command:

```
$ restor x file
```

where *file* is the inode number of the file extracted from the dump.

## backup and restore

**backup** and **restore** are standard System V UNIX commands. The **backup** utility is a front-end for **cpio**. You should use the **restore** to restore backups made with this utility. The syntax is

$ **backup**  [-t]  [-p¦-c¦-f *files* ¦-u *"user1* [*user2*]"* ]  -d *device*
$ **backup** -h

where **-h** produces a backup history, informing the user when the last complete and incremental/partial backups were done. The option **-c** generates a complete backup, all files changed since system installation. The **-p** option does an incremental/partial backup—only files modified since the last backup. The **-f** *files* backs up specified files. Filenames may contain characters to be expanded—i.e., asterisk (*) and period (.). Note that the argument must be in quotes. The **-u** option backs up all files in the user's home directory. At least one user must be specified. If more than one user is specified, the argument must be in quotes. The argument **all** backs up all users' home directories. Option **-d** specifies the backup device. Option **-t** indicates that the backup device is a tape. The **-t** option must be used with the **-d** option when a tape device is specified.

The **restore** command performs an incremental file system restore of a previous backup made with the System V **backup** utility. This utility acts as a front end to **cpio**. The syntax is

$ **restore** [-c] [-i]  [-o] [-t] [-d *device*] [*pattern* [*pattern*] ...]

where the  **-c** option does a complete restore. All files on the tape are restored. The **-i** option gets the index file off of the medium. The **-o** option overwrites existing files. If the file to be restored already exists, it will not be restored unless this option is specified. The **-t** option indicates that the tape device is to be used. The option must be used with the **-d** option when restoring from tape. The **-d** *device* option indicates the device to be used.

## fbackup and frestore

The **fbackup** and **frestore** commands are used on HP-UX System V. The **fbackup** command is used to selectively transfer files to an output device. **fbackup** combines the features of **dump** and **ftio** to provide a high-speed, flexible, file system backup mechanism. The syntax is as follows:

$ **/etc/fbackup** -f *device* [-f *device*..] [-0-9] [-uvyAH] [ -i *path*] [-e *path*][-g *graph_file*] [-I *path*] [-V *path*] [-c *config*]
$ **/etc/fbackup** -f *device* [-f *device*..] [-R *restart_file*] [-uvyAH][-I *path*] [-V *path*] [-c *config*]

The *Return Value* is 0 upon normal completion; 1 if it is interrupted but allowed to save its state for possible restart; and 2 if error conditions prevent the session from completing. The output device can be a file, standard output, a raw magnetic tape drive, a DDS-format tape, or a re-writeable magneto-optical disk.

The selection of files to back up is done by explicitly specifying trees of files to be included or excluded from a **fbackup** session. The user can construct an arbitrary graph of files by using the **-i** (include) or  **-e** (exclude) options on the command line, or by using the **-g** option with a graph file or multiple graph files. For backups being done on a regular basis, the **-g** option provides an easier interface for controlling the backup graph. **fbackup** selects files in this graph and attempts to transfer them to the output device. The selectivity depends on the mode in which **fbackup** is being used, i.e., full or incremental backups.

When doing full backups, all files in the graph are selected. When doing incremental backups, only files in the graph that have been modified since a previous backup of that graph are selected. If **fbackup** is used for incremental backups, a database of past backups must be kept. By default, **fbackup** maintains the data in the text file **/usr/adm/fbackupfiles/dates**. The directory **/usr/adm/fbackupfiles** must be created prior to the first incremental backup. The **-d** option can be used to specify another database file. Entries for each session are recorded on separate pairs of lines. The first line of each pair contains the graph file name, backup level, starting time, and ending time. The second line of each pair contains the same information; but in strftime (3C) format, **fbackup** does not use this line and it is included for readability. Graph filenames are compared character by character upon checking the previous backup database file to determine when a previous session was run for that graph.

The following example shows how to back up to tape a file that contains directories of files. Following that, we list the files that should be included in or excluded from the backup.

```
$ /etc/fbackup -f tape_device - g graph_file -u -0
$ /etc/fbackup -0I /usr -e /usr/lib -f /dev/rmt0h
$ cd /usr/adm/fbackupfiles
$ /etc/fbackup -0uc config -g graphs -I indices -f /dev/rmt0h
# graphs file
i          /dsk1
i          /dsk2
i          /dsk3/oracle
i          /dsk4/usr
e          /dsk1/usr/class
e          /dsk2/usr/test
```

The **frestore** reads media written by the **fbackup** command. The syntax is as follows:

$ **/etc/frecover** -r [-hmosvyAFNOX] [-c *config*] [-f *device*] [-S skip]
$ **/etc/frecover** -R *path* [-f *device*]
$ **/etc/frecover** -x [-hmosvyAFNOX] [-c *config*] [-e *path*] [-f *device*] [-g *graph*] [-i *path*] [-S skip]

Refer to the **man** pages in UNIX for descriptions of the various options.

**dd**

This command copies the specified input file to the specified output file with possible conversions. It can read input from a file or from standard input. It writes to a file or to standard output. The **dd** command is very useful because it allows raw device backups that cannot be done with the **tar** and **cpio** commands. With the **dd** command you can specify the input and output block size to perform raw physical I/O.

The **dd** command lets you copy data from one device to another that does not have the same block size, where **cpio** and **tar** might fail; you could use the **dd** command as a front end command that would extract the data from tape and convert it to a block size **cpio** and **tar** can utilize. The syntax is as follows:

$ **dd** [*option = value ...* ]

Some of the important options are described below:

- **bs=***n*   Sets the input and output block size to *n* bytes.
- **count =***n*   Allows only *n* blocks of input to be copied.
- **ibs=***n*   The input block size is set to *n* bytes. If the **ibs** option is not specified, a 512-byte block is used. Data corruption can occur on some systems if the ibs exceeds 1024 when copying data from tape to disk. As a workaround, use the **bs** option.
- **if=***file*   Specifies the input file, *file*. If the **if** option is not used, standard input is used.
- **obs=***n*   The output block size is set to *n* bytes. If the **obs** option is not used, a 512-byte block is used.
- **of=***file*   Specifies the output file, *file*. If the **of** option is not used, standard output is used.
- **seek=***n*   Skips over the first *n* blocks of the output file before it starts to write the data.
- **skip=***n*   Skips forward the first *n* blocks of the input file before copying.

To back up from a raw device to a raw tape device you have two options:

1. You can copy the raw device data to a regular UNIX file using the **dd** command and then use the normal UNIX backup commands such as **cpio** and **tar**.

2. Copy the raw device data directly to a raw tape device. The **dd** command does not handle multiple drives, so if the partition exceeds one tape,

multiple commands will need to be used. Check to see if **dd** requires special block size values to be used. The following steps will make the procedure clear:

■ Mount the first tape and back up the raw device to tape using the following command:

```
# dd if=raw_device of=tape_device bs=block_size count=number
```

■ If additional tapes are needed, enter the following when prompted. **skip** is incremented by the **count** value for each successive tape:

```
# dd if=raw_device of=tape_device skip=number bs=block_size count=number
```

To restore data from a raw tape device onto a raw partition use the following steps:

**1.** Mount the tape and then enter

```
# dd if=tape_device of=filename bs=block_size count=number
```

**2.** Mount subsequent tapes if needed, incrementing **seek** or **oseek** by **count**:

```
# dd if=tape_device of=raw_device [seek|oseek]=number bs=block_size
count=number
```

## ✭ crontab–UNIX Automated Scheduler Command

You can schedule physical backups or exports using **crontab**, an automated scheduler command. Chapter 4 gives an example of a UNIX script to do cold and hot backups. The script is scheduled to run using **crontab**. In this section we describe how this scheduler works.

The **crontab** command is used to designate a file whose lines schedule commands to be executed at regular intervals. The cron program reads, interprets, and executes the crontab file. The commands are usually executed by the Bourne shell (sh). The following is the syntax:

```
# crontab [ file ]
# crontab -e [ username ]
# crontab -l [ username ]
# crontab -r [ username ]
```

where *file* is the crontab file. Option **-e** lets you edit your crontab file using the editor defined by the EDITOR variable. The **-r** option removes your current crontab file. If username is specified, it removes that user's crontab file. Only root can remove other users' crontab files. The **-l** option lists the contents of your current crontab file. The argument *file* is the name of the file you want to use as your crontab file. The file is copied to a file named *username* in the system crontab directory. If you do not specify a filename for **crontab** to read as input, **crontab** reads the standard input until you press CTRL-D.

The **crontab** command reads a file or the standard input to a directory that contains all users' crontab files: **/usr/spool/cron/crontabs/username**. You can use **crontab** to remove your crontab file or display it. You cannot access other users' crontab files in the crontab directory. If you do not redirect the standard output and standard error of a command executed from your crontab file, the output is mailed to you. The crontab file contains lines that consist of 6 fields separated by blanks (tabs or spaces). The first five fields are integers that specify the time the command is scheduled. The sixth field contains the command that is executed by cron. Table 3-3 shows the first five fields of a line in the crontab file.

Each field can contain the following:

- An integer
- A range
- A list (of integers or ranges)
- An asterisk (*) (indicates all legal values, i.e., all legal times)

The days of the week and the day of the month fields are interpreted separately if both are defined. To specify days to run by only one field, the other field must be set to an asterisk (*). Following are some examples:

| | |
|---|---|
| 10 0 * * 3 | Run the command only on Wednesday at 12:10 A.M. |
| 0 6 1,9 * 1 | Run the command at 6 A.M. on the first and ninth of each month and every Monday. |
| 0,30 7-20 * * * | Run the command every 30 minutes from 7 A.M. to 8 P.M. every day. |

The sixth field contains the command that is executed by cron at the specified times. The command string is terminated by a new line or a percent sign (%). Any text following the percent sign is sent to the command as standard input. The percent sign can be escaped by preceding it with a backslash (\%). Lines beginning with a # sign are comment lines. To use the **crontab** command you must have access permission. The system administrator can make the **crontab** command available to all users, specific users, or no users. Two files that are used to control access are **/usr/sbin/cron.d/cron.allow** and **/usr/sbin/cron.d/cron.deny**. If the **cron.allow** file exists but is empty, then all users can use the **crontab** command. If neither file exists, then no users other than the *superuser* can use **crontab**.

| FIELD | RANGE | MEANING |
|---|---|---|
| 1 | 0 to 59 | Minutes |
| 2 | 0 to 23 | Hours (midnight is 0; 10 P.M. is 22) |
| 3 | 1 to 31 | Day of the month |
| 4 | 1 to 12 | Month of the year |
| 5 | 0 to 6 | Day of the Week (Sunday is 0; Saturday is 6) |

**TABLE 3-3.**   *Description of the First Five Fields of a Line in the crontab File*

Other related files are given below:

**/usr/sbin/cron.d**   The main directory for the cron process
**/usr/sbin/cron.d/log**   Accounting information for cron processing
**/usr/sbin/cron.d/crontab.allow**   A file containing a list of users allowed to use crontab
**/usr/sbin/cron.d/crontab.deny**   A file containing a list of users not allowed to use crontab
**/usr/spool/cron/crontabs**   Location of crontab text to be executed

# Backup/Restore in IBM MVS Environment

Backup and recovery procedures for Oracle on MVS are exactly the same as any other operating system. Externally, however, there are some differences because there are differences between MVS and other operating systems. In essence, Oracle for MVS files are VSAM files, and the ARCH process submits a batch job to archive online redo log files.

### Backing Up Data Files

Oracle files are backed up using *physical image* type backup utilities like IBM's DF/DSS or FDR. You can back up the database files using IDCAMS EXPORT with the CIMODE parameter. IDCAMS REPRO will not work because Oracle works on CI level and does not use VSAM records. Files belonging to a tablespace should be backed up as a unit by submitting a batch job. The following is an example of a *physical image* type backup.

```
//BACKUP    JOB (0000,O7),'ORACLE IMAGE COPY',CLASS=A
//STEP1     EXEC PGM=ADRDSSU
//SYSPRINT DD   SYSOUT=*
//DUMPOUT   DD   DSN=ORACLE.ORA1V.IMAGE.COPY,DISP=(NEW,CATLG,DELETE),
//               UNIT=TAPE,VOL=(,,,99,SER=(BKUP01,BKUP02,BKUP03,BKUP04)),
//               LABEL=(1,SL,EXPDT=98000)
//SYSIN     DD   *
```

```
     DUMP DATASET(INCLUDE(ORACLE.ORA1V.**))
          OUTDD(DUMPOUT)
/*
//
```

## Archiving Redo Log Files

Archiving redo log files is done differently on MVS compared to UNIX or other operating systems. If you are operating in the ARCHIVELOG mode, Oracle for MVS sets a timer of MAXWAIT duration and submits a batch job to archive the filled online log file. If the Archive job hasn't completed by the time the MAXWAIT timer expires, Oracle submits another batch job to archive the same log. Occasionally your robotic (or other) tape mount request may get delayed and a second job submitted before the tape gets mounted. The second job will recognize that the redo log it has been asked to archive has already been processed and will terminate. Oracle for MVS uses the INIT.ORA ACS (Archive Control String) parameter to control archiving. The following is an example of an ACS parameter.

```
ACS="TYPE=SUBMIT,INCJCL=/DD/ARCH,ODSN1=/DD/O1,ODSN2=/DD/O2,MAXWAIT=30"
```

This instructs the archiver to do the following:

**1.** Set a timer for 30 minutes.

**2.** Read the skeleton JCL from the ARCH DD statement.

**3.** Replace the substitute keywords with the appropriate values.

**4.** Submit a batch job to archive the recently filled online redo log file to the O1 DD statement and to the O2 DD statement. (Yes, Oracle for MVS has had dual archiving for years!)

**5.** When the timer expires, Oracle checks to see whether the online redo log was archived. If not, the process is repeated until it is.

The following is an archive JCL example:

```
//ARCHIVE   JOB (0000,O7),'ORACLE ARCHIVE',CLASS=A
//STEP1     EXEC PGM=ARCHIVE,PARM='++/DD/SYSPARM'
//STEPLIB   DD  DISP=SHR,DSN=ORACLE.ORA1.AUTHLOAD
//SYSERR    DD  SYSOUT=*
//SYSOUT    DD  SYSOUT=*
//SYSIN     DD  DUMMY
//O1        DD  DISP=(NEW,CATLG,DELETE),
//              DSN=ORACLE.AL%LOGSEQ%.LOG,
//              UNIT=SYSDA,DCB=(RECFM=FB,LRECL=4096,BLKSIZE=24576),
```

```
//              SPACE=(4096,(200,350),RLSE),VOL=SER=ORA001
//ORA$MMIO DD   DUMMY
//SYSPARM  DD   *
%LOGSEQ%
%LOGNAME%
%ODSN1%
%ODSN2%
/*
//
```

In the above JCL,

%LOGNAME% is the online redo log to be archived.
%LOGSEQ% is the redo log sequence number.
%ODSN1% is the ODSN1 string from the ACS parameter.
%ODSN2% is the ODSN2 string from the ACS parameter.

## Backing up Control Files

Control files should be backed up as part of the normal cold backup process in exactly the same way as the rest of the database and online redo log files. You can also do backups of the control file using the **alter database backup controlfile to 'file'** command. If you decide to back up the control file using this command, the file that will hold the backup control file is a VSAM file that has to be pre-created using the IDCAMS utility before the **alter database** command can be issued. If you want to submit a batch job to create the VSAM file, it is a good idea to do the backup of the control file as a second step in the same batch job. The following JCL example creates a VSAM file to hold a control file and then issues the **alter database** command to take control file backup.

```
//ORACLE1  JOB (0000,ORA),'ORACLE',CLASS=A,
//         MSGCLASS=X,PRTY=15,MSGLEVEL=(1,1),
//         REGION=4096K
//*------------------------------------------------------------*
//*          CREATE A VSAM FILE                                *
//*          TO HOLD A CONTROL FILE BACK                       *
//*------------------------------------------------------------*
//STEP1    EXEC PGM=IDCAMS
//SYSPRINT DD SYSOUT=*
//SYSIN    DD *
   DELETE (ORACLE.ORA1V.C020295)                   -
          CLUSTER PURGE
   DEFINE CLUSTER                                   -
     (                                              -
```

```
        NAME(ORACLE.ORA1V.C020295)                          -
             VOLUMES(ORA001)                                -
             CONTROLINTERVALSIZE(4096)                      -
             RECORDS(400)                                   -
             RECORDSIZE(4089 4089)                          -
             NONSPANNED                                     -
             UNIQUE                                         -
             NONINDEXED                                     -
             SPEED                                          -
             SHR(3 3)                                       -
        )                                                   -
        DATA                                                -
        (                                                   -
        NAME(ORACLE.ORA1V.C020295.DATA)                     -
        )
//*------------------------------------------------------------*
//*          RUN SQLDBA TO BACKUP THE CONTROL FILE        *

//*          TO A VSAM FILE AND TO TRACE                  *
//*------------------------------------------------------------*
//STEP2     EXEC PGM=SQLDBA
//STEPLIB   DD DSN=ORACLE.ORA1.CMDLOAD,DISP=SHR
//SYSMDUMP DD SYSOUT=*
//SYSOUT    DD SYSOUT=*,DCB=(LRECL=132,BLKSIZE=1320,RECFM=VB)
//SYSERR    DD SYSOUT=*,DCB=(LRECL=132,BLKSIZE=1320,RECFM=VB)
//ORAPRINT DD SYSOUT=*
//DBAINIT   DD DUMMY
//ORA@ORA1 DD DUMMY
//SYSIN     DD *
CONNECT SYSTEM/MANAGER
ALTER DATABASE BACKUP CONTROLFILE TO '/DSN/ORACLE.ORA1V.C020295';
ALTER DATABASE BACKUP CONTROLFILE TO TRACE;
/*
//
```

Note that the last **alter database** command creates a trace file with the SQL script to create a new control file. On MVS the trace files are created using the MPM TRACEDS parameter as a model. The INIT.ORA parameters USER_DUMP_DEST and BACKGROUND_DUMP_DEST are not used. The following is an example of the TRACEDS parameter.

```
TRACEDS="ORA1.PROD1.TRACE** UNIT=SYSDA"
```

# Backup/Restore in Desktop Environment

In this section we will discuss some of the backup commands and procedures used in the desktop environment, specifically with OS/2, Windows NT, and NetWare operating systems.

## Backup/Restore Procedures in Windows NT

One of the Windows NT database-management tools you can use with Oracle7 Release 7.1 is the Backup Manager. The Backup Manager runs in two modes, depending on whether you are operating the database in ARCHIVELOG mode or NOARCHIVELOG mode. If the database is running in ARCHIVELOG mode, the Backup Manager dialog appears, as described in Table 3-4.

| DIALOG ELEMENT | EXPLANATION |
|---|---|
| Database Status | Indicates the status of the database. |
| Offline - Full Database | If selected, this option does an offline backup for you. If the database is not open, it just takes a backup of the data files, log files, and control files. If the database is open, it shuts down the database, performs backup, and restarts database. |
| Online - Selected Tablespace | If selected, this allows you to do an online, partial database backup. It backs up the selected tablespaces for you. |
| Online - Control File only | If selected, backs up one copy of the control file. |
| Tape | If selected, backs up to tape. |
| Device | Indicates the tape device that stores the backup database files. |
| Disk, Directory and Browse | If selected, the database file is backed up to the directory specified on disk. Oracle recommends that you specify the complete path. The browse button can be used to select the location where the backup datafile should be stored. |
| Backup | Initiates the backup procedure. |

**TABLE 3-4.** *Backup Manager Dialog When Operating in ARCHIVELOG Mode*

| DIALOG ELEMENT | EXPLANATION |
|---|---|
| Database Status | Indicates the status of the database: NOARCHIVELOG mode or not running. |
| Backup Type | Indicates that only offline backup is possible in this mode. |
| Tape | If selected, backs up to tape. |
| Device | Indicates the tape device that stores the backup database files. |
| Disk, Directory and Browse | If selected, the database file is backed up to the directory specified on disk. Oracle recommends that you specify the complete path. The browse button can be used to select the location where the backup datafile should be stored. |
| Backup | Initiates the backup procedure. |
| Files | This button is enabled only when the database is not operating. You can use this button to review and change the list of database files before performing a backup. |

**TABLE 3-5.** *Backup Manager Dialog When Operating in NOARCHIVELOG Mode*

If the database is operating in NOARCHIVELOG mode, or the database is shut down, a different Backup Manager dialog appears, as described in Table 3-5.

If you choose the Files button to review or modify the database files, another dialog box appears. Using this dialog box, you can list all the database files and validate the file list by adding and/or deleting filenames.

The following backup procedure shows how to use the Backup Manager:

1. Open the Backup Manager. The Backup Manager dialog appears.

2. When prompted, enter the database password and choose OK.

3. If operating with NOARCHIVELOG mode or the database is not operating, skip this step. Else, select either *Offline Full Database*, *Online Selected Tablespace*, or *Online Control File only*, depending on what you want to back up.

4. Select either Tape or Disk as the destination for the backup database files.

**5.** If you selected Disk in the previous step, specify a full path name in the Directory field or by using the Browse button.

**6.** If the database is open, skip this step. Else choose the Files button to verify that you are backing up the right data files, log files, and the control files.

**7.** Choose Backup to begin the backup procedure. Note that if the database is open and an offline backup is requested, then the database is automatically shut down before the backup and restarted after the backup.

If you want to manually copy the data files during hot backups, you can use the **OCOPY*nn*** command (where *nn* is the version of OCOPY) to back up to disk or to a diskette. If copying to multiple diskettes, you can use the /B option to split large files. While restoring from multiple diskettes, you should use the /R option. The following examples show you how to back up to disk, back up to multiple diskettes, and to restore from multiple diskettes to disk, respectively.

```
C:\> OCOPY7.1 current_file backup_file
C:\> OCOPY7.1 /B current_file a:
C:\> OCOPY7.1 /R a: restore_dir
```

### Backup/Restore Procedures in NetWare
NBACKUP is a NetWare backup utility that allows you to back up and restore DOS and Macintosh files only. Regular network users can use the NBACKUP command to back up information on directories and only SUPERVISOR or its equivalent can back up a file server. Using this utility, you can also view the error and back up logs or restore the backed up data. Various third-party tools are very commonly used to back up the server as well.

### Backup/Restore Procedures in DOS/OS2
Standard DOS/OS2 and DOS **copy** commands are used to back up and restore database files to disk.There are backup and restore programs that are available in DOS, OS/2, and Windows. Third-party software products are also available.

## Backups in Special Environments

Before designing the appropriate backup procedure for your site, it is important that you understand the applications that are run at your site. First, determine if your applications are OLTP/OLQP (online transaction processing/query processing) or DSS-type applications. It is not wise to mix the two types of applications, if you can help it. For OLTP/OLQP, there will be some sustained TPS (transactions per second) rate and as the DBA, you must know where those changes (which tablespaces/data files) propagate to. Let's look into the various backup strategies for databases running these kinds of applications.

# Backup Considerations in an OLTP Environment

In an OLTP environment, there are several options that one can choose for backup strategy. Irrespective of the application type, if the databases are small (less than five gigabytes), and high availability is not a requirement (for example, you don't need to have the database available 24 hours a day, 7 days a week), then cold backups can be considered. However, if you operate your database 24 hours a day, 7 days a week, cold backups may not be feasible since the time to perform backups is longer than the window of time for maintenance. In such cases, the majority of the sites prefer using hot backups. Many sites elect to back up some tablespaces on one particular day and the others on another day. This is cycled until all tablespaces have been backed up. While designing such a backup strategy, careful thought must be given to MTTR (Mean Time To Recover), because the determining factor for the time to recover is the recovery of the oldest data file with the most changes. For this reason, if the online backups are chosen, ensure that the rollback segment tablespace(s) and all other tablespaces that undergo heavy changes are backed up frequently. The key issue with most of these sites is high availability. Let's look at some of the approaches that are used to maintain high availability and redundancy from a backup and recovery perspective.

One approach for ensuring availability of large OLTP systems is the deployment of RAID 1 or *mirroring* architecture, which provides fault tolerance. With disk mirroring, two drives store identical information so that one is a *mirror* of the other. Thus, for every disk write operation, the OS must write to both the disks. Mirroring of data files is not an Oracle feature but should be achieved at the OS or hardware level, depending upon the platform. Redo log files, control files, and all data files are mirrored. This is an expensive approach, as the number of disks is doubled.

The second approach is to take advantage of the new 7.1 feature called *read-only* tablespaces. Make the tablespaces read-only for tablespaces that contain data that does not undergo changes, such as lookup tables and monthly rollup data. Refer to Appendix A for details on read-only tablespaces. This means that the application must split up the data into appropriate tablespaces. However, you would still need to mirror redo log files, rollback segments, system tablespaces, and tablespaces that undergo changes. If you have a lot of read-only tablespaces, backup and restore time is significantly reduced since you don't have to take backups of the read-only tablespaces. It also reduces the number of disks because only the read-write tablespaces have to be mirrored.

The third approach to minimize database down time and increase fault tolerance is by using triple mirrors. Basically, the idea is to have a three-way mirror of a tablespace, and when you want to take a hot backup, simply issue the **alter tablespace begin backup** command and then break the mirror. You now have an on-disk hot backup while a two-way mirror is still in place. The broken mirror can be copied off to tape. This approach, though expensive, adds the benefit of having an on-disk hot backup of tablespaces, which drastically reduces MTTR because you don't need to restore data files from tape.

The last approach to minimize database downtime and maximize availability is to use a *hot standby database*. This is a new feature introduced in Oracle7 Release 7.3. The concept of standby databases is given in the last section of this chapter. For complete details on planning and maintenance of standby databases, refer to the *Disaster Recovery* section in Chapter 5.

# Backup Considerations in a DSS Environment

Typically, in DSS-class databases, such as data warehouses, many of the tablespaces will not undergo change, and thus can be made read-only. This means that backups need to be done only once for these tablespaces. This reduces the need to implement RAID unless availability is a factor. For DSS applications, backups will depend upon how often batch loads are completed. With some architectural improvements in Oracle7 Release 7.2, it is possible to add data through a parallel direct path loader and rebuild the indexes with the *parallel create index* option.

In a DSS environment, the backup and recovery strategy *must* dictate the overall operations of the system. For example, don't build tables with large amounts of data; instead, partition it into several smaller and more manageable pieces (for example a few gigabytes), so that you have the ability to back up and restore the individual pieces in a reasonable amount of time.

Before you design a backup procedure for a Very Large Database (VLDB), you should come up with a test model for predicting the length of time it takes to recover the database or portion of the database, given some failure scenario. The intent of such a model is to derive a set of best practice activities that can help you reduce MTTR (Mean Time To Recover) and increase MTBF (Mean Time Between Failures).

# Hot Standby Database

The growing need for high availability systems and the enormous expense resulting from downtime of database systems have given rise to many different approaches that are focused towards maximizing uptime. Oracle Corporation recognizes the importance of high availability and has come up with the *standby database* concept in Oracle7 Release 7.3. The objective of the standby database is to support the capability of maintaining a duplicate, or "standby" database of a "primary" or online production database for recovering from disasters at the production site. The goal is to be able to switch over from the primary database to the standby database in the case of a disaster in the least amount of time with as little recovery to perform as possible. Please note that this kind of *Disaster Recovery* strategy should be used only with Oracle7 Release 7.3. A few customers use standby databases today using a release less than 7.3. This is not officially supported by Oracle.

A brief description of standby databases follows. For a complete description on how to plan for disaster recovery and maintain standby databases, please refer to the *Disaster Recovery* section in Chapter 5.

A hot standby database is a backup copy of the production database that is maintained on an identical but different machine. Let's call the production database you use the *primary* database and the hot standby database the *standby* or *backup* database. Typically, an offline or online backup of the primary database is made and copied to the secondary machine. The secondary machine has a similar configuration as the primary (names of disk drives, directory paths, etc.) and the standby database is mounted but not opened. If keeping the same directory path is not feasible, Oracle provides some **init.ora** parameters so that renaming the files is not necessary. The archive log files are copied to the secondary machine and applied to the standby database at regular intervals. This means that the standby database is always a few log files (at least one log file) behind the primary database and is always in *mounted but not open* stage.

When the primary database fails (for example, due to a media failure), the secondary database can be opened or *activated* and all users can now be switched to the second machine and can continue to do work while the primary database is being recovered. After such a switch, the standby database becomes the primary database. Then, you will need another standby site. The mechanisms you use to deploy and maintain a standby database must be flexible. You should use environmental variables (in UNIX, for example) to identify the primary and standby sites. This way, you will not need to modify the scripts. Thus, after activation, you can create a new standby database simply by changing the variables to point to the new site names and running the scripts. This is particularly useful if you want to use the original site as the standby. Furthermore, you will need to make the original site the standby site if you wish that original site to once again house the production database.

A lot of things can go wrong with this administration intensive procedure if it is not implemented correctly. For example, if the primary database renames a data file, what are the ramifications of this on the standby database? A detailed description of design considerations, planning and maintenance of standby databases is given in Chapter 5.

# CHAPTER 4

# Backup Scripts in UNIX and VMS Environments

**T**his chapter gives sample scripts to automate your backup procedures in the VMS and UNIX environments. First, in the VMS environment, a generic backup script is presented. Due to the flexible design, this script should work at most shops without customizing it. For example, most of the variables, such as the data files that need to be backed up, are generated dynamically from the database. Hence after adding a new file, you don't need to modify your backup scripts to include the new data file. However, you should customize the scripts and test them thoroughly before using them to back up your production database. For this purpose, every script contains a *USER_PARAMETERS* section, where you can modify certain parameters to customize the scripts. In the UNIX environment, we keep the scripts simple by hardcoding certain parameters. All the assumptions made are clearly documented in the scripts and should be changed to fit your needs.

# Backup Scripts in VMS Environment

This script assumes that you are running a single-instance configuration. If you are running with the Parallel Server option, you should modify the script. The detailed operation of each script is documented in the script header. We assume that all the script files are located in a directory called ORACLE_UTILS, and we further assume that you are familiar with the VMS-specific directories.

The main command procedure that you should run is called BACKUP_MAIN.COM. Depending on the day of the week, this procedure calls other procedures to take either a cold backup, a hot backup, or a full database export. Note that this procedure doesn't copy from disk to tape, so you should run additional scripts to do this. The following tree of execution shows how the scripts are related. These command procedures can be executed separately as well.

```
BACKUP_MAIN.COM
    oracle_utils:env_symbols.com
    oracle_utils:export_database.com
    oracle_utils:hot_backup.com
    oracle_utils:cold_backup.com

EXPORT_DATABASE.COM
    oracle_utils:env_symbols.com
    oracle_utils:db_name_devices.com
    oracle_utils:instance_up.com
    oracle_utils:startup_dbamode.com
    ora_db:shutdown_db_name.com

HOT_BACKUP.COM
    oracle_utils:env_symbols.com
    oracle_utils:db_name_devices.com
    oracle_utils:instance_up.com
    oracle_utils:tbs_to_datafiles.sql
    oracle_utils:tablespace_state.sql
    oracle_utils:hot_backup_cmd_db_name.com
```

        oracle_utils:env_symbols.com
        oracle_utils:backup_tablespace.com
        oracle_utils:instance_up.com
        ora_db:ora_db_*db_name*.com

### COLD_BACKUP.COM
    oracle_utils:env_symbols.com
    oracle_utils:*db_name*_devices.com
    oracle_utils:instance_up.com
    oracle_utils:shutdown_immediate.com
    oracle_utils:startup_dbamode.com
    oracle_utils:tbs_logfiles.sql
    oracle_utils:backup_tablespace.com
    ora_db:ora_db_*db_name*.com
    ora_db:shutdown_*db_name*.com
    ora_db:startup_exclusive_*db_name*.com

### SHUTDOWN_IMMEDIATE.COM
    ora_db:ora_db_*db_name*.com
    oracle_utils:shutdown_immediate_*db_name*.com
        oracle_utils:shutdown_immediate_*db_name*.sql

### STARTUP_DBAMODE.COM
    ora_db:ora_db_*db_name*.com
    oracle_utils:startup_dbamode_*db_name*.com
        oracle_utils:startup_dbamode_*db_name*.sql

# BACKUP_MAIN.COM

This script performs cold and hot backups and an export of an Oracle database. We will get the current day of the week and perform the correct operation(s) on that day determined by the user configurable symbols (export_days, hot_backup_days, cold_backup_days). Look in the "USER_PARAMETERS" section of this script for details on these symbols. After the operation is complete we will check, and if necessary, re-submit this script for the following day at the same time. For more details, refer to the other DCL command procedures that this script is using.

```
$ vvv = 'f$verify(0)'  ! set noverify and remember what it was before
$! FILE:     ORACLE_UTILS:BACKUP_MAIN.COM
$! PURPOSE: Perform a cold/hot backup and export of an Oracle database.
$! USAGE:    submit backup_main.com -
$!                /parameters=(dbname, export mode, resubmit flag)
```

```
$!              OR
$!              @oracle_utils:backup_main dbname [export mode] [resubmit flag]
$!
$!          Example:  @backup_main TESTDB COMPLETE YES
$!
$! PARAMETERS:
$!          P1: The database name to perform operation on.
$!          P2: Type of export to do: INCREMENTAL, CUMULATIVE or COMPLETE.
$!          P3: Resubmit flag, optional: YES, NO  default=YES
$!              If set to NO, job will not resubmit itself for the next day.
$!
$! CALLS:  oracle_utils:env_symbols.com   ! Set up symbols to point to database
$!         oracle_utils:export_database.com   ! Export the database
$!         oracle_utils:hot_backup.com     ! Perform hot backup on the database
$!         oracle_utils:cold_backup.com    ! Perform cold backup on the database
$!
$! CALLED BY: Possibly called by submit_backup_dbname.com
$!            There is a sample file (submit_backup_TESTDB.sample) for
$!            users to modify.
$!
$! INPUT:  Symbols: Check the "USER_PARAMETERS" section of this script for
$!                  a list of symbols that you can change to control the
$!                  operation.
$!   Logical Names: ORACLE_UTILS must point to a directory with all
$!                  the backup scripts.
$!          Files: None.
$!
$! OUTPUT:  Symbols:  None.
$!    Logical Names:  None.
$!            Files:  None directly, but may include all or part of files
$!                    created by calls that it makes to export_database.com,
$!                    hot_backup.com and oracle_utils:cold_backup.com.
$!
$!
$! PRIVILEGES: There are no privilege checks done as this script is assumed
$!             to run from the Oracle account.
$!
$! HISTORY:
$!   Date         Name          Comments
$!   20-MAR-1995  Saar Maoz     Created
$!
$!!!!!!!!  This section could be changed by user to configure backup procedure
$ USER_PARAMETERS:
$!
$! These are the recommended values for the *_days symbols
$! If its Sunday, an export is performed; on Saturday a cold backup is
$! performed; any other day a hot backup is performed. You can change this to
$! fit your needs.
$  export_days := "/Sunday/"
$  hot_backup_days := "/Monday/Tuesday/Wednesday/Thursday/Friday/"
$  cold_backup_days := "/Saturday/"
$  userpasswd := system/manager
$  logfile := sys$scratch:save_database
$  mailuser = "SMAOZ"         ! set to "" if not interested in mail messages
$!!!!!!!!!!
```

```
$!
$ set noon
$!
$! Save time that we begin running, so we can resubmit at same time tomorrow.
$!
$ begin_time = f$time()
$!
$! Local symbols to this script
$!
$ say := write sys$output
$ wo := write outfile
$ delfile := delete/noconfirm/log
$ sendmail := mail nl: 'mailuser' /subject=
$ something_done =0
$!
$! Check for correct usage
$!
$ if p1 .eqs. "" then goto HELP
$ db_name = f$edit(p1,"UPCASE")
$ export_mode = f$edit(p2, "UPCASE")
$ submit_flag =  f$edit(p3, "UPCASE")
$ if submit_flag .eqs. "" then submit_flag := YES ! default value to submit flag
$!
$! Setup environment
$!
$ if f$trnlnm("oracle_utils") .eqs. "" then goto NO_LOGICAL
$ @oracle_utils:env_symbols.com
$!
$! The following command will point us to the right database. Note that there
$! must be a symbol as the database name defined in
$! ORACLE_UTILS:ENV_SYMBOLS.COM which will run the correct
$! ORA_DB:ORAUSER_DBNAME.COM which will point you to the right database.
$!
$ 'db_name'
$ if .not. $status then goto NO_SYMBOL
$ show logical ora_sid
$!
$ today = f$cvtime("TODAY",,"WEEKDAY")   ! get day of week.
$!
$! According to day of week, branch to the right place as defined by the user
$! Note that it is possible to perform more than one task per day.
$!
$ if f$locate("''today'",export_days) .ne. -
    f$length(export_days) then          call DO_EXPORT
$!
$ if f$locate("''today'",hot_backup_days) .ne. -
    f$length(hot_backup_days) then       call DO_HOT_BACKUP
$!
$ if f$locate("''today'",cold_backup_days) .ne. -
    f$length(cold_backup_days) then      call DO_COLD_BACKUP
$!
$! Go to resubmit this script for tomorrow if needed
$!
$ goto RESUBMIT
$!
```

```
$! If nothing done, give an informational message
$!
$ if something_done then goto FINISH
$ say " "
$ say "INFORMATION ** ORACLE_UTILS:BACKUP_MAIN.COM **"
$ say " There was no backup/export defined to be done today, if this is a"
$ say " mistake check the USER_PARAMETERS section in"+-
      " ORACLE_UTILS:BACKUP_MAIN.COM"
$ goto FINISH
$!
$ DO_EXPORT: SUBROUTINE
$!
$! Call the export routine
$!
$ something_done =1
$ @oracle_utils:export_database 'db_name' 'export_mode'
$ EXIT
$ ENDSUBROUTINE
$!
$ DO_HOT_BACKUP: SUBROUTINE
$!
$! Call the hot backup routine
$!
$ something_done =1
$ @oracle_utils:hot_backup 'db_name'
$ EXIT
$ ENDSUBROUTINE
$!
$ DO_COLD_BACKUP: SUBROUTINE
$!
$! Call the cold backup routine
$!
$ something_done =1
$ @oracle_utils:cold_backup 'db_name'
$ EXIT
$ ENDSUBROUTINE
$!
$ RESUBMIT:
$!
$! Submit this script for tomorrow if needed
$!
$ if .not. submit_flag  then goto FINISH
$ submit oracle_utils:backup_main.com -
      /parameters=("''db_name'","''export_mode'","''submit_flag'") -
      /after="''begin_time'+23:59:59" -
      /log='logfile'_'db_name'.log -
      /queue=sys$batch -
      /retain=error -
      /noprint
$ if f$search("''logfile'_''db_name'.log") .nes. "" then purge/nolog/keep=8 'logfile'
$!
$ goto FINISH
$!
$! ERROR-HANDLING SECTION
$!  The rest of this script is an error-handling routine.  After each
```

```
$! error message it branches to MAIL_FINISH (will send an email) or to FINISH
$! (will NOT send an email).  Default error notification is to send email;
$! change the label if you do not wish to send a mail message.
$!
$ NO_SYMBOL:
$  say " "
$  say "ERROR ** ORACLE_UTILS:BACKUP_MAIN.COM **"
$  say " a. No symbol found with the database name that runs the"
$  say "    ORAUSER_<dbname>.COM which will point us to the right database,"
$  say "    add it to ORACLE_UTILS:ENV_SYMBOLS.COM"
$  say " b. Some other error has occured while attempting to run the"
$  say "    ORAUSER_<dbname>.COM file, check the preceding VMS error message"
$  goto MAIL_FINISH
$!
$ NO_LOGICAL:
$  say " "
$  say "ERROR ** ORACLE_UTILS:BACKUP_MAIN.COM **"
$  say " The logical name ORACLE_UTILS is not defined please define it to point"
$  say " to the directory where all the backup scripts reside."
$  goto MAIL_FINISH
$!
$ HELP:
$  say " "
$  say "Usage of ORACLE_UTILS:BACKUP_MAIN.COM is:"
$  say " @ORACLE_UTILS:BACKUP_MAIN db_name [export mode] [submit]"
$  say " db_name : Database name"
$  say " export_mode : INCREMENTAL, CUMULATIVE or COMPLETE"
$  say " submit : YES ¦ NO (default=YES)"
$  goto FINISH
$!
$ MAIL_FINISH:
$  if mailuser .eqs. "" then goto FINISH
$!
$! Send correct mail whether run in interactive or batch mode
$!
$  msg = "Backup procedure run in interactive mode failed"
$  if f$mode() .eqs. "BATCH" then msg = "Backup procedure terminated"+-
       " with errors check ''logfile'_''db_name'.log for details"
$  sendmail "''msg'"
$  goto FINISH
$!
$ FINISH:
$  if vvv then set verify
$  Exit
```

# EXPORT_DATABASE.COM

Given a database name and export incremental type (either INCREMENTAL,
CUMULATIVE, or COMPLETE) as parameters, this script performs a full export of
that database. This is a logical backup of the database that can only be used in
conjunction with Import. The algorithm works as follows:

1. Make sure there is a device to export on to.

2. Check if database is up? If YES go to step 4.

3. Bring database up in restricted mode to export it.

4. Delete the previous export files from the export device.

5. Perform the actual export.

6. If database was down when export started (step 2), bring it back down.

7. Done.

```
$ vvv = 'f$verify(0)'  ! set noverify and remember what it was before
$! FILE:    ORACLE_UTILS:EXPORT_DATABASE.COM
$! PURPOSE: Performs a full export, of either INCREMENTAL, CUMULATIVE or
$!          COMPLETE of the database.
$! USAGE:    Usually called by oracle_utils:backup_main
$!           OR (if you want to use it separately)
$!           @oracle_utils:export_database dbname export_mode
$!
$!           Example:  @export_database TESTDB COMPLETE
$!
$! PARAMETERS:
$!          P1: The database name to perform export on
$!          P2: Incremental type can be: INCREMENTAL, CUMULATIVE or COMPLETE
$!              if not specified, defaults to COMPLETE
$!
$! CALLS:   oracle_utils:env_symbols.com       ! Set up symbols to point to DB
$!                oracle_utils:db_name_devices.com ! Get backup devices names
$!                oracle_utils:instance_up          ! Check if instance is up/down
$!                oracle_utils:startup_dbamode      ! Startup in restricted mode
$!                ora_db:shutdown_db_name           ! Shutdown normal
$!
$! CALLED BY:
$!          Usually this script will be called by BACKUP_MAIN.COM; however it
$!          could be called independently.
$!
$! INPUT:   Symbols:   Check the USER_PARAMETERS section of this script for
$!                     a list of symbols that you can change to control the
$!                     operation of this script
$!    Logical Names:   ORACLE_UTILS must point to a directory with all
$!                     the backup scripts.
$!          Files:   None.
$!
$! OUTPUT:  Symbols: None.
$!          Logical Names: None.
$!          Files: export_location:export_db_name_export_mode.dmp
$!                 The export file of the specified incremental level.
$!
$! PRIVILEGES: There are no privilege checks done, as we assume that this script
$!             is run from the Oracle account.
$!
$! HISTORY:
```

```
$!    Date        Name           Comments
$!    20-MAR-1995 Saar Maoz      Created
$!
$!
$!!!!!!!!!  This section can be changed by user to configure export procedure
$ USER_PARAMETERS:
$   export_buffer = 524288        ! make sure you have enough BYTLM for this user
$! userpasswd := system/manager
$! mailuser = "SMAOZ"            ! set to "" if not interested in mail messages
$!!!!!!!!!!!
$!
$ set noon
$!
$! Local symbols to this script
$!
$ say := write sys$output
$ wo := write outfile
$ delfile := delete/noconfirm/log
$ sendmail := mail nl: 'mailuser' /subject=
$!
$! Check for correct usage
$!
$ if p1 .eqs. "" then goto HELP
$ db_name = f$edit(p1,"UPCASE")
$ export_mode = f$edit(p2,"UPCASE")
$ if export_mode  .eqs. "" then export_mode := COMPLETE  !default value
$!
$ if export_mode .nes. "INCREMENTAL" .and. export_mode .nes. -
     "CUMULATIVE" .and. export_mode .nes.  "COMPLETE" then HELP
$!
$ if f$type(userpasswd) .eqs. "" .or. f$type(mailuser) .eqs. "" -
     then goto NO_SYMS
$!
$ say " "
$ say "ORACLE_UTILS:EXPORT_DATABASE.COM begins a ''export_mode' export on"
$ say " ''db_name' database at: "+f$time()
$ say " "
$!
$! Setup environment
$!
$ if f$trnlnm("oracle_utils") .eqs. "" then goto NO_LOGICAL
$ @oracle_utils:env_symbols !just to make sure
$!
$! The following command will point you to the right database. Note that there
$! must be a symbol as the database name defined in
$! ORACLE_UTILS:ENV_SYMBOLS.COM. This will run the correct
$! ORA_DB:ORAUSER_DBNAME.COM, which will in turn point you to the right
$! database.
$!
$ 'db_name'
$ if .not. $status then goto NO_SYMBOL
$ show logical ora_sid
$ @oracle_utils:'db_name'_devices.com    ! Define export location
$!
$! Check if export location exists and is a disk
```

```
$!
$ show logical export_location
$ if .not. f$getdvi("export_location","EXISTS") then goto NO_EXPORT_LOCATION
$ if f$getdvi("export_location","DEVCLASS") .ne. 1 then goto NOT_A_DISK
$ show device export_location
$!
$! Check whether instance is up
$!
$ @oracle_utils:instance_up 'f$trnlnm("ora_sid")'
$!
$ if instance_up then goto EXPORT
$!
$ say " "
$ say "ORACLE_UTILS:EXPORT_DATABASE.COM"
$ say " Instance was shutdown and an export is due so starting database up..."
$ say " "
$ @oracle_utils:startup_dbamode 'db_name'
$!
$ EXPORT:
$ say " "
$ say "ORACLE_UTILS:EXPORT_DATABASE.COM is now deleting last week's export"
$ say " "
$ if f$search("export_location:export_''db_name'_''export_mode'.dmp") .nes. ""
$ then
$   directory/date=(created,backup)/size=all -
      export_location:export_'db_name'_'export_mode'.dmp
$   delfile export_location:export_'db_name'_'export_mode'.dmp;*
$ endif
$!
$! Performing the actual export
$!
$ on error then goto EXPORT_ERROR
$ exp userid='userpasswd' -
      buffer='export_buffer' -
      file=export_location:export_'db_name'_'export_mode'.dmp -
      inctype='export_mode' -
      full=y -
      grants=y -
      indexes=y -
      rows=y -
      constraints=y -
      compress=n -
      statistics=none
$!
$ say " "
$ say "ORACLE_UTILS:EXPORT_DATABASE.COM finished a ''export_mode' export on"
$ say " ''db_name' database at: "+f$time()
$ say " "
$ if mailuser .nes. "" then  sendmail -
      "''export_mode' export finished successfully at ''f$time()'"
$!
$ if .not. instance_up
$ then
$   say " "
$   say "ORACLE_UTILS:EXPORT_DATABASE.COM"
```

```
$    say " The database was shutdown when export began, so bringing it back down"
$    say " "
$    @ora_db:shutdown_'db_name'
$ endif
$ goto FINISH
$!
$! ERROR-HANDLING SECTION
$!  The rest of this script is an error-handling routine.  After each
$!  error message it branches to MAIL_FINISH (will send an email) or to FINISH
$!  (will NOT send an email).  Default error notification is to send email;
$! change the label if you do not wish to send a mail message.
$!
$ NO_SYMS:
$  say " "
$  say "ERROR ** ORACLE_UTILS:EXPORT_DATABASE.COM **"
$  say " The local symbols userpasswd or mailuser are not defined"
$  say " This usually means that this script was called independently and the"
$  say " USER_PARAMETERS section of this script was not updated"
$  say " "
$  goto FINISH
$!
$ NO_LOGICAL:
$  say " "
$  say "ERROR ** ORACLE_UTILS:EXPORT_DATABASE.COM **"
$  say " The logical name ORACLE_UTILS is not defined. Please define it to"
$  say " point to the directory where all the backup scripts reside."
$  goto MAIL_FINISH
$!
$ NO_SYMBOL:
$  say " "
$  say "ERROR ** ORACLE_UTILS:EXPORT_DATABASE.COM **"
$  say " a. No symbol found with the database name that runs the"
$  say "    ORAUSER_dbname.COM which will point us to the right database,"
$  say "    add it to ORACLE_UTILS:ENV_SYMBOLS.COM"
$  say " b. Some other error has occured while attempting to run the"
$  say "    ORAUSER_dbname.COM file, check the preceding VMS error message"
$  goto MAIL_FINISH
$!
$ NO_EXPORT_LOCATION:
$  say " "
$  say "ERROR ** ORACLE_UTILS:EXPORT_DATABASE.COM **"
$  say " The logical name EXPORT_LOCATION which controls where the export file"
$  say " will be created is not defined."
$  goto MAIL_FINISH
$!
$ NOT_A_DISK:
$  say " "
$  say "ERROR ** ORACLE_UTILS:EXPORT_DATABASE.COM **"
$  say " The export location pointed to by EXPORT_LOCATION logical name is not"
$  say " a disk.  Sorry, this script does not currently do exports to tape."
$  goto MAIL_FINISH
$!
$ EXPORT_ERROR:
$  st=$status
$  say " "
```

```
$   say "ERROR ** ORACLE_UTILS:EXPORT_DATABASE.COM **"
$   say " An error has occured during the export, final VMS error code: ''st'"
$   say " Text: "+f$message(st)
$   goto MAIL_FINISH
$!
$ HELP:
$   say " "
$   say "Usage of ORACLE_UTILS:EXPORT_DATABASE.COM is:"
$   say " @ORACLE_UTILS:EXPORT_DATABASE db_name export_mode"
$   say " db_name : Database name to export"
$   say " export_mode : INCREMENTAL, CUMULATIVE or COMPLETE"
$   goto FINISH
$!
$ MAIL_FINISH:
$   if mailuser .eqs. "" then goto FINISH
$!
$! Send correct mail whether run in interactive or batch mode
$!
$   msg = "''export_mode' export run in interactive mode failed"
$   if f$mode() .eqs. "BATCH" then msg = "''export_mode' export terminated"+-
          " with errors check ''logfile'_''db_name'.log for details"
$   sendmail "''msg'"
$   goto FINISH
$!
$ FINISH:
$   if vvv then set verify
$   Exit
```

# HOT_BACKUP.COM

Given a database name as a parameter, this script performs a hot backup of that database. It copies all data files and one control file to backup devices designated for that purpose, and creates a DCL script that restores the files from the backup to their original locations. The algorithm works as follows:

1. Make sure there is at least one backup device.

2. Make sure the database is up, otherwise stop.

3. Call oracle_utils:tbs_to_datafiles.sql to generate a list of all data files and their sizes ordered by tablespace name.

4. Read this file and create a DCL script that will go into SQLDBA and perform an ALTER TABLESPACE BEGIN BACKUP, followed by a host command that will invoke backup_tablespace.com (with the tablespace as parameter), and then an ALTER TABLESPACE END BACKUP for each tablespace in the database to be backed up.

5. Delete the previous backup files from the backup devices.

6. Start creating the restore_database.com file needed to recover from this backup.

7. Call oracle_utils:tablespace_state.sql to show the status of all data files (any that have ACTIVE status are in backup mode; they should all have NOT ACTIVE status).

8. Invoke oracle_utils:hot_backup_cmd_*db_name*.com, which in turn issues the **alter tablespace** command and calls backup_tablespace.com for each tablespace.

9. Again call oracle_utils:tablespace_state.sql to show the status of all data files (any that have ACTIVE status are in backup mode; they should all have NOT ACTIVE status).

10. Search all the logs generated from the **alter tablespace** command and issue an error if the string "ORA-" is found.

11. Add final helpful notes to the restore_database.com file.

12. Done.

```
$ vvv = 'f$verify(0)'   ! set noverify and remember what it was before
$! FILE:      ORACLE_UTILS:HOT_BACKUP.COM
$! PURPOSE: Performs a "hot" backup of a database.
$! USAGE:    Usually called by oracle_utils:backup_main
$!           OR (if you want to use it separately)
$!           @oracle_utils:hot_backup dbname
$!
$!           Example:  @hot_backup TESTDB
$!
$! PARAMETERS:
$!           P1: The database name to perform hot backup on
$!
$! CALLS:    oracle_utils:env_symbols.com        ! Set up symbols to point to DB
$!           oracle_utils:db_name_devices.com ! Get backup devices names
$!           oracle_utils:instance_up            ! Check if instance is up/down
$!           oracle_utils:tbs_to_datafiles.sql   ! Generate tbs/datafiles list
$!           oracle_utils:tablespace_state.sql   ! View tablespace states
$!           oracle_utils:hot_backup_cmd_db_name.com ! Perform the hot backup
$!              !-> oracle_utils:env_symbols.com
$!              !-> oracle_utils:backup_tablespace ! Back up one tablespace
$!              !-> oracle_utils:instance_up
$!              !-> ora_db:ora_db_db_name          ! Get the ora_control* logicals
$!
$! CALLED BY:
$!           Usually this script will be called by BACKUP_MAIN.COM; however it
$!           can run independently.
$!
$! INPUT: Symbols: Check the "USER_PARAMETERS" section of this script for
$!                 a list of symbols that you can change to control the
$!                 operation of this script
```

```
$!  Logical Names: ORACLE_UTILS points to a directory with all backup scripts.
$!                 ORA_CONTROL* holds the logical names of the control files
$!                 defined by ora_db:ora_db_db_name.com
$!          Files: backup_location_1:tbs_to_datafiles.lis
$!                 Tablespaces/datafiles to back up
$!
$! OUTPUT:  Symbols: None.
$!   Logical Names:  None.
$!          Files:   * oracle_utils:hot_backup_cmd_db_name.com
$!                 This is a dynamically created DCL script that goes into
$!                 SQLDBA, alters the tablespaces to begin/end backup and
$!                 hosts out to backup that tablespace by calling
$!                 oracle_utils:backup_tablespace.  It does this for all
$!                 tablespaces. After finishing, it saves a copy of the
$!                 control file.
$!
$!              * backup_location_1:restore_database.com
$!                  This is a dynamically created DCL script that will perform
$!                  the restore operation of this hot backup.  If you plan
$!                  to use this file, please remember that you will need to
$!                  perform the actual database recovery after this script
$!                  restores the copy of the database.
$!                  Keep this file because it remembers to which backup
$!                  device it copied each file of the database during backup.
$!                  Look in this file for more details.
$!
$!              * backup_location_1:tbs_to_datafiles.lis
$!                  This is the output of a SELECT statement that identifies
$!                  the tablespaces and datafiles, and their sizes
$!                  in VMS blocks. Sample record of this file:
$!      "SYSTEM¦DISK$AXPVMSSYS:[ORACLE7.ROOT71.DB_TESTDB]ORA_SYSTEM.DBS¦12288"
$!                  This file is created by oracle_utils:tbs_to_datafiles.sql
$!
$!              * One control file of this database will be backed up to
$!                the first backup device.
$!
$! PRIVILEGES: There are no privilege checks done, as we assume that this script
$!             is run from the Oracle account.
$!
$! HISTORY:
$!   Date         Name          Comments
$!   20-MAR-1995  Saar Maoz     Created
$!
$!!!!!!!! This section can be changed by user to configure backup procedure
$ USER_PARAMETERS:
$!
$! uncomment the following 2 lines if you plan to use this script by itself
$! userpasswd := system/manager
$! mailuser = "SMAOZ"            ! set to "" if not interested in mail messages
$!!!!!!!!!
$!
$ set noon
$!
$! Local symbols to this script
$!
```

```
$ say := write sys$output
$ wo := write outfile
$ wo2 := write outfile2
$ delfile := delete/noconfirm/log
$ backupfile := backup/log/ignore=(interlock,nobackup)/new
$ sendmail := mail nl: 'mailuser' /subject=
$!
$! Check for correct usage
$!
$ if p1 .eqs. "" then goto HELP
$ db_name = f$edit(p1,"UPCASE")
$!
$ if f$type(userpasswd) .eqs. "" .or. f$type(mailuser) .eqs. "" -
     then goto NO_SYMS
$!
$ say " "
$ say "ORACLE_UTILS:HOT_BACKUP.COM begins a hot backup on"+-
     " ''db_name' database at: "+f$time()
$ say " "
$!
$! Setup environment
$!
$ if f$trnlnm("oracle_utils") .eqs. "" then goto NO_LOGICAL
$ @oracle_utils:env_symbols  !just to make sure
$!
$! The following command will point you to the right database. Note that there
$! must be a symbol as the database name defined in
$! ORACLE_UTILS:ENV_SYMBOLS.COM. This will run the correct
$! ORA_DB:ORAUSER_DBNAME.COM, which in turn will point you to the right
$! database.
$!
$ 'db_name'
$ if .not. $status then goto NO_SYMBOL
$ show logical ora_sid
$ @oracle_utils:'db_name'_devices.com     ! Define available backup locations
$!
$! Count the available devices (disks only)
$!
$ show log backup_location_*
$ device_cnt=1
$ DEV_LOOP:
$  if .not. f$getdvi("backup_location_''device_cnt'","EXISTS") -
     then goto DEV_VER  ! Make sure the device exists
$  if f$getdvi("backup_location_''device_cnt'","DEVCLASS") .ne. 1 -
     then goto DEV_VER   ! Make sure it's a disk
$  show device backup_location_'device_cnt'
$  device_cnt= device_cnt+1
$ goto DEV_LOOP
$!
$ DEV_VER:
$  device_cnt= device_cnt-1
$  if device_cnt .eq. 0 then goto NO_BACKUP_DEVICES ! if we have no devices
$!
$  say " "
$  say "ORACLE_UTILS:HOT_BACKUP.COM has recognized ''device_cnt' devices to"+-
```

```
                " use for backup."
$   say " "
$!
$! Check whether instance is up
$!
$ @oracle_utils:instance_up 'f$trnlnm("ora_sid")'
$ if .not. instance_up then goto UP_FOR_HOT    ! DB must be up for hot backup
$!
$! Generate the tablespace/datafiles listing file & detele old ones
$!
$ if f$search("backup_location_1:tbs_to_datafiles.lis") .nes. "" -
     then delfile/nolog backup_location_1:tbs_to_datafiles.lis;*
$ if f$search("oracle_utils:hot_backup_cmd_''db_name'.com") .nes. "" -
     then purge/nolog/keep=2 oracle_utils:hot_backup_cmd_''db_name'.com
$!
$ sqlplus -s 'userpasswd' @oracle_utils:tbs_to_datafiles.sql
$!
$! Open tablespace/datafiles listing file.  If it doesn't exist then something
$! went wrong.
$!
$ close/nolog infile
$ open/read/error=OPEN_TBS_ERROR infile backup_location_1:tbs_to_datafiles.lis
$ read/end=EMPTY_TBS_LIST infile rec  ! Skip first line in file - it's a comment
$!
$! Start writing the script that will go into sqldba and perform the actual
$! ALTER TABLESPACE BEGIN BACKUP, followed by the VMS backup, followed by an
$! ALTER TABLESPACE END BACKUP
$!
$ close/nolog outfile
$ open/write outfile oracle_utils:hot_backup_cmd_''db_name'.com
$!
$ wo "$! FILE:  oracle_utils:hot_backup_cmd_''db_name'.com"
$ wo "$! Dynamically created by ORACLE_UTILS:HOT_BACKUP.COM at: ''f$time()'"
$ wo "$! to perform hot backup of ''db_name' database"
$ wo "$ set noon"
$ wo "$ if f$search(""backup_location_1:alter_tbs_begin_end.log"") -"
$ wo " .nes. """" then delfile/nolog backup_location_1:tbs_tbs_begin_end.log;*"
$ wo "$ vvv = 'f$verify(1)' ! Turn verify on so we can see commands in sqldba"
$ wo "$ sqldba lmode=y"
$ wo "connect internal"
$ wo "alter system archive log current;"  ! To switch from and archive the
$!                                         ! current redolog
$ wo "  REM It is normal to get warning messages from backup in the form:"
$ wo "  REM %BACKUP-W-ACCONFLICT, <file name> is open for write by another user"
$!
$! Process each tablespace at a time
$!
$ prv_tbs = ""
$LOOP:
$ read/end=END_INFILE infile rec
$ tbs = f$element(0,"¦",rec)             ! extract tablespace name
$ file = f$element(1,"¦",rec)            ! extract the file specification
$ size = f$element(2,"¦",rec)            ! extract the size of this file
$!
$ if tbs .eqs. prv_tbs then goto LOOP    ! skip it if we already did it
```

```
$!
$ if prv_tbs .eqs. ""
$ then
$    wo "spool backup_location_1:alter_tbs_begin_end.log"
$    wo "alter tablespace ''tbs' begin backup;"
$    wo "spool off"
$ else
$    wo "spool backup_location_1:alter_tbs_begin_end.log"
$    wo "alter tablespace ''prv_tbs' end backup;"
$    wo "spool off"
$    wo "spool backup_location_1:alter_tbs_begin_end.log"
$    wo "alter tablespace ''tbs' begin backup;"
$    wo "spool off"
$ endif
$!
$ wo "host @oracle_utils:backup_tablespace ''tbs' ''db_name' ''device_cnt'"
$ prv_tbs = tbs
$!
$ goto LOOP
$END_INFILE:
$!
$! Add end backup command to last tablespace and save a copy of the controlfile
$!
$ wo "spool backup_location_1:alter_tbs_begin_end.log"
$ wo "alter tablespace ''tbs' end backup;"
$ wo "spool off"
$ wo "alter database backup controlfile to "+-
   "''''backup_location_1:ora_control_''db_name'.con'''';"
$ wo "exit"
$ wo "$ if vvv then set verify"
$ wo "$ exit"
$ close/nolog outfile
$ close/nolog infile
$!
$ say "ORACLE_UTILS:HOT_BACKUP.COM is now deleting previous backup files"
$ say " on all devices with the name BACKUP_LOCATION_*"
$ say " "
$ dev_cnt=1
$ DELETE_YESTERDAYS_BCK:
$!
$ delfile backup_location_'dev_cnt':*.*.* - ! don't delete the tbs/datafile
         /exclude=(*.lis.*,*.dmp.*)          ! listing file we just created
$!                                            ! or the export file
$ dev_cnt=dev_cnt+1
$ if dev_cnt .lt. device_cnt then goto  DELETE_YESTERDAYS_BCK
$!
$! Start writing the RESTORE_DATABASE.COM, which will be used to restore from
$! this backup.
$!
$ close/nolog outfile2
$ open/write outfile2 backup_location_1:restore_database.com
$ wo2 "$!FILE: backup_location_1:restore_database.com"
$ wo2 "$!Dynamically created by ORACLE_UTILS:HOT_BACKUP.COM at: "+-
        f$time()
$ wo2 "$!"
```

```
$ wo2 "$ type sys$input"
$ wo2 "  This script will restore all database files from their backup location"
$ wo2 "  to their location on production environment. It will first delete the"
$ wo2 "  database file if it exists in the production environment, and then"
$ wo2 "  copy a backup of that file to that location."
$ wo2 "  It will then copy all the control files to their location in"
$ wo2 "  the same fashion (deleting the production ones first)."
$ wo2 "  "
$ wo2 "  This script should be run only if you plan to perform a database"
$ wo2 "  recovery from a HOT backup."
$ wo2 "  To invoke this script edit it and remove the EXIT statement following"
$ wo2 "  this notice"
$ wo2 "$!"
$ wo2 "$ EXIT"
$ wo2 "$!"
$ wo2 "$ db_name := ''db_name'"
$ wo2 "$ if f$trnlnm(""oracle_utils"") .eqs. """" then goto NO_LOGICAL"
$ wo2 "$ @oracle_utils:env_symbols"
$ wo2 "$ ''''db_name''''"
$ wo2 "$ @ora_db:ora_db_''''db_name''''" ! to get ora_control* logicals
$ wo2 "$ if f$trnlnm(""ora_control1"") .eqs. """" then goto NO_CTL_LOGICALS"
$ wo2 "$!"
$ wo2 "$ @oracle_utils:instance_up ''''f$trnlnm(""ora_sid"")''''"
$ wo2 "$ if instance_up then goto INSTANCE_UP"
$ wo2 "$!"
$ wo2 "$ @oracle_utils:''db_name'_devices"
$ wo2 "$!"
$ wo2 "$ set noon"
$ wo2 "$!"
$ wo2 "$ delfile := ''delfile'"
$ wo2 "$ backupfile := ''backupfile'"
$ wo2 "$!"
$ close/nolog outfile2
$!
$! Call the script we just created, which will back up all tablespaces
$! one at a time
$!
$ sqlplus -s 'userpasswd' @oracle_utils:tablespace_state.sql  ! state before
$ @oracle_utils:hot_backup_cmd_'db_name'.com
$ sqlplus -s 'userpasswd' @oracle_utils:tablespace_state.sql  ! state after
$!
$! Search all the begin/end backup logs for any errors; if yes then report them
$!
$ search backup_location_1:alter_tbs_begin_end.log;* "ORA-"/exact/win=1
$ if $status .ne. %X08D78053 then goto HOT_BACKUP_PROBLEM
$!
$! Write final helpful notes to restore_database file
$!
$ close/nolog outfile2
$ open/append outfile2 backup_location_1:restore_database.com
$ wo2 "$!"
$ wo2 "$ type sys$input"
$ wo2 "  Restoration of all data files of database ''db_name' has"
$ wo2 "  been completed. Please review the log file or screen for any errors."
$ wo2 "  Since this restore was from a HOT backup, you will need to recover"
```

```
$ wo2 "  the database before you are able to use it.  Go into SQLDBA"
$ wo2 "  and issue:"
$ wo2 "  1. connect internal"
$ wo2 "  2. startup MOUNT ''db_name';"
$ wo2 "  3. set autorecovery ON;"
$ wo2 "  4. recover database; (or add the until clause)"
$ wo2 "  5. Then ALTER DATABASE OPEN; (use RESETLOGS in case of an"+-
       " incomplete recovery)"
$ wo2 " "
$ wo2 " Note: The controlfiles were not restored, if you need to use them"
$ wo2 "         please do so manually."
$ wo2 " "
$ wo2 "  Good Luck!"
$ wo2 "$ goto FINISH"
$ wo2 "$!"
$ wo2 "$ INSTANCE_UP:"
$ wo2 "$ type sys$input"
$ wo2 "ERROR ** BACKUP_LOCATION_1:RESTORE_DATABASE.COM **"
$ wo2 "  The database is UP.  One or more processes belonging to this database"
$ wo2 "  is still running.  This script should be run when the database is"
$ wo2 "  DOWN.  Make sure the database is down; if necessary, issue a SHUTDOWN"
$ wo2 "  ABORT, then rerun this script to restore a backup of this database."
$ wo2 "$ goto FINISH"
$ wo2 "$!"
$ wo2 "$ NO_LOGICAL:"
$ wo2 "$ type sys$input"
$ wo2 "ERROR ** BACKUP_LOCATION_1:RESTORE_DATABASE.COM **"
$ wo2 " The logical name ORACLE_UTILS is not defined. Please define it to point"
$ wo2 " to the directory where all the backup scripts reside."
$ wo2 "$ goto FINISH"
$ wo2 "$!"
$ wo2 "$ NO_CTL_LOGICALS:"
$ wo2 "$ type sys$input"
$ wo2 "ERROR ** BACKUP_LOCATION_1:RESTORE_DATABASE.COM **"
$ wo2 "  Can't find the controlfile logicals (ORA_CONTROL*)."
$ wo2 "  They are usually defined in ORA_DB:ORA_DB_''db_name'.COM, and not"
$ wo2 "  hardcoded as controlfile names in the init.ora file"
$ wo2 "$ goto FINISH"
$ wo2 "$!"
$ wo2 "$ FINISH:"
$ wo2 "$ Exit"
$ close/nolog outfile2
$!
$ say " "
$ say "ORACLE_UTILS:HOT_BACKUP.COM finished a hot backup on"+-
       " ''db_name' database at: "+f$time()
$ say " "
$ if mailuser .nes. "" then sendmail -
  "HOT backup operation for ''db_name' database completed at: ''f$time()'"
$!
$ goto FINISH
$!
$! ERROR-HANDLING SECTION
$!  The rest of this script is an error-handling routine.  After each
$!  error message it branches to MAIL_FINISH (will send an email) or to FINISH
```

```
$!  (will NOT send an email).  Default error notification is to send email;
$!  change the label if you do not wish to send a mail message.
$!
$ NO_SYMS:
$   say " "
$   say "ERROR ** ORACLE_UTILS:HOT_BACKUP.COM **"
$   say " The local symbols userpasswd or mailuser are not defined"
$   say " This usually means that this script was called independently and the"
$   say " USER_PARAMETERS section of this script was not updated"
$   say " "
$   goto FINISH
$!
$ NO_LOGICAL:
$   say " "
$   say "ERROR ** ORACLE_UTILS:HOT_BACKUP.COM **"
$   say " The logical name ORACLE_UTILS is not defined. Please define it to"
$   say " point to the directory where all the backup scripts reside."
$   goto MAIL_FINISH
$!
$ NO_SYMBOL:
$   say " "
$   say "ERROR ** ORACLE_UTILS:HOT_BACKUP.COM **"
$   say " a. No symbol found with the database name that runs the"
$   say "    ORAUSER_<dbname>.COM, which will point us to the right database."
$   say "    Add it to ORACLE_UTILS:ENV_SYMBOLS.COM."
$   say " b. Some other error has occured while attempting to run the"
$   say "    ORAUSER_<dbname>.COM file. Check the preceding VMS error message."
$   goto MAIL_FINISH
$!
$ NO_BACKUP_DEVICES:
$   say " "
$   say "ERROR ** ORACLE_UTILS:HOT_BACKUP.COM **"
$   say " No backup locations with the name BACKUP_LOCATION_* found."
$   say " Please define some backup locations in ''db_name'_DEVICES.COM"
$   say " and verify that the devices exist."
$   goto MAIL_FINISH
$!
$ UP_FOR_HOT:
$   say " "
$   say "ERROR ** ORACLE_UTILS:HOT_BACKUP.COM **"
$   say " The database ''db_name' is down, and a hot backup was attempted"
$   goto MAIL_FINISH
$!
$ OPEN_TBS_ERROR:
$   say " "
$   say "ERROR ** ORACLE_UTILS:HOT_BACKUP.COM **"
$   say " An error has occured opening the tablespace datafiles mapping file."
$   say " It is located in BACKUP_LOCATION_1:TBS_TO_DATAFILES.LIS."
$   say " Please verify that the location is a valid directory owned by Oracle"
$   say " or the person running this script.  Also make sure that the Oracle"
$   say " shareable images are installed using ORA_RDBMS:INSORACLE.COM, which"
$   say " is required to run sqlplus"
$   goto MAIL_FINISH
$!
$ EMPTY_TBS_LIST:
```

```
$  say " "
$  say "ERROR ** ORACLE_UTILS:HOT_BACKUP.COM **"
$  say " Found tablespace listings file empty"+-
$      " (BACKUP_LOCATION_1:TBS_TO_DATAFILES.LIS)"
$  goto MAIL_FINISH
$!
$ HOT_BACKUP_PROBLEM:
$  say " "
$  say "ERROR ** ORACLE_UTILS:HOT_BACKUP.COM **"
$  say " ALTER TABLESPACE BEGIN or END BACKUP command was issued."
$  say " Please check logfile or backup_location_1:alter_tbs_begin_end.log;*"
$  say " for more details."
$  goto MAIL_FINISH
$!
$ HELP:
$  say " "
$  say "Usage of ORACLE_UTILS:HOT_BACKUP.COM is:"
$  say " @ORACLE_UTILS:HOT_BACKUP <db_name>"
$  goto FINISH
$!
$ MAIL_FINISH:
$  if mailuser .eqs. "" then goto FINISH
$!
$! Send correct mail whether run in interactive or batch mode
$!
$  msg = "HOT backup procedure run in interactive mode failed"
$  if f$mode() .eqs. "BATCH" then msg = "HOT backup procedure terminated"+-
        " with errors check ''logfile'_''db_name'.log for details"
$  sendmail "''msg'"
$  goto FINISH
$!
$ FINISH:
$  close/nolog infile
$  close/nolog outfile
$  close/nolog outfile2
$  if vvv then set verify
$  exit
```

# COLD_BACKUP.COM

Given a database name as a parameter, this script performs a cold backup of that database. This means that the database must be shut down for the duration of the backup. This script will copy all data files and redo logs, one control file, and the parameter files (INIT.ORA and *nodename_SID*_INIT.ORA) to backup devices designated for this purpose. It will also create a DCL script that will restore the files from this backup to their original locations. The algorithm works as follows:

**1.** Make sure there is at least one backup device

**2.** Check if database is up; if NO goto step 7.

**3.** Notify users that database is going down in 10 minutes.

**4.** Shutdown immediate to force database shutdown.

**5.** Wait for PMON to clean up.

**6.** If waited more than user-defined wait period, stop; something is wrong.

**7.** Bring database up in restricted mode to SELECT the data file and redo log file names to back up and shut the database down clean.

**8.** Generate a list of all datafiles and redo logs and their sizes by calling oracle_utils:tbs_logfiles.sql.

**9.** Shutdown normal the database.

**10.** Delete the previous backup files from the backup devices.

**11.** Start creating the restore_database.com file needed to recover from this backup.

**12.** Read file created in step 8 and for each new tablespace call backup_tablespace.com, which will back up all files associated with that tablespace.

**13.** When getting a null for tablespace name, it will recognize that it is a redo log file and back it up while adding records to the restore_database.com.

**14.** After finishing all the redo logs, it will back up the control file indicated by ORA_CONTROL1.

**15.** Back up the INIT.ORA and *nodename_SID_*INIT.ORA files to the first backup device.

**16.** Add final records to the restore_database.com file.

**17.** If the database was up when the backup was started (step 2), bring it back up.

**18.** Done.

```
$ vvv = 'f$verify(0)'  ! set noverify and remember what it was before
$! FILE:    ORACLE_UTILS:COLD_BACKUP.COM
$! PURPOSE: Performs a "cold" backup of the database.
$! USAGE:   Usually called by oracle_utils:backup_main.com
$!          OR (if you want to use it separately)
$!          @oracle_utils:cold_backup dbname
$!
$!          Example:  @cold_backup TESTDB
$!
$! PARAMETERS:
$!          P1: The database name to perform cold backup on
$!
```

```
$! CALLS:     oracle_utils:env_symbols.com         ! Set up symbols to point to DB
$!            oracle_utils:db_name_devices.com     ! Get backup devices names
$!            oracle_utils:instance_up             ! Check if instance is up/down
$!            oracle_utils:shutdown_immediate      ! Shutdown immediate
$!            oracle_utils:startup_dbamode         ! Startup in restricted mode
$!            oracle_utils:tbs_logfiles.sql        ! tbs/datafile/redologs list
$!            oracle_utils:backup_tablespace       ! Backup one tablespace
$!            ora_db:ora_db_db_name                ! Get the ora_control* logicals
$!            ora_db:shutdown_db_name              ! Shutdown normal
$!            ora_db:startup_exclusive_db_name     ! Startup database
$!
$! CALLED BY:
$!            Usually this script will be called by BACKUP_MAIN.COM; however it
$!            can be called independently.
$!
$! INPUT:     Symbols: Check the "USER_PARAMETERS" section of this script for
$!                     a list of symbols that you can change to control the
$!                     operation of the script.
$!     Logical Names: ORACLE_UTILS must point to a directory with all
$!                     the backup scripts.
$!                     ORA_CONTROL* holds the logical names of the control files;
$!                     ORA_PARAMS points to the node_SID_INIT.ORA file;
$!                     both are defined by ora_db:ora_db_db_name.com.
$!            Files:   backup_location_1:tbs_to_datafiles.lis
$!                     Tablespaces/datafiles to backup.
$!
$! OUTPUT:    Symbols: None.
$!            Logical Names: None.
$!            Files: * backup_location_1:restore_database.com
$!                     This is a dynamically created DCL script that will perform
$!                     the restore operation of this cold backup.  After this file
$!                     is used to restore from the cold backup, the database
$!                     can be opened with no recovery needed.
$!                     Keep this file because it remembers to which backup
$!                     device it copied each file of the database during backup.
$!                     Look in this file for more details.
$!
$!                     * backup_location_1:tbs_to_datafiles.lis
$!                     This is an output of a SELECT statement for the purpose
$!                     of identifying the tablespaces, the datafiles, and their
$!                     sizes in VMS blocks.  In cold backup mode this file also
$!                     contains the redo log names and sizes.
$!                     Sample records of this file are:
$!    "SYSTEM|DISK$AXPVMSSYS:[ORACLE7.ROOT71.DB_TESTDB]ORA_SYSTEM.DBS|12288"
$!    "  |DISK$AXPVMSSYS:[ORACLE7.ROOT71.DB_TESTDB]ORA_LOG1.RDO|1000"
$!                     This file is created by oracle_utils:tbs_logfiles.sql
$!
$!                 * The redologs of this database will be backed up on to
$!                   one of the available backup devices.
$!
$!                 * One control file of this database will be backed up to
$!                   the first backup device.
$!
$!                 * The parameter files INIT.ORA and nodename_SID_INIT.ORA
$!                   will be backed up to the first backup device.
```

```
$!
$! PRIVILEGES: There are no privilege checks done, as we assume that this script
$!            is run from the Oracle account.
$!
$! HISTORY:
$!   Date          Name          Comments
$!   20-MAR-1995   Saar Maoz     Created
$!
$!!!!!!!!! This section can be changed by user to configure backup procedure
$ USER_PARAMETERS:
$   shutdown_immediate_wait = 20 ! wait for shutdown immediate to complete
$!
$! uncomment the following 2 lines if you plan to use this script by itself
$! userpasswd := system/manager
$! mailuser = "SMAOZ"                ! set to "" if not interested in mail messages
$!!!!!!!!!
$!
$ set noon
$!
$! Local symbols to this script
$!
$ say := write sys$output
$ wo := write outfile
$ delfile := delete/noconfirm/log
$ backupfile := backup/log/ignore=(interlock,nobackup)/new
$ sendmail := mail nl: 'mailuser' /subject=
$!
$! Check for correct usage
$!
$ if p1 .eqs. "" then goto HELP
$ db_name = f$edit(p1,"UPCASE")
$!
$ if f$type(userpasswd) .eqs. "" .or. f$type(mailuser) .eqs. "" -
    then goto NO_SYMS
$!
$ say " "
$ say "ORACLE_UTILS:COLD_BACKUP.COM begins a cold backup on"+-
    " ''db_name' database at: "+f$time()
$ say " "
$!
$! Setup environment
$!
$ if f$trnlnm("oracle_utils") .eqs. "" then goto NO_LOGICAL
$ @oracle_utils:env_symbols  !just to make sure
$!
$! The following command will point you to the right database. Note that there
$! must be a symbol as the database name defined in
$! ORACLE_UTILS:ENV_SYMBOLS.COM. This will run the correct
$! ORA_DB:ORAUSER_DBNAME.COM, which will in turn point you to the right
$! database.
$!
$ 'db_name'
$ if .not. $status then goto NO_SYMBOL
$ show logical ora_sid
$ @oracle_utils:'db_name'_devices.com     ! Define available backup locations
```

```
$!
$! Get the logical names of the control files so they can be backed up later.
$!
$ @ora_db:ora_db_'db_name'
$ if f$trnlnm("ora_control1") .eqs. "" then goto NO_CTL_LOGICALS
$!
$! Count the available valid devices (disks only)
$!
$ show log backup_location_*
$ device_cnt=1
$ DEV_LOOP:
$  if .not. f$getdvi("backup_location_''device_cnt'","EXISTS") -
      then goto DEV_VER  ! Make sure the device exists
$  if f$getdvi("backup_location_''device_cnt'","DEVCLASS") .ne. 1 -
      then goto DEV_VER  ! Make sure it's a disk
$  show device backup_location_'device_cnt'
$  device_cnt= device_cnt+1
$ goto DEV_LOOP
$!
$ DEV_VER:
$  device_cnt= device_cnt-1
$  if device_cnt .eq. 0 then goto NO_BACKUP_DEVICES  ! if we have no devices
$!
$  say " "
$  say "ORACLE_UTILS:COLD_BACKUP.COM has recognized ''device_cnt' devices to"+-
      " use for backup."
$  say " "
$!
$! Check whether instance is up, and rememeber that for later
$!
$ @oracle_utils:instance_up 'f$trnlnm("ora_sid")'
$ instance_was_up = instance_up
$ if instance_up
$ then
$! If instance UP, it needs to be shut down to perform COLD backup
$  say " "
$  say "ORACLE_UTILS:COLD_BACKUP.COM"
$  say " The ''db_name' database is UP and must be shut down in order to"
$  say " perform a COLD backup."
$  say " "
$!
$! Notify all users and shutdown immediate after 10 minutes.
$!
$   reply/node/all/urgent/bell -
   "Database ''db_name' shutting down in 10 minutes for backup. Please logout!"
$   say " "
$   say "ORACLE_UTILS:COLD_BACKUP.COM"
$   say " Now waiting 10 minutes before shutting down immediate"
$   say " "
$   wait 0:10:0.0
$   @oracle_utils:shutdown_immediate 'db_name'
$   wait 0:02:0.0
$   min = 2
$!
$! Wait for instance shutdown immediate to complete
```

```
$!
$   SHUTDOWN_WAIT:
$     @oracle_utils:instance_up 'f$trnlnm("ora_sid")'  ! Check if it's up
$     if .not. instance_up then goto BRING_DB_UP
$     wait 0:05:0.0
$     min = min + 5
$     if min .ge. shutdown_immediate_wait then -
         goto SHUT_IMMED_TIMEOUT   ! Waited too long, something is wrong
$     goto SHUTDOWN_WAIT
$ endif
$!
$ BRING_DB_UP:
$!
$! Now bring db up in dba mode for two reasons:
$! 1. To get the datafiles redologs listing file
$! 2. To later shut it down normal to get a clean COLD backup
$! Note that this will guarantee a backup of a normal shutdown database
$!
$ say " "
$ say "ORACLE_UTILS:COLD_BACKUP.COM"
$ say " Bringing ''db_name' database up to get the list of datafiles/redologs"
$ say " and also to make sure it is shut down normal before this backup"
$ say " "
$ @oracle_utils:startup_dbamode 'db_name'
$!
$! Generate the tablespace/datafiles listing file & delete old ones
$!
$ if f$search("backup_location_1:tbs_to_datafiles.lis") .nes. "" -
     then delfile/nolog backup_location_1:tbs_to_datafiles.lis;*
$ sqlplus -s 'userpasswd'  @oracle_utils:tbs_logfiles.sql
$!
$ say " "
$ say "ORACLE_UTILS:COLD_BACKUP.COM"
$ say " Shutting down ''db_name' database now for cold backup"
$ say " "
$ @ora_db:shutdown_'db_name'   ! Shutdown normal for a clean cold backup.
$!
$! Open tablespace/datafiles listing file.  If it doesn't exist then something
$! went wrong.
$!
$ close/nolog infile
$ open/read/error=OPEN_TBS_ERROR infile backup_location_1:tbs_to_datafiles.lis
$ read/end=EMPTY_TBS_LIST infile rec  ! Skip first line in file it's a comment
$!
$ say "ORACLE_UTILS:COLD_BACKUP.COM is now deleting previous backup files"
$ say " on all devices with the name BACKUP_LOCATION_*"
$ say " "
$ dev_cnt=1
$ DELETE_YESTERDAYS_BCK:
$!
$ delfile backup_location_'dev_cnt':*.*.* - ! don't delete the tbs/datafile
         /exclude=(*.lis.*,*.dmp.*)        ! listing file we just created
$!                                         ! or the export file
$ dev_cnt=dev_cnt+1
$ if dev_cnt .lt. device_cnt then goto  DELETE_YESTERDAYS_BCK
```

```
$!
$! Start writing the RESTORE_DATABASE.COM, which will be used to restore from
$! this backup
$!
$ close/nolog outfile
$ open/write outfile backup_location_1:restore_database.com
$ wo "$!FILE: backup_location_1:restore_database.com"
$ wo "$!Dynamically created by ORACLE_UTILS:COLD_BACKUP.COM at: "+-
      f$time()
$ wo "$!"
$ wo "$ type sys$input"
$ wo "  This script will restore all database files from their backup location"
$ wo "  to their location on production environment. It will first delete the"
$ wo "  database file if it exists in the production envrionment and then will"
$ wo "  copy a backup of that file to that location. The same will be done to"
$ wo "  restore all the logfiles."
$ wo "  After that it will copy all the controlfiles to their location in"
$ wo "  the same fashion (deleting the production ones first)."
$ wo "  "
$ wo "  This script should be run only if you plan to restore a database"
$ wo "  from a COLD backup."
$ wo "  To invoke this script edit it and remove the EXIT statement following"
$ wo "  this notice"
$ wo "$!"
$ wo "$ EXIT"
$ wo "$!"
$ wo "$ db_name := ''db_name'"
$ wo "$ if f$trnlnm(""oracle_utils"") .eqs. """" then goto NO_LOGICAL"
$ wo "$ @oracle_utils:env_symbols"
$ wo "$ ''''db_name''''"
$ wo "$ @ora_db:ora_db_''''db_name'''' ! to get ora_control* logicals"
$ wo "$ if f$trnlnm(""ora_control1"") .eqs. """" then goto NO_CTL_LOGICALS"
$ wo "$!"
$ wo "$ @oracle_utils:instance_up ''''f$trnlnm(""ora_sid"")'''' ! is db up?"
$ wo "$ if instance_up then goto INSTANCE_UP"
$ wo "$!"
$ wo "$ @oracle_utils:''db_name'_devices  ! define available backup devices"
$ wo "$!"
$ wo "$ set noon"
$ wo "$!"
$ wo "$ delfile := ''delfile'"
$ wo "$ backupfile := ''backupfile'"
$ wo "$!"
$ close/nolog outfile
$!
$! Process the datafiles listing file and backup all tablespaces
$!
$ prv_tbs = ""
$LOOP:
$ read/end=END_INFILE_ERROR infile rec
$ tbs = f$element(0,"|",rec)              ! extract tablespace name
$!
$! If tablespace name is blank, it is a logfile; go there.
$!
$ if f$edit(tbs,"compress") .eqs. " " then goto BACKUP_LOGFILES
```

```
$!
$! If it's a "new" tablespace then call the script that saves it
$!
$ if tbs .nes. prv_tbs then -
   @oracle_utils:backup_tablespace 'tbs' 'db_name' 'device_cnt'
$ prv_tbs = tbs
$ goto LOOP
$!
$ BACKUP_LOGFILES:
$  open/append outfile backup_location_1:restore_database.com
$  wo "$! Restore all logfiles by first deleting originals and then"
$  wo "$! copying the saved files into the production environment."
$  wo "$!"
$!
$ LOG_LOOP:
$  file = f$element(1,"¦",rec)          ! extract the file specification
$  size = f$element(2,"¦",rec)          ! extract the size of this file
$!
$! Announce file to be backed up.
$!
$  say " "
$  say "Attempting to back up ''file'"
$  dev_cnt = 1
$  FIND_DEVICE_LOOP:
$!
$!   Is there enough space on this disk?  Always leaving 2000 free blocks
$!   just in case (important not to fill location_1 completely)
$!
$    if f$getdvi("backup_location_''dev_cnt'","FREEBLOCKS") - 2000 .gt. size
$    then
$      say "                  to "+f$trnlnm("backup_location_''dev_cnt'")
$      say " "
$      backupfile 'file'; backup_location_'dev_cnt':/by=original
$      st = $status
$      if st .eq. %X10A38410 then goto BACKUP_OK   ! open for write by someone
$      if .not. st then goto BACKUP_ERROR          ! some other backup error
$!
$      BACKUP_OK:
$!
$!      Get full filename that you wrote. This is to make sure you get the
$!      version number of the file you just copied, in case there are files with
$!      the same name.
$!
$        fname=f$parse(file,,,"NAME")+f$parse(file,,,"TYPE")
$        full_name=f$search("backup_location_''dev_cnt':''fname'")
$!
$!      Write the commands to restore this redolog
$!
$        wo "$ if f$search("""''file'""") -"
$        wo " .nes. """" then -"
$        wo "      delfile ''file';"
$        wo "$ backupfile   ''full_name' -"
$        wo "               ''file'/by=original"
$        wo "$!"
$    else
```

```
$     dev_cnt = dev_cnt + 1                          ! skip to the next device
$     if dev_cnt .gt. device_cnt then goto NO_SPACE  ! no space on any device
$     goto FIND_DEVICE_LOOP
$   endif
$ read/end=COPY_CONTROLFILES infile rec     ! Finished copying redo logs
$ goto LOG_LOOP
$!
$ COPY_CONTROLFILES:
$!
$ close/nolog infile      ! We don't need this file anymore
$!
$! All we need is one controlfile
$!
$ backupfile ora_control1 -
            backup_location_1:ora_control_'db_name'.con/by=original
$ st = $status
$ if st .eq. %X10A38410 then goto COPY_PARAMS     ! open for write by someone
$ if .not. st then goto BACKUP_ERROR              ! some other backup error
$!
$ COPY_PARAMS:
$!
$! Find and backup INIT.ORA and <nodename>_<SID>_INIT.ORA
$!
$ initora=f$parse("ora_params",,,"device")+-       ! Get init.ora location in
          f$parse("ora_params",,,"directory")      ! case it's not in ora_db:
$ initora=f$search(initora+"init.ora")
$ backupfile ora_params:;,'initora'-
            backup_location_1:/by=original
$ st = $status
$ if .not. st then goto BACKUP_ERROR              ! some backup error
$!
$! Write the commands to restore all controlfiles and write final notes to
$! the restore file
$!
$ wo "$!"
$ wo "$! Now restore all control files"
$ wo "$!"
$ wo "$ cnt=1"
$ wo "$ REPLACE_CTL:"
$ wo "$ backupfile backup_location_1:ora_control_''''db_name''''.con; -"
$ wo "                ora_control''''cnt''''/by=original"
$ wo "$ cnt=cnt+1"
$ wo "$!"
$ wo "$ if f$trnlnm(""ora_control""+f$string(cnt)) .nes. """" then "+-
     "goto REPLACE_CTL"
$ wo "$!"
$ wo "$ type sys$input"
$ wo " Restoration of datafiles, logfiles and control files of database"+-
     " ''db_name'"
$ wo " has been completed. Please review the logfile or screen for any errors."
$ wo " Since this restore was from a COLD backup, you can proceed to startup"
$ wo " the database."
$ wo " Please note that the parameter files INIT.ORA and <node>_<SID>_INIT.ORA"
$ wo " were not restored, although they have been originally backed up."
$ wo " If you wish to restore them, please do so manually."
```

```
$ wo " "
$ wo "   Good Luck!"
$ wo "$ goto FINISH"
$ wo "$!"
$ wo "$ INSTANCE_UP:"
$ wo "$ type sys$input"
$ wo "ERROR ** BACKUP_LOCATION_1:RESTORE_DATABASE.COM **"
$ wo "   The database is UP.  One or more processes belonging to this database"
$ wo "   is still running.  This script should be run when the database is"
$ wo "   DOWN.  Make sure the database is down, if necessary, issue a SHUTDOWN"
$ wo "   ABORT and rerun this script to restore a backup of the database."
$ wo "$ goto FINISH"
$ wo "$!"
$ wo "$ NO_LOGICAL:"
$ wo "$ type sys$input"
$ wo "ERROR ** BACKUP_LOCATION_1:RESTORE_DATABASE.COM **"
$ wo " The logical name ORACLE_UTILS is not defined. Please define it to point"
$ wo " to the directory where all the backup scripts reside."
$ wo "$ goto FINISH"
$ wo "$!"
$ wo "$ NO_CTL_LOGICALS:"
$ wo "$ type sys$input"
$ wo "ERROR ** BACKUP_LOCATION_1:RESTORE_DATABASE.COM **"
$ wo "   Can't find the controlfiles logicals (ORA_CONTROL*)"
$ wo "   They are usually defined in ORA_DB:ORA_DB_''db_name'.COM, and not"
$ wo "   hardcoded as controlfile names in the init.ora file"
$ wo "$ goto FINISH"
$ wo "$!"
$ wo "$ FINISH:"
$ wo "$ Exit"
$ close/nolog outfile
$!
$ say " "
$ say "ORACLE_UTILS:COLD_BACKUP.COM finished a cold backup on"+-
        " ''db_name' database at: "+f$time()
$ say " "
$ if mailuser .nes. "" then sendmail -
  "COLD backup operation for ''db_name' database completed at: ''f$time()'"
$!
$! If db was up, then bring it back up and we are done!
$!
$ if instance_was_up
$ then
$   say " "
$   say "ORACLE_UTILS:COLD_BACKUP.COM"
$   say " The database was up when COLD backup started, so bringing it back up"
$   say " "
$   @ora_db:startup_exclusive_'db_name'
$ endif
$ goto FINISH
$!
$! ERROR-HANDLING SECTION
$!  The rest of this script is an error-handling routine.  After each
$!  error message it branchs to MAIL_FINISH (will send an email) or to FINISH
$!  (will NOT send an email).  Default error notification is to send email;
```

```
$!  change the label if you do not wish to send a mail message.
$!
$ NO_SYMS:
$   say " "
$   say "ERROR ** ORACLE_UTILS:COLD_BACKUP.COM **"
$   say " The local symbols userpasswd or mailuser are not defined."
$   say " This usually means that the script was called independently and the"
$   say " USER_PARAMETERS section of the script was not updated."
$   say " "
$   goto FINISH
$!
$ NO_LOGICAL:
$   say " "
$   say "ERROR ** ORACLE_UTILS:COLD_BACKUP.COM **"
$   say " The logical name ORACLE_UTILS is not defined. Please define it to"
$   say " point to the directory where all the backup scripts reside."
$   goto MAIL_FINISH
$!
$ NO_SYMBOL:
$   say " "
$   say "ERROR ** ORACLE_UTILS:COLD_BACKUP.COM **"
$   say " a. No symbol found with the database name that runs the"
$   say "    ORAUSER_<dbname>.COM, which will point us to the right database;"
$   say "    add it to ORACLE_UTILS:ENV_SYMBOLS.COM"
$   say " b. Some other error has occured while attempting to run the"
$   say "    ORAUSER_<dbname>.COM file; check the preceding VMS error message"
$   goto MAIL_FINISH
$!
$ NO_CTL_LOGICALS:
$   say " "
$   say "ERROR ** ORACLE_UTILS:COLD_BACKUP.COM **"
$   say " Can't find the controlfiles logicals (ORA_CONTROL*)"
$   say " They are usually defined in ORA_DB:ORA_DB_''db_name'.COM, and not"
$   say " hardcoded as controlfile names in the init.ora file"
$   goto MAIL_FINISH
$!
$ NO_BACKUP_DEVICES:
$   say " "
$   say "ERROR ** ORACLE_UTILS:COLD_BACKUP.COM **"
$   say " No backup locations with the name BACKUP_LOCATION_* found."
$   say " Please define some backup locations in ''db_name'_DEVICES.COM"
$   say " and verify that the devices exist."
$   goto MAIL_FINISH
$!
$ SHUT_IMMED_TIMEOUT:
$   say " "
$   say "ERROR ** ORACLE_UTILS:COLD_BACKUP.COM **"
$   say " Waited for instance "+f$trnlnm("ora_sid")+" to shutdown immediate for"
$   say " ''min' minutes, but instance has not shutdown yet."
$   goto MAIL_FINISH
$!
$ BACKUP_ERROR:
$   say " "
$   say "ERROR ** ORACLE_UTILS:COLD_BACKUP.COM **"
$   say " Received a VMS backup error final error code: ''st'"
```

```
$   say " Text: "+f$message(st)
$   goto MAIL_FINISH
$!
$ NO_SPACE:
$   say " "
$   say "ERROR ** ORACLE_UTILS:COLD_BACKUP.COM **"
$   say " Not enough space for ''file'"
$   say " on any backup device. please assign more backup devices or clear some"
$   say " space on existing ones"
$   goto MAIL_FINISH
$!
$ OPEN_TBS_ERROR:
$   say " "
$   say "ERROR ** ORACLE_UTILS:COLD_BACKUP.COM **"
$   say " An error has occured opening the tablespace datafiles mapping file."
$   say " It is located in BACKUP_LOCATION_1:TBS_TO_DATAFILES.LIS."
$   say " Please verify that the location is a valid directory owned by Oracle"
$   say " or the person running this script.  Also make sure that the Oracle"
$   say " shareable images are installed using ORA_RDBMS:INSORACLE.COM, which"
$   say " is required to run sqlplus."
$   goto MAIL_FINISH
$!
$ EMPTY_TBS_LIST:
$   say " "
$   say "ERROR ** ORACLE_UTILS:COLD_BACKUP.COM **"
$   say " Found tablespace listings file empty"+-
$       " (BACKUP_LOCATION_1:TBS_TO_DATAFILES.LIS)"
$   goto MAIL_FINISH
$!
$ END_INFILE_ERROR:
$   say " "
$   say "ERROR ** ORACLE_UTILS:COLD_BACKUP.COM **"
$   say " Unexpected end of file BACKUP_LOCATION_1:TBS_LOGFILES.LIS"
$   say " The file is created by this script, and contains all the tablespaces"
$   say " names and their associated files, followed by the logfile names."
$   say " The first argument of a logfile record should be blank."
$   goto MAIL_FINISH
$!
$ HELP:
$   say " "
$   say "Usage of ORACLE_UTILS:COLD_BACKUP.COM is:"
$   say " @ORACLE_UTILS:COLD_BACKUP <db_name>"
$   goto FINISH
$!
$ MAIL_FINISH:
$   if mailuser .eqs. "" then goto FINISH
$!
$! Send correct mail whether run in interactive or batch mode
$!
$   msg = "COLD backup procedure run in interactive mode failed"
$   if f$mode() .eqs. "BATCH" then msg = "COLD backup procedure terminated"+-
$           " with errors check ''logfile'_''db_name'.log for details"
$   sendmail "''msg'"
$   goto FINISH
$!
```

```
$ FINISH:
$  close/nolog infile
$  close/nolog outfile
$  if vvv then set verify
$  exit
```

# BACKUP_TABLESPACE.COM

Given as parameters a tablespace name, a database name, and the number of backup devices available, this routine will find all the data files associated with this tablespace and back them up. It will also add records to the restore_database.com file to restore the files being backing up. This uses the following algorithm:

1. Open backup_location_1:tbs_to_datafiles.lis for read.

2. Read one record from file in step 1 and check to see if the tablespace name matches the one that was passed as a parameter.

3. Find if the first device has enough space to hold the file to be backed up; if YES go to step 6.

4. Advance to the next device and check to see if there is enough space for this datafile; if YES go to step 6.

5. Repeat step 4 until you find a device with space; otherwise generate an error stating that there is not enough space on any of the backup devices.

6. Back up the file to the chosen backup device number denoted by backup_location_X, where X is the number of that device.

7. Append records to the restore_database.com file, which will delete the old copy of the file and restore the backup version of it.

8. If there are more records in file from step 1, go to step 2; otherwise step 9.

9. Done.

```
$ vvv = 'f$verify(0)'  ! set noverify and remember what it was before
$! FILE:    ORACLE_UTILS:BACKUP_TABLESPACE.COM
$! PURPOSE: Finds all datafiles associated with a tablespace and backs them up.
$! USAGE:   @oracle_utils:backup_tablespace tbs db_name num_of_devs
$!
$!          Example: @oracle_utils:backup_tablespace SYSTEM TESTDB 6
$!
$! PARAMETERS:
$!          P1: The tablespace to backup
$!          P2: The database name that tablespace belongs to
$!          P3: The number of backup devices available
$!
$! CALLS:   None.
```

```
$!
$! CALLED BY: oracle_utils:cold_backup
$!            oracle_utils:hot_backup
$!
$! INPUT:    Symbols: None.
$!     Logical Names: ORACLE_UTILS points to a directory with all
$!                    the backup scripts.
$!           Files:   backup_location_1:tbs_to_datafiles.lis
$!                    Tablespaces/datafiles to backup.
$!
$! OUTPUT:   Symbols: None.
$!           Logical Names: None.
$!           Files: * backup_location_1:restore_database.com
$!                    This is a dynamically created DCL script that will perform
$!                    the restore operation of this backup. It will also indicate
$!                    whether the file was created by a cold or hot backup.
$!
$!               * The datafiles of a specific tablespace will be backed up
$!                 on to one of the backup devices.
$!
$! HISTORY:
$!    Date         Name          Comments
$!    20-MAR-1995  Saar Maoz     Created
$!
$ set noon
$!
$! Local symbols to this script
$!
$ say := write sys$output
$ wo := write outfile
$ delfile := delete/noconfirm/log
$ backupfile := backup/log/ignore=(interlock,nobackup)/new
$!
$! Check for correct usage
$!
$ if p1 .eqs. "" then goto HELP
$!
$ tbs_to_copy = p1
$ db_name = p2
$ device_cnt = p3
$!
$! Open tablespace/datafiles listing file.  If it doesn't exist, something
$! went wrong.
$!
$ close/nolog infile2
$ open/read/error=OPEN_TBS_ERROR infile2 backup_location_1:tbs_to_datafiles.lis
$ read/end=EMPTY_FILE infile2 rec  ! Skip first record in file which is a comment
$!
$! Append commands to the RESTORE_DATABASE.COM, which will be used to restore
$! from this backup
$!
$ close/nolog outfile
$ open/append outfile backup_location_1:restore_database.com
$!
$ wo "$! Restore all files of tablespace ''tbs_to_copy' by first deleting"
```

```
$ wo "$! originals and then copying the saved files to the production"
$ wo "$! environment."
$ wo "$!"
$!
$! Identify the files for this tablespace
$!
$ MAIN_LOOP:
$    read/end=CLOSE_FILES infile2 rec
$    tbs = f$element(0,"¦",rec)            ! extract tablespace name
$    if tbs .nes. tbs_to_copy then goto MAIN_LOOP
$!
$!   found file to copy now find a disk for it.
$!
$    file = f$element(1,"¦",rec)           ! extract the file specification
$    size = f$element(2,"¦",rec)           ! extract the size of this file
$!
$! Announce file to be backed up.
$!
$    say " "
$    say "Attempting to backup ''file'"
$    dev_cnt = 1
$    FIND_DEVICE_LOOP:
$!
$!     Is there enough space on this disk?  Always leaving 2000 free blocks
$!     just in case (important not to fill location_1 completely)
$!
$      if f$getdvi("backup_location_''dev_cnt'","FREEBLOCKS") - 2000 .gt. size
$      then
$        say "                    to "+f$trnlnm("backup_location_''dev_cnt'")
$        say " "
$        backupfile 'file'; backup_location_'dev_cnt':/by=original
$        st = $status
$        if st .eq. %X10A38410 then goto BACKUP_OK  ! open for write by someone
$        if .not. st then goto BACKUP_ERROR
$!
$      BACKUP_OK:
$!
$!       Get full filename that we wrote, this is to make sure we get the version
$!       number of the file we just copied, in case there are files with the same
$!       name.
$!
$        fname=f$parse(file,,,"NAME")+f$parse(file,,,"TYPE")
$        full_name=f$search("backup_location_''dev_cnt':''fname'")
$!
$!       Write the commands to restore this datafile
$!
$        wo "$ if f$search(""''file'"") -"
$        wo "  .nes. """" then -"
$        wo "       delfile ''file';"
$        wo "$ backupfile   ''full_name' -"
$        wo "               ''file'/by=original"
$        wo "$!"
$        goto MAIN_LOOP
$      endif
$    dev_cnt = dev_cnt + 1                              ! skip to the next device
```

```
$     if dev_cnt .gt. device_cnt then goto NO_SPACE  ! no space on any device
$     goto FIND_DEVICE_LOOP
$!
$ CLOSE_FILES:
$ close/nolog infile2
$ close/nolog outfile
$!
$ goto FINISH    !Done
$!
$! ERROR-HANDLING SECTION
$! The rest of this script is an error-handling routine.  After each
$! error message it branchs to MAIL_STOP (will stop execution and send an
$! email). It is important to stop, because other scripts are relying on this
$! script to complete successfully.
$!
$ OPEN_TBS_ERROR:
$  say " "
$  say "ERROR ** ORACLE_UTILS:BACKUP_TABLESPACE.COM **"
$  say " An error has occured opening the tablespace datafiles mapping file."
$  say " It's located in BACKUP_LOCATION_1:TBS_TO_DATAFILES.LIS"
$  say " Please verify that the location is a valid directory owned by Oracle"
$  say " or the person running this script.  Also make sure that the Oracle"
$  say " shareable images are installed using ORA_RDBMS:INSORACLE.COM which"
$  say " is required to run sqlplus"
$  goto MAIL_STOP
$!
$ EMPTY_FILE:
$  say " "
$  say "ERROR ** ORACLE_UTILS:BACKUP_TABLESPACE.COM **"
$  say " Tablespace datafiles mapping file is empty.  The file is created by"
$  say " ORACLE_UTILS:HOT/COLD_BACKUP.COM which calls"
$  say " ORACLE_UTILS:TBS_TO_DATAFILES.SQL or ORACLE_UTILS:TBS_LOGFILES.SQL"
$  say " respectively."
$  goto MAIL_STOP
$!
$ BACKUP_ERROR:
$  say " "
$  say "ERROR ** ORACLE_UTILS:BACKUP_TABLESPACE.COM **"
$  say " Received a VMS backup error final error code: ''st'"
$  say " Text: "+f$message(st)
$  goto MAIL_STOP
$!
$ NO_SPACE:
$  say " "
$  say "ERROR ** ORACLE_UTILS:BACKUP_TABLESPACE.COM **"
$  say " Not enough space for ''file'"
$  say " on any backup device. Please assign more backup devices or clear some"
$  say " space on existing ones."
$  goto MAIL_STOP
$!
$ HELP:
$  say " "
$  say "Usage of ORACLE_UTILS:BACKUP_TABLESPACE.COM is:"
$  say " @ORACLE_UTILS:BACKUP_TABLESPACE.COM <tbsname> <db_name> <num_devs>"
$  say " look in ORACLE_UTILS:HOT/COLD_BACKUP for correct usage"
```

```
$  goto FINISH
$!
$ MAIL_STOP:
$  if mailuser .nes. "" then  sendmail -
      "Backup procedure terminated with error check logfile for details"
$!
$  STOP ! Exit this script and all calling scripts because of serious error
$!
$ FINISH:
$  if vvv then set verify
```

# INSTANCE_UP.COM

Given the SID (System Identifier) name of an instance, this script sees if any of the background processes of that instance are up. The algorithm is as follows:

1. Set the global symbol instance_up to 1, assuming it is up.

2. Scan all processes on this node (requires WORLD privilege) for any processes with the name of ORA_*sid*_*

3. If no processes are found in step 2, set instance_up to 0 to signal that the instance is down.

```
$! FILE:    ORACLE_UTILS:INSTANCE_UP.COM
$! PURPOSE: Check if any of the background processes are up.
$! USAGE:   @oracle_utils:instance_up SID
$!          Example: @oracle_utils:instance_up TEST
$!
$! PARAMETERS:
$!          P1 The System Identifier (SID) of the instance
$!
$! CALLS:   None.
$!
$! CALLED BY: oracle_utils:cold_backup
$!            oracle_utils:hot_backup
$!            oracle_utils:export_database
$!
$! INPUT:   Symbols: None.
$!          Logical Names: None.
$!          Files: None.
$!
$! OUTPUT:  Symbols: instance_up   1 for up, 0 for down.
$!          Logical Names: None.
$!          Files: None.
$!
$! HISTORY:
$!   Date         Name          Comments
$!   20-MAR-1995  Saar Maoz     Created
$!
$ set noon
```

```
$!
$! Check for correct usage
$!
$ if p1 .eqs. "" then goto HELP
$ sid = p1
$!
$ instance_up == 1
$ ctx = ""
$!
$! Look for any process with a name ORA_sid_* on this node. This would mean
$! that this is one of the background processes belonging to this instance.
$!
$ tmp = f$context("PROCESS",ctx,"NODENAME","''f$getsyi("nodename")'","EQL")
$ tmp = f$context("PROCESS",ctx,"PRCNAM","ORA_''sid'_*","EQL")
$ pid = f$pid(ctx)
$ if pid .eqs. "" then instance_up == 0
$ goto FINISH
$!
$ HELP:
$  say " "
$  say "Usage of ORACLE_UTILS:INSTANCE_UP.COM is:"
$  say " @ORACLE_UTILS:INSTANCE_UP SID"
$  goto FINISH
$!
$ FINISH:
$  exit
```

# ENV_SYMBOLS.COM

This script defines the symbols that will point to the right orauser_*dbname*.com file. The symbol should be the database name and should point to the orauser_*dbname*.com located in ora_db.

```
$! FILE:     ORACLE_UTILS:ENV_SYMBOLS.COM
$! PURPOSE: Set up a symbol for each database.
$! USAGE:    @oracle_utils:env_symbols
$! PARAMETERS:  None.
$! CALLS:    None.
$!
$! CALLED BY: Preferably by login.com or sylogin.com
$!
$! INPUT:    Symbols: None.
$!           Logical Names: None.
$!           Files: None.
$!
$! OUTPUT:   Symbols: db_name
$!           Logical Names: None.
$!           Files: None.
$!
$! HISTORY:
$!   Date        Name         Comments
$!   20-MAR-1995 Saar Maoz    Created
```

```
$!
$ set noon
$!
$! Setup a symbol for each database on this node as follows:
$!
$! dbname :== @location_of_orauser_file.com
$!
$! Example:
$!
$! testdb :== @sys$sysdevice:[oracle7.root71.db_testdb]orauser_testdb
$!
$ Exit
```

# SHUTDOWN_IMMEDIATE.COM

Given a database name, this script generates the DCL and SQLDBA scripts
necessary to shut down the database with the immediate option. It does so in the
following way:

1. Create oracle_utils:shutdown_immediate_*db_name*.com with the DCL
   commands to go into SQLDBA, and call
   oracle_utils:shutdown_immediate_*db_name*.sql.

2. Create the SQLDBA command file that will connect internal, then issue a
   shutdown immediate.

3. Invoke DCL file created in step 1.

4. Done.

```
$! FILE:     ORACLE_UTILS:SHUTDOWN_IMMEDIATE.COM
$! PURPOSE: Shuts down the database immediate.
$! USAGE:    @oracle_utils:shutdown_immediate db_name
$!           Example: @oracle_utils:shutdown_immediate TESTDB
$!
$! PARAMETERS:
$!           P1: The database name
$!
$! CALLS:    oracle_utils:shutdown_immediate_'db_name'.com
$!               \->oracle_utils:shutdown_immediate_'db_name'.sql
$!           ora_db:ora_db_db_name
$!
$! CALLED BY: oracle_utils:cold_backup
$!
$! INPUT:    Symbols:      None.
$!          Logical Names: ORACLE_UTILS points to a directory with all
$!                         the backup scripts.
$!                         ORA_PARAMS points to the node_SID_INIT.ORA file
$!                         defined by ora_db:ora_db_db_name.com
$!           Files:        None.
$!
```

```
$! OUTPUT:  Symbols: None.
$!  Logical Names:   None.
$!      Files: * oracle_utils:shutdown_immediate_db_name.sql
$!                  This is a dynamically created script that contains the
$!                  SQLDBA commands necessary to shut down the database.
$!             * oracle_utils:shutdown_immediate_db_name.com
$!                  This is a dynamically created DCL script that goes into
$!                  SQLDBA and calls the above-mentioned file to shut down
$!                  the database.
$!
$! HISTORY:
$!   Date        Name          Comments
$!   20-MAR-1995 Saar Maoz     Created
$!
$ set noon
$!
$! Local symbols to this script
$!
$ say := write sys$output
$ wo := write outfile
$ wo2 := write outfile2
$!
$! Check for correct usage
$!
$ if p1 .eqs. "" then goto HELP
$ db_name = p1
$ @ora_db:ora_db_'db_name'            ! to get ora_params logical
$ if f$trnlnm("ora_params") .eqs. "" then goto NO_PARAM_FILE
$!
$! Purge old logs
$!
$ if f$search("oracle_utils:shutdown_immediate_''db_name'.*") .nes. "" then -
    purge/nolog/keep=3 oracle_utils:shutdown_immediate_'db_name'.*
$!
$! Create the DCL script and SQL script that will actually do the shutdown
$!
$ close/nolog outfile
$ close/nolog outfile2
$ open/write outfile oracle_utils:shutdown_immediate_'db_name'.com
$ open/write outfile2 oracle_utils:shutdown_immediate_'db_name'.sql
$!
$ wo "$!Dynamically created by ORACLE_UTILS:SHUTDOWN_IMMEDIATE.COM at: "+-
    f$time()
$ wo "$!This script will go into sqldba and call a SQL script that will "
$ wo "$! shut down the ''db_name' database with the immediate option"
$ wo "$!"
$ wo "$ sqldba lmode=y"
$ wo "@oracle_utils:shutdown_immediate_''db_name'"
$ wo "exit"
$ wo "$exit"
$ close/nolog outfile
$!
$ wo2 "rem Dynamically created by ORACLE_UTILS:SHUTDOWN_IMMEDIATE.COM at: "+-
    f$time()
```

```
$ wo2 "rem This script issues the SQL statements to shutdown the ''db_name'"
$ wo2 "rem database with the immediate option"
$ wo2 "set echo on"
$ wo2 "connect internal"
$ wo2 "shutdown immediate"
$ close/nolog outfile2
$!
$! Execute the created script - to shutdown immediate the database
$!
$ @oracle_utils:shutdown_immediate_'db_name'.com
$ goto FINISH
$!
$ NO_PARAM_FILE:
$  say " "
$  say "ERROR ** ORACLE_UTILS:SHUTDOWN_IMMEDIATE.COM **"
$  say " The logical name ORA_PARAMS which points to the init.ora file of"
$  say " this ("+f$trnlnm(""ora_sid"")+") instance is not defined. The usual"
$  say " place where this logical is defined is ora_db:ora_db_''db_name'.com"
$  say " Please check why this logical was not defined and rerun this script."
$  goto FINISH
$!
$ HELP:
$  say " "
$  say "Usage of ORACLE_UTILS:SHUTDOWN_IMMEDIATE.COM is:"
$  say " @ORACLE_UTILS:SHUTDOWN_IMMEDIATE <db_name>"
$  goto FINISH
$!
$ FINISH:
$  Exit
```

# STARTUP_DBAMODE.COM

Given a database name, this script generates the DCL and SQLDBA scripts necessary to bring the database up in restricted mode. It does so in the following way:

**1.** Create oracle_utils:startup_dbamode_*db_name*.com with the DCL commands to go into SQLDBA, and call oracle_utils:startup_dbamode_*db_name*.sql.

**2.** Create the SQLDBA command file, which will connect internal and issue the startup restrict command.

**3.** Invoke DCL file created in step 1.

**4.** Done.

```
$! FILE:    ORACLE_UTILS:STARTUP_DBAMODE.COM
$! PURPOSE: Bring a database up in restricted mode (or the DBA mode)
$! USAGE:   @oracle_utils:startup_dbamode db_name
$!          Example: @oracle_utils:startup_dbamode TESTDB
$!
```

```
$! PARAMETERS:
$!          P1: The database name
$!
$! CALLS:    oracle_utils:startup_dbamode_db_name.com
$!                \->oracle_utils:startup_dbamode_db_name.sql
$!          ora_db:ora_db_db_name
$!
$! CALLED BY: oracle_utils:cold_backup
$!            oracle_utils:export_database
$!
$! INPUT:    Symbols:        None.
$!          Logical Names: ORACLE_UTILS points to a directory with all
$!                          the backup scripts.
$!                          ORA_PARAMS points to the node_SID_INIT.ORA file
$!                          defined by ora_db:ora_db_db_name.com
$!          Files:          None.
$!
$! OUTPUT:   Symbols: None.
$!          Logical Names: None.
$!          Files: * oracle_utils:startup_dbamode_db_name.sql
$!                      This is a dynamically created script that contains the
$!                      SQLDBA commands necessary to start the database
$!                      up in restricted mode.
$!                  * oracle_utils:startup_dbamode_db_name.com
$!                      This is a dynamically created DCL script that goes into
$!                      SQLDBA, and calls the above-mentioned file to bring
$!                      the database up in restricted mode.
$!
$! HISTORY:
$!   Date         Name          Comments
$!   20-MAR-1995  Saar Maoz     Created
$!
$ set noon
$!
$! Local symbols to this script
$!
$ say := write sys$output
$ wo := write outfile
$ wo2 := write outfile2
$!
$! Check for correct usage
$!
$ if p1 .eqs. "" then goto HELP
$ db_name = p1
$ @ora_db:ora_db_'db_name'                    ! to get ora_params logical
$ if f$trnlnm("ora_params") .eqs. "" then goto NO_PARAM_FILE
$!
$! Purge old logs
$!
$ if f$search("oracle_utils:startup_dbamode_''db_name'.*") .nes. "" then -
   purge/nolog/keep=3 oracle_utils:startup_dbamode_'db_name'.*
$!
$! Create the DCL script and SQL script that will actually do the startup
$!
$ close/nolog outfile
```

```
$ close/nolog outfile2
$ open/write outfile oracle_utils:startup_dbamode_'db_name'.com
$ open/write outfile2 oracle_utils:startup_dbamode_'db_name'.sql
$!
$ wo "$!Dynamically created by ORACLE_UTILS:STARTUP_DBAMODE.COM at: ''f$time()'"
$ wo "$!This script will go into sqldba and call a SQL script that will start"
$ wo "$!the ''db_name' database in restricted mode"
$ wo "$!"
$ wo "$ sqldba lmode=y"
$ wo "@oracle_utils:startup_dbamode_''db_name'"
$ wo "exit"
$ wo "$exit"
$ close/nolog outfile
$!
$ wo2 "rem Dynamically created by ORACLE_UTILS:STARTUP_DBAMODE.COM at: "+-
      f$time()
$ wo2 "rem This script issues the SQL statements to startup the ''db_name'"
$ wo2 "rem database in restricted mode."
$ wo2 "set echo on"
$ wo2 "connect internal"
$ wo2 "startup restrict open ""''db_name'"""
$ close/nolog outfile2
$!
$! Execute the created script - to startup the database in restricted mode
$!
$ @oracle_utils:startup_dbamode_'db_name'.com
$ goto FINISH
$!
$ NO_PARAM_FILE:
$  say " "
$  say "ERROR ** ORACLE_UTILS:STARTUP_DBAMODE.COM **"
$  say " The logical name ORA_PARAMS which points to the init.ora file of"
$  say " this ("+f$trnlnm(""ora_sid"")+") instance is not defined. The usual"
$  say " place where this logical is defined is ora_db:ora_db_''db_name'.com."
$  say " Please check why this logical was not defined and rerun this script."
$  goto FINISH
$!
$ HELP:
$  say " "
$  say "Usage of ORACLE_UTILS:STARTUP_DBAMODE.COM is:"
$  say " @ORACLE_UTILS:STARTUP_DBAMODE <db_name>"
$  goto FINISH
$!
$ FINISH:
$ Exit
```

# SUBMIT.COM

This is a sample file that shows how to submit ORACLE_UTILS:BACKUP_MAIN.COM to run as a batch job. Copy this script and modify all that is in uppercase to match your environment and needs. If you specify the resubmit flag (3rd parameter) as

YES, you will need to run this script only once. After that, the backup script will run a similar command to resubmit itself every day at the same time.

```
$ submit oracle_utils:backup_main.com -
    /parameters=("TESTDB","COMPLETE","YES") -
    /after="23:00" -
    /log=sys$scratch:save_database_TESTDB.log -
    /queue=sys$batch -
    /retain=error -
    /noprint
```

# db_name_DEVICES.COM

This is a sample file that defines the backup and export devices for a database. This file should be copied from this sample form and named ORACLE_UTILS:*db_name*_DEVICES.COM. Currently only disks are supported as backup and export devices.

```
$! Define only one export location which is a valid directory on a disk
$!
$ define/nolog export_location userdisk1:[export_testdb]
$!
$! Define as many backup directories as you wish
$!
$ define/nolog  backup_location_1  sys$sysdevice:[hot_backup_testdb]
$ define/nolog  backup_location_2  userdisk21:[hot_backup_testdb]
$ define/nolog  backup_location_3  userdisk33:[hot_backup_testdb]
$ define/nolog  backup_location_4  userdisk14:[hot_backup_testdb]
$ define/nolog  backup_location_5  userdisk5:[hot_backup_testdb]
$ define/nolog  backup_location_6  userdisk4:[hot_backup_testdb]
```

# Tbs_To_Datafiles.sql

The following SQL script is used by the hot backup script to create a list of the tablespace and data file names. The output contains a list of all data files that are part of the database.

```
set feedback off
set pagesize 0
set heading off
set echo off
set termout off
set timing off
spool backup_location_1:tbs_to_datafiles

SELECT '! Dynamically created by ORACLE_UTILS:HOT_BACKUP.COM at: '||
       to_char(sysdate,'dd-mon-yyyy hh:mi:ss')
FROM dual;
```

```
rem Get all the datafiles for this database

SELECT tablespace_name||'|'||file_name||'|'||ceil(bytes/512)
FROM    sys.dba_data_files
ORDER BY tablespace_name,bytes desc;

spool off;

EXIT
```

## Tbs_Logfiles.sql

The following SQL script is run by the cold backup script. The output file lists all the data files as well as the online log file names.

```
set feedback off
set pagesize 0
set heading off
set echo off
set termout off
set timing off
spool backup_location_1:tbs_to_datafiles

SELECT '! Dynamically created by ORACLE_UTILS:COLD_BACKUP.COM at: '||
        to_char(sysdate,'dd-mon-yyyy hh:mi:ss')
FROM dual;

rem Get all the datafiles for this database

SELECT tablespace_name||'|'||file_name||'|'||ceil(bytes/512)
FROM    sys.dba_data_files
ORDER BY tablespace_name,bytes desc;

rem Get all the redologs for this database

SELECT '    '||'|'||member||'|'||ceil(bytes/512)
FROM    v$log,v$logfile
WHERE   v$log.group# = v$logfile.group#;
spool off;

EXIT
```

# Backup Scripts in a UNIX Environment

In this section we give a very similar script as in the last section. The main backup script reads the schedule to determine the kind of backup to be taken. Then it calls other procedures to actually take a cold backup, a hot backup, or an export of the database. The scripts should give you an idea on the kind of logic to use while automating backup procedures. A lot of variables are hardcoded in this script. For example, we assume that all the control files have a .ctl extension when we make a backup of the control file. If you have a control file with a different name, you have to modify the scripts. You should customize the scripts for your business needs and test them before using them in a production environment.

The main procedure is called **dbbackup.** This procedure always does the following:

- Sets up the environment variables specific to the database by running the shell script **dbname_backup_admin.sh**

- Reads the backup schedule from **dbbackup_sched.dat** file to determine whether to take a hot backup, cold backup, or an export of the database

- Calls the procedure **dbbackup_begin** to do a hot or cold backup

- Calls the procedure **dbexport_begin** to do a full database export

The procedure **dbbackup_begin** does the following:

- Builds a dynamic listing of database files for use by hot and cold backups

- Performs hot backup by executing the following steps:

  - Each tablespace is put into hot backup mode

  - Data files are copied

  - Ends hot backup mode for all tablespaces

  - A log switch is forced before the archive logs are copied

  - Control file backup is made

- Performs cold backups by executing the following steps:

  - Send warning messages to users notifying them of the impending database shutdown

  - Shuts the database down and copies all database files

  - Starts the database in restricted mode and performs DBA tasks

  - Shuts database down, restarts the database, and sends message to users

The procedure **dbexport_begin** does the following:

- Takes a backup of the previous export file by copying it from the current location to a backup location

- Deletes the export file in the current location

■ Performs the export using the parameter file *dbname_export.par*

The following files are used in this section with a brief description.

| | |
|---|---|
| $TOOLS/db_mgmt/backup/dbbackup | main routine |
| $TOOLS/db_mgmt/backup/dbbackup_begin | called by **dbbackup** |
| $TOOLS/db_mgmt/backup/dbexport_begin | called by **dbbackup** |
| $TOOLS/db_mgmt/backup/dbbackup_sched.dat | schedule file |
| $TOOLS/system/crontab.dat | crontab schedule |
| $DBNAME/tools/backup/dbname_backup_admin.sh | environment variables |
| $DBNAME/tools/backup/dbname_backup_date.dyn | dynamic SQL written by **dbbackup_begin** |
| $DBNAME/tools/log/dbname_backup_date.log | log written by **dbbackup** |
| $DBNAME/tools/log/dbname_backup_date.err | error log written by **dbbackup** |
| $DBNAME/tools/log/dbname_backup_date.msg | email message written by **dbbackup** |
| $DBNAME/tools/log/dbname_export.par | export parameter file |
| $DBNAME/log/dbbackup.log | crontab log |

Following is the tree of execution of the scripts included in this section:

**dbbackup** *dbname*
    ***dbname*_backup_admin.sh**
    **dbbackup_sched.dat**
    **dbbackup_begin** *dbname  hot ¦ cold ¦ nobackup  special_task*
    **dbexport_begin** *dbname  export ¦ noexport  special_task*

While creating scripts in UNIX always remember the following general rules:

■ Never use **cd** in a script; always use absolute paths of files.

■ Never refer to files with wildcards.

■ Always verify file copies using the **cksum** command.

■ Always check the return status of shell commands to verify their success or failure.

■ Always check whether a file or directory exists with the -f option.

The scripts **dbbackup**, **dbbackup_begin**, and **dbexport_begin** are described below. The UNIX backup procedure is not as flexible as the backup script described in the VMS section. In this example, the database is backed up from disk to disk on the same machine. For every production disk you have, we assume you have a backup disk. You need to determine whether you want to copy all data files to one disk, to more than one disk, or to tape, and customize the scripts accordingly.

# dbbackup

This is the main backup script. It reads the backup schedule and calls scripts to take hot and cold backups and exports.

```
#! /bin/sh
#
# name                    $TOOLS/db_mgmt/backup/dbbackup
#
# $TOOLS variable is set to the directory where all system administration scripts
# reside
#
# purpose               Perform a backup of the database.
#
# usage                 $TOOLS/db_mgmt/backup/dbbackup dbname
#                             Calls $TOOLS/db_mgmt/backup/dbbackup_begin
#                             Calls $TOOLS/db_mgmt/backup/dbbackup_export
# parameters            $1=dbname
# HISTORY:
#   Date          Name              Comments
#   02-MAR-1995   Susie Ehrsam      Created
#   20-MAR-1995   Sumant Chaudhari  Modified and documented
# ..............................................................
# set environment
# ..............................................................
. /db_admin/tools/system/crontab.env >> /dev/null


# ..............................................................
# set local variables: Files to log messages, errors, etc.
# ..............................................................
BEGIN_JOB="`date`"
ERRMSG='$TOOLS/db_mgmt/backup/dbbackup: syntax error, parameter=<dbname>'

if [ "$1" ]
then DBNAME=$1
else echo $ERRMSG
exit
fi

LOGFILE="/db_admin/db_$DBNAME/tools/log/${DBNAME}_backup_`date '+%y%m%d'`.log"
LOGFILE2="/db_admin/db_$DBNAME/tools/log/${DBNAME}_backup_`date '+%y%m%d'`_old.log"
ERRFILE="/db_admin/db_$DBNAME/tools/log/${DBNAME}_backup_`date '+%y%m%d'`.err"
```

```
ERRFILE2="/db_admin/db_$DBNAME/tools/log/${DBNAME}_backup_`date '+%y%m%d'`_old.err"
MSGFILE="/db_admin/db_$DBNAME/tools/log/${DBNAME}_backup_`date '+%y%m%d'`.msg"
# ADMIN_FILE is the file that runs some administrative commands on a given database
# SCHED_FILE is the file containing the backup schedule
# JOBNAME is the current script.
# DBBACKUP_BEGIN is the backup script that performs hot or cold backup
# DBEXPORT_BEGIN is the script for exporting the database.
#
ADMIN_FILE="/db_admin/db_$DBNAME/tools/backup/${DBNAME}_backup_admin.sh"
SCHED_FILE="/db_admin/tools/db_mgmt/backup/dbbackup_sched.dat"
JOBNAME="$TOOLS/db_mgmt/backup/dbbackup"
DBBACKUP_BEGIN="$TOOLS/db_mgmt/backup/dbbackup_begin"
DBEXPORT_BEGIN="$TOOLS/db_mgmt/backup/dbexport_begin"
TODAY="`date`"
THIS_DAY="`date '+%a'`"
MSG="$DBNAME Backup succeeded at `date`"


# ............................................................
# Begin script processing, save old log files and error files
# ............................................................
if [ -f "$LOGFILE" ]; then
#
# Save old log file
#
cat $LOGFILE >> $LOGFILE2
fi
if [ -f "$ERRFILE" ]; then
#
# Save old error file
#
cat $ERRFILE >> $ERRFILE2
fi
#
# Enter name of the current script in message file and logfile,
# script_header is a generic script that marks beginning of this
# script for readability of message and log files.
#
$TOOLS/system/script_header $JOBNAME > $MSGFILE
$TOOLS/system/script_header $JOBNAME > $LOGFILE

#
# Read backup schedule. awk command is used to process the backup schedule file
# and extract record for the specified database for a given day.  Please refer
# to UNIX man pages for more information on awk.
#
awk -v dbname=$DBNAME -v this_day=$THIS_DAY '{
#
# get a record
#
cmd=$0
sizeofarray=split(cmd,rec," ")
dbname2=rec[1]
day_of_week=rec[2]
backup=rec[3]
export=rec[4]
```

```
special_task=rec[5]
#  if the database name and today's day match an entry in the schedule data file,
#  print the entry and feed it to the do loop for further processing
#
if (( dbname2 == dbname ) && ( this_day == day_of_week ))
print " " backup " " export " " special_task
}' $SCHED_FILE ¦ while read BACKUP EXPORT SPECIAL_TASK
do
. /db_admin/db_$DBNAME/.orauser_$DBNAME
#
# Print all parameters before beginning backup.
#
PARAMETER_MSG="
\n..................................................................
\nBackup Job Parameters:
\n
\nDatabase Name = $DBNAME
\nBackup Type   = $BACKUP
\nExport Type   = $EXPORT
\nSpecial Task  = $SPECIAL_TASK
\n
\nEnvironment Variables:
\nORACLE_HOME   = $ORACLE_HOME
\nORACLE_SID    = $ORACLE_SID
\nORACLE_BASE   = $ORACLE_BASE
\nPATH          = $PATH
\n..................................................................
\n
"
echo $PARAMETER_MSG >> $LOGFILE 2> $ERRFILE
echo $PARAMETER_MSG >> $MSGFILE
df >> $LOGFILE 2> $ERRFILE
echo " " >> $LOGFILE 2> $ERRFILE
#
# Backup: if the backup option is not nobackup proceed with backup by calling
# the procedure dbbackup_begin
#
if [ "$BACKUP" != "nobackup" ]; then
echo "..................................." >> $LOGFILE 2>> $ERRFILE
echo "Begin backup at `date`" >> $LOGFILE 2>> $ERRFILE
echo "..................................." >> $LOGFILE 2>> $ERRFILE
$DBBACKUP_BEGIN $DBNAME $BACKUP $SPECIAL_TASK >> $LOGFILE 2>> $ERRFILE
echo "..................................." >> $LOGFILE 2>> $ERRFILE
echo "End backup at `date`" >> $LOGFILE 2>> $ERRFILE
echo "..................................." >> $LOGFILE 2>> $ERRFILE
fi


#
# Export: if the export option is not noexport proceed with export by calling
# the procedure dbexport_begin
#
if [ "$EXPORT" != "noexport" ]; then
echo "..................................." >> $LOGFILE 2>> $ERRFILE
echo "Begin export at `date`" >> $LOGFILE 2>> $ERRFILE
echo "..................................." >> $LOGFILE 2>> $ERRFILE
```

```
$DBEXPORT_BEGIN $DBNAME $EXPORT $SPECIAL_TASK >> $LOGFILE 2>> $ERRFILE
echo "................................" >> $LOGFILE 2>> $ERRFILE
echo "End export at `date`" >> $LOGFILE 2>> $ERRFILE
echo "................................" >> $LOGFILE 2>> $ERRFILE
fi

echo " " >> $MSGFILE
echo "Backup log file errors and warnings:" >> $MSGFILE

echo " " >> $LOGFILE 2>> $ERRFILE
df >> $LOGFILE 2>> $ERRFILE
echo " " >> $LOGFILE 2>> $ERRFILE

#
# Errors: search for any errors or warning messages in the logfile and place them in
# message file.  grep is a unix utility for searching specific patterns, please
# refer to unix man pages for more information.
#
grep -e error -e warning -e ORA- -e EXP- -e fatal $LOGFILE | grep -v "No errors." >>
$MSGFILE
ERRCNT=`grep -e error -e ORA- -e EXP- -e fatal $LOGFILE | grep -c -v "No errors."`
grep -e error -e warning -e ORA- -e EXP- -e fatal $ERRFILE | grep -v "Export
terminated successfully" >> $MSGFILE
ERRCNT2=`grep -e error -e ORA- -e EXP- -e fatal $ERRFILE | grep -c -v "Export
terminated successfully"`
END_JOB="`date`"
if [ "$ERRCNT" -gt 0 -o "$ERRCNT2" -gt 0 ]
then MSG="$DBNAME backup failed at ${END_JOB}"
else MSG="$DBNAME backup succeeded at ${END_JOB}"
fi

echo " " >> $MSGFILE
echo "Log files: " >> $MSGFILE
echo "Log file=$LOGFILE" >> $MSGFILE
echo "Error file=$ERRFILE" >> $MSGFILE
echo "Message file=$MSGFILE" >> $MSGFILE
# script.footer is a banner of some kind
$TOOLS/templates/script.footer "$BEGIN_JOB" "$END_JOB" >> $MSGFILE
$TOOLS/templates/script.footer "$BEGIN_JOB" "$END_JOB" >> $LOGFILE

#
# Send mail to all DBAs
#
$TOOLS/mail/dba_mail_list "$MSG" $MSGFILE $DBNAME 0
```

# dbbackup_begin

```
#! /bin/sh
# name          $TOOLS/db_mgmt/backup/dbbackup_begin
#
# purpose       Perform a backup of a database.
#
```

```
# usage          $TOOLS/db_mgmt/backup/dbbackup_begin dbname backup special_task
# parameters     $1=dbname
#                $2=backup type
#                $3=special task
# HISTORY:
#   Date         Name          Comments
#   02-MAR-1995  Susie Ehrsam    Created
#   20-MAR-1995  Sumant Chaudhari Modified backup logic

# ...........................................................
# set local variables
# ...........................................................
ERRMSG='
$TOOLS/db_mgmt/backup/dbbackup_begin: syntax error:
dbbackup_begin <dbname> <hot|cold|nobackup> <special task>.
'
#
# check command parameters, if null, exit the procedure.
#
if [ "$1" ]
then DBNAME=$1
else echo $ERRMSG
exit 1
fi
if [ "$2" ]
then BACKUP=$2
else echo $ERRMSG
exit 1
fi
if [ "$3" ]
then SPECIAL_TASK=$3
else SPECIAL_TASK=" "
fi
#
# booleans
#
TRUE=0
FALSE=1
SHUTDOWN_FAILED_B=1
RESTART_FAILED_B=1
#
# local variables
#
JOBNAME="$TOOLS/db_mgmt/backup/dbbackup_begin"
JOBNAME_SHORT="dbbackup_begin"
ADMIN_FILE="/db_admin/db_$DBNAME/tools/backup/${DBNAME}_backup_admin.sh"
DBBACKUP="/db_admin/db_$DBNAME/tools/backup/${DBNAME}_backup_`date '+%y%m%d'`.dyn"
WALL="/etc/wall"
CKSUM="/bin/cksum"
CMP="/bin/cmp"
 BANNER="/db_admin/db_${DBNAME}/banner/status"
CKSUM_SIZE_ERR="${JOBNAME_SHORT}: fatal error in cksum size comparison."
CKSUM_VALUE_ERR="${JOBNAME_SHORT}: fatal error in cksum value comparison."
CKSUM_VALUE_WAR="${JOBNAME_SHORT}: warning in cksum value comparison."
CMP_ERR="${JOBNAME_SHORT}: fatal error in cmp."
```

```
DBSERR="${JOBNAME_SHORT}: fatal error in dbs file copy."
DBSWAR="${JOBNAME_SHORT}: warning with database file copy."
ARCERR="${JOBNAME_SHORT}: fatal error in archive log copy."
THISNODE=`uname -n`
TSLIST=="/db_admin/db_$DBNAME/tools/backup/${DBNAME}_tablespaces"
ERRORLOGFILE="/db_admin/db_$DBNAME/tools/backup/${DBNAME}_backup_errors"
#    CURRENT_TABLESPACE variable should be initialized to a tablespace name that does
#      not exist
CURRENT_TABLESPACE="CURRENT"

#
# node-specific logic: customize according to your needs
#
if [ "$THISNODE" = "prodhp1" ]
then TMP='/bugtmp'
else TMP='/dbatmp'
fi

# .............................................................
# begin the backup process
# .............................................................

#
# orauser script sets environment variables such as ORACLE_HOME, SID, PATH etc.
#
. /db_admin/db_$DBNAME/.orauser_$DBNAME
. $ADMIN_FILE

#
# check for database online
#
STATUS=`ps -fu oracle | grep $DBNAME | grep ora_ | grep -v grep`
if [ $? != 0 ]; then
# There are no background processes running, or database is down
if [ "$BACKUP" = "hot" ]; then
# hot backup does not make sense.
echo "${JOBNAME_SHORT}: Error - database is not online."
echo "${JOBNAME_SHORT}: process listing is to follow..."
echo "${JOBNAME_SHORT}: ps -fu oracle | grep -v grep | grep $DBNAME | grep ora_"
ps -fu oracle | grep -v grep | grep $DBNAME | grep ora_
echo "${JOBNAME_SHORT}: exiting."
exit
else
# for cold backup this is fine
echo "${JOBNAME_SHORT}: Database is already down.  Continuing."
echo "${JOBNAME_SHORT}: kill sqlnet v1 processes."
# Kill lingering processes since the DB is already down
$TOOLS/unix/kill_processes.sh oracle${DBNAME}
fi
else
# since database is already up
if [ "$BACKUP" = "cold" ]; then
#
# broadcast shutdowns, write your own banners
#
```

```
• $WALL /db_admin/db_${DBNAME}/banner/${DBNAME}_shutdown_15min.banner
  $WALL /db_admin/db_${DBNAME}/banner/${DBNAME}_shutdown_5min.banner
  $WALL /db_admin/db_${DBNAME}/banner/${DBNAME}_shutdown_1min.banner
  #
  # shutdown using appropriate shutdown scripts
  #
  echo "${JOBNAME_SHORT}: Shutting down immediate."
  /db_admin/db_${DBNAME}/sql/shutdown_immediate_${DBNAME}.sh
  #
  # kill sqlnet processes
  #
  echo "${JOBNAME_SHORT}: kill sqlnet v1 processes."
  $TOOLS/unix/kill_processes.sh oracle${DBNAME}
  fi
  fi

  if [ "$BACKUP" = "cold" ]; then
  echo "${JOBNAME_SHORT}: Starting up restrict."
  /db_admin/db_${DBNAME}/sql/startup_restrict_${DBNAME}.sh
  fi

  # ................................................................
  # begin backup
  # ................................................................
  #
  # Build database file list.  The file list has name of the tablespace, name of
  # file, and backup destination.  It is assumed that for each partition with
  # datafiles,there is a partition for backup of these files. For example, if
  # dbf1, dbf2...dbf12 are datafile partitions, there should be 12 partitions for
  # backing up these files.Thus, each time more disk space is added for datafiles,
  # disk space should be added for backup. The distribution of datafiles and the
  # strategy of copying must be robust enough to overcome space problems that
  # could cause failure in backup. Plan and design your backup strategy carefully
  # to accomodate space constraints. The following logic should be customized if
  # you want a different backup scheme.

  echo "${JOBNAME_SHORT}: building dynamic parameter file."
  sqlplus -s / > $DBBACKUP <<EOF
  set pagesize 0
  set linesize 2048
  set heading off
  set feedback off
  column TNAME format a20
  column FNAME format a80
  select tablespace_name TNAME,
  file_name FNAME,
  ' \$BACKUPDIR'||
  substr(file_name,instr(translate(file_name,'1234567890','0000000000'),'0'),
  instr(file_name,'/',1,2)- instr(translate(file_name,'1234567890','0000000000'),'0'))
  from sys.dba_data_files
  order by tablespace_name,file_name;
  exit
  EOF

  #
```

```
# Check dynamic file for size. A sample line in this file is as follows:
#   SYSTEM        /dbf1/DB1_system.dbf      /backup1/DB1
#
DYNSIZE=`ls -al  $DBBACKUP | awk '{print $5}'`
if [ $DYNSIZE = 0 ]; then
echo "${JOBNAME_SHORT}: fatal error during backup file creation.  Backup aborting."
echo "${JOBNAME_SHORT}: cat $DBBACKUP"
cat $DBBACKUP
return
fi


#
# Create a list of all tablespaces in the database
echo "${JOBNAME_SHORT}: building list of tablespaces."
sqlplus -s / > $TSLIST <<EOF
set pagesize 0
set linesize 2048
set heading off
set feedback off
column TNAME format a20
column FNAME format a80
select tablespace_name TNAME from sys.dba_tablespaces;
exit
EOF
cat $TSLIST
# shutdown if the backup option is for cold backup
#
if [ $BACKUP = "cold" ]; then
echo "${JOBNAME_SHORT}: Shutting down normal."
. /db_admin/db_${DBNAME}/sql/shutdown_${DBNAME}.sh

STATUS=`ps -fu oracle | grep -v grep | grep $DBNAME | grep -v ${DBNAME}1 | grep ora_`
if [ $? = 0 ]; then
echo "${JOBNAME_SHORT}: error in shutdown. Cold backup aborting."
SHUTDOWN_FAILED_B="$TRUE"
else
echo "${JOBNAME_SHORT}: Database is shutdown."
echo "${JOBNAME_SHORT}: move alert log."
mv /db_admin/db_${DBNAME}/bdump/alert_${DBNAME}.log \
/db_admin/db_${DBNAME}/bdump/alert_${DBNAME}.log_`date '+%y%m%d'`
fi
fi


#
# Check for the database files from previous backup in the backup partitions.
# Delete the files to create space for the new backup. Customize this part
# for your backup partitions.
#
if [ $SHUTDOWN_FAILED_B = $TRUE ]; then
echo "${JOBNAME_SHORT}: Skipping backup file deletion."
else
echo " "
echo "${JOBNAME_SHORT}: Deleting previous backup..."
if [ -f $BACKUPDIR1/${DBNAME}_*.dbf ]; then rm $BACKUPDIR1/${DBNAME}_*.dbf; fi
if [ -f $BACKUPDIR2/${DBNAME}_*.dbf ]; then rm $BACKUPDIR2/${DBNAME}_*.dbf; fi
```

```
if [ -f $BACKUPDIR3/${DBNAME}_*.dbf ]; then rm $BACKUPDIR3/${DBNAME}_*.dbf; fi
if [ -f $BACKUPDIR4/${DBNAME}_*.dbf ]; then rm $BACKUPDIR4/${DBNAME}_*.dbf; fi
if [ -f $BACKUPDIR5/${DBNAME}_*.dbf ]; then rm $BACKUPDIR5/${DBNAME}_*.dbf; fi
if [ -f $BACKUPDIR6/${DBNAME}_*.dbf ]; then rm $BACKUPDIR6/${DBNAME}_*.dbf; fi
if [ -f $BACKUPDIR7/${DBNAME}_*.dbf ]; then rm $BACKUPDIR7/${DBNAME}_*.dbf; fi
if [ -f $BACKUPDIR8/${DBNAME}_*.dbf ]; then rm $BACKUPDIR8/${DBNAME}_*.dbf; fi

if [ -f $BACKUPDIR1/${DBNAME}_*.ctl ]; then rm $BACKUPDIR1/${DBNAME}_*.ctl; fi
if [ -f $BACKUPDIR2/${DBNAME}_*.ctl ]; then rm $BACKUPDIR2/${DBNAME}_*.ctl; fi
if [ -f $BACKUPDIR3/${DBNAME}_*.ctl ]; then rm $BACKUPDIR3/${DBNAME}_*.ctl; fi
if [ -f $BACKUPDIR4/${DBNAME}_*.ctl ]; then rm $BACKUPDIR4/${DBNAME}_*.ctl; fi
if [ -f $BACKUPDIR5/${DBNAME}_*.ctl ]; then rm $BACKUPDIR5/${DBNAME}_*.ctl; fi
if [ -f $BACKUPDIR6/${DBNAME}_*.ctl ]; then rm $BACKUPDIR6/${DBNAME}_*.ctl; fi
if [ -f $BACKUPDIR7/${DBNAME}_*.ctl ]; then rm $BACKUPDIR7/${DBNAME}_*.ctl; fi
if [ -f $BACKUPDIR8/${DBNAME}_*.ctl ]; then rm $BACKUPDIR8/${DBNAME}_*.ctl; fi

if [ $BACKUP = "cold" ]; then
if [ -f $BACKUPDIR1/${DBNAME}_*.log ]; then rm $BACKUPDIR1/${DBNAME}_*.log; fi
if [ -f $BACKUPDIR2/${DBNAME}_*.log ]; then rm $BACKUPDIR2/${DBNAME}_*.log; fi
if [ -f $BACKUPDIR3/${DBNAME}_*.log ]; then rm $BACKUPDIR3/${DBNAME}_*.log; fi
if [ -f $BACKUPDIR4/${DBNAME}_*.log ]; then rm $BACKUPDIR4/${DBNAME}_*.log; fi
if [ -f $BACKUPDIR5/${DBNAME}_*.log ]; then rm $BACKUPDIR5/${DBNAME}_*.log; fi
if [ -f $BACKUPDIR6/${DBNAME}_*.log ]; then rm $BACKUPDIR6/${DBNAME}_*.log; fi
if [ -f $BACKUPDIR7/${DBNAME}_*.log ]; then rm $BACKUPDIR7/${DBNAME}_*.log; fi
if [ -f $BACKUPDIR8/${DBNAME}_*.log ]; then rm $BACKUPDIR8/${DBNAME}_*.log; fi
else
if [ -f $CONBACK1/${DBNAME}_*.ctl ]; then rm $CONBACK1/${DBNAME}_*.ctl; fi
fi
fi


#
# Begin backup procedure
#
if [ $SHUTDOWN_FAILED_B = $FALSE ]; then
echo " "
echo "${JOBNAME_SHORT}:  Starting $BACKUP backup using $DBBACKUP..."
#
# check hot backup status for datafiles
#
if  [ $BACKUP = "hot" ]; then
sqldba lmode=y <<EOF
connect internal
select * from v$backup;
exit
EOF
fi
# If any datafile is in hot backup mode, end the backup. Do an end backup for
# all tablespaces. Ignore the warnings in log file.
#
cat $TSLIST | while read TABLESPACE
    do
        if [ $BACKUP = "hot" ]; then
          sqldba lmode = y  << EOF
          connect internal
          alter tablespace $TABLESPACE end backup;
```

```
            exit
            EOF
        fi
    done

# begin reading file list
#
cat $DBBACKUP | while read TABLESPACE FILE DIR
do
if [ $BACKUP = "hot" ]; then
#  If it is the first tablespace to be backed up
        if  [ $CURRENT_TS = "current" ]; then
            sqldba lmode = y << EOF
            connect internal
            alter tablespace $TABLESPACE begin backup;
            exit
            EOF
        fi
#
#  When the next tablespace has to be backed up (TABLESPACE),  end backup of the
#  current tablespace, make the next tablespace CURRENT_TS, and begin its backup.
#
if [ $BACKUP = "hot" ]; then
        if [ $CURRENT_TS != `eval echo \$TABLESPACE` ]; then
            sqldba lmode = y << EOF
            connect internal
            alter tablespace $CURRENT_TS   end backup;
            exit
            EOF
        CURRENT_TS =  `eval echo \$TABLESPACE`
            sqldba lmode = y << EOF
            connect internal
            alter tablespace $TABLESPACE begin backup;
            exit
EOF
        fi
fi


#
# copy a database file, verify sizes, do checksum etc.
#
BACKUPDIR=`eval echo \$DIR`
echo "${JOBNAME_SHORT}: cp $FILE $BACKUPDIR"
cp $FILE $BACKUPDIR
STATUS=$?
if [ "$STATUS" != 0 ]; then
echo  "${JOBNAME_SHORT}: error during file copy $FILE."
fi
DATAFILE=`basename $FILE`
if [ $BACKUP = "hot" ]; then
echo "${JOBNAME_SHORT}: $CKSUM $FILE $BACKUPDIR/$DATAFILE"
$CKSUM $FILE $BACKUPDIR/$DATAFILE
CKSUM_OUT=`$CKSUM $FILE $BACKUPDIR/$DATAFILE`
echo $CKSUM_OUT | read VALUE1 SIZE1 NAME1 VALUE2 SIZE2 NAME2
if [ "$VALUE1" != "$VALUE2" ]; then
```

```
echo "$CKSUM_VALUE_WAR"
fi
if [ "$SIZE1" != "$SIZE2" ]; then
echo "$CKSUM_SIZE_ERR"
fi
else
echo "${JOBNAME_SHORT}: $CMP $FILE $BACKUPDIR/$DATAFILE"
$CMP $FILE $BACKUPDIR/$DATAFILE
STATUS="$?"
if [ "$STATUS" != 0 ]; then
echo "$CMP_ERR"
fi
fi
done
#
# check hot backup status
#
if  [ $BACKUP = "hot" ]; then
sqldba lmode=y <<EOF
connect internal
select * from v$backup;
exit
EOF
fi
# If any tablespace is in hot backup mode, Do an end backup for the tablespace.
# Ignore the warnings in the log file.
#
cat $TSLIST | while read TABLESPACE
    do
        if [ $BACKUP = "hot" ]; then
          sqldba lmode = y  << EOF
          connect internal
          alter tablespace $TABLESPACE end  backup;
          exit
          EOF
        fi
    done
#
# Backup control files and online redo logs
#
if [ $BACKUP = "hot" ]; then
echo "${JOBNAME_SHORT}: backing up controlfile to
${CONBACK1}/${DBNAME}_control01.ctl"
sqldba lmode=y <<EOF
connect internal
alter database backup controlfile to '${CONBACK1}/${DBNAME}_control01.ctl';
exit
EOF
#
else
#
# copies control files; assumes all control files have .ctl extension
#
echo "${JOBNAME_SHORT}: backing up all control files..."
if [ -f /dbf1/$DBNAME/${DBNAME}_*.ctl ]; then cp /dbf1/$DBNAME/${DBNAME}_*.ctl
```

```
$BACKUPDIR1; fi
if [ -f /dbf2/$DBNAME/${DBNAME}_*.ctl ]; then cp /dbf2/$DBNAME/${DBNAME}_*.ctl
$BACKUPDIR2; fi
if [ -f /dbf3/$DBNAME/${DBNAME}_*.ctl ]; then cp /dbf3/$DBNAME/${DBNAME}_*.ctl
$BACKUPDIR3; fi
if [ -f /dbf4/$DBNAME/${DBNAME}_*.ctl ]; then cp /dbf4/$DBNAME/${DBNAME}_*.ctl
$BACKUPDIR4; fi
if [ -f /dbf5/$DBNAME/${DBNAME}_*.ctl ]; then cp /dbf5/$DBNAME/${DBNAME}_*.ctl
$BACKUPDIR5; fi
if [ -f /dbf6/$DBNAME/${DBNAME}_*.ctl ]; then cp /dbf6/$DBNAME/${DBNAME}_*.ctl
$BACKUPDIR6; fi
if [ -f /dbf7/$DBNAME/${DBNAME}_*.ctl ]; then cp /dbf7/$DBNAME/${DBNAME}_*.ctl
$BACKUPDIR7; fi
if [ -f /dbf8/$DBNAME/${DBNAME}_*.ctl ]; then cp /dbf8/$DBNAME/${DBNAME}_*.ctl
$BACKUPDIR8; fi
if [ -f /dbf9/$DBNAME/${DBNAME}_*.ctl ]; then cp /dbf9/$DBNAME/${DBNAME}_*.ctl
$BACKUPDIR9; fi
if [ -f /dbf10/$DBNAME/${DBNAME}_*.ctl ]; then cp /dbf10/$DBNAME/${DBNAME}_*.ctl
$BACKUPDIR10; fi
if [ -f /dbf11/$DBNAME/${DBNAME}_*.ctl ]; then cp /dbf11/$DBNAME/${DBNAME}_*.ctl
$BACKUPDIR11; fi
if [ -f /dbf12/$DBNAME/${DBNAME}_*.ctl ]; then cp /dbf12/$DBNAME/${DBNAME}_*.ctl
$BACKUPDIR12; fi
#
# copies redo log files; assumes all log files have .log extension
#
echo "${JOBNAME_SHORT}: backing up all online redo logs..."
if [ -f /dbf1/$DBNAME/${DBNAME}_*.log ]; then cp /dbf1/$DBNAME/${DBNAME}_*.log
$BACKUPDIR1; fi
if [ -f /dbf2/$DBNAME/${DBNAME}_*.log ]; then cp /dbf2/$DBNAME/${DBNAME}_*.log
$BACKUPDIR2; fi
if [ -f /dbf3/$DBNAME/${DBNAME}_*.log ]; then cp /dbf3/$DBNAME/${DBNAME}_*.log
$BACKUPDIR3; fi
if [ -f /dbf4/$DBNAME/${DBNAME}_*.log ]; then cp /dbf4/$DBNAME/${DBNAME}_*.log
$BACKUPDIR4; fi
if [ -f /dbf5/$DBNAME/${DBNAME}_*.log ]; then cp /dbf5/$DBNAME/${DBNAME}_*.log
$BACKUPDIR5; fi
if [ -f /dbf6/$DBNAME/${DBNAME}_*.log ]; then cp /dbf6/$DBNAME/${DBNAME}_*.log
$BACKUPDIR6; fi
if [ -f /dbf7/$DBNAME/${DBNAME}_*.log ]; then cp /dbf7/$DBNAME/${DBNAME}_*.log
$BACKUPDIR7; fi
if [ -f /dbf8/$DBNAME/${DBNAME}_*.log ]; then cp /dbf8/$DBNAME/${DBNAME}_*.log
$BACKUPDIR8; fi
if [ -f /dbf9/$DBNAME/${DBNAME}_*.log ]; then cp /dbf9/$DBNAME/${DBNAME}_*.log
$BACKUPDIR9; fi
if [ -f /dbf10/$DBNAME/${DBNAME}_*.log ]; then cp /dbf10/$DBNAME/${DBNAME}_*.log
$BACKUPDIR10; fi
if [ -f /dbf11/$DBNAME/${DBNAME}_*.log ]; then cp /dbf11/$DBNAME/${DBNAME}_*.log
$BACKUPDIR11; fi
if [ -f /dbf12/$DBNAME/${DBNAME}_*.log ]; then cp /dbf12/$DBNAME/${DBNAME}_*.log
$BACKUPDIR12; fi
fi

#
# archive logs
```

```
#
#
# force a log switch
#
if [ $BACKUP = "hot" ]; then
sqldba lmode=y <<EOF
connect internal
alter system switch logfile;
exit
EOF
#
# wait for archive log copy to complete
#
sleep 120
fi
#
# copy archive logs
#
if [ -f $ARCOLD/${DBNAME}_*.arc ]; then
echo " "
echo "${JOBNAME_SHORT}: Delete previous backup archive logs..."
ls -l $ARCOLD/${DBNAME}_*.arc
for I in $ARCOLD/${DBNAME}_*.arc
do
ls -l $I
ARCNAME=`basename $I`
rm $ARCOLD/$ARCNAME
STATUS="$?"
if [ "$STATUS" != 0 ]; then
echo "${JOBNAME_SHORT}: error deleting old archive log: $ARCOLD/$ARCNAME"
fi
done
else    echo " "
echo "${JOBNAME_SHORT}: No old archive logs to delete."
fi

if [ -f $ARC/${DBNAME}_*.arc ]; then
echo " "
echo "${JOBNAME_SHORT}: Copying archive logs..."
for I in $ARC/${DBNAME}_*.arc
do
ls -l $I
ARCNAME=`basename $I`
echo "${JOBNAME_SHORT}: cp $ARC/$ARCNAME $ARCOLD"
cp $ARC/$ARCNAME $ARCOLD
STATUS="$?"
if [ "$STATUS" != 0 ]; then
echo "$ARCERR"
fi
echo "${JOBNAME_SHORT}: $CMP $ARC/$ARCNAME $ARCOLD/$ARCNAME"
$CMP $ARC/$ARCNAME $ARCOLD/$ARCNAME
STATUS="$?"
if [ "$STATUS" != 0 ]; then
echo "$CMP_ERR"
echo "${JOBNAME_SHORT}: Archive log deletion skipped."
```

```
else echo "${JOBNAME_SHORT}: $CKSUM $ARC/$ARCNAME $ARCOLD/$ARCNAME"
$CKSUM $ARC/$ARCNAME $ARCOLD/$ARCNAME
CKSUM_OUT=`$CKSUM $ARC/$ARCNAME $ARCOLD/$ARCNAME`
echo $CKSUM_OUT | read VALUE1 SIZE1 NAME1 VALUE2 SIZE2 NAME2
if [ "$VALUE1" != "$VALUE2" -o "$SIZE1" != "$SIZE2" ]; then
echo "$DIFFERR"
echo "${JOBNAME_SHORT}: Archive log deletion skipped."
else rm $ARC/$ARCNAME
if [ $? != 0 ]; then
echo "${JOBNAME_SHORT}: Archive deletion failed."
fi
fi
fi
done
else echo "${JOBNAME_SHORT}: Found no archives to copy."
fi


#
# startup
#
if [ $BACKUP = "cold" ]; then
#
# dba mode tasks
#
echo "${JOBNAME_SHORT}: Begin startup restrict..."
/db_admin/db_${DBNAME}/sql/startup_restrict_${DBNAME}.sh
STATUS=`ps -fu oracle | grep -v grep | grep $DBNAME | grep ora_`
if [ $? != 0 ]; then
echo "${JOBNAME_SHORT}: error in restrict startup."
#
# special task
#
if [ "$SPECIAL_TASK" != " " ]; then
echo "${JOBNAME_SHORT}: Running DBA mode task..."
. ${SPECIAL_TASK} > $TMP/${DBNAME}_restrict.log 2> $TMP/${DBNAME}_restrict.err
# sqlplus / @${SPECIAL_TASK} ${SPECIAL_TASK}.log 2>> ${SPECIAL_TASK}.err
fi
fi
echo "${JOBNAME_SHORT}: Shutdown..."
/db_admin/db_${DBNAME}/sql/shutdown_${DBNAME}.sh
STATUS=`ps -fu oracle | grep -v grep | grep $DBNAME | grep ora_`
if [ $? = 0 ]; then
echo "${JOBNAME_SHORT}: error in shutdown following analyze..."
else
echo "${JOBNAME_SHORT}: End shutdown..."
fi
#
# startup
#
/db_admin/db_${DBNAME}/sql/startup_exclusive_${DBNAME}.sh
STATUS=`ps -fu oracle | grep -v grep | grep $DBNAME | grep ora_`
if [ $? != 0 ]; then
echo "${JOBNAME_SHORT}: error in database startup."
RESTART_FAILED_B=0
else
```

```
echo "${JOBNAME_SHORT}: Database restarted."
echo "1" > $BANNER
$WALL /db_admin/db_${DBNAME}/banner/${DBNAME}_db_online.banner
fi
fi
```

# dbexport_begin

```
#! /bin/sh
# name            $TOOLS/db_mgmt/backup/dbexport_begin
#
# purpose         Perform a backup of a database.
#
# usage           $TOOLS/db_mgmt/backup/dbexport_begin dbname export special task
#
# parameters      $1=dbname
#                 $2=export
#                 $3=special task
# HISTORY:
#    Date         Name            Comments
#    02-MAR-1995  Susie Ehrsam      Created
#    20-MAR-1995  Sumant Chaudhari Documented


# ............................................................
# local variables
# ............................................................
ERRMSG='
$TOOLS/db_mgmt/backup/dbexport_begin: syntax error:
dbexport_begin <dbname> <export;noexport> <special task>.
'
#
# parameters
#
if [ "$1" ]
then DBNAME=$1
else echo $ERRMSG
exit 1
fi
if [ "$2" ]
then EXPORT=$2
else echo $ERRMSG
exit 1
fi
if [ "$3" ]
then SPECIAL_TASK=$3
else SPECIAL_TASK=" "
fi


# ............................................................
# booleans
# ............................................................
TRUE=0
```

```
FALSE=1
SHUTDOWN_FAILED_B=1
RESTART_FAILED_B=1


#..............................................................
# local variables
#..............................................................
JOBNAME="$TOOLS/db_mgmt/backup/dbexport_begin"
JOBNAME_SHORT="dbexport_begin"
ADMIN_FILE="/db_admin/db_$DBNAME/tools/backup/${DBNAME}_backup_admin.sh"
CMP="/bin/cmp"
PARFILE="/db_admin/db_$DBNAME/tools/backup/${DBNAME}_export.par"
CMP_ERR="${JOBNAME_SHORT}: fatal error in cmp."
EXPERR="${JOBNAME_SHORT}: fatal error in export file copy."


# .............................................................
# begin
# .............................................................
#
# run the orauser to setup oracle environment
#
. /db_admin/db_$DBNAME/.orauser_$DBNAME
. $ADMIN_FILE
#
# check for database online
#
STATUS=`ps -fu oracle ¦ grep -v grep ¦ grep $DBNAME ¦ grep ora_`
if [ $? != 0 ]; then
echo "${JOBNAME_SHORT}: error - database not online."
echo "${JOBNAME_SHORT}: process listing is to follow..."
echo "${JOBNAME_SHORT}: ps -fu oracle ¦ grep -v grep ¦ grep $DBNAME ¦ grep ora_"
ps -fu oracle ¦ grep -v grep ¦ grep $DBNAME ¦ grep ora_
echo "${JOBNAME_SHORT}: exiting."
exit 1
fi


# .................................................................
# Delete export files from backup location (2nd copy on disk). Then copy the export
# file from current location to backup location. Finally take an export
# of the database to the current location.  You can choose your own strategy here.
# .................................................................
echo " "
echo "${JOBNAME_SHORT}: List previous export files..."
ls -l $EXPORTDIR/${DBNAME}.exp*
ls -l $EXPORTDIROLD/${DBNAME}.exp*


#
# delete old export
#
if [ -f $EXPORTDIROLD/${DBNAME}.exp_old ]; then
rm $EXPORTDIROLD/${DBNAME}.exp_old
if [ $? != 0 ]; then
echo "${JOBNAME_SHORT}: error deleting previous export."
else
echo "${JOBNAME_SHORT}: Deleted previous export file."
```

```
fi
else echo "${JOBNAME_SHORT}: Found no previous export file."
fi
#
# copy current export to old
#
if [ -f $EXPORTDIR/${DBNAME}.exp ]; then
chmod 642 $EXPORTDIR/${DBNAME}.exp
echo "${JOBNAME_SHORT}: cp $EXPORTDIR/${DBNAME}.exp $EXPORTDIROLD"
cp $EXPORTDIR/${DBNAME}.exp $EXPORTDIROLD
if [ $? != 0 ]; then
echo "$EXPERR"
else echo "${JOBNAME_SHORT}: $CMP $EXPORTDIR/${DBNAME}.exp
$EXPORTDIROLD/${DBNAME}.exp"
$CMP $EXPORTDIR/${DBNAME}.exp $EXPORTDIROLD/${DBNAME}.exp
STATUS="$?"
if [ "$STATUS" != 0 ]; then
echo "$CMP_ERR"
fi
echo "${JOBNAME_SHORT}: mv ${EXPORTDIROLD}/${DBNAME}.exp
${EXPORTDIROLD}/${DBNAME}.exp_old"
mv ${EXPORTDIROLD}/${DBNAME}.exp ${EXPORTDIROLD}/${DBNAME}.exp_old
if [ $? != 0 ]; then
echo "$EXPERR"
fi
rm $EXPORTDIR/${DBNAME}.exp
if [ $? != 0 ]; then
echo "${JOBNAME_SHORT}: error deleting export file."
exit
fi
fi
else echo "${JOBNAME_SHORT}: Found no current export file to copy."
fi

#
# Begin export
#
exp parfile=$PARFILE
echo " "
echo "${JOBNAME_SHORT}: Export complete.  "
ls -l $EXPORTDIR/${DBNAME}.exp*
ls -l $EXPORTDIROLD/${DBNAME}.exp*
```

# dbbackup_sched.dat

This section presents a sample schedule file that describes the schedule for taking physical and logical backups. A typical line in this file has the following format:

```
V7PROD     Sat     cold     export     /bugdev/db_management/bug_restrict1.sh
```

where *V7PROD* is name of the database, *Sat* is the day of the week, *cold* is the physical backup type (hot or cold), and *export* is the logical backup procedure.

You can specify a shell script in the last column to perform additional administrative tasks, such as deleting certain files.

```
V7PROD     Sun     hot        noexport
V7PROD     Mon     hot        noexport
V7PROD     Tue     hot        noexport
V7PROD     Wed     hot        noexport
V7PROD     Thu     hot        noexport
V7PROD     Fri     cold       export      /bugdev/db_management/bug_restrict1.sh
V7PROD     Sat     cold       export      /bugdev/db_management/bug_restrict1.sh
V7test     Sun     hot        export
V7test     Mon     hot        export
V7test     Tue     hot        export
V7test     Wed     hot        export
V7test     Thu     hot        export
V7test     Fri     cold       export
V7test     Sat     nobackup   export
```

You should modify this schedule and the backup procedures to fit your business needs. For example, in addition to the full export backup, you might want to take a *user* or *table* mode export as well. Or you might want to take a *complete* export once a week and an *incremental* export every night. Building a robust backup procedure will help you reduce the Mean Time To Recover (MTTR) during a failure.

# CHAPTER 5

# Recovery Principles

To understand recovery principles and strategies, you need to understand the underlying data structures used in recovery. This chapter is divided into three sections. First, we define the fundamental data structures of the Oracle RDBMS followed by a detailed discussion of some of the basic concepts that relate to recovery. An overview of the contents of the control file, log files, and data files is given. Later, we shift our focus to the various recovery options provided by Oracle. We discuss the three main options of recovery—database, tablespace, and data file recovery. In addition to learning the syntax, you will also learn when and how to apply different recovery procedures, depending on the kind of failure.

The final section is on *failure analysis*. In this section, we first discuss a survey that was done with several Oracle customers regarding system outages. The results show the Mean Time Between Failures (MTBF) of various systems and the Mean Time to Recover (MTTR) when a failure occurs. When a production or a development database goes down, Oracle customers usually call Oracle

Worldwide Support and open a priority 1 Technical Assistance Request (TAR). An analysis was done on a sample of priority 1 TARs that shows how the databases are recovered (i.e., what kind of recovery method was chosen). The results of this analysis is given in detail. Based on this information and the real life experience that we have gained while dealing with mission critical applications, some recommendations are made on how to plan for a disaster recovery site.

# Definitions and Internal Recovery Concepts

The following definitions introduce some fundamental data structures that are used in recovery. Each definition is also followed by a discussion or an example to make the concepts clear.

## Redo Generation and Estimation

As mentioned in Chapter 2, the redo log files contain changes made to the database. In this section, we will discuss some of the basic concepts, such as change vectors and redo records, that relate to redo. Some SQL scripts are also provided, which help you estimate the amount of redo generated at your site. This is very important, for when you design a backup procedure to back up the archived redo log files, the frequency of this backup depends on it.

### Change Vector
A *change vector* describes a single change made to any single block in the database. Among other information, the change vector contains a *version number*, the operation code of the transaction, and the address of the data block that this change belongs to. The version number is copied from the data block when the change vector is constructed. During recovery, Oracle reads the change vector and applies the change to the appropriate data block. When a change vector is applied to the data block, the data block's version number is incremented by one.

**NOTE**
A data block could belong to a data segment, index segment, or a rollback segment in the database. Redo is not generated for temporary segments.

### Redo Record and Its Contents
A *redo record* is a group of change vectors describing a single atomic change to the database. Some transactions may generate multiple redo records, and each redo record can have a collection of change vectors. Recovery guarantees that all

or none of the change vectors of a redo record are applied, no matter what type of system failure occurs. In other words, a *transaction* is the unit of recovery, so as a unit, all changes are either applied or not applied.

To illustrate the creation of change vectors and redo records, consider the following example transaction, which updates one record in the EMP table:

```
UPDATE EMP
SET EMPNO = 1234
WHERE EMPNO = 9999;
```

When this UPDATE statement is executed, the sequence of operations is as follows:

1. Change vectors of the redo record are generated.

2. The redo record is saved in a redo log buffer (which eventually gets flushed to the redo log file on disk).

3. The change vectors are applied to the data blocks.

In the example we are using here, the redo record generated in step one contains three change vectors:

1. The transaction has to write an undo entry to the transaction table of the rollback segment (refer to Chapter 2 for contents of a rollback segment). Since the transaction table is also another block in the database, entering an undo entry would modify this block and thus generate redo. So the first change vector of the redo record contains the change for the transaction table.

2. Next, the old value of empno (which is 9999) has to be stored in a block within the rollback segment. This is another modification to a block within the database and therefore generates redo. So the second change vector contains redo for the undo block.

3. The last and most obvious change is the change to the data block where the empno value is changed to 1234. So the third change vector is the redo for the data block.

To summarize, the redo record for this transaction contains three change vectors:

■ Change to the transaction table of the rollback segment

■ Change to the rollback segment data block

■ Change to the data segment block belonging to the EMP table

Of course, this may not be the only redo record generated. If, for example, the EMP table has an index on the EMPNO column, then the index key needs to be modified as well and will generate a second redo record (also containing multiple change vectors). Similarly, if a COMMIT statement is issued after this transaction, a third redo record will be created. So if you lose the data files and have to restore a backup and roll forward, since the unit of recovery is a transaction, *all* three of these redo records will be applied to keep the database consistent, or none will be applied at all.

In Oracle7 some optimization has been done to generate less redo. If more space is available in the rollback segment block, the transaction uses it without modifying the transaction table again. This way, fewer change vectors are created.

### Estimating the Amount of Redo

To estimate how much redo is generated at your site, use the following two procedures. The first procedure estimates the amount of redo generated in one day; the second procedure gives you the amount of redo generated for a specific transaction. Knowing this information and the transaction rate, you can calculate the amount of redo generated at your site.

**Amount of Redo per Day**   The **archive log list** command gives information regarding the online log sequence number. For example,

```
SQLDBA> archive log list
Database log mode               ARCHIVELOG
Automatic archival              ENABLED
Archive destination             DISK$WR3:[ ORA7.DB_RDBMS3]ARCHnnn.ARC
Oldest online log sequence      1742      17439
Next log sequence to archive    1744
Current log sequence            1744
```

Issuing this command on two consecutive days at the same time and taking the difference between the *current log sequence* numbers will give a general idea of how many redo log files are created in 24 hours. Multiply that number by the redo log file size to estimate the amount of redo generated at your site (in bytes).

**Amount of Redo per Transaction**   This procedure calculates the amount of redo generated for a particular transaction. You can then multiply this value by the transaction rate (the number of transactions that are run on the database in 24 hours) to estimate the amount of redo generated at your site in bytes. Use the following steps to estimate the amount of redo generated by a specific transaction.

**1.** Run the following script before executing your transaction. This will mark the redo's "begin value" (taken from the V$SYSSTAT view) before you run the transaction in step 2.

```
COLUMN NAME FORMAT a40
COLUMN redo_i NEW_VALUE redo
SET TERMOUT OFF
SELECT VALUE redo_i
FROM v$sysstat
WHERE statistic# = 71;
SET TERMOUT ON
```

2. Execute your transaction. At this time, we assume that this is the only transaction that is running in your database.

3. Run the following script, which gives the difference between the "end value" of the redo and the "begin value" taken from step 1. This number gives you the amount of redo generated (in bytes) by running the transaction in step 2.

```
SELECT (value - &redo) redo
FROM v$sysstat
WHERE statistic# = 71;
```

Note that the *statistic#* in step 3 can change in future releases of Oracle.

## System Change Number (SCN)

The *System Change Number* (or simply the *SCN*) is a crucial data structure that defines a committed version of the database at a precise moment in time. When a transaction commits, it is assigned an SCN that uniquely identifies the transaction. SCNs provide Oracle's internal clock mechanism and can be viewed as logical clocks, but must not be confused with the system clock—think of SCNs as a way to provide read-consistent *snapshots* of the database that are crucial for recovery operations (Oracle performs recovery based on SCNs only). For example, if transaction 1 does an UPDATE and commits, it will be assigned an SCN value of, say, 20. The next transaction that commits 5 minutes later will receive an SCN value of 21 or greater. If the second transaction receives a higher value than 21, say 25, that means between the two transactions, Oracle has done some work internally (for example, block cleanout) which has used SCNs 21 through 24. So, SCNs are guarenteed to be unique to a database and increase with time but may not be sequential. SCN values never get reset to zero unless the database is re-created. You don't need to worry about running out of SCNs—even if you were to commit 16,000 transactions per second, it would take more than 500 years to run out of SCN numbers.

SCNs play a very important role in distributed transactions. When a distributed transaction is committed, the highest SCN of all the database instances involved is given to the distributed transaction. Thus, there will never be a problem with read consistency. For example, if database 1 has an SCN value of 200 (i.e., the next transaction that commits in this database gets an SCN value of 200), and database 2 has an SCN value of 20,000, and if you do a distributed transaction from database 1 and commit, this transaction will be given an SCN value of 20,000 instead of 200. This means that for some databases (involved in distributed transactions), the SCN value can jump from one value to another, much higher value.

In times of high activity, multiple transactions may commit simultaneously. Then the LGWR process may write multiple commit records to the online redo log file for each write I/O. This is known as *group commits.* (Using group commits has some effects on time-based recovery and will be discussed in Chapter 7.)

While using the Parallel Server option, since there are multiple instances accessing the same database, Oracle maintains some information in the SGA of each instance for controlling the allocation of redo and SCNs. Each instance stores a *local SCN* value, and there is one *global SCN* value for all the instances. This global SCN is protected by a global lock. Every time a transaction does a commit on any instance, it updates the global SCN and copies the global SCN value to the local SCN. This way, the SCN value is still unique to the database and two transactions running on two different instances will never get the same SCN value.

SCNs are used in transaction tables, block headers, control files, data file headers and redo records. Let's now look at some of the important data structures that store SCNs in the redo log files (low and high SCN), data files (offline normal SCN and checkpoint SCN), and the control file (stop SCN).

### Low and High SCN

Every redo log file has a *log sequence number* to uniquely identify that file. When a redo log file gets filled with redo records, it gets closed and a new redo log file is opened. The redo log file is marked with a *low SCN,* which is one greater than the high SCN of the previous log file, and the high SCN value of the current log is set to infinity since Oracle doesn't know how many SCNs will be recorded in the current log file. The low SCN represents the lowest value of the change number that is stored in that log file. Similarly, when the log file gets closed, the high SCN marker is set to the highest SCN recorded in the log file. This information can be obtained by selecting from the V$LOG_HISTORY view:

```
SQL> select * from v$log_history where rownum < 3;
```

```
THREAD#   SEQUENCE# TIME              LOW_CHANGE# HIGH_CHANGE#
-------   --------- ----------------- ----------- ------------
ARCHIVE_NAME
----------------------------------------
      1          12 03/30/95 20:33:14       6706         6723
C:\ORACLE7\RDBMS70\ARCHIVE\ARC00012.001

      1          11 02/11/95 14:18:26       6689         6705
C:\ORACLE7\RDBMS70\ARCHIVE\ARC00011.001
```

In this example, log sequence number 12 belongs to thread number 1 (its name and time that the log file was created is also given). The lowest SCN recorded in this log file is 6706 and the highest SCN is 6723. If any one of these changes is required in the future to do recovery, Oracle will request that this log file be applied to roll forward the backup of the database.

## Offline Normal SCN
An *offline normal SCN* is an SCN that is kept in the data dictionary table **ts$** for each tablespace that is taken offline with the *normal* option. When a tablespace is taken offline with the *normal* option, a checkpoint is performed on all the data files that belong to the tablespace; and at this point, the offline normal SCN is assigned. The offline normal SCN is used by Oracle while bringing a tablespace online. This is especially useful while bringing a tablespace online after the database is opened with the RESETLOGS option (we will discuss the RESETLOGS option in greater detail later in this chapter).

The offline normal SCN will be zero if the tablespace is taken offline with the *immediate* or *temporary* option. This way, you cannot bring the tablespace online after the database is opened with the RESETLOGS option.

There is an SCN value stored in every data file header called the *checkpoint SCN*, which gets updated when a checkpoint is done on a data file. We will discuss this data structure in detail later in this chapter, when we discuss checkpoint structures.

## Stop SCN
In the control file, corresponding to every data file, there is a *stop SCN* that is recorded. When a data file is online, and any instance has the database open, the stop SCN for that corresponding data file will be set to infinity. When you take a

tablespace offline, the stop SCN is recorded in the control file for each data file that belongs to the tablespace. This means that no redo will be generated for the data file after the stop SCN is allocated.

The stop SCN is used while doing media recovery to ensure that media recovery will end when recovery reaches an SCN value equal to the stop SCN of the data file when recovering an offline data file.

# Redo Threads

An online redo log file contains the changes made to the database. The redo records that are created by modifying data are stored in these online log files. Online log files are essential for normal operation of the database. As discussed in Chapter 2, each instance of an Oracle database has at least two online redo log groups; a *redo log group* contains one or more online log files (known as members) that are identical and reside on different disk drives. Oracle recommends maintaining at least two members for each group to protect against online redo log file failures.

A collection of online redo log files is referred to as a *thread of redo log files*. Each instance records changes in its own set of online log files or its own thread of redo. If you have a single-instance database, Oracle creates the first thread of redo log files when you create the database. If you are using the Parallel Server option, you have to create a thread of redo log files for each instance (except for the first one). Each thread is uniquely identified by a thread number. After creating a thread of redo log files, you have to enable the thread using the PUBLIC or PRIVATE option. The PUBLIC option indicates that the redo thread may be used by any instance. If the keyword PUBLIC is omitted, the thread is enabled PRIVATE. This means that you have to specifically include the INIT.ORA parameter THREAD = n, where n is the thread number, to use the thread. Every instance that opens a database needs a thread of redo log files. The following example illustrates how to create a thread of redo log files:

Let's assume that instance A has opened the database and uses thread 1. Thread 1 has three log groups with one member each. From instance A, we issue the following commands in SQL*DBA to create a second thread:

```
SQLDBA> Alter database add logfile thread 2 group 4  'log4.rdo';
SQLDBA> Alter database add logfile thread 2 group 5  'log5.rdo';
SQLDBA> Alter database enable public thread 2;
SQLDBA> Alter database disable thread 2;
```

The first two commands create a new thread (thread number 2) with two redo log groups. Each log group has one member. By default, the new thread is disabled after creation. The thread then needs to be enabled before it can be opened by an instance. The last two commands in the above example show how to enable and disable a thread, respectively. Note that the thread is publicly enabled. When an instance opens the database, it needs to open a thread of redo log files to store the changes made to the database by that instance.

If multiple threads are available to the database, one of the threads is chosen at mount time. The INIT.ORA parameter THREAD can be specified if you want the instance to open a specific thread number. Otherwise, any publicly enabled thread can be used if it is available. A *thread mount lock* is used to prevent two instances from mounting the same thread at the same time. When a thread is opened, a new checkpoint is done and used as the *thread checkpoint*. If this is the first instance to open the database, this becomes the new *database checkpoint*, and Oracle ensures that all the online data files have the same checkpoint SCN in their headers. We will discuss *thread checkpoints* and *database checkpoints* in detail later in this section.

A thread must have at least two online redo log files (groups) while it is enabled. An enabled thread always has one online log file as its current log file. The *high SCN* value of the current log file is set to infinity so that any new SCN allocated will be recorded within the current log file. A special redo record is written when a thread is enabled. This record is used by media recovery to start applying redo from the new thread. For example, given two threads of a database, if you want to enable thread 2, you have to enable it by issuing the command from thread 1, which implies that it takes an open thread to enable another thread.

This chicken and egg problem is resolved by having the first thread automatically enabled publicly at database creation time. Only if you are running the database with the Parallel Server Option will you need to create/enable a second thread. If you are running a single-instance database, you don't need a second thread.

When an instance closes the database or when a thread is recovered by instance/crash recovery (discussed later in this chapter), the thread is closed. The first step in closing a thread is to ensure that no more redo is generated in it. Next, all the changes to the online files must be in the data files. For a normal database close, Oracle accomplishes this by doing a checkpoint. Thread recovery does this by applying the redo since the previous thread checkpoint. Once all the changes are in the data files, the thread's checkpoint is advanced to the end of the thread. This may advance the database checkpoint just like a normal thread checkpoint. If this is the last thread to close, the database checkpoint will be left pointing at this thread even after it is closed.

If a thread is not going to be used for a long time, it is best to disable it. A thread must be closed first before it can be disabled. This ensures that all the changes have been written to the data files. Then, as part of the disable process, a new SCN is allocated as the *next SCN* for the current log file. The log header is marked with this SCN and flags saying that it is the end of a disabled thread. Similar to enabling a thread, when you disable a thread, you need to issue the **disable thread** command from SQL*DBA. This means that a thread must be open in order to disable another thread. Thus, it is not possible to disable all the threads of a database. Once you have disabled a thread, it means that crash recovery will not expect any redo to be found in the thread. However, you need to be very careful in discarding redo log files of a disabled thread as the log files might be required if media recovery is done later. The following example should make this concept clear:

Consider that a new thread, say thread 2, is created with two log files log4.rdo and log5.rdo, and by default the thread is disabled. Then we perform the following two commands in the order given:

```
SQLDBA> Alter database enable thread 2;
SQLDBA> Alter database disable thread 2;
```

The first command above enables the thread. In other words, in the control file, the *low SCN* value is set for log4.rdo, and the log is marked *current*. Let's assume that the low SCN value is 200. The second command disables the thread. This sets the *high SCN* value in the control file for log4.rdo to, say, 201. Note that thread 2 is never opened by any instance, and so no redo is recorded in log file log4.rdo. However, if you ever do media recovery starting at an SCN that is less than 200, log4.rdo is required as part of the recovery.

The above example shows that you need to be careful in discarding the redo files once a thread is disabled because redo from a thread that was once enabled but is currently disabled is required for media recovery, but not required for crash recovery.

# Redo Log Switching

*Log switching* is the process whereby the LGWR process stops writing to the current log file and switches to the next available online log file. When Oracle creates redo, it uses the redo log buffer in memory and the redo log files on disk. The redo log buffer is flushed to disk, to the redo log files, and the redo log buffer is reused to store further redo. The same is true for the redo log files on disk. As the log file on disk fills up, Oracle switches to the next available log file while the ARCH process archives the filled log file. Each log has a sequence number to identify it. As mentioned earlier, Oracle needs a minimum of two log files on disk, and a redo buffer in memory. The LGWR process writes to only one log file on disk at a time, but the redo buffer can be written to by several processes concurrently.

A log switch is triggered on one of the following two conditions:

■ Foregrounds are no longer able to allocate space in the redo log buffer.

■ The **alter system switch logfile** command is issued by the DBA.

The processing of the log switch, regardless of which event triggers it, causes redo generation to resume in the next allocated log file. The steps are summarized here.

1. *Select a Log File to Switch Into*  Oracle gets the thread information from the control file and scans the log files. Using criteria including the checkpoint information, archiving status, and the availability, Oracle selects a log file to switch into. If several log files are good candidates for switching into, Oracle chooses the one with the lowest log sequence number. Once a log file is chosen Oracle sets various status flags to make it the next log file. These changes are made in a manner such that if the process doing the changes dies, crash recovery will recognize that the switch was not complete.

2. *Flush the Current Log and Disable Redo Generation*  Oracle maintains information in the SGA regarding several structures, including information to indicate whether redo can be generated or disabled. During a log switch, redo generation is disabled. Once this information is written in the SGA, redo generation by foregrounds is stopped. The buffers filled so far are then written out to disk. While the LGWR process is taking care of the log switch, processes that are allocated redo space in the redo log buffer continue to generate redo. Once Oracle flushes the last buffer, it closes the log.

3. *Perform the Switch in the Control File/Data File Headers and Close the Log*  The information in the thread record and also for the log file entries is updated. This is written out to disk so that it is visible to other threads. A new SCN is allocated and used during the operation. The log file is now closed.

4. *Open the New Log File*  This opens the new log group for access as the current log. All the members are attempted, including members previously marked as STALE (members that could not be written to). If there is a write error with a specific log file member, LGWR doesn't write to it and updates the status of the member accordingly. For the members that it can write to, the log header status is set to OPEN, indicating that the log switch is complete.

## Archiving Log Switches

Each thread switches log files independently. Thus when running the Parallel Server option, the SCN ranges in the current log can vary. However, it is desirable to have roughly the same range of SCNs in the archived log files of all enabled threads. This ensures that the last log archived in each thread is reasonably current. For example, we don't want a situation in which instance A has a low SCN value of 200 in its current online log file and instance B has a low SCN value of 2 million. In this situation, if the current online log file of instance A is lost due to a media failure, you can apply media recovery to a backup of the database, but you can only roll forward up to an SCN value of 200. This means that all changes made to the database from SCN = 201 to SCN = 2 million are lost.

This problem is solved by forcing log switches in other threads when their current SCNs are significantly behind the log just archived. For example, if instance A has two log files and instance B has five, and if instance B is a very active instance, then, for every five log switches at instance B, instance A will be forced to switch once. This way, instance A will keep up with the SCN range and you will not lose a significant amount of data, should you lose an online log file of an inactive or less active instance.

**NOTE**
Multiplexing online log files is very strongly recommended, as it addresses the single point of failure caused by losing the online log files.

What happens if there is a thread that is closed but enabled? For open threads, a lock is used to trigger the other inactive instances, which then will do a log switch and archive as soon as they can. For a closed thread, the ARCH process of the active thread (instance B, in the above example) will do a log switch of the closed thread. It will then archive the log files for the closed threads. You don't need to worry about wasting disk space because all the archived redo log files that are created by the closed threads will have only a file header, since no redo is generated in those threads. So the archive log files are very small and don't take up much disk space.

To implement the above feature of archiving redo log files from disabled threads, Oracle maintains a *force SCN* in the control file. Oracle will archive any log file that contains an SCN that is less than the *force SCN*. In general, the log file with the lowest SCN is archived first.

Note that you can manually archive the current log files of all enabled threads by using the **archive log next** command from SQL*DBA. This command forces all threads (open and closed) to switch to a new log file. All necessary log files of all threads are archived. This command doesn't return to the prompt until all redo generated before the command was entered is archived. This is useful for ensuring that all redo log files necessary for the recovery of a hot backup are archived.

## Checkpoints

A *checkpoint* is a database event that flushes the modified data from cache to disk and updates the control file and data files. After a checkpoint, the redo in the redo log files is no longer useful for crash/instance recovery. If the redo log file size on disk were unlimited and crash recovery time were not a consideration, perhaps checkpoints wouldn't be needed; all we would do is apply the changes to the backup database using all the archive log files generated. But given the circular nature of the redo log file, there is a need to guarantee that before we allocate space in the redo log file and overwrite redo, the redo is copied to an archived log file.

In the recovery scheme, Oracle makes sure that, before a change to the data block is made, the redo for the change has made its way into the redo log buffer; and before the data block is flushed to the data file on disk, its redo is flushed to the redo log file. So to determine that a particular piece of redo is no longer useful for crash/instance recovery, Oracle makes sure that all the blocks changed up to the cutoff point in the log file do actually make it to the disk and into the database files. This is sufficient to guarantee that the redo is no longer of use and the redo log files can be allocated for reuse.

### Events Triggering Checkpoints

Checkpoints are triggered automatically when an event occurs during the normal operation of the database, but can be triggered manually by issuing a SQL*DBA command. For example, the command

```
SQLDBA> alter system checkpoint local;
```

will explicitly trigger a checkpoint from the instance that is executed from. When a log file gets full and the log is switched, this operation implicitly triggers a checkpoint. The *Oracle7 Server Concepts Manual* gives a good explanation of checkpoints and the events that trigger them. There are three types of checkpoints:

1. *Local (Thread) checkpoint*   Here, a particular instance performs a checkpoint on all the data files of the database. In other words, all the dirty buffers from a specific instance are written to all the data files of the database. For example, the **alter system checkpoint local** command will perform a local checkpoint.

2. *Global (Database) checkpoint*   Here, all the instances perform a checkpoint on all the data files of the database. For example, the **alter system checkpoint global** command performs a global checkpoint.

3. *File checkpoint*   Here, all the instances perform a checkpoint on a subset of the data files. For example, the command **alter tablespace SYSTEM begin backup** performs a global checkpoint on all the data files that belong to the SYSTEM tablespace.

Global checkpoints are specific to Parallel Server configuration (multiple threads). Local checkpoints are instance specific, and restricted to the local thread. A global checkpoint may be done in response to a SQL command or when a database-wide checkpoint is done. Local checkpoints may be started due to a log file switch, execution of a SQL command, or on reaching the checkpoint interval specified by the INIT.ORA parameter LOG_CHECKPOINT_INTERVAL. Global and local checkpoints are always done on all data files of the database. On successful completion, the redo prior to the checkpoint is no longer useful, except during media recovery. A file checkpoint is always done in response to a SQL command. For example, database operations such as hot backups or taking a tablespace offline require the RDBMS to do a checkpoint from all the instances, but only on a specific tablespace. The command **alter tablespace** *tablespace_name* **offline** requires that all the dirty buffers in cache (of all instances) that belong to the tablespace be written to the disk. Similarly, when you issue an **alter tablespace begin backup** command, all the dirty buffers from all instances that belong to this tablespace are flushed.

Checkpoints can be triggered with *fast* or *slow* priority and are discussed in detail later in this section. There are certain occasions when completion of a checkpoint becomes critical. A good example is when a log switch occurs and the LGWR process has to wait because the log file it has to write to is still involved in the checkpoint process.

Checkpoints are an integral part of the normal functioning of the database. You can control the frequency of checkpoints, but be aware that performing a checkpoint can be an I/O- and CPU-intensive operation, and should be tuned carefully.

Since checkpoints can be triggered by users or by database events, and checkpoint processing is done concurrently with normal activity in the database, there can be multiple checkpoints triggered in an overlapped fashion. To avoid this, each type of checkpoint event carries with it a privilege to *override* or be *ignored* when it is activated. When a checkpoint with override is triggered, the earlier checkpoint is replaced by the current checkpoint. This means that no matter where you are in processing the earlier checkpoint, Oracle will start another one as if the previous one did not exist. Overriding of checkpoints can be done for local or global checkpoints only.

Table 5-1 gives all the SQL commands, database events, and INIT.ORA parameters that trigger checkpoints. The global, local, and file checkpoints are denoted by G, L, and F, respectively (N/A in the table means "not applicable"). The table also gives the priority of the checkpoints (fast or slow) and if they have override privilege.

In Table 5-1, the operation *log file switch stuck* means that a log file switch may be unsuccessful if a checkpoint has started and not yet finished. A typical case is when you have two log files, the second log file is completely filled, and the instance needs to switch to log 1. If log 1 is still involved in a previous checkpoint, then it needs to be sped up. To do this, another checkpoint is not started—starting another checkpoint would only delay things. Instead, the process requests that Oracle speed up the checkpoint process.

| CHECKPOINTS TRIGGERED BY FOREGROUND AND BACKGROUND PROCESSES | FAST/SLOW | OVERRIDE | G/L/F |
|---|---|---|---|
| alter system switch logfile | Slow | Yes | L |
| alter system checkpoint (local or global) | Fast | Yes | G/L |
| alter tablespace begin backup | Fast | NA | F |
| alter tablespace offline (*normal, temporary*) | Fast | NA | F |
| instance shutdown (*normal, immediate*) | Fast | Yes | L |
| log file switch *normal* | Slow | Yes | L |
| log file switch *stuck* | Fast | N/A | L |
| INIT.ORA parameter: LOG_CHECKPOINT_TIMEOUT | Slow | No | L |
| INIT.ORA parameter: LOG_CHECKPOINT_INTERVAL | Slow | No | L |

**TABLE 5-1.** *Checkpoints and Their Attributes*

For single-process databases, all the work is done by the same process; messaging is done away with. Blocks are written out immediately upon being found to be checkpoint-marked.

## Checkpoint Processing

The work done in processing a checkpoint is more or less the same in any case; which process doing the work depends on the event triggering the checkpoint. If a checkpoint is initiated by a user command such as **alter system checkpoint local**. then a checkpoint is performed by the foreground process. In all other cases, the checkpoint processing is done either by the CKPT process (if CHECKPOINT_PROCESS parameter is set to *true* in the INIT.ORA file) or by the LGWR process.

For a global checkpoint, the work done to process the checkpoint involves the following steps:

### 1: Getting/Holding the Instance State Enqueue
The *instance state enqueue* is acquired during instance-state transitions. Oracle acquires this enqueue to ensure that the database is kept open over the duration of the checkpoint processing.

### 2: Capturing the Current Checkpoint Information
This step involves setting up a structure to record information including the current checkpoint time,

the active threads at this time, the current thread doing the checkpoint, and most importantly, obtaining the address in the redo log file that will be the cutoff point for recovery.

### 3: Identifying the Dirty Buffers

The next step is to identify all the dirty buffers. This is done by scanning each buffer in cache and looping through until all dirty buffers are found. If Oracle finds a dirty buffer within the range of files that are being checkpointed, the buffer header is marked as *to be flushed*. Oracle skips temporary segment buffers and unmodified (read-only) buffers, since no redo is generated for them. Once the dirty buffers are identified, the DBWR process is posted to do the writes.

### 4: Flushing the Dirty Buffers

This step involves flushing all the dirty buffers to disk using the DBWR process. (How this works is explained in Fast/Slow checkpoints, which will be discussed presently.) Once the DBWR flushes all the buffers, it sets a flag to indicate that it has finished flushing the buffers to disk. The LGWR (or CKPT) process continuously keeps checking until it recognizes that the DBWR process is done.

### 5: Updating the Data Files and Control Files

The last step is to update the data file headers and the control file with the information captured in step 2. The control file contains a checkpoint structure for each enabled thread. Each data file header contains a checkpoint structure as well. The information in these structures is updated as part of this step. Later in this chapter, we will discuss the checkpoint structure in greater detail.

In two cases, the checkpoint information (captured from step 2 above) is not updated in the file header. The first case is when the data file is in hot backup mode. In this case, Oracle doesn't know when the OS backup will read the file header, and the backup copy must have the checkpoint SCN when the copy started. The second case is if the checkpoint SCN is less than what is in the file header. This means that the changes made by the checkpoint are already on the disk. This can happen if a hot backup fast checkpoint updates the file header when a global checkpoint is in progress. Remember that Oracle captures the checkpoint SCN before it really gets into doing the hard work of processing the checkpoint, and it's quite possible that a command like **begin backup**, which does a fast tablespace checkpoint, might beat it.

Oracle verifies the data file headers for consistency before updating them. Once verified, the data file headers are updated to reflect the current checkpoint. Unverified files, and files that error out while doing the update write, are ignored.

A file would need media recovery if the log files get overwritten, and in this case, the DBWR process takes the data file offline.

Taking a data file offline is always perfomed by the DBWR process. A data file cannot be taken offline if you are operating the database in NOARCHIVELOG mode or if the data file belongs to the SYSTEM tablespace. If Oracle can write all dirty blocks (in step 4 above) or if nothing needs to be written (because the data blocks are in the future of the redo, hence all changes already exist in the data file on disk), then no damage has been done.

Oracle keeps a counter of checkpoints in the data file headers. This is used to verify that you are using the current version of the data file during normal operation, and to prevent you from restoring the wrong version of a data file during recovery. This counter is incremented even if the data files are in hot backup mode. The checkpoint counter for each data file is also kept in the control file for the corresponding data file entry.

## Fast and Slow Checkpoints

The speed of performing a checkpoint is really determined by the DBWR process and not by the LGWR or CKPT process, as it may seem. The LGWR (or CKPT) process merely conveys to the DBWR process how it needs to handle the writes for the buffers marked for checkpoint write. Once the DBWR process is posted, it starts scanning all buffer headers looking for dirty buffers that need to be flushed to disk. In doing the scan, all the buffers that are read in *consistent read* mode (i.e., blocks that are read into memory with the SELECT statement) and temporary segment buffers are ignored, as no redo is generated for them. All other buffers are scanned, and if a buffer is found dirty, it is saved for write. If Oracle is doing a *slow* checkpoint, the DBWR process stops to process the checkpoint if one of the two following conditions occurs:

- If the threshold size of the **db_checkpoint_write_batch** (number of buffers) is reached

- When over 1,000 buffers are scanned and a dirty buffer can't be found to write to disk

The idea is to give up the CPU, which would otherwise get wasted, affecting the foreground response. Also, if large values are set for **db_checkpoint_write_batch**, I/O will clobber the foregrounds. If, however, Oracle is doing a *fast checkpoint,* the DBWR simply continues scanning all the buffers in cache. In this case, such things as the overhead of message handling and passing, and possible context switching, are avoided. Once started, the DBWR process will not do anything else until all the dirty buffers are written to disk as part of the fast checkpoint process.

## Thread Checkpoint

When an instance checkpoints, it's called a *thread checkpoint*. Every thread will perform checkpoints independent of other threads; and every time a thread checkpoints, it updates the checkpoint information in the control file.

There is a *checkpoint structure* that is maintained in the control file for each thread. This means only dirty buffers from the instance that is performing the checkpoint are guaranteed to be written to disk. Oracle guarantees that all the redo generated in this thread before the checkpoint SCN has been applied to the online data files, and the blocks are written to the data files on disk. Among other things, the checkpoint structure contains the following information:

- The *current SCN* at which the checkpoint occurred
- The thread that did the checkpoint
- All threads that are enabled at the time
- The timestamp at which the current SCN is recorded
- Other information regarding redo

When a checkpoint occurs, Oracle records the SCN value and time stamp as of that point in the control file. Oracle guarantees that all changes made to the database before this checkpoint SCN are on disk. This means that in the event of a database crash, crash recovery will apply changes only from that SCN value.

## Database Checkpoint

When a database has multiple threads, there is one checkpoint structure for each thread in the control file. One of these checkpoint structures is also written to the data file headers and is referred to as the *database checkpoint structure, database checkpoint information,* or simply the *database checkpoint*. The thread checkpoint structure that is chosen to be the database checkpoint structure is the one with the lowest checkpoint SCN. For example, if there are three open threads with thread checkpoint SCN values of 300, 350, and 400, the database checkpoint SCN will be equal to 300, since that's the lowest value of all the thread checkpoint SCNs.

Oracle guarantees that all the changes that have an SCN value lower than the database checkpoint SCN have been written to the database files on disk. In the case of a single-instance database, the thread checkpoint in the control file is the same as the database checkpoint in the data files. If there are no open threads, the database checkpoint is the highest thread checkpoint of all the enabled threads, because all changes before the database checkpoint are written to the online data files. The database checkpoint is used to update the file headers when an instance checkpoints its thread.

### Data File Checkpoint

Every data file header contains the checkpoint information (checkpoint structure). The SCN corresponding to the checkpoint guarantees that all changes previous to this SCN are on disk. The checkpoint information in all the online data files gets updated when a *file checkpoint* or a *global checkpoint* is performed. The only exception is when a hot backup is in progress. For example, if the checkpoint SCN of a data file is 500, then when the data file is put in hot backup mode, this value doesn't change until the **end hot backup** command is issued. Since this SCN value is not updated, the backup data file is guaranteed to have the same checkpoint SCN value of 500. So if we ever restore this data file to do media recovery, recovery starts from SCN 500 for this file. As discussed earlier, the checkpoint SCN value is stored in the control file for every data file as well.

## Log History

The control file can be configured to contain the history records for every redo log file that is used by the database. Each record in this table gives information of one redo log file. Each history record contains the thread number, log sequence number, low SCN and high SCN. This information can be obtained by selecting from the **V$LOG_HISTORY** view. The parameter MAXLOGHISTORY can be used while creating a database to specify how much history you want to store in the control file.

The purpose of maintaining this information is to reconstruct archived log file names from the SCN and thread number. Since the log sequence number is part of the checkpoint information, databases opened with single instances don't need this log history table to reconstruct the log filenames during recovery.

With the Parallel Server option, when media recovery processes a data file, it reads the thread number from the checkpoint information recorded in the data file header and starts recovery with that thread. However, when Oracle switches threads (the concept of *thread switching* is discussed later in this chapter in the section "Thread Recovery"), it needs the names of the log files for the other threads. The log history table is used for this purpose. The log history table is a circular table, which means that the records are overwritten in a fashion such that the oldest information is lost first.

## Structures of Control Files, Data Files, and Log Files

The *control file* describes the schema of the database. It holds state information about the other database files. Several types of records are stored in the control file.

Control file transactions allow updates to the control file to be committed atomically. It is recommended that you maintain redundant copies of the control file.

The *data files* contain the data blocks that hold the users' data. Each tablespace contains one or more data files. The first block of the data file is the file header and is not used for user data. This block stores structures to keep track of the state of the data file. The rest of the file is a collection of blocks that can be accessed through the buffer cache.

Log files contain redo that is generated in the process of modifying the data blocks. A log file is divided into blocks that must be the same size as the operating system block size. The first block of the redo log file is the header, and doesn't contain redo.

## Contents of a Control File

The information in the control file is divided into five parts. The first part contains information about the database. It has information about the total number of data files, log files, and threads that are enabled and open. If you are not using the Parallel Server option, you will have only one thread.

The second part of the control file gives information about the redo threads. Among other things, it contains information such as whether it is privately or publicly enabled. Information about each log group and the current log group that the LGWR is writing to is also recorded.

The third part of the control file contains information about each log member of each log group. The size of each log file, its full path name, the log sequence number, the low and high SCN values, and the thread to which each log file belongs are some of the important data structures.

The fourth part contains the data file information. A text string giving the fully expanded filename is recorded, along with its size in Oracle blocks, and the Oracle block size in bytes. In addition, each data file has a status indicating whether the file is readable, writable, online or offline, whether media recovery is required, and so on. The stop SCN for each data file is also recorded.

The last part of the control file contains the log history information (discussed earlier in this chapter).

## Contents of a Data File

As discussed earlier, the first block of the data file contains the file header information. Almost all of the information that is stored in the data file header is also stored in the control file for each data file. This includes, among other things, the file size, checkpoint information, block size, and creation time stamp. In addition, there is some information stored in the file header to indicate whether the data file is in hot backup mode or not.

Every data block contains header information such as the data block address, the block type (whether it's a data segment block, index segment block, etc.), and the version of the data block. The version of the block always increases by one when the block is read into cache for modification. This is crucial during recovery because the redo needs to be applied to a block with a specific version.

If the INIT.ORA parameter **_db_block_compute_checksum** is set to *true*, the block header will also contain some checksum information. This is used for special debugging purposes and is discussed in Chapter 6. Finally, at the end of the Oracle block, the version number is recorded. This is used to determine if the front and back halves of a block match. This is especially useful while recovering from hot backups, because there is a possibility of a block split (as discussed in Chapter 3).

### Contents of a Log File

The contents of an online redo log file and an archive log file are identical. (Note that each log file only holds redo for one thread.) The first block of the log file is the log file header. It contains the log sequence number, the thread number it belongs to, the low SCN, the high SCN, and some other flags to indicate the thread status.

One of the interesting data structures is the *resetlogs counter*. This is the same value from the database portion stored in the control file. It is used to prevent applying log files that were generated before the *resetlogs SCN*. Opening the database with the RESETLOGS option is discussed later in this chapter.

# Recovery Methods

This section focuses on the recovery methods used by Oracle and various options available to the DBA. There are three basic types of recovery—*online block recovery, thread recovery,* and *media recovery.* In all three cases, the algorithm that applies the redo records against an individual block is the same. But first, you need to understand the concepts of *redo application, roll forward*, and *rollback* mechanisms and how Oracle determines that recovery is required for a data file(s).

## Redo Application

When a database is started with the **startup** command from SQL*DBA, there are various stages that the database goes through. The database first goes into the *nomount* state. In this state Oracle reads the INIT.ORA file to determine the size of the SGA, creates the SGA, and starts the background processes. The DBA sees a message on the terminal at this time that says "instance started."

Next, the instance *mounts* the database. In this state, the control file is opened and the "database mounted" message is displayed. In the mounted state commands such as **recover database** or any **alter database** command can be issued. The **alter session** command can be used to dump trace information from the control file, redo log file headers, data file headers, and data blocks to trace files.

In the third and final stage, the instance *opens* the database displaying the "database opened" message to the user screen. In this stage, it is verified that all the data and log files can be opened. If the instance is opening the database for the first time after a database crash, crash recovery needs to be performed. There are two steps to crash recovery. The first is to *roll forward* the database, where all the redo stored in the redo log files will be applied to the database files and a new thread is opened. As part of the second step (known as *transaction recovery*), all uncommitted transactions are rolled back.

A common question asked is how does Oracle know when to apply recovery to a particular data file or data files? We have learned that each data file, in its header, has a checkpoint counter that gets incremented every time Oracle performs a checkpoint on the data file. The control file keeps a checkpoint counter for every data file as well. We have also learned that every data file header contains an SCN as part of its checkpoint structure. This is called the *start SCN.* Corresponding to every data file, the control file has a *stop SCN.* During normal operation of the database, the stop SCN in the control file is set to infinity. The start SCN in the data file is incremented every time a checkpoint is done.

When the database is shut down with the *normal* or *immediate* option, the checkpoint that is issued will set the stop SCN in the control file equal to the corresponding start SCN in the data file header for each data file. When the database is opened the next time, Oracle makes two checks. The first check is to see if the checkpoint counter in the data file header matches its corresponding checkpoint counter in the control file. Once it is the same, it does the second check. This check compares the start SCN value in the data file header to its corresponding stop SCN in the control file. If the stop SCN equals the start SCN, then no recovery is required for that file. This check is performed for every data file and then the database is opened. As part of the open, the stop SCNs are set to infinity again.

Now take the case where you shut the database down hard using the **shutdown abort** command. In this case, a checkpoint is not performed and the stop SCN remains at infinity when the database goes down. During the next startup, the checkpoint counters are again matched first. If they are the same (i.e., you didn't replace the data files with a backup copy), then Oracle compares the stop and start SCNs. In this case, since the stop SCN is infinite and the start SCN has some value, Oracle determines that they are not the same so thread recovery needs to be performed. In this case, since you are starting up the instance after a crash, crash recovery will be performed. As part of the crash recovery, Oracle reads the online log files and applies the changes to the database as part of the *roll forward* and reads the rollback segment's transaction table to perform transaction recovery (roll backward). Thread recovery is discussed later in this section.

After shutting down the database, if you replace one of the data files with a backup copy, Oracle detects this as part of the checkpoint counter check and asks you to apply media recovery. From the data file header, Oracle also knows the beginning log sequence number of the archived redo log file where recovery starts. Oracle requests that you apply media recovery starting from that log file sequence number.

## Roll Forward

Any kind of recovery (thread or media) is done in two parts. The first part is the *roll forward*. Roll forward involves sequentially applying the redo records to the corresponding data blocks. Oracle will apply all or none of the changes in an atomic redo record.

This is done in the following manner. First, the log file is opened for each thread that was enabled at the time the SCN was allocated. If the log file is online (as in the case of crash recovery), then it is automatically opened. If the log is an archived log file, then you are prompted to enter the name of the log file. The redo is applied from all the threads in the order it was generated, switching threads if needed. Thread switching is discussed later in the "Media Recovery" section of this chapter.

The order of application of redo records without an SCN is not precise, but it is good enough for rollback to make the database consistent. If the next log file in a thread is needed, an online copy is used if available. If not, the dirty recovery buffers are written to the disk, and the checkpoints on the data files are advanced so that the redo does not need to be reapplied—this is known as a *redo checkpoint*. Then you are prompted for the next log file. Note that redo application does occasionally need to back up and reapply redo that was skipped. This can happen when a corrupted block is repaired and redo for it was skipped.

Every data block has a version number. Every change made to the data block is recorded in the log file as a change vector. The change vector will have a version number one greater than that of the block. When recovery is done, for example, change 11 needs to be applied to the block that has a version number of 10. After applying the change, the block's version number will be incremented by 1, and made 11. Then change 12 needs to be applied to this block, and so on.

Figure 5-1 shows that changes 6 and 7 from the redo log file are being applied to a data block, thus rolling it forward. In this figure, you can see that in the redo log file, there are two redo records that belong to block number 20 of file 10. Let's assume that at the beginning of recovery, the data block on disk has a block version of 5, and so change 6 needs to be applied from the redo log file. So the first redo record will be applied to block 20. As part of rolling forward, after the change is applied to the block, the block's version number is now incremented to 6. Now the second redo record (corresponding to file 10, block 20) in the redo log file has change 7, which needs to be applied to the data block with version number 6. This will change the block's version number to 7, as shown in Figure 5-1.

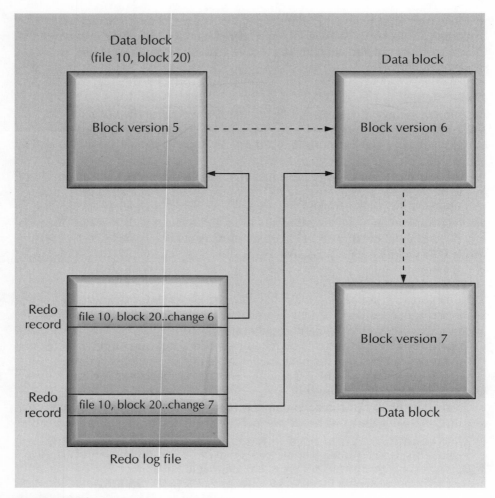

**FIGURE 5-1.** *Rolling a data block forward*

Now, if another redo record exists for this data block that has a change number of 9, this redo record cannot be applied to the data block, since the data block's version number is 7. This means that change 8 has to be applied before change 9. In other words, all changes have to be sequentially applied to the block. However, at some point in time, when change 15 needs to be applied to a block and the version of the block is, say, 19, that means the block is ahead of the redo change (i.e., the change is already in the data block). In this case, the redo is skipped and the next redo record in the redo log file is read. A data block can be in the future of the redo, for example, if database recovery is being performed but only one data file has been restored, and the other files are the current files. Then redo is applied only to that one file that really needs recovery. However, since all the redo is examined during recovery, it will try applying redo to the files that don't need recovery as well. This doesn't require Oracle to actually read the data block but it checks the redo SCN against the checkpoint SCN of the file header. If the checkpoint SCN is ahead of the redo SCN, then Oracle realizes that the data block is in the future of the redo (which means that the block already contains the change). So the redo record is skipped and the next record in the redo log file is examined.

## Rolling Backward

Once all the redo has been applied (rolled forward), the second part of the recovery process is the *roll back.* This process is also known as *transaction recovery.* Rollback segments are the mechanism that allow Oracle to roll back the uncommitted transactions. Because rollback segments reside in data files, and are protected by the redo mechanism, all redo must be applied before any transactions can be rolled back.

Oracle finds the transaction tables by querying the base dictionary table, **undo$**. It scans the transaction tables of the rollback segments for active transactions. For each uncommitted transaction, Oracle chains through the undo and rolls back all changes. It is reasonable to see redo being generated, and thus log files being archived, if many or large transactions are being rolled back. This is because rolling back transactions causes changes to blocks inside the data files, thus generating redo.

The INIT.ORA parameter ROLLBACK_SEGMENTS has no effect on this. All transactions in all the rollback segments are looked at and uncommitted transactions are rolled back. Once this is finished, all rollback segments acquired by the instance will be ONLINE, and all others OFFLINE. Rollback segments containing dead transactions that cannot be cleaned up are marked as NEEDS RECOVERY. The SYSTEM rollback segment is always ONLINE for the database to function, and should not be listed in the INIT.ORA parameter ROLLBACK_SEGMENTS. At this point, transaction recovery is complete and users can log on.

The SYSTEM rollback segment is unique and special, and this has consequences for recovery. Undo generated by all transactions involving **undo$** (the base data dictionary table, owned by the user SYS) use the SYSTEM rollback segment. This means that SYSTEM rollback segment corruptions are very serious.

# Block Recovery

Block-level recovery is automatically performed by Oracle during normal operation of the database and is transparent to the user. When a process dies while changing a buffer, Oracle reconstructs the buffer using the online redo log files for the current thread and writes it to disk. The buffer header contains information regarding the range of redo records that needs to be applied to it.

When Oracle detects a corrupted block in the cache, it attempts to pull the block off disk and recover it using the online log files. It starts with the online log file that contains redo records that haven't been checkpointed against the data file holding the block. This is because no buffer should need recovery from any time before the last checkpoint. The redo log files are scanned in order and the redo records for the block are applied. Recovery stops at the end of the redo log file with the version number that was current during the time the block recovery started. If an error occurs in doing recovery, the block is marked as corrupted and a *corrupt block error* is signaled.

If the PMON process is perfoming the block recovery, Oracle does not allow it to spend large amounts of time working on the recovery of one buffer. PMON makes some progress in doing the recovery and then checks for other things to clean up (such as abnormally terminated processes, or rollback transactions). To control the amount of recovery done by PMON, Oracle limits the amount of redo that is applied in one call to block recovery. The maximum number of redo blocks to apply in one call to block recovery by PMON is a port-specific constant, and users don't have control over this.

Block-level recovery is a normal operation performed automatically by Oracle during normal operation of the database, and does not involve any action from the DBA.

# Thread Recovery

In this discussion, we assume that you are running the Parallel Server option and have multiple instances accessing the database. A single-instance database uses the same structures and recovery methods described below—it is just a simpler case, in which only one thread exists.

If an instance crashes while it has the database open, it is necessary to do *thread recovery*. This involves applying to the database all the redo changes in the thread that have occurred since the last time the thread was checkpointed. The checkpoint SCN stored in the control file for the thread ensures that any blocks that were dirty in the buffer cache when the instance died will have the lost changes applied.

Thread recovery also does a clean close of the thread that the instance had open. If the thread was in the middle of a log switch when the instance died, thread recovery rolls back the appropriate information and calculates the *next available block*. The next available block is the block number in the redo log file from which the thread starts writing redo information. Thread recovery also calculates the highest SCN used by the dead instances.

Thread recovery is done either as a part of *instance recovery* or *crash recovery*. Instance recovery is done while the database is open and one instance detects that another instance has died. This is possible only if you are running multiple instances using the Parallel Server option. Oracle determines whether there really is a dead instance, and if so, it does thread recovery for its redo thread. It also clears the locks held by the dead instance, if any, after any required thread recovery is complete. If you restart the dead instance before instance recovery is done, then Oracle will do crash recovery. In general, the first instance to open the database after an abnormal termination (**shutdown abort** or a database crash) does crash recovery.

**NOTE**
If running a single-instance database, there is only one thread. In this case, if the instance crashes there is no concept of instance recovery as there is only one instance. When you restart the instance, thread recovery is done as part of crash recovery.

While running the Parallel Server option, if another instance attempts to open the database while the first one is doing crash recovery, it waits until crash recovery is complete. Crash recovery determines which threads are left open, and calls thread recovery to close them cleanly. The reason for this is that if crash recovery dies in the middle for some reason, a data file can be replaced with a backup that was taken just before crash recovery started. This file would then look like a current file but it would be missing the changes for any threads that were recovered.

Remember that before attempting thread recovery, the checkpoint counter in the control file for every data file is checked with the corresponding checkpoint counter in the data file header. This ensures that none of the data files have been restored from a backup. If there is a restored file, then media recovery needs to be performed.

Each thread's redo can be applied independently because for any given block, only one cache at a time can have changes that have not been written to disk. This means that to recover a specific thread, only the redo log files for that thread are required. If multiple threads are being recovered, they will be recovered one at a time. In other words, thread recovery is single threaded. The following example should illustrate this concept.

Let's assume that a DBA is running the Parallel Server option, with two instances accessing the database, and with T1 as the thread for instance one and T2 as the thread for instance two. Let's further assume that there are two transactions running simultaneously (one from each instance) and modifying the same block in the database. Figure 5-2 shows the changes recorded in the log files of T1 and T2. If the first instance crashes, thread recovery needs to be performed and can be applied independently, as mentioned earlier. You may wonder how change 5 can be applied to the block without applying change 4, which belongs to T2.

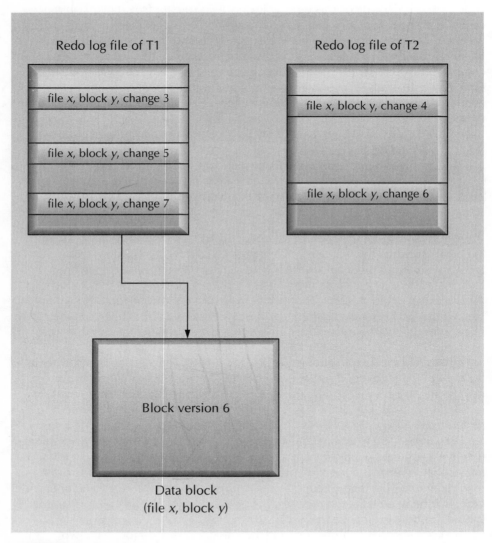

**FIGURE 5-2.** *Thread recovery*

The explanation is that at the time of thread recovery, the version of the block on disk has to be at least 6. This is because when the transaction of instance 1 wants to modify the block to create change 7, the block needs to be *pinged* (pinging is the process of flushing the dirty buffer from one instance's cache to disk so that the second instance can modify it), and change 6 has to be written to disk. So during thread recovery of T1, changes 3 and 5 will be skipped because the version of the data block on disk is ahead of the redo, and therefore these changes don't need to be applied to the data block.

For crash recovery, however, it is important to note that none of the threads are closed until all the redo from all threads is applied. If this is not done, a DBA can restore a backup copy of a data file and Oracle wouldn't know that it needs recovery. It would be possible to have multiple instances cooperating on crash recovery. Each instance would recover one thread at a time until all threads were recovered. As shown in the above example, no thread needs to wait for another thread to apply recovery first, as in the case of thread recovery. In the next section we will learn that media recovery is dependent on multiple threads.

Thread recovery doesn't attempt to apply redo that is before the checkpoint SCN of a data file. The end of a thread recovery almost always advances the data file checkpoints, and always advances the checkpoint counters.

# Media Recovery

While block and thread recovery is done by the database automatically, *media recovery* is done in response to a recovery command issued by the DBA. It is used to make backup data files current, or to restore changes that were lost when a data file went offline without a checkpoint. For example, if you take a tablespace offline using the *immediate* option, the data files will go offline without a checkpoint being performed by Oracle. Media recovery can apply archived log files, as well as online log files.

## When to Do Media Recovery

A restored data file backup always needs media recovery, even if it can be accomplished with the online log files. The same is true of a data file that went offline without a checkpoint. The database cannot be opened if any of the online data files needs media recovery. A data file cannot be brought online while the database is open if it needs media recovery. Depending on the failure and the recovery procedure you want to use, you can recover the database while a portion of the database is open; but if the database is open, the file to be recovered must be offline. We will get into details on the options that you have for doing media recovery later in this section.

### Media Recovery Operation: Database, Tablespace, and Data File Recovery

Oracle detects that media recovery is needed when the checkpoint counter in the data file header is not equal to the corresponding checkpoint counter in the control file. When you issue the **recover** command from SQL*DBA, recovery starts at the lowest checkpoint SCN of the data files being recovered. This means Oracle checks for the SCN value in the file header for all data files and chooses the one that has the oldest SCN value. As we have discussed earlier, associated with this checkpoint SCN is the thread that issued the checkpoint. Oracle starts applying media recovery to this file starting with this thread. The checkpoint SCN of every file is saved to eliminate applying redo from before its checkpoint. The highest stop SCN is also saved (recorded in the control file) to know if recovery should stop before all the redo is applied.

There are primarily three options you can choose while doing media recovery. First, you can do *database recovery*. This means that you can restore all (or some) data files from the backup and recover the entire database. The second type is a *tablespace recovery*. While a portion of the database is open and running, you can perform media recovery on a specific tablespace. This means all data files that belong to the tablespace will be recovered. The third type of recovery is *data file recovery*. Here you can recover a specific data file while the rest of the database is in use. All three of these options use the same criteria for determining if the files can be recovered

When a process recovers a data file, first it locks the data file in exclusive mode. If the process cannot lock the file because some other process has a lock on it (since the file is online or another process is recovering the data file), then Oracle gives you an error saying that the data file is in use. This prevents two recovery sessions from recovering the same data file, and it prevents media recovery of a file that is in use.

During media recovery, the redo of all enabled threads is applied. Oracle has an initial list of enabled threads that it has to recover. As it starts reading the redo log files, it knows if any new threads have been enabled. If so, it will apply recovery for those threads as well. The last redo record in each redo thread is an *end_of_thread* record, which tells Oracle that there is no more redo to be applied for that specific thread. Recovery for a particular thread is complete when this record is applied. Media recovery is complete when all enabled threads have been recovered through the end of each thread.

While applying redo, Oracle may have to switch between threads to roll blocks forward enough to apply the next piece of redo. Oracle may have to apply the same archive log file multiple times if it contains a lot of blocks that were modified by other threads. During media recovery, a thread's redo will be applied until it hits the end-of-thread marker, or until it needs to apply a redo change that is in the future of a block. If a thread finds that it has redo in the future of a block, recovery will switch to another thread. Eventually, the block should be rolled forward enough to apply this piece of redo. The example in Figure 5-3 illustrates the concept of switching threads.

Figure 5-3, shows two database blocks and redo for two threads. Redo record 1 of thread 1 contains change 4 of data block *y*. Since data block *y* has version number 3 on disk, this is the next change that needs to be applied. However, redo

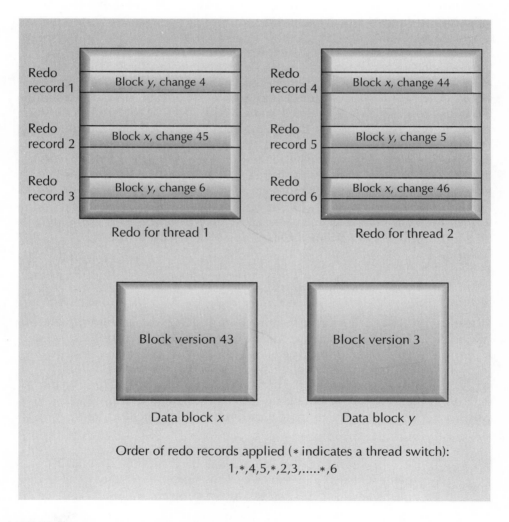

**FIGURE 5-3.** *Thread switching during recovery*

record 2 of thread 1 contains change 45 and this cannot be applied to block *x*, as the redo is in the future of the block. In other words, change 44 needs to be applied to block *x* before change 45 can be applied, so Oracle has to switch threads and starts applying recovery starting from redo record 4 of thread 2. Note that after redo record 4 is applied, Oracle continues to apply redo in this thread until it is forced to switch again or until it completes recovery for this thread. Figure 5-3 gives the order in which the redo records are applied in this example. The asterisk (*) indicates that a thread switch happened.

## Prerequisites for Using Media Recovery

If a media failure occurs while the database is operating in NOARCHIVELOG mode, complete recovery using physical backups might not be possible. In other words, if you take weekly offline backups, then you should be prepared, in a worst-case scenario, to lose a week's worth of data if there is a media failure. This is because the changes made to the database are not archived to the archive log files, since the database is running in NOARCHIVELOG mode. So running the database in this mode is suitable only if the data can be reconstructed, if necessary, during a media failure. In summary, if the DBA opts to operate the database in NOARCHIVELOG mode, the only recovery methods available are

- Restoring from an offline backup—which involves restoring all data files, control files, and online log files—and restarting the database.

- Rebuilding the database using a full database export. This method involves re-creating the schema of the database and importing all the data from a previously taken full database export.

On the other hand, if a media failure occurs while the database is operating in ARCHIVELOG mode, there are many ways to recover, depending on the types of files that are damaged and what type of media failure has occurred. Complete recovery can be done, which involves restoring the data file(s) from backup, applying *all* changes made since the backup was taken, and rolling forward the database completely, without losing any data. For the purpose of this discussion, we assume that you are operating the database in ARCHIVELOG mode.

**NOTE**
It is very important that you run your database in ARCHIVELOG mode. Otherwise, it is almost certain that you will lose data if a media failure occurs and you lose your database files.

As mentioned earlier, there are three kinds of recovery commands that you can use:

```
Recover database
```

```
Recover tablespace
```

```
Recover datafile
```

The recovery command to use depends on the kind of failure that occurred and whether you want to keep the database open while recovering. If you recover a data file or a tablespace when the database is open, it is called *online recovery*. If the database is closed when you perform recovery, it is called *offline recovery*. Table 5-2 summarizes which type of recovery can be performed while recovering the database, a tablespace, or a data file.

When the **recover database** command is used, the database always has to be mounted but not open. Since a tablespace is a logical entity, Oracle recognizes it only when the database is open; therefore, when using the **recover tablespace** command, the database needs to be open, but with the tablespace being recovered offline. (The SYSTEM tablespace can never be recovered using the **recover tablespace** command since it cannot be taken offline.) To recover a data file, you can use the **recover datafile** command and the database can be open or closed, depending on the files being recovered. For example, if the SYSTEM data files are being recovered, the database has to be closed since the database cannot be open with SYSTEM data files offline. If files belonging to a *user* tablespace are being recovered, the database can be open but the files that are being recovered need to be offline.

| RECOVERY COMMAND | DATABASE ONLINE | DATABASE OFFLINE |
| --- | --- | --- |
| Recover database | No | Yes |
| Recover tablespace | Yes | No |
| Recover datafile | Yes | Yes |

**TABLE 5-2.**  *Online and Offline Recovery*

# Database Recovery and Implementation

This section describes various media recovery options that Oracle provides to DBAs at a database-wide level. Regardless of the method used, the fundamental concept of recovery is very straightforward: *Before opening the database, all data files must be recovered to the exact same point in time, and not have any changes in the future from this point.* For example take a look at this illustration:

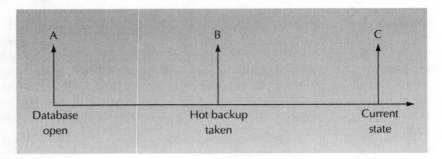

The database is opened at state A, a hot backup is taken at state B, and the current state of the database is state C. Let's assume that a media failure occurred and a data file belonging to the user tablespace is lost. At this point you have two recovery options:

- You can recover all the data files from state B and recover all of them to state C by using the **recover database** command.

- The one data file that was damaged can be restored from the backup, the database mounted, the data file taken offline, and the database opened before recovering it with the **recover datafile** command.

In either case, at the end of recovery, all data files have to be at state C (or the current state, whatever it is). You should never start the database with one data file at state B and the rest of the data files at state C. This would cause database inconsistency. Oracle keeps track of the fuzziness of the files to avoid such situations.

It is possible, and might be necessary in some drastic situations, to start up the database in an inconsistent mode—such cases should be handled by an Oracle Worldwide Support Analyst. In cases like this, there are a number of precautions that you need to take, and the database needs to be rebuilt after opening it. The main reason for facing such a drastic situation is usually due to the DBA not having a proper backup procedure in place. It is unlikely that DBAs who plan a good backup and recovery scheme would face a situation like this. The syntax to use database recovery is as follows:

```
RECOVER [AUTOMATIC]  [FROM 'location']  [DATABASE]
  [UNTIL CANCEL]
  [UNTIL TIME date]
  [UNTIL CHANGE integer]
[USING BACKUP CONTROLFILE]
```

All keywords in square brackets are optional. If the AUTOMATIC option is used, recovery is done automatically without asking the DBA for the names of the redo log files during media recovery.

Alternatively, the command **set autorecovery on/off** can be used from SQL*DBA to turn on/off automatic recovery. However, when you request Oracle to do automatic recovery, the archived redo log files should be in the location specified by the INIT.ORA parameter LOG_ARCHIVE_DEST, and the format of the filename should be the same as specified in the INIT.ORA parameter LOG_ARCHIVE_FORMAT. If you don't want Oracle to do media recovery automatically, you should omit this option while using the **recover** command. This will force Oracle to prompt you for the next archived redo log filename, and you should specify the next log filename. Alternatively, you can use the **alter database recover** command to perform database media recovery.

> **NOTE**
> Oracle recommends using the **recover** command rather than the **alter database** command with the **recover** clause to do media recovery because it is easier to use.

The next keyword is FROM, which is optional as well. This should be used if the file location is different from what is specified in the INIT.ORA parameter LOG_ARCHIVE_DEST. If you don't use the UNTIL keyword, Oracle assumes that complete database recovery is requested. For example, the command

```
SQLDBA> RECOVER DATABASE
```

does media recovery on all the data files that are online, if required. If all instances are cleanly shut down and no backup files are restored, this command will signal an error saying no recovery is required. This command will also fail if any one of the instances have the database open, since they will have the data file locks. Database-wide recovery can be performed *only* when the database is not open and mounted.

The other options, such as UNTIL CANCEL, UNTIL TIME, and UNTIL CHANGE, will be discussed in the next section as part of incomplete recovery.

Oracle7 release 7.1 introduces the new *parallel recovery* option. Appendix A gives complete details of the new features of releases 7.1 and 7.2. A brief description of the parallel recovery option is discussed below.

As shown in Figure 5-4, the Oracle server uses one process to read the redo log files and dispatches the redo information to several recovery processes. The recovery processes apply the changes from the redo log files to the data files. Recovery processes are not dedicated to a specific file, but recover a range of data blocks. The INIT.ORA parameter RECOVERY_PARALLELISM determines the number of recovery processes desired.

### Complete Versus Incomplete Recovery

Recovering the database from a media failure without losing any data is known as *complete recovery*. If you have lost some data after recovering the database, it is known as *incomplete recovery*. Complete recovery should be implemented when all the required redo log files, backup data files (for all the lost or damaged data files), and a current valid control file are available. Incomplete recovery should be used only when you cannot recover all the data completely (for example, to recover from the loss of an archived or online redo log file and the loss of control

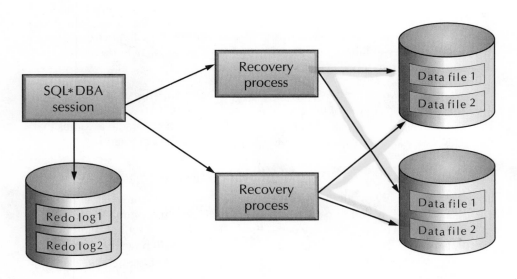

**FIGURE 5-4.** *Parallel Recovery in Oracle7, release 7.1*

files). Incomplete recovery can also be implemented to restore the database to a previous point in time. For example, if you drop a table by accident at 10 A.M. and want to recover the table, you can restore the appropriate data files from a backup and do point-in-time, incomplete recovery to a point before 10 A.M. Chapter 7 gives a case study on point-in-time recovery. When incomplete recovery is done, the database must be opened using the **alter database open resetlogs** command. This marks the database so that the redo that was skipped can never be accidentally applied.

There are three options to choose from when doing incomplete recovery. The **recover database** command should be used with one of the following options: **until cancel**, **until time**, and **until change**. These options allow you to perform cancel-based, time-based, and SCN-based recovery, respectively.

If the **until cancel** option is chosen, Oracle allows you to roll forward one log file at a time. When recovery needs to be stopped, just issue the **cancel** command. Online log files are not automatically applied in this mode. If multiple threads of redo are being recovered, there may be log files in other threads that are partially applied when the recovery is canceled.

The **until time** option allows the DBA to do recovery to a specific point in time within a redo log file. The *SQL Language Reference Manual* gives the date format that needs to be specified with this command. This option works just like the **until change** option, except that a time is given instead of an SCN.

The **until change** option recovers the database to a transaction-consistent state. The SCN that is specified with this option is noted by Oracle as a reference, and any redo records that have an SCN less than the reference SCN are applied. This is very similar to the *point-in-time recovery* option in version 6. This option terminates redo application for any redo associated with that SCN or higher. Thus, the transaction that is committed exactly at the SCN is rolled back. If the DBA needs to recover through a transaction that committed at a specific SCN, then the DBA needs to add one to the SCN specified in this command. The following are some examples of incomplete recovery:

```
SQLDBA> recover database until cancel;

SQLDBA> recover database until time '1995-04-15:17:55:00';

SQLDBA> recover database until change integer;

SQLDBA> recover database until cancel using backup controlfile;
```

The first command above does recovery until you issue the command **cancel**. The second command does point-in-time recovery. All changes up to 5.55 P.M. on April 15th, 1995, are applied to the database. The third command does recovery up to a specific SCN, specified as an integer. The last command is the same as the first one except that a backup control file is used to do recovery. When is it appropriate to use the above commands? Let's look at the following example.

John doesn't multiplex his redo log files, and one day he lost his online redo log files due a media failure. If he opens his database now, the data will be inconsistent, since data from committed transactions after the last checkpoint may or may not be in the data files on disk. As discussed earlier, the fundamental rule of recovery is that all blocks have to be at the same point in time before starting up the database. In this case, incomplete recovery needs to be done.

The recommended procedure is to restore the complete database backup from a recent online or offline backup, and issue the command **recover database until cancel** from the SQL*DBA prompt. Once all the archived redo log files are applied, open the database using the **alter database open resetlogs** command. This command creates the online log files for you.

### NOTE
From the example given here, it is clear that multiplexing online log files is very important.

If a data file is offline during incomplete recovery, it will not be recovered. This is all right if the file is part of a tablespace that was taken offline with the *normal* option. But if the tablespace is taken offline with the *immediate* option and the data file is still offline when the RESETLOGS option is used to open the database, the tablespace containing the data file will have to be dropped and re-created. This is because the data file needs media recovery from a point before the RESETLOGS option was used. In Chapter 7, one case study (Case 11) shows that it is not possible to do recovery on a data file that is restored from before a point where RESETLOGS was done. In general, the view V$DATAFILE should be checked to ensure that all necessary data files are online before an incomplete recovery is done. The only data files that can be offline are files that belong to a tablespace that was taken offline with the *normal* option or read-only data files.

Doing incomplete recovery can sometimes be tricky. The following example will make this clear: Let's assume that at time T1 a hot backup of the database was taken. At time T2 a tablespace containing file F1 was dropped. Let's assume that you need a table that resides in the tablespace that was dropped at time T2. In this case, you need to restore from the backup taken at time T1, perform point-in-time recovery, and stop before T2. Since media recovery recovers only online data files, you need to make sure that the data file you need is online; otherwise, it will not be recovered. This means that if you are using a *current* control file during recovery, you can't recover file F1, as it no longer exists.

Therefore, you must use the backup control file from time T1 (or any time before T2) to perform recovery. Another option is to create a new control file using the **create controlfile** command and then perform recovery.

**NOTE**
Data files can be taken offline by using the **alter database datafile** *'filename'* **offline** command; the control file can be created using the **create controlfile** command. Both these commands are described in the *Oracle7 Server SQL Language Reference Manual.*

If recovery is done with a control file other than the current one, you must use the **using backup controlfile** option with the **recover database** command. This is the case if a control file backup was restored, or if the control file was created with the RESETLOGS option. A **create controlfile** command with the NORESETLOGS option makes the new control file current. A backup control file wouldn't have valid information about the online log files and the data file stop SCNs. Therefore, Oracle can't use the online log file during recovery, and hence assumes infinite stop SCNs for the data files. In order to correct this information, when you open the database you must have the RESETLOGS option specified. An error is signaled if a NORESETLOGS option is used while opening the database.

The **using backup controlfile** option can be used either alone or in conjunction with an incomplete recovery option. For example, it is quite common to use a command such as **recover database until cancel using backup controlfile**. Unless an incomplete recovery option is included, all threads must be applied to the end of thread. This is validated when the log files are reset at database open. Failure to specify the **using backup controlfile** option when it is required can frequently be detected by Oracle. The old checkpoint counter in the data file headers will never be greater than the checkpoint counter in the current control file, but this may not catch the problem if the data files are also backups. The online log file headers are also validated against their control file entries, but this too may not always catch an old control file. So if you are using a backup copy of the control file, always use the **using backup controlfile** option with the **recover** command.

## RESETLOGS Option

The RESETLOGS option is needed when you open the database after one of the following is performed:

- Incomplete recovery
- Recovery using a backup control file
- Recovery with a control file that was created using the **create controlfile** command with the RESETLOGS option

When you use this option to open the database, Oracle throws away the redo that was not applied during the recovery, and ensures that it can never be applied again. It also reinitializes the control file information about online log files and redo threads.

While doing complete recovery of the database, if all threads of redo have been completely applied to all online data files, then we can be sure that the database is consistent. However, when incomplete recovery is done, there is the possibility that a file was not restored from a sufficiently old backup. This is definitely the case if the file has a different checkpoint than the other files. For this reason, before you open the database with the RESETLOGS option, you have to make sure that all data files are recovered to the same point in time to ensure consistency of the database.

A *resetlogs SCN* and *counter* are kept in the control file to uniquely identify each execution of a database open with the RESETLOGS option. The values are written into the header of every data file and redo log file as well. A redo log file cannot be applied by recovery if its log sequence number doesn't match what is expected by Oracle. A data file can't be recovered from a backup that was taken before the database was opened with the RESETLOGS option. This ensures that changes discarded by resetting the log files do not get back into the database. So it is very important to note that a database backup (online or offline) should be performed immediately after opening the database with the RESETLOGS option. However, read-only tablespaces and any tablespaces that were taken offline with the *normal* option can be brought online even after opening the database with the RESETLOGS option.

> **NOTE**
> Oracle strongly recommends taking an offline or online backup of the entire database after the database is opened with the RESETLOGS option.

Here is a brief description of what happens when you open the database using the RESETLOGS option. First, the redo is thrown away by zeroing all the online log files. This means that redo in online log files may be lost forever if it is not backed up—it would only be needed if it were decided to do the recovery all over again. One log is picked to be the current log file for every enabled thread. That log header is written as log sequence number one. Note that the set of log files and their thread association is picked up from the control file. If it is a backup control file, this may be different from what was current the last time the database was open.

Next, the file headers of all the online data files are updated to the new database checkpoint. The new *resetlogs* data is written into the header. The offline data files are marked as *needing media recovery* in the control file. This recovery can never be done, as no redo can be applied after the database is open with the RESETLOGS option. This means that the tablespace that contains the offline data file needs to be dropped. The only exception is if the file was taken offline using the *normal* option. In this case, the checkpoint SCN written to the file headers is recorded in the data dictionary. Thus, no recovery is required to bring a tablespace and its files online if the files are not fuzzy and are checkpointed at exactly the SCN saved in the dictionary. The following example shows the log sequence numbers of the online log files before and after the RESETLOGS option is used to open the database.

```
SQLDBA> archive log list
Database log mode                ARCHIVELOG
Automatic archival               ENABLED
Archive destination              /home/orahome/product/7.2.1/dbs/arch
Oldest online log sequence       61
Next log sequence to archive     63
Current log sequence             63

SQLDBA> recover database until cancel;
Media recovery complete.
SQLDBA> alter database open resetlogs;
Statement processed.
SQLDBA> archive log list;
Database log mode                ARCHIVELOG
Automatic archival               ENABLED
Archive destination              /home/orahome/product/7.2.1/dbs/arch
Oldest online log sequence       0
Next log sequence to archive     1
Current log sequence             1
```

When you open the database with the RESETLOGS option, after transaction recovery, the data files listed in the data dictionary are compared with the data files listed in the control file. This is also done on the first open after executing a **create controlfile** command. Oracle does this check because there is a possibility that incomplete recovery ended at a time when the files in the database were different from those in the control file used for the recovery. Using a backup control file or creating a new control file can have the same problem.

Checking the dictionary doesn't do any harm, so it could be done on every database open; but it could be time consuming. As part of the check, the entry in **file$** is compared with the entry in the control file for every file number. Since **file$** reflects the space allocation information in the database, it is correct, and the control file might be wrong. If the file doesn't exist in **file$**, but the control file record says it does, the file is dropped from the control file. If a file exists in **file$** but not in the control file, a fake entry is created in the control file. The fake file is named MISSING*xxxx* where *xxxx* is the file number in decimal form. This file is marked as offline and needs media recovery. If this data file is unavailable, the tablespace containing the file must be dropped. If the data file is available, the entry for MISSING*xxxx* can be renamed to point to the real file. If the data file is part of a tablespace that has been taken offline with the *normal* option, it may be brought online without recovery. Another option is to repeat the entire operation that led up to the dictionary check with the correct control file. For incomplete recovery, this would involve restoring all backups and repeating the recovery.

To summarize, opening up the database with the RESETLOGS option has many implications on the database, and impacts the database backups. So you should use this option only after doing incomplete recovery or after recovering using a backup control file. The most important point to remember is that after opening the database with the RESETLOGS option, you should immediately take an online or offline backup of the entire database.

## Checklist for Complete and Incomplete Database Recovery

In this section we summarize the requirements and discuss the advantages of using database recovery. Implementation plans are described for doing complete recovery and incomplete recovery.

### Description

- Database recovery recovers all the data files in the database that are online.
- Complete or incomplete recovery is possible.
- You can recover from an online or offline backup.

### Requirement

- You have to do offline recovery only (i.e., database cannot be open during recovery).
- All data files to be recovered should be online.

### Required Files

- Archived and/or online redo log files.
- Current or backup control file.
- Backup of data files (for the lost or damaged data files).

### Advantages

- It recovers the database in one step.
- You can do incomplete recovery.

■ You can recover data files that belong to SYSTEM tablespace.

## Disadvantages

■ The database is inaccessible during recovery.

■ It can take a long time based on the amount of redo to be applied and frequency of backups.

## Complete Recovery Implementation

The following steps show how to do complete recovery.

**1.** Restore all (or the damaged) data files at the OS level. For example, in UNIX, you can issue the following command:

```
mcs% cp /home/orahome/backup/*.dbf /home/orahome/data/721
```

**2.** Start the instance in RESTRICT mode and mount the database:

```
SQLDBA> startup restrict mount [dbname];
```

**3.** This step is optional and should be used only if the original location of a lost or damaged database file has become invalid (i.e., a disk crash). The path stored in the control file must be renamed to the new restored file location. Use the following command to rename data or log files:

```
SQLDBA> alter database rename file 'old_filename' to 'new_filename';
```

**4.** Make sure that all the data files you want to recover are online. Select from the V$DATAFILE view to get the file status.

```
SQLDBA> select file#, status, name from V$DATAFILE;
SQLDBA> alter database datafile 'filename' online;
```

**5.** Recover the database:

```
SQLDBA> RECOVER DATABASE [dbname];
```

Oracle now prompts for the names of the archived redo log files that it needs to apply, beginning with the earliest. When recovery is complete, you will see the message "Media recovery complete."

**6.** Now you can open the database:

```
SQLDBA> alter database [dbname] open;
```

**NOTE**
A database can be opened only if all the online data files have been recovered to the same point in time.

## Incomplete Recovery Implementation

Let's assume that a DBA running Oracle Financial applications accidentally ran a batch job twice, thereby logically corrupting the data. This requires restoring from the backup and rolling forward point-in-time before the batch job was run the second time. The steps involved in doing this are as follows:

1. Shut down first Oracle Financial applications, then the database, and back up all the database files in case you make an error in doing incomplete recovery of the database. This involves stopping the concurrent managers and shutting down the database clean before taking a backup:

```
SQLDBA> shutdown [dbname]
```

2. Restore all the data files from backup. You can use the current control file. For example, in VMS:

```
$ copy disk$wr3:[backup]*.dbs disk$wr4:[oracle7.data]
```

3. Start the instance in the RESTRICT mode and mount the database:

```
SQLDBA> startup restrict mount [dbname];
```

4. This step is optional and should be used only if the original location of a lost or damaged database file has become invalid (i.e., a disk crash). The path stored in the control file must be renamed to the new restored file location. Use the following command to rename data or log files:

```
SQLDBA> alter database rename file 'old_filename' to 'new_filename';
```

5. Make sure that all the data files you want to recover are online. Select from the V$DATAFILE view to get the file status:

```
SQLDBA> select file#, status, name from V$DATAFILE;
SQLDBA> alter database datafile 'filename' online;
```

6. Recover the database using the UNTIL CANCEL or UNTIL TIME option. For example, to recover up to 1.55 P.M. on the 15th of May, 1995, use the following command:

```
SQLDBA> recover database until time '1995-05-15:13:55:00';
```

Oracle prompts you for redo log files and you should get the message "Log applied" after each redo log file is applied. Recovery ends at the specified time and returns the message "Media recovery complete."

**7.** Open the database using the RESETLOGS option:

```
SQLDBA> ALTER DATABASE OPEN RESETLOGS;
```

**8.** Take an offline or online backup. This is a very important step.

# Tablespace Recovery

The syntax for using tablespace recovery is as follows:

```
RECOVER [AUTOMATIC] [FROM location]
  TABLESPACE tablespace_name [, tablespace_name...]
```

It is very important to note that you can use tablespace recovery only while doing complete recovery—incomplete recovery cannot be done.

The **recover tablespace** command does media recovery on all the data files in the tablespace(s) listed. We have learned that a tablespace is a logical entity that corresponds to one or more physical data files on the disk. Oracle knows which tablespace contains what data only when the database is open. Therefore, you can do tablespace recovery only when the database is open.

Before doing tablespace recovery, you have to take the tablespace offline. Tablespaces that cannot be taken offline (such as SYSTEM) cannot be recovered using the **recover tablespace** command. If none of the data files of a tablespace need recovery, an error is signaled.

## Checklist for Tablespace Recovery

A summary of tablespace recovery and an implementation plan is given here.

## Description

- Tablespace recovery allows online recovery of all restored data files in the listed tablespace(s).
- You can recover from an online or offline backup.
- You can do complete recovery only.

## Requirements

- Database must be open.

■ The tablespace to be recovered should be offline.

## Required Files

■ Archived and online redo log files.

■ Current control file.

■ Backup of the data files (for lost or damaged files).

## Advantages

■ Recovers all lost or damaged data files in the listed tablespace(s) in one step.

■ It is faster than doing database recovery, since redo doesn't need to be applied to all data files.

■ Other tablespaces in the database are accessible to users during recovery.

■ Multiple SQL*DBA sessions can be used to recover tablespaces in parallel.

## Disadvantages

■ You cannot perform online recovery for tablespaces that cannot be taken offline, such as SYSTEM. To recover the SYSTEM tablespace, you have to use the **recover database** command.

■ Incomplete recovery cannot be performed.

## Tablespace Recovery Implementation

**1.** Take the tablespace(s) that needs recovery offline:

```
SQLDBA> alter tablespace ts_name offline;
```

**2.** Restore all (or any) data files that belong to the tablespace(s) that need recovery.

**3.** If the original location of a lost or damaged data file has become invalid (i.e., a disk crash), the path stored in the control file must be renamed to the new, restored file location:

```
SQLDBA> alter database rename file 'old_filename' to 'new_filename';
```

**4.** Recover the tablespace(s):

```
SQLDBA>  RECOVER TABLESPACE ts_name [,ts_name ...]
```

Oracle now prompts for the names of the archived redo log files that it
needs to apply, beginning with the earliest log file needed. When all
changes are applied to the database, Oracle displays a message saying
"Media recovery complete."

**5.** Bring the tablespace online:

```
SQLDBA>  alter tablespace ts_name online;
```

# Data File Recovery

The syntax for using data file recovery is as follows:

```
RECOVER [AUTOMATIC] [FROM location]
¦ DATAFILE 'filename' ['filename',...]
```

It is very important to note that you can use data file recovery only while doing
complete recovery—incomplete recovery cannot be done.

The **recover datafile** command does recovery on all the data files listed. Online
or offline recovery is possible, as long as media recovery locks can be acquired on
data files. If the database is open by any instance, then the data file recovery can
recover only offline data files—online recovery cannot be performed while
recovering the SYSTEM data files.

## Checklist for Data File Recovery

A summary of data file recovery and an implementation plan is given here.

## Description

- Data file recovery allows recovery of a data file(s). You can use separate
  terminal sessions to perform parallel recovery of database files.

- It allows recovery from an offline or online backups.

- Online or offline recovery (i.e., with database open or mounted) can be
  implemented, depending on the data files.

## Requirements

- The data file must be taken offline for online recovery.

### Required Files

- Archived and online redo logs.
- Current control file.
- Backup of data files (for the lost files).

### Advantages

- Offline or online recovery can be performed.
- Multiple SQL*DBA sessions can be implemented to recover data files in parallel.

### Disadvantages

- For online recovery, the data file must be taken offline. Therefore, SYSTEM data files cannot be recovered with the **recover datafile** command.
- Cannot perform incomplete recovery.

### Online Recovery Implementation

**1.** Mount the database:

```
SQLDBA> startup mount [dbname]
```

**2.** Take all the damaged or lost data files offline:

```
SQLDBA> alter database datafile 'filename' offline;
```

**3.** Open the database:

```
SQLDBA> alter database open;
```

**4.** Restore the data files that need to be recovered (i.e., the files that were taken offline in step 2). If the original location of a lost or damaged database file has become invalid (i.e., a disk crash), the path stored in the control file must be renamed to the new, restored file location:

```
SQLDBA> alter database rename file 'old_filename' to 'new_filename';
```

**5.** Recover the data file(s):

```
SQLDBA> RECOVER DATAFILE 'datafile' [, 'datafile'...]
```

Oracle now prompts for the names of the archived redo log files that it needs to apply, beginning with the earliest log file needed. When all changes are applied to the database, Oracle displays a message saying "Media recovery complete."

**6.** Bring the data file(s) online:

```
SQLDBA> alter database datafile 'filename' online;
```

## Offline Recovery Implementation

**1.** Restore any data files that need recovery. If the original location of a lost or damaged database file has become invalid (i.e., a disk crash), the path stored in the control file must be renamed to the new, restored file location:

```
SQLDBA> alter database rename file 'old_filename' to 'new_filename'
```

**2.** Mount the database:

```
SQLDBA> startup restrict mount [dbname]
```

**3.** Since the database is closed, the data files can be offline or online. You can use the following commands to take data files online or offline, respectively:

```
SQLDBA> alter database datafile 'filename' online
SQLDBA> alter database datafile 'filename' offline
```

**4.** Recover the data file(s):

```
SQLDBA> RECOVER DATAFILE 'datafile' [, 'datafile'...]
```

Oracle now prompts for the names of the archived redo log files that it needs to apply, beginning with the earliest log file needed. When all changes are applied to the database, Oracle displays a message saying "Media recovery complete."

**5.** If the data file(s) was offline during recovery (i.e., in step 4) you need to bring it online before startup. You can skip this step if the data file(s) is online:

```
SQLDBA> alter database datafile 'filename' online;
```

**6.** Open the database:

```
SQLDBA> alter database [dbname] open;
```

Table 5-3 compares the three media recovery options.

| RECOVER DATABASE | RECOVER TABLESPACE | RECOVER DATA FILE |
|---|---|---|
| Recovers all data files of the database in one step. | Can recover one tablespace, multiple tablespaces, or all tablespaces in a single step. | Can recover a single database file, multiple database files, or all database files in one step. |
| Used with the database closed and with files to be recovered online. | Used with the database open, but with the tablespace being recovered offline. | Used with the database closed or open. If open, data files to recover should be offline. |
| Must be used if the damaged tablespace is the SYSTEM. | Cannot be used to recover a tablespace that cannot be taken offline, such as SYSTEM. | Cannot be used when the database is open to recover files in the SYSTEM tablespace. |
| Two sessions cannot recover the database simultaneously. | Can be used with multiple SQL*DBA sessions to recover multiple tablespaces in parallel. | Can be used with multiple SQL*DBA sessions to recover multiple data files in parallel. |
| Incomplete recovery can be done. | Complete recovery only. | Complete recovery only. |

**TABLE 5-3.** *Comparison of the Three Media Recovery Options*

## Creating Control File and Data Files

While doing media recovery, it is always suggested to use the current control file if you have one. If the current control file is lost as part of the media failure, you can use a backup copy of the control file or create a new control file. The syntax to create a new control file is given here:

```
CREATE CONTROLFILE [REUSE] [SET]
DATABASE [dbname]
LOGFILE filespec [, filespec, ...]
RESETLOGS : NORESETLOGS
DATAFILE filespec [, filespec, ...]
[MAXLOGIFLES integer]
[MAXLOGMEMBERS integer]
[MAXLOGHISTORY integer]
[MAXDATAFILES integer]
```

```
[MAXINSTANCES integer]
[ARCHIVELOG | NOARCHIVELOG]
```

For a complete description of the keywords, refer to the *Oracle7 Server SQL Language Reference Manual*.

The **create controlfile** command can be used to create a new control file when all the existing control files are lost or corrupted. This command is very commonly used to alter some of the parameters, such as MAXDATAFILES and MAXLOGFILES. Note that these parameters are set when the database is originally created, and the only way to alter them is to re-create the database or the control file. Obviously, re-creating the entire database is impractical, so you should use the **create controlfile** command to modify these parameters.

The **create controlfile** command can be issued only after the database is started with the **startup nomount** option. After executing this command, a new control file is created and the database is automatically mounted. The new control file can then be used for recovery, if needed. The first database open will verify if the data dictionary is consistent with the information in the new control file. After the database is open, it is strongly recommended that you shut the database down cleanly and take a complete backup. This is particularly important if the RESETLOGS option was used while creating the control file. The following example illustrates how to create a new control file:

1. Take a backup of all available redo log files, data files, and control files before attempting this operation.

2. Start up the instance but don't mount the database:

```
SQLDBA> STARTUP NOMOUNT
```

3. Issue the **create controlfile** command.

4. Recovery may be implemented if needed; otherwise, go to next step.

5. Open the database.

```
SQLDBA> ALTER DATABASE OPEN [NO]RESETLOGS;
```

In step 3, you should specify all the data files and log files that are part of the database. It may be difficult for you to remember them unless you have written them down somewhere. For this purpose, the following command should be used:

```
SQLDBA> ALTER DATABASE BACKUP CONTROLFILE TO TRACE;
```

This command creates a SQL script that can be used to create a new control file. This command should be used as part of your backup procedure. Here is a sample trace file that is created by executing the above SQL command:

```
SQLDBA> ALTER DATABASE BACKUP CONTROLFILE TO TRACE;
Dump file /home/orahome/admin/721/udump/ora_19210.trc
Oracle7 Server Release 7.2.1.0.0 - Beta Release
With the distributed and parallel query options
PL/SQL Release 2.2.1.0.0 - Beta
ORACLE_HOME = /home/orahome/product/7.2.1
ORACLE_SID = 721
Oracle process number: 8 Unix process id: 19210
System name:SunOS
Node name:cosmos
Release:5.3
Version:Generic
Machine:sun4m


Wed Apr  5 15:09:54 1995
Wed Apr  5 15:09:54 1995
*** SESSION ID:(7.1)
# The following commands will create a new control file and use it
# to open the database.
# No data other than log history will be lost. Additional logs may
# be required for media recovery of offline data files. Use this
# only if the current version of all online logs are available.
STARTUP NOMOUNT
CREATE CONTROLFILE REUSE DATABASE "721" NORESETLOGS ARCHIVELOG
    MAXLOGFILES 16
    MAXLOGMEMBERS 2
    MAXDATAFILES 30
    MAXINSTANCES 1
    MAXLOGHISTORY 100
LOGFILE
  GROUP 1 '/home/orahome/data/721/redo01.log'  SIZE 500K,
  GROUP 2 '/home/orahome/data/721/redo02.log'  SIZE 500K,
  GROUP 3 '/home/orahome/data/721/redo03.log'  SIZE 500K
DATAFILE
  '/home/orahome/data/721/system01.dbf' SIZE 500K,
  '/home/orahome/data/721/rbs01.dbf' SIZE 500K,
  '/home/orahome/data/721/tools01.dbf' SIZE 500K,
  '/home/orahome/data/721/users01.dbf' SIZE 500K,
  '/home/orahome/data/721/test1.dbf' SIZE 500K,
  '/home/orahome/data/721/temp.dbf' SIZE 500K
;
# Recovery is required if any of the data files are restored backups,
# or if the last shutdown was not normal or immediate.
RECOVER DATABASE
# All logs need archiving and a log switch is needed.
ALTER SYSTEM ARCHIVE LOG ALL;
# Database can now be opened normally.
ALTER DATABASE OPEN;
```

When you add a new data file to a tablespace or create a new tablespace, you should take a backup of the new data file(s) and the control file immediately. If you forget to take a copy of the data file(s), and you lose the current data file due to a media failure, you can create the data file(s) using the following command:

```
SQLDBA> ALTER DATABASE CREATE DATAFILE 'filename';
```

This is a very useful command introduced in Oracle7. It can be used to create a new empty data file that will replace the existing one. At this point, media recovery should be performed to roll forward the data file. This means that all the changes made to the data file since its creation should be saved by retaining the necessary archived redo log files. Oracle records the SCN value in the control file when a new data file is created; so when you apply recovery, Oracle tells you where to start recovery. In order to use this command to create SYSTEM data files, the database should be created with the ARCHIVELOG option; otherwise, this command can be used only for data files that were created after the database is put in ARCHIVELOG mode. Chapter 7 provides a case study (Case 12) on how to use this command.

# Recovery with the Import Utility

Oracle provides the *Import* utility for DBAs who rely on logical backups to restore the data. Import reads data from export files (DDL and DML SQL statements), executes them to create the tables, and populates the data into the Oracle database. Import automatically does any character set translation (ASCII or EBCDIC) necessary.

The Import utility can be used to restore or reorganize a database. One of the main advantages of using the Import utility is that you can be sure that no physical data block corruptions will be imported, since no data block corruptions will be propagated to the backup file when exported. This is because the Export utility does a full table scan on all the tables that are backed up (exported). Another advantage is that data can be exported from a database on one machine, and imported into another. This is useful for DBAs running in a heterogeneous environment.

To view the contents of the export file without importing it, the SHOW=Y import option can be used. Import can be performed from the command line or by using a parameter file (PARFILE = *parameter_file*). To import data using the import utility, the DBA must have access to the *connect* and *resource* roles of an Oracle database, and to the export file. Only a DBA can import an export file that was exported by a DBA. The rollback segment should be sized appropriately to perform the import, or it will roll back to the last commit, only partially importing the data. By default, Import commits after loading each table, unless the COMMIT=Y parameter is used to commit after each array insert. This will guarantee that data imported remains in the database (doesn't get rolled back, since commit is issued after an insert), but will have an overhead on performance.

The RECORDLENGTH parameter is required when a DBA imports into another operating system that by default uses a different value. The BUFFER size must be set high enough to import a table row containing long fields. If rows contain LONG data, only one row at a time is fetched. The *Oracle 7 Server Utilities User's Guide* gives complete details on the Import utility.

Table 5-4 gives the names of the parameters that you can use with the Import utility, their default values, and brief descriptions.

# Re-Creating the Database from an Incremental Export

In Chapter 3 we discussed various incremental export options such as COMPLETE, CUMULATIVE, and INCREMENTAL. Once the data is exported, you can use the following steps to import data from an incremental export.

**1.** Using the *most recent* export file (whether COMPLETE, CUMULATIVE, or INCREMENTAL) restore the database definitions using the command

```
$ imp DBA/passwd inctype=system full=Y file=exp_file
```

**2.** Bring necessary rollback segments ONLINE.

**3.** Import the most recent COMPLETE export file using the following command:

```
$ imp DBA/passwd inctype=restore full=Y file=file_spec
```

**4.** Import, in chronological order, all the CUMULATIVE export files since the most recent COMPLETE export:

```
$ imp DBA/passwd inctype=restore full=Y file=file_spec
```

If no CUMULATIVE exports were taken, skip to step 5.

**5.** Import, in chronological order, all the INCREMENTAL export files since the most recent CUMULATIVE (or COMPLETE) export, using the following command:

```
$ imp DBA/passwd inctype=restore full=Y file=file_spec
```

| PARAMETER | DEFAULT | DESCRIPTION |
|---|---|---|
| USERID | Undefined | The username/password of the user performing the import |
| BUFFER | OS dependent | The size in bytes of the buffer used to transport data rows |
| FILE | expdat.dmp | The name of the export file to import |
| SHOW | No | A flag to indicate whether to list only the contents of the export file, and not import the table data, not create any object, and not modify the database |
| IGNORE | Yes | A flag to indicate whether to ignore errors if the object already exists during import |
| GRANTS | Yes | A flag to indicate whether to import grants |
| INDEXES | Yes | A flag to indicate whether to import indexes |
| ROWS | Yes | A flag to indicate whether to import the rows of table data |
| FULL | No | A flag to indicate whether to import the entire file |
| FROMUSER | Undefined | A list of user names whose objects are exported |
| TOUSER | Undefined | A list of user names to whom data is imported |
| TABLES | Undefined | A list of table names to import |
| RECORDLENGTH | System dependent | The length in bytes of the file record |
| INCTYPE | Undefined | The type of incremental import. Valid values are SYSTEM and RESTORE |
| COMMIT | No | A flag to indicate whether to commit after each array insert. By default, import commits after loading each table |
| PARFILE | Undefined | The name of an import parameter file that contains one or more parameter specifications |

**TABLE 5-4.**  *Description of Import Parameters*

# Recovery Strategy

For smooth operation of the database and prompt recovery from failures, you need to plan a robust backup and recovery strategy. The first step in doing this is to determine the business goals. Operation requirements cannot be met if they are unknown or undefined. The second step is to do an operations review on the current backup and recovery strategy against the reliability and availability requirements stated in the business goals.

A DBA should be able to do an operations audit on the recovery strategy to identify remedial action where the present backup and recovery implementation does not meet operations requirements, or in the case of a new system, to provide a robust backup and recovery strategy. If this is done, the risk of losing data can be minimized and the DBA can have peace of mind.

The first step is to establish the requirements. You should be able to answer the following questions before planning a backup and recovery strategy:

- How much data can I afford to lose?

- How long can the database be offline to perform backups?

- Should recovery be needed, how quickly do I need to recover the data?

- What resources are available for me to do backup and recovery?

- Do I need the capability to reverse changes made to the database ?

These are all important factors. For example, if you can afford to lose a week's worth of data if a failure occurs (i.e., you can easily populate the last one week's worth of data), then you can take weekly backups. Similarly, how long the database can be down while taking backups will determine whether a hot or cold backup should be taken.

The following are some issues to consider while designing a backup and recovery strategy:

- Redo log files need to be sized according to operational requirements. The size of the online redo log files should be determined by estimating the amount of redo the transactions would be generating per hour. A point of failure in version 6 was the loss of online redo log file. So, multiplexing of online redo log files is very important (i.e., maintaining multiple log members for each log group).

- At least three copies of the control file should be maintained on different disks. Disks should be mounted under different controllers.

■ Database design considerations, such as planning to keep archived redo log files and online log files on different disks, are important.

■ In many cases, the procedure of rolling forward a database or database file from a backup can be simplified and made faster by keeping, on disk, a recent backup of all the data files and all the associated archived redo log files. For many systems, much of the time necessary for recovery is spent restoring the data and archived redo log files from tape.

■ Operate in ARCHIVELOG mode to utilize greater flexibility in recovery options.

■ A higher level of security can be achieved by maintaining a second backup of offline archived redo log files. This copy should ideally be to tape, requiring a dedicated tape drive and some operator monitoring. Disk mirroring might not be a safe option in some cases.

■ The use of the UNIX "compress" should be verified with the hardware vendor.

■ The physical copying of disks to tape should detect disk errors. An additional check on database health may be achieved via the export mechanism. This has the advantage of reading and optionally analyzing all data tables. It is recommended that the production instances be automatically exported to disk prior to the nightly backup. An export should be completed with the database operating in RESTRICT mode, while no data is being modified. Two forms of export are recommended, *schema* and *full*. Both should use a parameter file including tables, synonyms, sequences, indexes, grants, and constraints.

■ In the event of object loss, it is often advantageous to have a complete set of object-creation scripts available outside the database. This is particularly useful for re-creating indexes, views, constraints. Similarly, scripts should be maintained for grants.

■ You should have battle-tested rebuild strategies. It is highly recommended to prepare and test recovery scripts for each instance. Tests should address at least the following scenarios:

   ■ Loss of a SYSTEM tablespace

   ■ Loss of a non-SYSTEM tablespace

   ■ Loss of a non-SYSTEM tablespace with active rollback segments

   ■ Loss of redo logs (online and archived)

   ■ Loss of static or dynamic user tables

   ■ loss of control file

# Disaster Recovery

This section gives you details on design considerations, planning and maintenance of standby databases. Refer to *Hot Standby Database* section in Chapter 3 for a definition of standby databases.

## Concepts and Terminology

This section describes the concepts and terminology behind the standby database feature. First, we will briefly review the Oracle7 recovery mechanism. Emphasis is placed on areas affecting the standby mechanism. Next, we will briefly review the standby database feature and how changes are propagated from the primary to the standby database.

### Archiving and Recovery

Let us consider a production database. When the database is running, Oracle guarantees transaction durability by logging changes to data in the form of *redo*. When the Oracle recovery mechanism is invoked, redo is applied to data to restore database consistency. *Redo* is written to the online redo log files by *LGWR*, a background process. The online redo log is composed of two or more online redo log files. LGWR writes to one online log at a time, the *current* or *active* log. When the active log is filled, LGWR performs a *log switch* and begins writing to the next available online log. When all online logs are filled, the next available online log will be re-used, and so on, in a cyclic fashion.

Let us assume that the database is now running in ARCHIVELOG mode and automatic archiving is enabled. Let us now consider the following events, diagrammed in Figure 5-5:

- at time $T_{Backup}$, an *offline backup* of the database completes successfully

- at time $T_{FirstArchive}$, an archive log file is successfully created after the backup

- at time $T_{LastArchive}$, archiving successfully creates an archive log file before a failure

- at time $T_{Failure}$, a failure occurs making the database unusable, such that *media recovery* is necessary

**NOTE**
At the point of failure, it is possible that at least one inactive online log was being copied to an archive log file. Such archive log files are not available for recovery. If available, the online redo log can be used to recover to the last committed transaction before the failure.

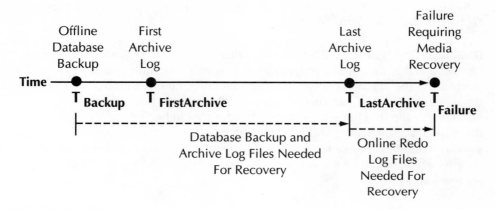

**FIGURE 5-5.**   *Backup and Recovery timelines*

Let us now consider media recovery. After the media failure is repaired and the system is brought back online, the database is restored from the offline database backup. The backed up archive log files from time T$_{FirstArchive}$ to T$_{LastArchive}$ are also restored. Recovery commands are issued such that the archive log files are used to *apply* redo to the database. The database is now consistent up to time T$_{LastArchive}$; that is, the point in time at the end of the last committed transaction in the last archive log file used in the recovery. However, the database is not completely recovered up to the time of failure, T$_{Failure}$. If a valid copy of the online redo logs are available as of T$_{Failure}$, then, and only then, can those redo logs be used to recover the database up to the point in time of the failure. If the online redo logs are not available, then committed transactions that occurred after the last recovered archive log are lost; that is, transactions committed during the period T$_{LastArchive}$ to T$_{Failure}$.

## The Standby Database Feature-Overview

In this section, the standby database feature is briefly reviewed before describing how changes in the primary database are propagated to the standby. Administrative tasks are briefly outlined in this section; detailed descriptions are provided later in this section.

A *primary database* is a database that contains production data that must be protected against any kind of loss. A *standby database* is a copy of the primary database and can be brought online quickly to become the production database. When the standby database is *activated*, it becomes the production database and the older version of the production database is no longer valid. Once the standby is activated, production users can then connect to the new production database. Figure 5-6 shows a standby database.

**Database Configuration and Implementation**   It is recommended that the hardware at the standby site be configured in exactly the same manner as the hardware at the primary. (However, different configurations are possible as discussed later in the *Database Design* section.) The only notable difference between the file structures of the two databases should be that the standby database has a special controlfile. Archiving must be enabled before deploying the standby feature. From that point on, archiving must remain enabled so that the standby database can be made reasonably concurrent with the primary by applying archive log files.

**NOTE**
Although manual archiving can be used, it is *always* better to use automatic archiving.

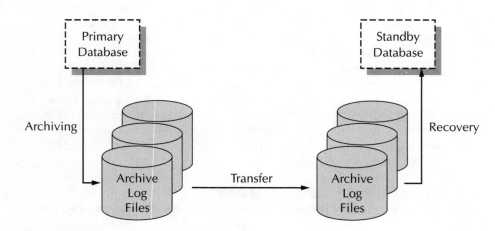

**FIGURE 5-6.**   *Standby Database*

Deployment of the standby database can be briefly outlined as follows:

**I.** Primary site

    **A.** backup initialization file(s) and database files

    **B.** create standby database control file

**II.** Transfer files to the standby site

**III.** Standby site

    **A.** restore files

    **B.** mount the standby database using the standby control file

    **C.** leave the standby database in recovery mode

After deployment, the standby database needs to be maintained to ensure that changes (archive log files) at the primary are *propagated* to the standby database. Maintenance should be automatic so that propagation occurs quickly to ensure that the standby database is reasonably *concurrent* with the primary. How closely the standby database concurs with the primary depends on how quickly changes are propagated to the standby database.

Maintenance can be briefly outlined as follows:

**I.** Primary site

    **A.** continue archiving to archive log files

**II.** Transfer "completed" archive log files to the standby site

**III.** Standby site

    **A.** apply archive log files to standby database

The redo in the archive log files from the primary is applied to the standby database. Thus, the standby database is in a constant state of recovery. This is the primary mechanism for propagating changes to the standby database.

**NOTE**
The archive stream must not be interrupted at the primary site. If this occurs, then the standby database must be rebuilt.

When a failure occurs, it is possible that one or more archive log files are not completed and are not available for recovery. In a standby database environment, if one or more complete archive log files are not transferred to the standby, then these archive log files are also not available for recovery. In other words, the standby database is only concurrent with the primary database to the last transaction in the last archive transferred and applied to the standby database. Transactions in archive log files that are not transferred are lost. This is a design issue that must be kept in mind when considering the transfer mechanism and the tuning of the archiving mechanism.

**Redo Generation**     You must ensure that transactions occurring at the primary are propagated to the standby database through the archive log files. It is important to note that Oracle's redo logging and transaction consistency mechanisms work independently. The purpose of redo is to record changes to the database, which can be replayed during recovery.

A few database operations deliberately do not generate redo. For example, it is unnecessary to generate redo for sort segments because the segments are transient in nature and changes to the segments are not needed during recovery. Furthermore, performance of some transactions can be improved by interfering with redo logging mechanism using the UNRECOVERABLE option. For details on the UNRECOVERABLE option, refer to *Oracle7 Server Administrator's Guide.* Obviously, it is not possible to replay changes at the standby database that are *not* stored in the redo. In almost all cases, performing recovery at the standby database will bring the database to a state that is concurrent with the primary. For a few specific cases, as noted below, changes at the primary are recovered in a slightly different manner at the standby database. Furthermore, in some cases, it may be desirable not to propagate changes to the standby database.

**Invalidating the Standby database**     If the archive stream is interrupted, then the standby database must be rebuilt. Any command issued at the primary that forces media recovery will interrupt the archive stream. Furthermore, media recovery is always necessary when the online redo logs are *cleared*. For more information on clearing logs, refer to *Oracle7 Server Administrator's Guide*. Thus, **avoid using commands that interrupt the archive stream**.

**Full Propagation**     Full propagation occurs when a transaction at the primary is completely propagated to the standby database. At the primary site, almost all transactions generate the necessary redo to completely propagate a transaction. However, there are some transactions that are not completely propagated or only partially propagated through the archive log files. These transactions *can* be propagated with some extra administration. Conversely, you may choose to *not* propagate some transactions.

**Normal Propagation**    Normal propagation occurs when a complete transaction is propagated to the standby database through the archive log files. Assuming no errors occur at the standby database, normal propagation results in full propagation. This is the general case and almost all transactions are propagated in this way.

For example, datafile size changes are normally propagated. If the standby database's hardware is configured the same as the primary's hardware, then any successful datafile size changes at the primary should normally result in full propagation. Standby database's hardware that is not configured the same as the primary's is more susceptible to failure. In particular, a propagated resize command attempting to increase the size of a datafile might fail for lack of disk space. Furthermore, normal propagation that needs to increase the size of an autoextend datafile might fail for lack of disk space. When a space availability problem is encountered, normal propagation can continue after freeing disk space. Normally, such problems can be avoided by ensuring that the standby database has available disk space.

*Tablespace Status*—Changing the status of a tablespace is normally propagated to the standby database.

*Offline or Read-Only Tablespaces*—The redo propagated to the standby database allows the recovery process to update the data dictionary and controlfile. Because no further redo is generated at the primary, no redo is subsequently propagated to the standby database. Thus, no action is needed at the standby site. If the standby database is activated then the status in the controlfile is updated to offline or read-only. Note that after an offline or read-only status change, the datafiles can be brought online or made read-write, but only if the datafiles are recovered.

**Avoiding Propagation**    Sometimes, it may be desirable to *not* propagate transactions from the primary database to the standby database. For example, the redo generated for a heavily updated tablespace that is not mission-critical may slow down propagation to an unacceptable level. In this case, you can OFFLINE DROP the desired tablespace at the standby database. However, if the affected tablespace is needed when the standby database is activated, then the tablespace must be brought online at activation time and may need recovery.

> **NOTE**
> Obviously, an **offline drop** at the standby database does not stop redo being generated at the primary. The redo is still stored in the archive log files that are transferred to the standby database, but it is ignored by the standby recovery process. Furthermore, even though the redo is not applied, the standby recovery process must still read past the redo records. Thus, the front-end of the propagation method will still affect the time to propagate, which may heavily influence propagation times for VLDBs. Conversely, the back-end of the propagation method, which would write to datafiles, does *not* occur. This could be a considerable time saving during propagation.

**Partial Propagation**   Partial propagation occurs when application of redo does not completely propagate the transaction at the standby database.

*New Datafiles*—The redo propagated to the standby database allows the recovery process to update the standby controlfile. If the file does not exist at the standby site, the recovery process will fail. Such a failure can be prevented by copying the datafile to the standby database before the redo is applied. However, this may not be practical when very large datafiles are added at the primary. In this case, it may be more efficient to issue the same datafile creation command at the standby database as was issued at the primary. Once the datafile is created, recovery can continue. When recovery successfully propagates the transaction, the data dictionary and file headers are updated.

**Non-Propagation**   Some actions at the primary interfere with redo generation and are not propagated through the archive log files to the standby database.

*Renaming Database Files*—Renaming a datafile or online log file at the primary does not generate redo, but only changes the file pointers in the primary control file. Thus, it is left to the discretion of the database administrator to move files to different locations without affecting the configuration of the standby database. (This is useful if files need to be migrated to larger disks.) To fully propagate *file name changes*, rename the files at the standby database using operating system commands and refresh the standby controlfile.

*Online Redo Log Configuration*—Adding or dropping online redo log files at the primary are reflected in the primary controlfile, but no redo is generated that will propagate the change to the standby controlfile. Thus, it is left to the discretion of the database administrator how the online redo log is configured at both sites. To fully propagate a changed online redo log configuration to the standby database, either refresh the standby controlfile or issue the same commands as issued at the primary. However, refreshing the standby controlfile is recommended because this guarantees that the configuration is the same for the primary and standby controlfiles.

**NOTE**
Reconfiguring the online redo log could invalidate the standby database.

*Temporary Tablespaces and Sort Segments*—Changes to sort segments do not generate redo because such changes are not needed during recovery. Thus, at the standby database, you do not need to offline drop temporary tablespaces used *only* for sort operations.

*Unrecoverable Commands*—The UNRECOVERABLE option can be used to improve performance for some database operations, such as table creation. For such operations, a small amount of redo is generated that marks affected objects as unrecoverable. Any redo generated *after* the unrecoverable command cannot be used. Although redo is still stored in the archive log files transferred to the standby database, the redo is not applied to affected objects since they are deemed inconsistent. Thus, changes to objects at the primary after an unrecoverable command are not propagated through the archive log files to the standby database.

# Choice, Design, and Planning

This section gives some insight into answering the following questions: Does the standby feature fulfill my business need? What design and planning issues must be resolved? What will the feature cost? Answering these questions may be apparent only after you read this section in its entirety.

### Standby Database—The Correct Choice?

What business need are you trying to fulfill? The answer should be that you are implementing a disaster recovery mechanism. Answering the following questions will decide whether the standby feature is a suitable choice for you.

Do you want to access data in the standby database while it is in standby mode? Unfortunately, this is not possible with the current implementation of the feature. (Once activated, the standby database cannot be re-used as a standby unless it is rebuilt.) This might be changed in the future releases of Oracle. If your transaction rates are within certain limits, then replication may suit your business needs. Alternatively, you might consider incremental exports and imports to another database.

How much data can you lose? If you cannot afford to lose *any* transactions in your production database, then the standby feature may not be acceptable. However, fault-tolerant systems that guarantee no data loss tend to be extremely expensive. If well implemented, switching over to a standby database may take only a few minutes. If the transactions lost during the switch-over period is an acceptable loss, then the standby feature may be a very suitable choice. Also, if you can transfer the online redo log or archive the outstanding redo, you will not lose any committed transactions.

The number of transactions lost during switch-over to a standby database depends on the number of transactions that were not propagated to the standby database; that is, committed transaction in the online redo log and in archive log files that are not transferred to the standby database. Generally, in a well-tuned standby environment, transaction loss can be minimized.

What quantity of data must be protected? If you want to protect only a small percentage of the data in your production database, then there may be a simpler and cheaper alternative.

Let us consider a data warehouse where one tablespace is critical. The tablespace contains calculated summary information that cannot be lost. This summary information is garnered from very large tables in other tablespaces, which are not critical because they can be easily rebuilt. The large tables are heavily updated and generate very large quantities of redo. In this case, the time to propagate the mission critical tablespace to a standby database is adversely affected by the non-critical tablespaces. However, if the large tablespaces do not need to be propagated, then use of the unrecoverable option during loading will have a considerable impact on reducing propagation time.

MTTR—What is the desired recovery time? For a standby environment, mean time to recover (*MTTR*) is calculated as follows:

```
MTTR = Detection + Apply Remaining Redo + Standby Activation + Switch Users
```

Generally, the major influence on MTTR is the time needed to apply outstanding archive log files to the standby database. This depends on the number and size of the archive log files, which can be tuned. Activating the standby database and switching users over to the standby database should be accomplishable within minutes. Switch-over times to a standby of a few minutes are often possible. Conversely, a large MTTR might be suitable. If the standby database is kept a couple of hours behind the primary, then it is possible to recover to a point in time before a logical corruption. For example, a logical corruption would occur if a table was loaded with obsolete data.

What will it cost? The largest direct cost will be the purchase of any new hardware. It is recommended that the standby site hardware duplicates the primary site as much as possible. Other possible direct costs are: hiring an administrator, upgrading software or operating systems, and so on. One potential indirect cost might be performance on the primary database. (However, tuning the archiving mechanism on the primary database for the standby feature may actually increase performance on the primary database). Reducing risk of downtime by implementing several standby databases is sensible, but is obviously more expensive.

## Design and Planning Issues
In this subsection, design and planning issues are briefly discussed.

### Software Upgrades
You must have Oracle7 release 7.3 installed to use the standby database feature. If an upgrade is required, then it is necessary to consider the effect on your production database. You may need to upgrade your application software or your operating system. After such upgrades, system re-tuning is often required.

### Hardware and Oracle Version
The primary and standby sites *must* use the same version of Oracle 7.3 for a specific operating system and platform. Preferably,

the primary and standby databases should reside on systems at separate locations some distance apart and do not share resources such as the same power source, hard disks, etc. It is recommended that hardware configurations are exactly the same at the primary and standby sites. If the hardware is configured the same, then this ensures that on activation of the standby database, the same resources are available and that performance will be the same. Likewise, disk configurations and disk space usage should be the same at both sites to ensure that adding datafiles or increasing datafile sizes at the primary also succeed at the standby database. Administration of both sites is also simplified. Although not recommended, it is possible to have different hardware configurations. In which case, you must ensure that the standby database has sufficient disk space and that the standby database's initialization file is adequately tuned to reflect the available system resources.

**Lost Transactions and MTTR**     How many transactions can be lost during the MTTR? Begin by determining the maximum number of transactions that occur in a period of time and the minimum time for an archive log file to fill. (These numbers must be determined during the busiest periods of the business day and when ARCH does not fall behind LGWR.) You can then calculate an approximate maximum number of transactions that can be propagated in an archive. If only one archive is not successfully transferred at the time of a failure, then the potential number of transactions lost will not exceed twice the calculated maximum in an archive. (This assumes that the number of lost transactions in the online redo log will not exceed the maximum calculated for an archive.) Now time how long it takes to transfer and apply an archive (filled during the busy period) to the standby database. Using the formula on the previous page, you can determine the MTTR. At this point, you have MTTR and transaction loss metrics for the configuration of the online redo log at the primary. If the metrics are too high, then you must review your archiving strategy and tune the primary or standby databases, possibly both.

**Tuning**     Once release 7.3 is available on your system, then deployment and maintenance of the standby feature can be made relatively straightforward. Tuning for the standby feature may be simple or complex. On the primary, the database is tuned to ensure that archiving does not interfere with normal operations. On the standby database, you might tune the initialization file to optimize the application of archive log files to reduce the MTTR. (When the standby database is activated you would use another initialization file that is tuned to the standby hardware configuration.)

A tuning goal for the primary site is to avoid ARCH falling behind LGWR, which is normally achievable. In a standby environment, there is usually a secondary goal; that is, to get the archive log files transferred and applied to the standby database as quickly as possible. These tuning goals may conflict. For example, small archive log files are ideal for speedy propagation, but this requires small online redo logs. If there are too few online redo logs, then ARCH will fall behind LGWR. Furthermore, creating small archive files is unrealistic in some processing environments; in particular, high volume OLTP environments.

Tuning may be relatively straightforward. For example, ensuring that the online redo log and archive log files are on their own disks separate from other database files. As another example, you might consider not propagating some tablespace to improve performance. (It is a good practice to store similar database objects in their own tablespace and put the corresponding datafiles on their own disks to optimize I/O performance.)

**Transfer Mechanism**     A fast interconnect between the primary and standby database will reduce the MTTR. Other network traffic must not interfere with the transfer of archive log files. Archive log files should be transferred and applied to the standby database as soon as possible. However, you must ensure that only completely finished archive log files are transferred.

**Switching Users to the Standby Database**     You must choose a mechanism for users to switch over from the primary to the standby database. The most effective method requires that software detect a failure and choose a different network route to the standby database. The software could reside in the user application, which may need re-coding.

**Standby Database Automation**     The deployment and maintenance of the standby feature should be automated as much as possible. When a failure occurs, the standby database becomes the new primary. At this point, you can switch back to the original primary or use it as a standby database. If you decide to maintain the original primary site as the standby database, the transfer and application of archive log files should be automatic. Furthermore, any partially propagated or non-propagated changes that must be fully propagated on a regular basis should be automated. Lastly, error detection should be automated.

**Error Detection**     You must implement mechanisms to automatically detect failures. First, a mechanism must initiate switch-over to the standby database when the primary site fails. Second, a mechanism must detect problems at the primary site affecting the standby feature; in particular, the archiving mechanism. Third, a mechanism must detect failures in the transfer mechanism. And fourth, a mechanism must detect failures in full propagation at the standby database.

Most of the above detection mechanisms can be accomplished by writing scripts that run at regular intervals at both the primary and standby database sites. For example, a script run at the standby database could ping the primary to detect a network failure and thus a potential break in the transfer mechanism. If the ping does not succeed, but the network is not malfunctioning, then this indicates that there may be a failure at the primary. At which point, a process could use a dial-out modem to page the database administrator.

A site must not be entirely responsible for detecting its own failures. Rather, *both* sites must perform bi-directional error detection. For example, the same script ran at both sites can *grep* for recovery errors in the standby database **alert log**. If errors are detected, then the error log will be available at both sites, even if one of the sites becomes unavailable.

**Backups and Standby Rebuilds**    Although the standby feature is a robust disaster recovery mechanism, backups are still necessary. The standby site or sites are also susceptible to failure! Thus, you must prepare for the eventuality of performing media recovery at the primary using backups of the database files, including the archive logs. However, there is an additional benefit. The backups can be used to rebuild the standby database during strategically convenient periods.

**Training and Preventing Problems**    Application developers must be made aware of issues that will affect the standby database. For example, developers must be cautioned against usage of the unrecoverable option to modify tables that are needed after the standby database is activated.

# Preparation

This section reviews preparations before deploying the standby feature. We assume that we are using a UNIX operating system.

## Upgrading, Testing, and Automation

It is good practice to test upgrades before upgrading in a production environment. The introduction of a new system to host the standby database provides a useful opportunity to perform thorough testing before implementing the standby feature. You can experiment with a new operating system and version of Oracle7 to ensure that your production system will run properly on the new system. In particular, you should test the effects of setting COMPATIBILITY to 7.3 and the use of new 7.3 features. It is also the time to determine and test any changes in client software needed to switch over to standby database.

Scripts for automating deployment, propagation, problem prevention, and error detection must also be written and tested. You may find the following tips useful.

*Problem prevention*—at the primary, modify the global *.login* script to halt execution of batch scripts that contain SQL commands that will interfere with the standby mechanism. The *.login* script will *grep* for commands that are listed later in this chapter, in Table 5-7. At the standby database, queue a *cron* job that regularly checks that the amount of disk space available for datafiles matches the space available at the primary. (This is particularly useful when the configurations for the primary and standby databases are different.) The same cron job can also check for unexpected changes in the datafile directory at the primary.

*Error detection*—cron jobs to detect errors must run at both sites. See "Error Detection" in the previous section. Scripts to detect errors at the primary or standby database can grep for errors in the alert logs and trace files. A grep for errors in the range ORA-250 to ORA-299 will detect archiving errors, ORA-300 to 369 will detect some redo log errors, and so on. Refer to the *Oracle7 Server Message Manual* for other appropriate ranges. If possible, check the online message file, which will be more up to date and include platform specific messages.

### Database Design

Make any necessary changes to the database layout during the testing period. The goal is to avoid making unnecessary physical structural changes after the standby feature is implemented. Thus, now is the time to perform any re-organization or defragmentation tasks. In particular, now is the time to make any controlfile changes; for example, if you anticipate that MAXDATAFILES may need to be increased in the near future.

It is good practice to place similar objects in the same tablespace. This facilitates administration and performance improvements. For example, sorts using a temporary tablespace placed on its own set of disks on one disk controller will not cause I/O contention with full table scans in another tablespace.

If you choose to *not* propagate some objects, then place these objects in a separate tablespace that will be offline dropped at the standby database. Candidates for non-propagation are: tablespaces that are not needed after activation, tablespaces that can be rebuilt easily and quickly with minimal effect on the MTTR when the standby database is activated, and, tablespaces not immediately needed at activation that can be rebuilt some time thereafter.

### Timing Metrics, Tuning Archiving, and Deployment Time

When testing the standby feature, keep timing metrics for major tasks. These metrics are needed to determine the MTTR and potential transaction loss. See *Lost Transactions and MTTR* in previous section. If these numbers are unacceptable, you can tune archiving at the standby site before introducing major archiving changes at the primary. See *Tuning* in previous section.

When deploying the standby feature, a window of opportunity is needed to perform backups at the primary. Here again, timing metrics are useful. The larger the production database, the more critical are the metrics, especially if online backups are used.

**NOTE:**
For large databases, caution must be taken when performing online backups because extra redo is generated for the backup. This will affect the archiving rate and may cause ARCH to fall behind LGWR. It may be necessary to online backup a few or only one tablespace at a time.

The backup and restore phases of deployment consume most of the time. Deployment time can be roughly calculated as follows:

```
deployment = backup + archive current logs + file transfer + restore +
archive application
```

It may be possible to dramatically reduce deployment time by parallelizing the backup, transfer, and restore. For example, each datafile might be copied, transferred, and restored by a single process.

**Example Metrics**    Timings for your environment will be dependent on hardware limitations and database size. However, it is useful at this point to have some numbers as a frame of reference. The following metrics are typical for Sequents using a FDDI network: approximately three hours for a complete standby database rebuild of a 20 GB database; *ftp* transfer rate at approximately 3.5 MB per second; approximately 300 KB per second when archiving up to current log. Lastly, for a 10 drive tape array, a backup rate of 20 GB per hour. These metrics are provided by Oracle Worldwide Support. Please note that these metrics will change based on the platform and hardware you use.

## Initialization Parameters
The standby and primary sites must have their own unique initialization files. If the two sites are configured the same, then the only difference is that CONTROL_FILE will point to the standby controlfile. See Table 5-5 for details.

## Standby Site Specifics
Ensure that the production database will run at the standby site. This is especially important if different configurations are used for the standby and primary databases. Also check that environment variables are correctly set; in particular, ORACLE_HOME, ORACLE_SID, and any other variable specified in your installation guide.

Ensure that the initialization parameters are set correctly for the standby site. (See Table 5-5). If the two sites have different hardware configurations, then you

| Initialization Parameter | Primary Site Value | Standby Site Value |
| --- | --- | --- |
| COMPATIBLE | Must be 7.3 or higher. | Identical to primary value. |
| COMPATIBLE_NO _RECOVERY | Must default to COMPATIBLE. | Identical to primary value. |
| CONTROL_FILE | Primary control file path and name. | Standby control file path and name. |
| DB_BLOCK_SIZE DB_FILES DB_NAME | Same as at database creation time. | Identical to primary value. |
| %%%_DUMP_DEST LOG_ARCHIVE_DEST ORACLE_TRACE _%%%_PATH | As needed | Must be the same as at primary, if the same configurations are used at both sites. However, these parameters may be different. |
| DB_FILE_STANDBY _NAME_CONVERT LOG_FILE_STANDBY _NAME_CONVERT | Not needed—however, if these values are set at the standby database, then it is a good policy to have these parameters identical to the standby values. | Only use these parameters if the directory paths to datafiles or online redo logs are different at both sites. Values are used to convert primary path names to standby path names. |

**TABLE 5-5.** *Initialization Parameters for Primary and Standby Databases*

must ensure that parameters are tuned for the standby configuration. If standby directory paths are different than at the primary, then the standby paths must be reflected in the standby controlfile and initialization file.

Ensure that the database directory paths for the standby database are valid and have sufficient disk space.

## Primary Site Specifics
Ensure that initialization parameters are set correctly for the primary site as discussed earlier in this section. In particular, COMPATIBLE must be set to 7.3. Check that directory paths and file names are correctly set in the parameters. Ensure that automatic archiving is working correctly. Instigate measures to prevent untimely alterations to the production database during deployment, such as

revoking privileges from users that can add datafiles. Also, start up cron jobs to detect if untoward changes occur to the database during deployment. (These scripts should have been written during the testing period, as described earlier in this section in *Upgrading, Testing, and Automation*). Finally, ensure that the control file is consistent.

# Deployment

This section describes how to deploy the standby database feature. Table 5-6 shows the steps involved in deploying the standby feature. The examples show real commands, but may not be complete. References to **cron** jobs assume that scripts to be queued are already available. Notes and scripting information is provided in the sections following the table.

### Deployment Notes and Scripting
This section provides useful information for steps listed in the previous section.

| | **Example Commands and Comments** |
|---|---|
| **Primary Site**<br>Check automatic archiving | `ARCHIVE LOG LIST`<br>Check ARCH is running and initialization parameter LOG_ARCHIVE_START=TRUE.<br>`SELECT STATUS FROM V$LOGFILE`<br>`   WHERE STATUS IS NOT NULL;`<br>No rows should be returned. INVALID or STALE indicates problems that need to be resolved before continuing. (DELETED indicates a log file is no longer used.) |
| Start change detection | Queue cron job that looks for changes to the physical structure of the database. |
| Check tablespaces | `SELECT TABLESPACE_NAME, STATUS FROM DBA_TABLESPACES;`<br>Ensure that desired tablespaces are online or read-only. |

**TABLE 5-6.** *Deploying the Standby Database Feature*

| | **Example Commands and Comments** |
|---|---|
| Backup database<br><br>(Note 1, Note 2) | For offline backup:<br>`svrmgrl <<EOF`<br>`connect internal`<br>`shutdown immediate`<br>`exit`<br>`EOF`<br>`cp $ORACLE_HOME/dbs/*.dbf $BACKUP` |
| Archive to current online log | `ALTER SYSTEM ARCHIVE LOG CURRENT;` |
| Create standby controlfile | `ALTER DATABASE CREATE STANDBY`<br>`CONTROLFILE AS 'ctlstby.ora';` |
| **Transfer files to standby site**<br>(Note 2) | Files from *offline* backup, standby controlfile, and archive log files:<br>`foreach FILE ('ls -1 $BACKUP')`<br>`  dd if=$FILE | resh $STDBYSITE`<br>`of=\$BACKUP/$FILE`<br>`end`<br>`dd if=ctlstby.ora | resh $STDBYSITE`<br>`of=\$BACKUP`<br>`foreach FILE ('ls -1`<br>`$LOG_ARCHIVE_DEST')`<br>`  dd if=$FILE | resh $STDBYSITE`<br>`of=\$LOG_ARCHIVE_DEST/$FILE`<br>`end` |
| **Standby Site**<br>Check environment | `echo $ORACLE_HOME $ORACLE_SID`<br>`du $ORACLE_HOME/dbs`<br>`Check Oracle environment and disk`<br>`space availability.`<br>`resh $PRIMARYSITE cat`<br>`\$ORACLE_HOME/dbs/init.ora \`<br>`| comm -3`<br>`$ORACLE_HOME/dbs/initstby.ora`<br>If both sites are configured the same, then the above comparison of initialization files should only show that the CONTROLFILE parameters are different. |

**TABLE 5-6.** *Deploying the Standby Database Feature (continued)*

**Example Commands and Comments**

| | |
|---|---|
| Restore backups[(Note 2)] | `cp $BACKUP/*.dbf $ORACLE_HOME/dbs` Archive log files are already in correct directory from transfer. |
| Start standby database | `svrmgrl` `connect internal` `startup nomount pfile=$ORACLE_HOME/` `dbs/initstby.ora` |
| Take unwanted tablespaces offline | `ALTER TABLESPACE unwanted OFFLINE DROP;` |
| Start recovery | `RECOVER STANDBY DATABASE;` |
| Start failure detection | Queue cron job to ping primary. (This step could be in auto propagation scripts.) |
| Start automatic propagation | Queue cron job to find and transfer archive log files from primary to standby database. |

**Both Sites**

| | |
|---|---|
| Start error detection | Queue cron jobs to detect errors at either site. |

Note 1:  Archive log files must also be backed up to ensure a complete database backup is available for recover.

Note 2: The "backup", "transfer", and "restore" steps shown in the above table could be one action; that is, copying the files directly to the standby database. However, backups are required at the primary.

**TABLE 5-6.**  *Deploying the Standby Database Feature* (continued)

**Backups**    UNIX commands *cpio, ufsdump, dd, tar*, and so on, can be used for copying file system datafiles. For raw partition datafiles, use the *dd* command. See Chapter 3 for various backup commands in different operating systems.

**Offline Backups**    Before performing an offline backup, make sure that the database is shut down cleanly by examining the alert file. A SHUTDOWN ABORT or shutdown due to a crash is not acceptable. In this case, you must restart and shutdown the database until you get a clean shutdown. However, a **SHUTDOWN IMMEDIATE** is acceptable.

When performing offline backups for standby database deployment, ensure that you backup all datafiles, control files, and initialization files. You can use the backup to rebuild the standby database or recover the primary if the standby becomes unavailable.

**Online Backups**    Online backups generate extra redo. For large databases, performing online backups for all tablespaces may not be acceptable because of the increased burden on ARCH. In this case, online backups should only be performed for a few or only one tablespace at a time. The following script creates and executes another script that performs online backups of one tablespace at a time. The $BACKUP variable must be defined globally, probably in .login or .cshrc. Note that to conserve disk space, compress is used to create the backup file, which must be reversed when the files are restored at the standby database.

```
sqlplus <<EOD
connect system/manager
set echo off
set termout off
set feedback off
set heading off
spool backup.sh

SELECT
'svrmgrl <<EOS'||CHR(10)||
'connect internal'||chr(10)||
'ALTER TABLESPACE '||TABLESPACE_NAME||' BEGIN BACKUP;'||CHR(10)||
'EXIT'||CHR(10)||
'EOS'||CHR(10)||
'compress <'||FILE_NAME||' \$BACKUP'||CHR(10)||
'svrmgrl <<EOS'||CHR(10)||
'connect internal'||CHR(10)||
'ALTER TABLESPACE '||TABLESPACE_NAME||' END BACKUP;'
||CHR(10)||'EXIT'||CHR(10)||
'EOS'||CHR(10)
FROM DBA_DATA_FILES WHERE STATUS = 'AVAILABLE';

spool off
EOD
chmod u+x backup.sh
backup.sh
```

**Archive up to Current Online Log**    The ALTER SYSTEM ARCHIVE LOG CURRENT command is used to ensure that all redo is archived. This forces a log switch (on all threads in a parallel server environment). The archive log files contain all redo at an SCN existing after the datafiles were backed up. This guarantees that the standby recovery process can successfully apply the archive log files against the backed up datafiles.

**Transfer Files to Standby Database**    Ensure that all files are transferred to the standby database. This includes: backup datafiles, backup archive log files, standby control file. The initialization file for the primary should not be copied because the standby database has its own initialization file. When raw partitions are used, ensure that the raw files end up in the correct location. Preferably, the locations are named the same, which simplifies administration.

When transferring to the standby database, ensure that the files are valid. While transferring offline datafiles or archive log files to the standby database, ensure that the files are not still being accessed by the database. The following script can be used as an outline for scripts performing such checks. Note that the following script performs the backup, transfer, and restore of the primary's archive log files.

```
foreach FILE ($LOG_ARCHIVE_DEST/arch1_*.dbf)


    echo "Backing up archive: $FILE"

    if (! -F $FILE) then
        echo "Error: `$FILE' is not a regular file."
        exit
    end

    cp $FILE $BACKUP
    if ($status == 1) then
        echo "Error: backup failed on archive `$FILE'"
        exit
    end

    cmp -s $FILE $BACKUP/$FILE
    if ($status == 1) then
        echo "Error: Oracle still using archive `$FILE'"
        rm $BACKUP/$FILE
        exit
    end
```

```
dd if=$FILE | resh $STDBYSITE of=\$BACKUP/$FILE
if ($status == 1) then
      echo "Error: failed to transfer archive `$FILE`"
      exit
end

resh $STDBYSITE cp \$BACKUP/$FILE \$ORACLE_HOME/dbs
if ($status == 1) then
      echo "Error: restore failed at standby site for archive `$FILE`"
      exit
end
end
```

# Maintenance

This section describes how to maintain the standby feature after deployment. Maintenance of the standby database ensures that changes made to the primary are fully propagated to the standby database. Whenever possible, these tasks should be automated with scripts that run at regular intervals. Most changes to the primary are propagated using normal propagation, which is fairly easy to automate. See *Transfer and Applying Archive Log Files* later in this section. However, special attention is needed if partially propagated and non-propagated changes must be fully propagated. Table 5-7 indicates whether a command is normally propagated or requires extra administrative efforts to be fully propagated.

### Maintenance Notes and Scripting
This section provides some useful information for maintaining standby databases.

**Upgrades**    If it is your intention to upgrade either the operating system or the Oracle software, you must ensure that the upgrades occur at both the primary and standby databases. The safest route is to shutdown both databases, upgrade, and rebuild the standby database.

**Logical Transaction Grouping**    During normal operations there may be groups of transactions that are critical, such that it is advantageous if these transactions are propagated more quickly than usual to the standby database. To do so, after the transactions are committed, issue the **ALTER SYSTEM ARCHIVE LOG CURRENT** command. This forces a log switch (on all threads in a parallel server environment), such that all redo up to an SCN higher than the last commit in the transaction group is written out to completed archive log files. The completed archive log files can then be transferred and applied at the standby database.

| Command Issued at Primary Site | Effect at Standby Site |
|---|---|
| `sqlldr direct=false` (RECOVERABLE) | Propagated. |
| `sqlldr direct=false` (UNRECOVERABLE) | NOT PROPAGATED. If the affected objects are needed after activation, then, at the standby database, either: rebuild the standby, backup up the affected datafiles at the primary and restore at the standby database. If the affected objects are not needed, then ensure that the tables exist in a tablespace that can be offline dropped at the standby database. |
| ALLOCATE | Not applicable—session based command. |
| ALTER CLUSTER | Propogated. |
| ALTER DATABASE | |
|    ACTIVATE STANDBY DATABASE | Not applicable—rejected at primary. |
|    ADD LOGFILE<br>   ADD LOGFILE MEMBER | NOT PROPOGATED. If the online redo log configuration should be the same as at the primary, then refresh the standby controlfile. |
|    ARCHIVELOG | No effect. |
|    BACKUP CONTROLFILE | No effect. |
|    BACKUP CONTROLFILE TO TRACE | No effect—unless the SQL commands in the trace file are used to re-create the primary database, which then *INVALIDATES STANDBY* if online redo logs are cleared. |
|    CONVERT | *INVALIDATES STANDBY*—must rebuild. |
|    CLEAR LOGFILE | *INVALIDATES STANDBY*—must rebuild. |

**TABLE 5-7.**   *Command Propagation from Primary to Standby Database*

| Command Issued at Primary Site | Effect at Standby Site |
|---|---|
| `CREATE DATAFILE` | Partial propagation. Recovery process at standby database will fail during application of archive if datafiles do not already exist. Datafiles should be created in advance at the standby database to prevent automatic recovery from failing. However, if the recovery process fails, then the problem can be fixed creating the datafile(s) and restarting recovery. |
| `CREATE STANDBY CONTROLFILE` | No effect—new standby control file should be used to refresh control file at standby site. |
| `DATAFILE AUTOEXTEND` | Propagated—future propagation will **FAIL** if disk space is not available. |
| `DATAFILE END BACKUP` | Propagated—no action needed. |
| `DATAFILE OFFLINE` | Propagated—no action needed because no further redo is generated at the primary for an offline datafile. |
| `DATAFILE ONLINE` | Propagated—only possible if complete media recovery of affected tablespace at primary was successful *before* archive log files are transferred to the standby database. |
| `DATAFILE RESIZE` | Propagated—command will **FAIL** if disk space available for increase in datafile size is insufficient. |
| `DISABLE THREAD` `ENABLE THREAD` | NOT PROPAGATED. (Parallel Server Option only.) |
| `DROP LOGFILE GROUP` `DROP LOGFILE MEMBER` | NOT PROPAGATED. If the online redo log configuration should be the same as at the primary, then refresh the standby controlfile. |
| `MOUNT` | No effect. |

**TABLE 5-7.** *Command Propagation from Primary to Standby Database* (continued)

| Command Issued at Primary Site | Effect at Standby Site |
|---|---|
| `MOUNT STANDBY DATABASE` | Not applicable—rejected at primary. |
| `NOARCHIVELOG` | *INVALIDATES STANDBY*—must rebuild because the archive stream is interrupted. |
| `OPEN RESETLOGS` | *INVALIDATES STANDBY*—must rebuild. |
| `OPEN NORESETLOGS` | No effect. |
| `RECOVER`<br>　`AUTOMATIC`<br>　`DATAFILE`<br>　`LOGFILE`<br>　`TABLESPACE`<br>　`UNTIL CANCEL`<br>　`UNTIL TIME`<br>　`UNTIL CHANGE`<br>　`USING BACKUP CONTROLFILE` | *INVALIDATES STANDBY* if incomplete or media recovery is performed, which requires the standby database to be rebuilt.<br>However, if you can perform complete recovery without resetting the logs, then the standby database is *not* invalidated. |
| `RENAME FILE` | NOT PROPAGATED—the standby controlfile is not updated.<br>If the redo log configuration at the standby database is different than at the primary, then no action is needed. Else, rename as for datafiles.<br>Datafiles at standby database must be renamed at the operating system level and then at the database level; that is, repeat the commands issued at the primary. |
| `RENAME GLOBAL_NAME` | NOT PROPAGATED—refresh controlfile. |
| `RESET COMPATIBILITY` | *INVALIDATES STANDBY*—must rebuild. |
| `SET` | Propagated. |
| `ALTER FUNCTION`<br>`ALTER INDEX` | Propagated. |
| `ALTER INDEX REBUILD RECOVERABLE` | Propagated. |
| `ALTER INDEX REBUILD UNRECOVERABLE` | NOT PROPAGATED. See `sqlldr` `unrecoverable` |

**TABLE 5-7.** *Command Propagation from Primary to Standby Database* (continued)

| Command Issued at Primary Site | Effect at Standby Site |
|---|---|
| `ALTER PACKAGE`<br>`PROCEDURE`<br>`PROFILE`<br>`RESOURCE COST`<br>`ROLE`<br>`ROLLBACK SEGMENT`<br>`SEQUENCE` | Propagated. |
| `ALTER SESSION` | Not applicable—session based command. |
| `ALTER SNAPSHOT`<br>`SNAPSHOT LOG` | Propagated. |
| `ALTER SYSTEM`<br>`ARCHIVE LOG SEQUENCE`<br>`ARCHIVE LOG CHANGE`<br>`ARCHIVE LOG CURRENT`<br>`ARCHIVE LOG LOGFILE`<br>`ARCHIVE LOG NEXT`<br>`ARCHIVE LOG ALL`<br>`ARCHIVE LOG START`<br>`ARCHIVE LOG STOP` | No effect. |
|  | *INVALIDATES STANDBY*—if archive stream is interrupted. In which case, you must rebuild standby database. However, if this is a temporary halt in archiving, then it has *no effect*. |
| `SWITCH LOG` | No effect. |
| `ALTER TABLE` | Propagated. |
| `ALTER TABLESPACE`<br>`ADD DATAFILE` | Partial propagation—treated the same as `ALTER DATABASE CREATE DATAFILE`. |
| `BEGIN BACKUP` | May increase number of archive log files because extra redo is generated during the online backup.<br>Ensure that the online backup completes at primary. |

**TABLE 5-7.** *Command Propagation from Primary to Standby Database (continued)*

| Command Issued at Primary Site | Effect at Standby Site |
|---|---|
| **END BACKUP** | Backed up primary tablespace can be used to refresh tablespace at standby database. |
| **COALESCE** | Propagated. |
| **DEFAULT STORAGE** | Propagated. |
| **RENAME DATAFILE** | NOT PROPAGATED—treated the same as ALTER DATABASE RENAME FILE |
| **OFFLINE** | Propagated—no action needed. See ALTER DATABASE DATAFILE OFFLINE |
| **ONLINE** | Propagated—treated the same as ALTER DATABASE DATAFILE ONLINE |
| **PERMANENT** | Propagated. |
| **READ ONLY** | Indirect propagation—treated the same as ALTER TABLESPACE OFFLINE NORMAL |
| **READ WRITE** | Propagated—no action needed. See ALTER DATABASE DATAFILE ONLINE NORMAL |
| **TEMPORARY** | Propagated. |
| **ALTER TRIGGER** | Propagated. |
| **USER** | |
| **VIEW** | |
| **ANALYZE** | Propagated. |
| **AUDIT** | |
| **COMMIT** | |
| **CREATE CLUSTER** | |

**TABLE 5-7.** *Command Propagation from Primary to Standby Database* (continued)

| Command Issued at Primary Site | Effect at Standby Site |
|---|---|
| `CREATE CONTROLFILE` | *INVALIDATES STANDBY*—if the archive stream is interrupted, in which case, rebuild standby database.<br>However, if you are performing complete recovery without resetting the online redo logs, then the standby database is not invalidated. For example, if all primary controlfiles are lost but all other files are available, then the controlfile can be created with `NORESETLOGS`.<br>Furthermore, if you create a control file to increase maximum values, such as MAXDATAFILES and do not reset the redo logs, then you should refresh the standby controlfile if the change must be propagated. |
| `CREATE DATABASE` | NOT PROPAGATED because primary database destroyed, which *INVALIDATES STANDBY*. If command was not intended at primary, then switch over to standby database. |
| `CREATE DATABASE`<br>     `LINK`<br>     `FUNCTION` | Propagated. |
| `CREATE INDEX` | Propagated. |
| `CREATE INDEX`<br>  `REBUILD RECOVERABLE` | Propagated. |
| `CREATE INDEX`<br>  `REBUILD UNRECOVERABLE` | NOT PROPAGATED. See `sqlldr unrecoverable` |

**TABLE 5-7.**  *Command Propagation from Primary to Standby Database* (continued)

| Command Issued at Primary Site | Effect at Standby Site |
|---|---|
| `CREATE PACKAGE`<br>`       PACKAGE BODY`<br>`       PROCEDURE`<br>`       PROFILE`<br>`       ROLE`<br>`       ROLLBACK SEGMENT`<br>`       SCHEMA`<br>`       SEQUENCE`<br>`       SNAPSHOT`<br>`       SNAPSHOT LOG`<br>`       SYNONYM` | Propagated. |
| `CREATE TABLE   RECOVERABLE` | Propagated. |
| `CREATE TABLE   UNRECOVERABLE` | NOT PROPAGATED. See `sqlldr`<br>`unrecoverable` |
| `CREATE TABLESPACE` | Partial propagation—treated the same as `ALTER TABLESPACE ADD DATAFILE` |
| `CREATE TRIGGER`<br>`       USER`<br>`       VIEW` | Propagated. |
| `DELETE`<br>`DROP INDEX`<br>`DROP PACKAGE`<br>`     PROCEDURE`<br>`     PROFILE`<br>`     ROLE`<br>`     ROLLBACK SEGMENT`<br>`     SEQUENCE`<br>`     SNAPSHOT`<br>`     SNAPSHOT LOG`<br>`     SYNONYM`<br>`DROP TABLE`<br>`     TABLESPACE` | Propagated. |

**TABLE 5-7.** *Command Propagation from Primary to Standby Database* (continued)

| Command Issued at Primary Site | Effect at Standby Site |
|---|---|
| `DROP TRIGGER`<br>`     USER`<br>`     VIEW`<br>`EXPLAIN PLAN`<br>`GRANT`<br>`INSERT`<br>`LOCK TABLE`<br>`NOAUDIT`<br>`RENAME`<br>`REVOKE`<br>`ROLLBACK`<br>`SAVEPOINT`<br>`SELECT`<br>`SET ROLE`<br>`SET TRANSACTION`<br>`TRUNCATE`<br>`UPDATE` | Propagated. |

**TABLE 5-7.**    *Command Propagation from Primary to Standby Database* (continued)

**Transferring and Applying Archive Log Files**    In this section, code and script outlines are provided that can be used to automatically transfer and apply the archive log files to the standby database. The idea is to have a stored procedure running every few minutes at the primary, which writes out a file identifying the latest archive completed. On the standby database, a job runs that reads the identifier and if the identifier is greater than the last archive applied at the standby database, then the job transfers the newest archive log files and applies them at the standby database. The examples do not contain error checking and are not intended to be complete, but merely to provide you with a basis to write your own code.

In the code and scripts it is assumed that the same configuration is used at the primary and standby sites, thus:

**I.** directory paths used are the same at both sites

   **A.** `LOG_ARCHIVE_FORMAT = arch%S.log`

**II.** the operating system default for %S produces four characters; e.g. arch0234.log

**III.** the following initialization parameters are the same at both sites

    **A.** `LOG_ARCHIVE_FORMAT`

    **B.** `LOG_ARCHIVE_DEST`

    **C.** `UTIL_FILE_DIR`

**IV.** the following environment variables are the same at primary and standby sites

    **A.** `LOG_ARCHIVE_DEST`

At the primary, the following procedure is queued to run every three minutes. This procedure writes out a file with information identifying the latest archive created. The identifying information is the latest archive sequence number. Archive sequence numbers are used in the %S part of the archive filename.

```
CREATE OR REPLACE PROCEDURE Note_Latest_Archive AS
   LatestSeqNum INT;
   fno INT;
BEGIN
   SELECT MAX(SEQUENCE#) INTO LatestSeqNum FROM V$LOG
     WHERE ARCHIVED = 'YES';
   fno :=
   UTL_FILE.FOPEN('$LOG_ARCH_DEST', 'latest.arc', 'W');
   UTL_FILE.PUTLINE(fno, LatestSeqNum);
   UTL_FILE.FCLOSE(fno);
END;
```

**NOTE**
Archive sequence numbers do not necessarily represent the order in which archive log files are completed or applied. However, the method used in these samples works because all archive log files are eventually transferred.

The following anonymous block can be issued in SQL*Plus at the primary to put the above procedure in the database queue. The job then executes every three minutes.

```
VARIABLE jobno INT;
BEGIN
   DBMS_JOB.SUBMIT(:jobno,'note_latest_archive',SYSDATE,'SYSDATE + 1/480');
END;
```

At the standby site, the following script runs continuously. The script checks whether the latest archive log files at the primary site are newer than the last archive log file applied at the standby database. If so, then the newest archive log files are transferred from the primary to the standby database and applied. Thereafter, the script waits three minutes and repeats the cycle.

```
while (1)
  set LastApplied = `ls -1 $LOG_ARCHIVE_DEST | tail -1`
  @ LastApplied    = `basename $LastApplied:r | cut -c7-10`
  @ NextToApply    = `expr $LastApplied + 1 `
  @ NewestArchive = `resh $PRIMARYSITE cat $LOG_ARCHIVE_DEST/latest.arc`

  if ( $NextToApply < $NewestArchive ) then

    foreach Archive (`echo $NextToApply $NewestArchive | \
        awk '{for(i=$1;i<=$2;i++) {printf("arch%04.log\n",i)} }' )

      resh $PRIMARYSITE dd if=$LOG_ARCHIVE_DEST/$Archive | \
          resh dd of=$LOG_ARCHIVE/$Archive

      svrmgrl <<EOF
      connect internal
      recover standby database until cancel
      auto
      cancel
      EOF
    end
  end
  sleep 180
end
```

**NOTE**
The above script only takes normal propagation into account. You will need to modify the above script to fully propagate other changes. For example, you could add code to check for new datafiles added at the primary, and if found, then copy the datafiles to the standby database before the recovery process starts. This prevents the recovery process from failing when a new datafile is not found. However, this is impractical if very large datafiles are added at the primary. Thus, you should add small datafiles and resize the datafiles thereafter.

**Initialization Parameters**     If parameter values are changed in the initialization file at the primary, then ensure that corresponding changes are made to the standby initialization file.

**Refreshing Controlfile**     Refreshing the standby controlfile is performed as described in Table 5-8

| | |
|---|---|
| **Primary Site** | |
| Create new standby controlfile | `ALTER DATABASE CREATE STANDBY CONTROLFILE;` |
| Archive up to current log | `ALTER DATABASE ARCHIVE LOG CURRENT;` |
| **Transfer files to standby site** | Transfer the new standby controlfile and archive files to the standby database. |
| **Standby Site** | |
| Shutdown recovery, if necessary | Kill automatic maintenance script, or, `CANCEL` if performing manual recovery. Ensure standby database is shutdown normally. |
| Start and mount standby database | `svrmgrl`<br>`connect internal`<br>`startup mount`<br>`pfile=$ORACLE_HOME/dbs/`<br>`initstby.ora` |
| Offline drop unwanted tablespaces | `ALTER TABLESPACE unwanted OFFLINE DROP;`<br>Only needed if unwanted tablespaces at primary were added since last refresh. |
| Recover remaining archive log files | `RECOVER STANDBY DATABASE;` |
| Restart maintenance | Restart automatic maintenance scripts. |

**TABLE 5-8.**   *Refreshing Controlfile*

# Activation

This section describes how to switch over to the standby database after a failure of the production database, and, how to switch back, once the failure is fixed. Table 5-9 shows the steps involved in activating the standby feature. The examples show real commands, but are not intended to be complete.

### After Activation and Switching Back to Original Production Site

After switching over to a standby database, it becomes the primary. In which case, you will need another standby site. The mechanisms you use to deploy and maintain a standby database must be flexible. Preferably, scripts will not need modification because environment variables are used to identify the primary and standby sites. Thus, after activation, you can create a new standby database simply by changing the variables to point to the new site names and running the scripts. This is particularly useful if you want to use the original site as the standby database. Furthermore, you will need to make the original site the standby site (and then activate) if you wish that original site to once again house the production database.

### Activation Notes

Activating the standby database clears the online redo logs before opening the database unless the logs are already cleared. You can reduce your MTTR, by creating in advance and clearing the online redo logs just before activation using the **ALTER DATABASE CLEAR LOGFILE** command. When the online redo logs are reset in this manner, a special flag is set. Oracle recognizes the flag at activation and does not clear the logs, thus saving time.

# Failure Analysis

In today's ever-changing technological world, businesses are finding it harder to maintain high availability of crucial business information systems. This problem is further complicated by the diversity in heterogeneous networks, and the increasing trend toward client/server architecture. Maintaining high availability is no small task in a client/server environment, yet many companies are moving toward a high availability (24 hours a day, 7 days a week), mission-critical type of operation for three main reasons.

The first reason is *globalization of businesses*. These days, with international markets opening up, many companies are opening up branches in various countries; yet due to business reasons, they are keeping operations centralized. This essentially means that a database or an application running on a machine needs to be available at all times.

| | |
|---|---|
| **Transfer files to standby site** | If possible, transfer any remaining archive log files to be applied from the primary. |
| | If possible, transfer the online redo log from the primary, *but only if* the online redo log configurations are the same at both sites. This will allow the standby database to be recovered up to the last transaction committed at the primary. |
| **Standby Site** | |
| Start and mount standby database | `svrmgrl`<br>`connect internal`<br>`startup mount`<br>`pfile=$ORACLE_HOME/dbs/`<br>`initstby.ora` |
| Recover remaining archive log files | `RECOVER STANDBY DATABASE;` |
| Activate standby database | `ALTER DATABASE ACTIVATE`<br>`STANDBY DATABASE;` |
| Offline unwanted tablespaces | `ALTER TABLESPACE unwanted`<br>`OFFLINE;`<br>`Possibly because tablespace`<br>`was offlined at primary.` |
| Change tablespaces to Read-Only | `ALTER TABLESPACE wanted READ`<br>`ONLY;`<br>`Possibly because tablespace`<br>`was read-only at primary.` |
| Online tablespaces | `ALTER TABLESPACE wanted`<br>`ONLINE;`<br>`Possibly because tablespace`<br>`was offline at standby`<br>`database to improve`<br>`performance.` |
| Switch over users | Contact users directly, or, initiate network switching software. |
| Instigate new standby | Your new primary database must be safeguarded. Instigate backups, and, when possible, build a new standby database. |

**TABLE 5-9.**  *Steps involved in Activating a Standby Database*

The second reason is competitive pressure. For example, if a bank extends its business hours to Saturdays and Sundays, other banks have to meet their competitor's challenge. This means keeping the databases up and running on Saturdays and Sundays as well.

The third and final reason why more companies are moving towards high availability systems is cost of downtime. A survey done by *SVP Strategic Research Division* shows that businesses, on an average, incur $1,300 of mean revenue loss per outage minute. This survey was done on 450 companies in manufacturing, securities, health insurance, transportation, banking, retail, and telecommunications industries. This implies that a shop that operates 24 hours a day, 7 days a week, and maintains a 99 percent availability, faces 1 percent downtime (accounts for more than 5,000 minutes of downtime), which is equivalent to 6 million dollars of revenue loss per year.

# System Outage Survey

A *system outage* survey and a *Down System and Recovery* survey conducted by Oracle Worldwide Support found very interesting information on why systems go down, how often, and how customers recover them. Consider the following outage categories:

- Physical outages
- Design outages
- Operational outages
- Environmental outages
- Scheduled outages

The first four outage types in this list are *unscheduled* outages, according to IEEE. *Physical outages* are usually caused by hardware failures. Media failure or a CPU failure is a typical example of a Physical outage. *Design outages* are caused by software failures, more commonly known as software *bugs*. Any software bug, whether in the operating system, database software, or application software, contributes to a design outage. *Operational outages,* on the other hand, are caused by human intervention. Failures attributed to poor DBA skills, user errors, inappropriate system setup, or inadequate backup procedures are examples of Operational outages. Outages such as earthquakes, power surges, and failures due to abnormal temperature conditions are typical examples of *Environmental outages.*The last category is the *scheduled* outage, which is necessary for the maintenance of the system—for example, configuring/reconfiguring hardware and software.

Oracle Worldwide Support has done a survey on 30 Oracle customers running mission critical applications. Not all customers surveyed have high availability requirements. The operational logs at each site were reviewed with the help of the DBAs and system managers for the years 1994 to 1995. The total outage minutes were calculated at each site. Each outage was analyzed and the cause for the outage was categorized according to the outage classes mentioned above. Under each outage class, the total amount of downtime was calculated and averaged out over 30 customers.

Figure 5-7 gives the outage categories as a percentage of the total outage time. The figure shows that the outages caused by design failures cause the most downtime (36 percent). This includes software bugs caused by the operating system, Oracle, third-party software that runs on top of Oracle, and in-house developed applications.

Figure 5-8 gives a detailed analysis of design-related outages. While documentation is the main cause and accounts for almost 50 percent of the downtime caused by design outages, the downtime for code bugs is significant (40 percent), as well.

Figure 5-7 shows that 34 percent of the outage time is caused by Operational outages, an outage that you can control. As you can see, this is quite significant. Figure 5-9 gives further details on the Operational outage category. While 80 percent of the operations-related downtime was due to lack of DBA skills, the survey showed that improper recovery handling, improper network setup, improper system setup, and DBA/user errors were some of the main reasons for Operational outages.

Finally, Figure 5-7 shows that Physical outages cause 25 percent of the total downtime. Since the survey was done on a small sample of 30 customers, the Environmental outages are zero percent, which leaves the scheduled downtime to be 5 percent.

To summarize, the survey showed that of the total system downtime, 95 percent was due to unscheduled outages, and the other 5 percent of the time, the systems were down due to maintenance. In addition, the average Mean Time Between Failures (MTBF) is calculated for the sample surveyed. This gives the mean time elapsed between two consecutive failures, which is calculated to be 102 days. The average Mean Time To Recover (MTTR) when a failure occurs is estimated to be 17 hours and 53 minutes.

# Down System and Recovery Survey

Most Oracle customers might be familiar with Oracle Worldwide Support's processes and procedures. When a customer calls into the Support Organization, a *technical assistance request* (or a TAR) is created to track the call. Oracle Worldwide Support has done a study on the priority 1 TARs that were logged by the analysts. A *priority 1 TAR* is logged when an Oracle database is not operational, and critically impacts the

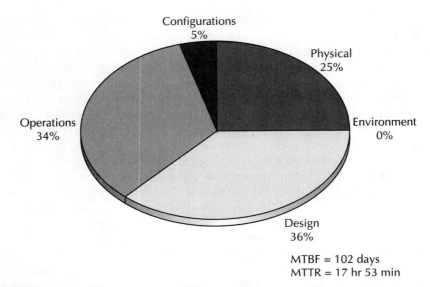

**FIGURE 5-7.** *Outage analysis survey conducted at 30 Oracle customer sites*

customer's business. The total TARs surveyed were 208. Of the total TARs, 18 percent of them (38 TARs) show that DBAs had to do media recovery to bring the production database back to normal operation.

An important observation in this survey is that, of the 38 TARs that ended up in doing recovery, 17 of them did *complete recovery* and the other 21 had to do *incomplete recovery*, which usually implies data loss. In these 38 cases the root cause for doing media recovery was due to OS/hardware problems, loss of data files due to user errors, block corruptions, instance crashes, inadequate DBA skills, and Oracle bugs. Figure 5-10 gives a breakdown of these 38 TARs. Note that this survey was done on a very small sample of TARs and may have a significant margin of error.

# Recommendations for Disaster Recovery

In today's world, businesses are beginning to demand more from their information systems, while at the same time pushing the outer limits of technology. This poses a daunting challenge on the service organizations. A reactive service paradigm no longer provides adequate solutions. A proactive approach is required to meet the demands of running mission critical operations in today's heterogeneous client/server networks.

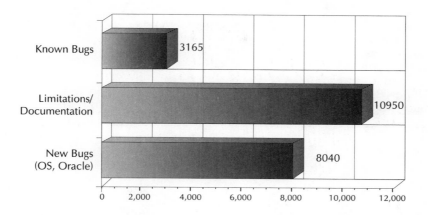

**FIGURE 5-8.** *Design-related outages*

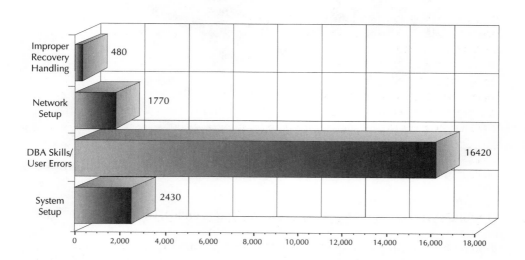

**Downtime in Minutes**

**FIGURE 5-9.** *Operations-related outages*

| Problem | Count | Complete Recovery | Incomplete Recovery |
|---|---|---|---|
| OS/Hardware problems | 14 | 9 | 5 |
| Loss of files | 15 | 3 | 12 |
| Block Corruptions | 4 | 2 | 2 |
| Crashed Instance | 2 | 2 | |
| DBA Skills | 2 | 1 | 1 |
| Bugs | 1 | | 1 |
| | 38 | 17 | 21 |

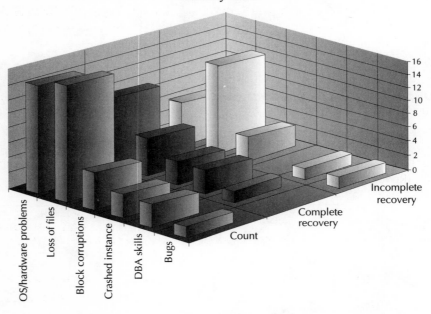

**FIGURE 5-10.** *Recovery detail graph*

## Customer Requirements

The following are some general requirements you need to consider while designing disaster recovery procedures for your site. When they are properly designed, you should be able to increase the Mean Time Between Failures (MTTR) and decrease the Mean Time To Recover (MTTR).

■ Sites must have a premium level of support from their hardware and software vendors.

■ Uninterrupted Power Supply units must be used for mission-critical systems.

■ A system monitoring tool should be used to proactively detect problems. Monitoring tools should be able to do event monitoring and problem reporting. For example, the tool should be able to beep/email/fax the DBA in the event of any fatal problems. In addition, it should be able to proactively monitor space usage and other crucial data structures in the database. Various third-party tools exist that can be customized to monitor your database and applications.

■ Have access to the world via Internet. In addition, have dedicated phone lines and high bandwidth modems connected to your machine for you to access from home or on the road. When problems occur, the hardware and software vendors can use the modem to dial into your site to monitor, diagnose, and fix problems.

■ Sites should have a qualified system administrator, and proper system administration procedures should be practiced. The system administrator must successfully complete required education programs with the hardware vendor. The DBAs should do the same with the database vendors.

■ Proper hardware protection should be available at each production site. Required hardware protection may include hard disk mirroring, keeping on-site spare parts, and implementing a backup and recovery plan. RAID (Redundant Arrays of Inexpensive Disks) technology is becoming very popular for building fault tolerance and improving data availability. RAID technology is built on the fact that disk arrays generally improve performance, but how much it improves depends on the RAID level used and how the manufacturer has implemented it. The following is a brief description of the RAID levels:

   ■ RAID 0: A disk array that doesn't have redundancy but implements striping is referred to as RAID 0. This level doesn't offer any fault tolerance and improves speed.

   ■ RAID 1: Mirroring of disks is referred to as RAID 1. Mirroring is a concept where two disk drives store identical information. The system writes to both the disk drives for every write operation. When one disk fails, the other keeps working, thereby providing fault tolerance.

   ■ RAID 2: This level provides check disks with data bit-striped across the data and check disks. With this technology, you can detect and correct single-bit errors and detect double-bit errors. The check disks take about 30 percent of the total disk array space. RAID 2 is relatively complex to implement.

   ■ RAID 3: This level is commonly implemented in workstations. A parity disk is used for a group of drives and the data written to the disk array is bit-striped across the data disks. This level of RAID reduces overhead for check disk (about 80 percent of the space in the array can be used for data storage).

- RAID 4: This level is used for transaction-processing applications, due to better optimized disk array architecture. At this RAID level, block or sector striping is done on the data disks, which allows multiple unrelated sectors to be read simultaneously. However, write operations might become a bottleneck.

- RAID 5: The primary advantage of RAID 5 is the distributed check-data approach, which allows multiple read and write operations to take place simultaneously.

- If using Oracle, sites must be able to operate the machine in production with all the Oracle diagnostic events turned on (if and when required), with adequate performance from the machine. If the machine performance is not adequate, the machine will have to be correctly sized.

- All Oracle sites must be Optimal Flexible Architecture (OFA)-compliant.

- Machines running in production must be housed in a proper hazard-resilient environment. It is recommended that an environmental audit be requested from the hardware vendor.

- DBAs, system managers, and application developers should analyze the in-house applications and develop clear expectations on the response time and availability goals for each application.

- Oracle database administrators need to be certified by Oracle. The administrator is expected to be at a certain knowledge level of the Oracle database. The *Oracle Education Services* gives a certification test and does a skills assessment when requested. They also recommend the classes a DBA should take.

- Sites *must* maintain a test bed that should be a replica of their production environment. If running a Very Large Database (VLDB), a percentage of the data should be maintained on the test database. This is absolutely required to perform on-site testing and migration planning for future software releases. This machine should also be used for testing backup and recovery procedures at regular intervals.

- Last, but not least, the system managers and DBAs have to maintain an operations log at each production site. Any kind of Physical, Design, Operational, Environmental, or scheduled outage should be recorded promptly. If an automated procedure doesn't exist, at least manual logging should be practiced.

# CHAPTER 6

# Diagnostic Facilities and Debugging the RDBMS

This chapter familiarizes the DBA with the diagnostic facilities that are available in Oracle7. In order for a DBA to diagnose any RDBMS-related problems, he or she should be familiar with all the debugging utilities that are provided by Oracle. In addition, certain concepts such as reading the control file dumps or reading the trace files are necessary. All the information recorded in any trace file might not be useful to the DBA or the user. Some of the information is specifically used by Oracle Worldwide Support analysts and the Oracle development teams. We will first start off by discussing the various trace files that are generated by Oracle automatically. We will then discuss various diagnostic tools available to debug the RDBMS. Note that this chapter is dedicated to learning the diagnostic tools pertaining to the RDBMS only. Tools to debug/tune applications such as SQL_TRACE and TKPROF or database tuning scripts such as UTLBSTAT/UTLESTAT are not discussed in this chapter as they are beyond the scope of this book.

# Oracle Trace Files

The alert log file is very helpful in pointing the DBA toward the trace files with crucial information, and should usually be the first file to take a look at when diagnosing a database problem. The ability to use the information contained in a trace file is very dependent on your experience with the various messages printed in the file. Many messages printed to the log are not associated with any error conditions.

During startup of the database, if the alert log file doesn't exist, Oracle will create one for you to write to the file with information such as "DBWR started." Figure 6-1 gives the dump of an alert file after starting up the Oracle7 database on Microsoft Windows.

When the database is started, all the INIT.ORA parameters and messages indicating that the background processes have started are recorded in the alert log file. The thread that this instance is using, and the log sequence number that LGWR is currently writing to, are also recorded. In general, the alert log file keeps a log of all database startups, shutdowns, tablespace creations, rollback segment creations, some **alter** statements issued, information regarding log switches, and error messages. Each entry has a time stamp associated with it, and for non-error messages, there is usually an entry for the beginning of an action plus an entry indicating its successful completion. It is very important for DBAs to regularly check this file for error messages. If there is an error message in the alert log file, it will often direct you to a specific trace file (or files) for more information.

In addition to the alert log file, there are two types of trace files that Oracle generates automatically. One is the *background trace file* created by background processes such as DBWR and LGWR. The background trace files might or might not be created on startup, depending on if there is any information that the background process needs to write at that time. Initially, when the file is created, it contains some header information indicating the version numbers of the RDBMS and the operating system. These files are created in a directory specified by the INIT.ORA parameter, **background_dump_dest**.

The second type of trace file is produced by the user connection to Oracle and is known as the *user trace file*. These files are only created when the user session encounters an error condition and information can be dumped to the trace files. In

```
Dump file C:\ORACLE7\RDBMS70\trace\ALERT.LOG
Thu Nov 24 01:56:11 1994
ORACLE V7.0.16.6.0 - Beta vsnsta=1
vsnsql=7 vsnxtr=3
MS-WINDOWS Version 3.10
Thu Nov 24 01:56:11 1994

Starting up ORACLE RDBMS Version: 7.0.16.6.0.

System parameters with non-default values:
processes                = 50
license_max_sessions     = 15
control_files            = %RDBMS70_CONTROL%\ctl1.ora,
    %RDBMS70_ARCHIVE%\ctl1.ora
db_block_buffers         = 400
log_archive_start        = TRUE
log_archive_dest         = %RDBMS70_ARCHIVE%
log_buffer               = 65596
log_checkpoint_interval  = 1000
row_locking              = ALWAYS
sequence_cache_hash_buckets= 10
distributed_lock_timeout = 0
distributed_recovery_connection_hold_time= 0
mts_servers              = 0
open_links               = 20
audit_trail              = NONE
sort_area_size           = 262144
sort_area_retained_size  = 262144
db_name                  = oracle
background_dump_dest      = %RDBMS70%\trace
user_dump_dest           = %RDBMS70%\trace
max_dump_file_size       = 5120

PMON started
Dump file C:\ORACLE7\RDBMS70\trace\ALERT.LOG
Thu Nov 24 01:56:11 1994
ORACLE V7.0.16.6.0 - Beta vsnsta=1
vsnsql=7 vsnxtr=3
MS-WINDOWS Version 3.10
Thu Nov 24 01:56:11 1994
```

**FIGURE 6-1.**   *Output of ALERT.LOG file for Oracle7 on Microsoft Windows*

```
DBWR started
Dump file C:\ORACLE7\RDBMS70\trace\ALERT.LOG
Thu Nov 24 01:56:11 1994
ORACLE V7.0.16.6.0 - Beta vsnsta=1
vsnsql=7 vsnxtr=3
MS-WINDOWS Version 3.10
Thu Nov 24 01:56:11 1994

ARCH started
Dump file C:\ORACLE7\RDBMS70\trace\ALERT.LOG
Thu Nov 24 01:56:11 1994
ORACLE V7.0.16.6.0 - Beta vsnsta=1
vsnsql=7 vsnxtr=3
MS-WINDOWS Version 3.10
Thu Nov 24 01:56:11 1994

LGWR started
Dump file C:\ORACLE7\RDBMS70\trace\ALERT.LOG
Thu Nov 24 01:56:14 1994
ORACLE V7.0.16.6.0 - Beta vsnsta=1
vsnsql=7 vsnxtr=3
MS-WINDOWS Version 3.10
Thu Nov 24 01:56:14 1994

alter database  mount exclusive
Thu Nov 24 01:56:15 1994

Completed: alter database  mount exclusive
Thu Nov 24 01:56:15 1994

alter database  open
Thu Nov 24 01:56:16 1994

Thread 1 opened at log sequence 4

Current log# 1 seq# 4 mem# 0: C:\ORACLE7\DBS\wdblog1.log
Dump file C:\ORACLE7\RDBMS70\trace\ALERT.LOG
Thu Nov 24 01:56:16 1994
ORACLE V7.0.16.6.0 - Beta vsnsta=1
vsnsql=7 vsnxtr=3
```

**FIGURE 6-1.**   *Output of ALERT.LOG file for Oracle7 on Microsoft Windows (continued)*

```
MS-WINDOWS Version 3.10
Thu Nov 24 01:56:16 1994

SMON: enabling cache recovery
Thu Nov 24 01:56:29 1994

SMON: enabling tx recovery
Thu Nov 24 01:56:31 1994

Completed: alter database  open
```

**FIGURE 6-1.**   *Output of ALERT.LOG file for Oracle7 on Microsoft Windows (continued)*

addition, if a user session requests a trace file by using the **alter session** command, then they are created as a user trace as well. The user trace files are created in a directory specified by the INIT.ORA parameter, **user_dump_dest**.

Trace file names have a standard format so you can locate them easily. The names of the trace files give information that can help users locate the correct one more easily. The naming convention is operating system specific. For example, on VMS, the file has the name *IMAGE_NAME_SID_PROCESS_ID*.TRC. The *IMAGE_NAME* is the name of the executable image that created the trace file. The *SID* is the system identifier of the instance. The *PROCESS_ID* is the process ID of the process that created the trace file. In the UNIX environment, the background trace file will look something like *ORA_PID_PROCESS_ID*.trc and the user trace file has the name *PROCESS_ID*.trc. The *ORA_PID* is the Oracle process ID and the *PROCESS_ID* is the system process ID for the process creating the trace file. Note that all messages written to the user trace files might not be critical but it is always a good practice for the DBA to monitor the trace files at periodic intervals.

There is a lot of information contained in the trace files that the DBA can use to resolve some of the problems. Later in this chapter, we will discuss in detail some of the common errors, causes, and resolutions. But before we do that, we need to examine some of the diagnostic features and better understand how to read the information in certain trace files.

# Diagnostic Tools

Oracle provides various diagnostic tools for debugging the RDBMS. Certain events can be turned on to dump diagnostic information of various data structures to trace.

Next, some special INIT.ORA parameters are available that can be used while diagnosing memory and disk corruptions. These parameters are not set during normal operation of the database, as they affect the performance of the database. Some special tools such as Oradbx are available on some operating systems. A brief overview of such tools will be given as well.

## Setting Trace Events

The Oracle RDBMS contains a facility that allows the DBA to dump information contained in various structures and to trace the occurrence of particular events. There are two ways to turn on the event trace. The first way is to set the required event in the INIT.ORA file, which will turn on event trace for all the sessions. The second way is to enter the **alter session set events** command, usually from SQL*DBA. This will turn on event trace for just the ongoing session.

The syntax while using INIT.ORA is

EVENT = "*event syntax* ¦ ,LEVEL n¦: *event syntax* ¦ ,LEVEL n¦.."

The syntax while using SQL is

ALTER SESSION SET EVENTS '*event syntax* LEVEL *n*: *event syntax* LEVEL *n*:....';

For example, to dump the complete contents of the control file, the syntax is

```
ALTER SESSION SET EVENTS 'IMMEDIATE TRACE NAME CONTROLF LEVEL 10';
```

The *event syntax* contains multiple keywords. The first keyword of the event syntax can be an *event number* or a special keyword, **immediate**. Event numbers can be Oracle error numbers (ones prefixed by "ORA-" in the *Oracle7 Server Messages and Codes Manual* ) or internal *event codes* defined in the Oracle RDBMS. The event codes are implemented by logic in the kernel that takes some action depending on its value. These internal event codes can be found in the rdbms/mesg/oraus.msg file on UNIX, or in the error.msg file in the ora_rdbms directory on VMS. In some operating systems, this file might be in binary format and not as a text file. The internal event codes are in the range 10000 to 10999. Some of the event codes that are commonly used by DBAs and Oracle Worldwide Support will be discussed later in this chapter.

If the keyword **immediate** is specified as the first word in the event syntax, it's an indication to Oracle that it is an unconditional event, and the structure specified should be dumped to trace immediately after the command is issued. This keyword is issued in the **alter session** command (it doesn't make sense to use it in the INIT.ORA file).

The second and third keywords in the event syntax are almost always **trace** and **name**, respectively. The keyword **trace** indicates that the output will be dumped to a trace file and the keyword **name** comes before the actual *event name*. There are qualifiers other than **trace** that can be used as well, but are used only by the Oracle development team for internal use. The last keyword of the event syntax is the *event name*, which is the actual structure that you want to dump.

If you are not using the **immediate** option as the first keyword in the event syntax, then you need to indicate how long the specified tracing should be enabled. Specifying the keyword **forever** will keep the event active for the life of the session or instance, depending on whether the event is set from INIT.ORA or at a session level.

After the event syntax, the **LEVEL** keyword is specified for most events. An exception would be while dumping the **errorstack** where there is no level (**errorstack** is discussed later in this section ). Usually the **LEVEL** needs to be set between 1 and 10. A value of 10 would mean to dump all the information for that event. So, for example, setting **LEVEL** to 1 while dumping the control file would dump only the control file header, whereas setting **LEVEL** to 10 would dump the entire contents of the control file. **LEVEL** has a special meaning while using the **blockdump** keyword to dump a data block. Here, the **LEVEL** is the actual address of the datablock, specified in decimal form. Oracle Worldwide Support would advise you on what the value of **LEVEL** should be depending on the structure you are dumping to trace.

Putting all this together, here are some examples. The following are examples that can be used while using the INIT.ORA file to set events:

```
EVENT = "604 TRACE NAME ERRORSTACK FOREVER"

EVENT = "10210 TRACE NAME CONTEXT FOREVER, LEVEL 10"
```

The above two lines need to be typed in the INIT.ORA file exactly as shown. The first statement would dump the error stack every time a process encounters the ORA-604 error. The second statement is a block-checking event that would check every block's integrity when read from disk to cache. Remember that setting these events in the INIT.ORA file would create a trace when the above conditions occur by any session in the database.

The following are examples that can be used while using SQL to set events:

```
ALTER SESSION SET EVENTS 'IMMEDIATE TRACE NAME BLOCKDUMP LEVEL 67109037';

ALTER SESSION SET EVENTS 'IMMEDIATE TRACE NAME CONTROLF LEVEL 10';

ALTER SESSION SET EVENTS 'IMMEDIATE TRACE NAME SYSTEMSTATE LEVEL 10';
```

The first statement would dump the data block 67109037 to a trace file. Every data block in the Oracle database is uniquely identified by a block number and a file number combination. In the above example, 67109037 is the decimal representation of the file number and the block number. This information is operating system dependent. The second statement would dump the entire contents of the control file to trace. The third statement would dump the *systemstate* to trace, which includes all *process state* dumps (system state and process state are discussed later in this chapter). This system state dump will be useful while diagnosing *system hang* problems.

### Event Names
This section gives a partial list of the event names that can be set. It includes the definition of each event name, a brief description of the trace it produces, and when this event should be used.

**Buffers**    Setting this trace event will dump all the buffers in the SGA buffer cache. This event is useful while diagnosing corruptions happening in memory. If a proper **LEVEL** is not set, setting this event can affect performance of the database. Setting the **LEVEL** to 1 would dump only the buffer header whereas setting it to 10 would dump the entire contents of the buffer. Depending on the problem that is being diagnosed, Oracle Worldwide Support will suggest the appropriate **LEVEL** to set. This event should be used only when requested by Oracle Worldwide Support. For example,

```
alter session set events 'immediate trace name buffers level 1';
```

would dump the buffer header to trace.

**Blockdump**    Use this command to dump a specific database block belonging to any segment, such as data, index, or rollback. The block's address should be specified after the **LEVEL** keyword as a decimal value. This command should be used under Oracle Worldwide Support's supervision. This event is normally set to debug data corruptions in data or index blocks. For example,

```
alter session set events 'immediate trace name blockdump level 134219181';
```

would dump the contents of the datablock that has an address of 134219181.

**Controlf**   This event is the one most commonly used to dump the contents of the control file. Setting the **LEVEL** to 1 will dump only the control file header. Setting the **LEVEL** to 10 would dump the entire contents of the control file. For example,

```
alter session set events 'immediate trace name controlf level 10';
```

would dump the entire control file to trace. A detailed description on control file dumps is provided in the following section.

**Locks**   When set, this event dumps all locks held by the lock process. It is usually used to debug locking problems while using the *parallel server* option. For example,

```
alter session set events 'immediate trace name locks level 5';
```

would dump the information regarding the locks held by the LCK process to trace.

**Redohdr**   This is also a common event, which dumps the redo log file's header to trace. Setting the **LEVEL** to 1 would dump the control file entry of the redo information only. **LEVEL** 2 would dump the generic file header (discussed later in this chapter). Any **LEVEL** greater than 2 would dump the complete log header to trace. Sometimes, while starting up the database after a media failure, Oracle reports that some data files have failed the verification checks that it performs. In such cases, using this event along with **file_hdrs** and **controlf** is useful for debugging. For example,

```
alter session set events 'immediate trace name redohdr level 10';
```

would dump the redo header information to trace.

**Loghist**   This event dumps the log history entries from the control file. If **LEVEL** 1 is set, it only dumps the earliest and latest log history entries. If **LEVEL** 2 or greater is specified, it dumps the most recent 2**LEVEL** (2 to the power **LEVEL**) entries. For example,

```
alter session set events 'immediate trace name loghist level 4';
```

Here, **LEVEL** is set to 4, so 2**4 = 16 most recent log-history entries would be dumped from the control file.

**File_hdrs**    This event dumps all data file headers to trace. The **LEVEL** setting is the same as for the event **Redohdr**. For example,

```
alter session set events 'immediate trace name file_hdrs level 10';
```

would dump the contents of all data file headers to trace.

**Errorstack**    Oracle will create a stack called the *error stack* to store the information relating to a particular error that a process has encountered. Usually, when an error occurs the Oracle foreground process gets an error message. However, while running some applications (e.g., SQL*FORMS) the foreground process may not get all the information related to the error. This event dumps the entire error stack to trace, and is very useful for debugging any Oracle error. For example, if an application is failing with the ORA-604 error,

```
alter session set events '604 trace name errorstack forever';
```

would dump the error stack and also the process stack to trace. For more information on stack traces, refer to "Oracle Internal Errors," later in this chapter.

**Systemstate**    This event dumps the entire system state, which includes all processes' state dumps. This event is very useful for diagnosing problems when experiencing performance degradation, process hangs, or system hangs. System state and process state dumps are discussed in the "Oracle Internal Errors" section of this chapter. This event should be used under the supervision of Oracle Worldwide Support. For example,

```
alter session set events 'immediate trace name systemstate level 10';
```

would dump the system state to trace.

**Coalesce**    For DBAs, this is an extremely useful space-management event. When set, this event coalesces free space in **fet$** for the specified tablespace (**fet$** gives information regarding the free space that's available in the database, and is discussed in Chapter 2). For example, if blocks 1 through 5 indicate the first chunk of free space and blocks 6 through 10 indicate the second chunk, by setting this event, the two records can be replaced by a single record in the **fet$** table, indicating that one chunk of free space is available that contains blocks 1 through 10. The tablespace and number of entries to coalesce is specified after the **LEVEL** as follows:

```
alter session set events 'immediate trace name coalesce level X';
```

where $X$ is a decimal number constructed by taking the high-order 2 bytes as number of extents to coalesce and low-order 2 bytes as the tablespace number. So for example, let's assume that we want to coalesce up to 5 entries in the system tablespace. Then, the high-order 2 bytes in hexadecimal representation would be 0x0005. Since the system tablespace has a tablespace number of zero, the low-order two bytes are 0x0000. Combining the low-order and high-order bytes, the value in hex is 0x00050000. This represents a value of 327680 in decimal form, which is the value of $X$:

```
alter session set events 'immediate trace name coalesce level 327680';
```

Note that this event needs to be explicitly set while using Oracle7 (7.0.x) of the RDBMS only. In future releases of Oracle, this will be a feature built into the RDBMS and the event will not exist.

Some other event names exist in addition to the ones described above, but they are not used as often. Some of them are **Latches**, **Processstate**, **Row_Cache**, **Enqueues**, and **Contextarea**.

## Event Codes

Note that some codes that are available in one version of Oracle may be changed or deleted in the following version. In addition, some of the event codes are destructive and can crash the database, so these event codes are not supported by Oracle Worldwide Support unless advised by them. It is suggested that you try some of these events on your test database and *don't* experiment on your production database. Following is the description of some of the common event codes used by Oracle Worldwide Support.

**Event Codes 10013 and 10015**    These event codes are used while diagnosing problems induced by a corrupted rollback segment. In such cases, the database cannot be started and gives the ORA-1578 error, indicating that a block in the database is corrupted for whatever reason. If Oracle Worldwide Support determines the cause to be due to a rollback segment, setting the above events in the INIT.ORA file would create a trace file that will be helpful in determining the bad rollback segment. The syntax for setting event 10015 in the INIT.ORA file is

```
event = "10015 trace name context forever"
```

**Event Codes 10029 and 10030**    These event codes give information on the session logons and session logoffs, which are used by some DBAs. If you want to know the number of logons and logoffs to the database, you can use these events.

**Event Codes 10210 and 10211** These are *block-checking* and *index-checking* events, respectively. Normally when a block is read from disk to cache, some basic integrity checks are performed. By setting these events, Oracle does additional checks, which could be very crucial while diagnosing some block corruptions. PMON always has block checking turned on. It is good practice to use the block-checking and index-checking events even during normal operation of the database, but there is an overhead involved. Running the database with these events turned on is especially advisable for customers running a VLDB shop with high availability requirements. For example,

```
event = "10210 trace name context forever, level 10"
```

would turn on block checking for every data block read into the SGA.

**Event Codes 10231 and 10232** These are probably the most important event codes. Assume that due to a physical outage, one of the blocks on disk is zeroed out—that is, all the data in that block is gone. To salvage the remaining data in that table, one needs to export that table. However, a full table scan of the table would fail when the bad block is read. To work around the corruption, event 10231 needs to be set. This event would skip corrupted blocks during full table scans. If event 10232 is set, these corrupted blocks are dumped to a trace file. There are certain conditions that need to be met in order for event 10231 to work.

■ This block should be *soft-corrupted* by Oracle. This means that, when Oracle detects a corrupt block, it marks the block as corrupt by setting certain bits in the block to zero. In order for Oracle to soft-corrupt the block, you have to use the event 10210. So using event 10231 along with event 10210 is recommended.

■ The **LEVEL** should be set correctly. Oracle Worldwide Support can provide this information to you.

■ Accessing the blocks through an index wouldn't work. Only full table scans should be done on the table. Note that if this event is set in a session, it would work only if that session does the full table scan. If you need to export the table, then this event should be set in the INIT.ORA file.

Two examples are given below. The first one is used with SQL and the other in the INIT.ORA file.

```
alter session set events '10231 trace name context off';

event = "10231 trace name context forever, level 10"
```

The first statement would turn off block checking for that session. The second statement would turn on block checking database-wide for all data blocks read into the SGA by any process.

**Event Code 10061**    This event code has been added with version 7.0.15. After a database crash or **shutdown abort** statement is issued, during next startup, SMON cleans up temporary segments. When set, this event will disable cleanup of temporary segments by SMON at startup time. Sometimes, depending on the outage that caused the failure, it might be necessary to take such an action to start the database up. After starting up the database, Oracle Worldwide Support analysts can troubleshoot the problem and fix it, at which point this event should be removed from the INIT.ORA file and the database restarted.

# INIT.ORA Parameters

Almost every DBA will be familiar with the documented INIT.ORA parameters. Parameters such as LOG_BUFFERS, DB_BLOCK_WRITE_BATCH, and DB_FILE_MULTIBLOCK_READ_COUNT are usually used by DBAs to tune the database (for example, tuning memory allocation or tuning I/O). Other parameters, such as SQL_TRACE and TIMED_STATISTICS, are used while debugging or tuning application-specific problems.

The INIT.ORA parameters we are about to discuss are not documented. Some DBAs know about these parameters and might have used them as well. Any INIT.ORA parameter that starts with an underscore is an undocumented, unsupported Oracle feature. The idea behind keeping these parameters undocumented should be obvious—there are risks involved in using these parameters. If not used properly, the data might become inconsistent, thereby having logical corruptions in the database.

Two such parameters are _OFFLINE_ROLLBACK_SEGMENTS and _CORRUPTED_ROLLBACK_SEGMENTS.

### _OFFLINE_ROLLBACK_SEGMENTS and _CORRUPTED_ROLLBACK_SEGMENTS

These undocumented parameters help you solve problems that are related to rollback segments. For example, if you have problems opening the database due to a corrupted rollback segment, using the _CORRUPTED_ROLLBACK_SEGMENTS parameter will help you open the database. These parameters have drastic effects on the database and should be used under Oracle Worldwide Support's supervision.

To use these parameters, set the following line in the INIT.ORA file.

*parameter = (rollback segment name, rollback segment name,...)*

For example,

```
_offline_rollback_segments =  (rbs1, rbs2)
```

would take the rollback segments **rbs1** and **rbs2** offline while doing transaction recovery.

Due to hardware or software failures, if a block in a rollback segment gets corrupted, it will cause problems while starting up the database. Consider the following scenario: A DBA was getting the ORA-1578 error on a rollback segment block during startup. By setting events, an Oracle Worldwide Support analyst dumped a trace file on startup and all Oracle indicated was that Oracle error ORA-1578 was encountered while recovering transaction $X$. No additional information was given (such as the object name or number). By using the _OFFLINE_ROLLBACK_SEGMENTS parameter, the database was brought online. Is the database consistent at this time? Is rebuilding the database necessary? To answer these questions, one needs to understand the ramifications of using these parameters.

When the _OFFLINE_ROLLBACK_SEGMENTS parameter is used, Oracle takes the rollback segment(s) offline during transaction recovery (roll backward) for those rollback segments listed in this parameter when the database is started. In other words, Oracle temporarily prevents SMON from cleaning up the uncommitted transactions in the rollback segments involved. However, when a data/index/cluster/cluster index block, which is part of this uncommitted transaction, is needed at a later time, Oracle tries to read the block and detects a corruption. So using this parameter gives the DBA or the Oracle Worldwide Support analyst a chance to determine which objects still have uncommitted transactions in the rollback segment by dumping the transaction table and corresponding pieces of the rollback segment itself.

If the problem is due to inability to roll back a transaction because an object is corrupt, it may be possible to drop the object and bring the rollback segment back online without further damage taking place, and still have any remaining uncommitted transactions roll back normally. If the status of the rollback segment changes from NEEDS RECOVERY to IN USE or AVAILABLE, then it is generally safe to say that you can continue operating the database without a rebuild. If rebuilding your database is necessary, depending on the size of the database and the kind of backup and recovery procedures used, it may sometimes be faster to go back to a good backup and recover the database instead of going through a rebuild.

When the _CORRUPTED_ROLLBACK_SEGMENTS parameter is used, it works the same way while starting up the database as described in the previous case. However, once the database is open, the blocks needing read consistency are read *as is*. In other words, the uncommitted transactions are marked as *committed*. As a result, the blocks are made *good enough*, yet might be out of sync with respect to the application data. Applications handling financial-type transactions, which need a very high degree of accuracy, can run into problems here as the outcome of a query can give different results than expected. In addition, using this parameter can lead to worse problems down the road if, for example, a data dictionary cluster index becomes inconsistent with the clustered tables because it was only partially rolled back. Note that one of the main differences of using this parameter versus the _OFFLINE_ROLLBACK_SEGMENTS parameter is that, once the _CORRUPTED_ROLLBACK_SEGMENTS parameter is used to corrupt the rollback segments, they can never be brought online and used again.

To summarize, using the _CORRUPTED_ROLLBACK_SEGMENTS parameter to start up the database, and dropping the rollback segments involved, almost immediately guarantees database inconsistency if not loss of data integrity, which may or may not be detected immediately. There is no quick and simple way to find that out ahead of time. Even a database rebuild does not guarantee user data integrity. So you need to consider, very carefully, your options before using any of these parameters.

### _DB_BLOCK_COMPUTE_CHECKSUMS

_DB_BLOCK_COMPUTE_CHECKSUMS is the next INIT.ORA parameter worth mentioning. This parameter is not documented before release 7.2, and is normally used to debug corruptions that happen on disk. When this parameter is set, while reading a block from disk to cache, Oracle will compute and write a checksum to the block. Next time the same block is read, Oracle computes the checksum again and compares it with the value that's in the block. If that differs, it's an indication that the block is corrupted on disk. Oracle marks the block as corrupt and signals an error. There is an overhead involved in using this parameter, and it should normally be used only when advised by Oracle Worldwide Support.

### _DB_BLOCK_CACHE_PROTECT

Another diagnostic INIT.ORA parameter is _DB_BLOCK_CACHE_PROTECT. If this parameter is set to *true*, Oracle will catch stray writes made by processes in the buffer cache. Using operating system–dependent utilities and system calls, it forces every process to lock a block in memory before writing to it. If a process writes to a location in memory that it hasn't locked, then an access violation occurs, giving diagnostic trace information. The following operating systems have this feature implemented.

VMS
MVS
OS/2 2.0 (6.0.36+ and 7.0.12+ of Oracle)
NEC (port# 476)
DG Aviion

The _DB_BLOCK_CACHE_PROTECT parameter is not implemented on most UNIX ports since memory management under UNIX does not make it as easy to implement this parameter. On some operating systems, using this parameter might have severe impact on performance.

One problem with setting any of these events or event codes in the INIT.ORA file is that the database needs to be shut down and started up, which is not very practical for a lot of customers with high availability requirements. For example, if a block of a particular user's table gets corrupted, and the DBA decides to work around the corruption by setting event code 10231 and exporting the table, the DBA has to shut the database down and include this event in the INIT.ORA parameter, start up the database, and finally export the table. In the future releases of Oracle, the INIT.ORA parameter EVENT will modify the scope of the **alter session set events** command from a session level to the instance level. Note that this parameter is syntactically available with Oracle7 and reserved for future implementation.

## Other Diagnostic Utilities

There are a number of other utilities, such as the debugger program ORADBX on UNIX operating system, and Mailboxes on VMS. In addition, various V$ tables are also useful for debugging the RDBMS. A few of them are discussed here.

### ORADBX

This utility has existed for a long time and is used by Oracle Worldwide Support analysts extensively. ORADBX is a debugger program implemented in 6.0.29 on UNIX for debugging active Oracle processes. ORADBX sends messages asynchronously to the active Oracle process to dump to trace information of different data structures of Oracle, such as the SGA, PGA, state objects, context area, system states, stack trace, core, control file, data file, and *ipc* information. It also allows the user or DBA to turn *on* event trace when the process is already running. Following is the output of the help screen of ORADBX. Note that some of these diagnostic traces can be obtained by using the **alter session set events** command as well.

```
oradbx: Release 7.1.3.0.0 - Production on Thu Jan 19 14:13:35 1995
Copyright (c) Oracle Corporation 1979, 1994.  All rights reserved.

(oradbx) help
help                     - print help information
show                     - show status
debug <pid>              - debug process
dump SGA                 - dump SGA
```

```
dump PGA              - dump PGA
dump stack            - dump call stack
dump core             - dump core without crashing process
dump level 0          - dump error buffer
dump level 1          - level 0 + call stack
dump level 2          - level 1 + process state objects
dump level 3          - level 2 + context area
dump system 1         - brief system states dump
dump system 2         - full system states dump
dump ipc              - dump ipc information
dump controlfile #    - dump control file at level #
dump datafile #       - dump data file header at level #
dump procstat         - dump process statistics
event <event-trace>   - turn on event trace
unlimit trace         - unlimit the size of trace file
exit                  - exit this program
!                     - shell escape
```

The following example illustrates how to take a process state dump of a process using the ORADBX utility.

1. Start ORADBX.

2. Initiate a user process—for example, SQL*PLUS.

3. Determine the pid for the user process via a **ps** command.

4. In ORADBX, enter **debug** *pid*.

5. In ORADBX, enter **dump level 2**.

This will create a trace file with the process state dump.

## V$ Views

Oracle maintains a set of tables called *dynamic performance tables*. The data in these tables keep changing during normal operation of the database. Though most of these tables contain data relating to the performance of the database, there are some tables that contain information regarding the control file, data files, log files, and backup information. There are a set of V_$ views created on top of these tables and public synonyms are created on top of these views, which are prefixed with V$. Some of the V$ objects (commonly referred to as V$ views) are extremely useful while diagnosing common problems on a day-to-day basis, and to monitor the normal database activity and its status. Some V$ views are very useful while diagnosing problems relating to backup and recovery. A list of some of the important V$ views is given here:

| | | |
|---|---|---|
| V$ACCESS | V$INSTANCE | V$RECOVERY_FILE |
| V$ARCHIVE | V$LOCK | V$ROLLNAME |
| V$BACKUP | V$LOG | V$ROLLSTAT |
| V$BGPROCESS | V$LOGFILE | V$SESSION |
| V$DATABASE | V$LOG_HISTORY | V$SESSION_WAIT |
| V$DATAFILE | V$PROCESS | V$THREAD |
| V$DB_OBJECT_CACHE | V$RECOVERY_LOG | V$WAITSTAT |

## Lock Utility

Locking is an essential aspect of any dynamic system where there are many users or many processes sharing access to a single object or resource. Depending on the applications being used, or on the circumstances of process termination, there are situations that can cause processes to hang while waiting for a particular resource. For many DBAs, determining which process is "holding up" the rest involves intense scrutinization of the MONITOR LOCK screen.

There are two types of locks that are managed by the Oracle RDBMS: Internal Locks and Data (DML) Locks.

The two categories of internal locks are *latches* and *enqueues.* Both latches and enqueues protect shared-memory data structures. Enqueues, however, protect other objects as well, such as access to control files, redo logs, and rollback segments. Latches are internal locks that are only held for short periods of time. Structures such as the LRU chain in the buffer cache are protected by this latch, meaning processes that make modifications to the LRU chain need to acquire this latch before doing so.

When a process wishes to acquire a latch, most of the time it tries to acquire it with a *willing to wait* request. This means that it is willing to retry in the event that it cannot acquire the latch on the first try. The overall assumption here is that, since latches will be held for very short periods of time, a short waiting period followed by a retry will be successful. Enqueues are also internal locks, but they differ from latches in that there is a built-in mechanism for processes to wait in line for the resource. Enqueues can be held in shared or exclusive mode, depending on the degree of sharing allowed for the given transaction. One of the most common types of enqueue is the Row Cache Enqueue.

Data Locks, which are present to protect the consistency of the data, can be held in exclusive or shared mode at the row or table level. With row-level locking, this category of locks is the most common source of contention.

To diagnose locking problems, or systems hung on locks, Oracle provides a file called UTLLOCKT.SQL. This script file can be quite useful for filtering out relevant information from the MONITOR LOCK screen, especially when there may be many other users whose shared locks are not really interesting to the problem at hand. The UTLLOCKT.SQL script is normally found in the **rdbms/admin** directory and clearly describes how to use this script and interpret the output. Figure 6-2 gives a sample output when script file UTLLOCKT.SQL is run.

According to the documentation in the UTLLOCKT.SQL script, "if a process id is printed immediately below and to the right of another process, then it is waiting for that process. The process ids printed at the left hand side of the page are the ones that everyone is waiting for." In Figure 6-2, process 10 is waiting for process 7. The lock information to the right of the process ID describes the lock that this process is waiting for. By definition, process 7 is not waiting for any locks. What this implies is that 7 is the process that is *blocking* or *holding up* the other processes from acquiring the resources that they wait for. Also shown is the fact that process 10 is waiting for a transaction (TX) lock.

# Debugging the RDBMS

In this section we discuss when and why you would want to take dumps of control files, datablocks, log file headers, and data file headers using the **ALTER SESSION** command. The **ALTER SYSTEM** command to dump contents of redo log files is discussed as well. Then, using some sample dumps, some of the data structures useful to the DBA are discussed.

## Control File Dump

The control file can be dumped using the **ALTER SESSION** statement while the database is open or mounted. Oracle Worldwide Support uses the control file dump to diagnose various problems. Sometimes the wrong version of a data file or log file might be used by the DBA to start up the database. Oracle will normally give an error, for example,

```
ORA—01130: data file version num incompatible with ORACLE Version num.
```

| WAITING SESSION | LOCK TYPE | MODE_REQUESTED | MODE_HELD | LOCK_ID1 | LOCK_ID2 |
|---|---|---|---|---|---|
| 7 | None | | | | |
| 10 | Transaction | Exclusive | Exclusive | 327731 | 721 |

**FIGURE 6-2.**  *Sample output of a Lock Wait Tree*

Other reasons for dumping the control file would include

- To check the status of the data files
- To see the status of the threads
- To see if the database was ever started using the **RESETLOGS** option
- To check *compatibility version*
- To see checkpointing information
- To see the status of online log file information

There is much more information that Oracle Worldwide Support and developers use from a control file dump while debugging various RDBMS problems.

One common reason DBAs would dump the control file would be to see the full path names of all the data files and log files when the database is down. When the database is open or mounted, selecting from V$DATAFILE gives the same information gotten by reading the control file dump.

Figure 6-3 gives a partial dump of a control file. Each line of the dump is numbered for reference in the discussion that follows. This dump is taken on a VMS system running Oracle7 release 7.1.2.

Lines 1 through 17 of Figure 6-3 give the trace file header information. This includes information of the foreground process that created this trace file, the executable this process was running, a timestamp, the Oracle version number, and finally, information concerning the operating system. Line 18 indicates that this is the dump of a control file. At the beginning of any file dump, Oracle records a similar set of information regarding the database files, and this is known as the *generic file header* information. Lines 19 through 23 give the generic file header information. Note that this generic file header information would be the same for any data file or log file in this database.

Line 20 shows the *software version* to be 0x700c000. This is the hexadecimal representation that is equivalent to 7.0.12.0.0 in the decimal form. This is the Oracle version under which this control file was created. Note that the current version of the software is release 7.1.2, which means that the Oracle software version has been upgraded after the original install. The *compatibility version* (7.0.9.0.0) is the lowest version of Oracle software with which the format of this control file is compatible.

The *Db Id* (0xc3b1c389) on line 21 is the database identification number, which is created by the hashed database name and creation time. This identification number is placed in all generic file headers and verified when the database is started. *Db Name* is the database name.

The control file sequence number on line 22 indicates the number of times this control file has been updated. This can be considered as the version of the control

```
1.   Dump file ORA_DUMP:WRVMS_RDBMS5_FG_SQLDBA_009.trc
2.   15-APR-1994 17:53:34.01:
3.   Oracle7 Server Release 7.1.2.0.0 - Beta Release
4.   With the procedural, distributed, parallel query and Parallel Server options
5.   PL/SQL Release 2.1.2.0.0 - Beta
6.   Parallel server mode inactive
7.   Proc: 0x3d4251f0 RVELPURI2 User: [113,040] RVELPURI Term: VTA824:
8.   Image: $1$DUA41:[V7ROOT.RDBMS]SQLDBA.EXE;8
9.   Enqueue Quota: 200
10.  vsnsql=a vsnxtr=3
11.  cpu 4700 13000202 vms V5.5-2H4 clustered with 35 nodes
12.  scsnd: WRVMS, ndname: WRVMS, sys$node WRVMS::
13   cpuid 13 rev 01CB00000000000013000202 archflg 38F0
14.  hwmdl: 459 hwnm: VAX 4000-700A cpus: FFFFFFFF cpush: 0 active: 1, avail: 1
15.  locktbl size 160000 max 480001 resource hash size 65535
16.  15-APR-1994 17:53:33.46:

17.  *** SESSION ID:(7.51)

18.  DUMP OF CONTROL FILES, Seq # 12181 = 2f95
19.  FILE HEADER:
20.  Software vsn=117489664=700c000, Compatibility Vsn= 117477376= 7009000
21.  Db Id=3283207049=c3b1c389, Db Name='RDBMS5'
22.  Control Seq=12181=2f95, File size=280=118
23.  File Number=0, Blksiz=512, File Type=1

24.  DATABASE ENTRY:
25.  (offset = 0x163, size = 129, max = 1, hi = 1)
26.  DF Version:creation=0x700c000 compatable=0x700b000, Date 01/08/93 11:30:17
27.  DB Name RDBMS5
28.  Database flags = 0x00000041
29.  Incmplt recovery scn: 0.00000000 Resetlogs scn: 0.00000000 count: 0x0
30.  Redo Version: creation=0x700c000 compatable=0x700c000
31.  #Data files = 8, #Online files = 5
32.  Database checkpoint: Thread=1 scn: 1f4.912955e8
33.  Threads: #Enabled=3, #Open=1, Head=1, Tail=1
34.  enabled  threads:  01110000 00000000 00000000 00000000 00000000 00000000 00000000
35.  Max log members = 2, Max data members = 1
36.  Log hist = 1134, Arch list: Head=4, Tail=1, Force scn: 1f4.01068bb6

37.  REDO THREAD ENTRIES:
38.  (offset = 0x200, size = 80, max = 16, hi = 3)
39.  THREAD #1 - status:0x7 thread links forward:0 back:0
40.  #logs:2 first:1 last:2 current:1 last used seq#:0x3c5
41.  enabled at scn: 1f4.010687d6 01/04/94 12:49:59
42.  opened at 04/14/94 23:25:04 by instance RDBMS5
43.  Checkpointed at scn: 1f4.912955e8 04/15/94 17:52:56
44.  thread:1 rba:(3c5.2.10)
45.  enabled  threads:  01110000 00000000 00000000 00000000 00000000 00000000 00000000
46.  THREAD #2 - status:0x6 thread links forward:0 back:0
47.  #logs:3 first:3 last:7 current:4 last used seq#:0x87
48.  enabled at scn: 1f4.010686fc 01/03/94 16:10:17
```

**FIGURE 6-3.** *Partial dump of control file on Oracle7 release 7.1.2*

```
49.  opened at 02/14/94 17:32:22 by instance RDBMS5
50.  Checkpointed at scn: 1f4.01068b6f 02/18/94 17:18:04
51.  thread:2 rba:(87.1b.0)
52.  enabled threads:  01110000 00000000 00000000 00000000 00000000 00000000 00000000
53.  THREAD #3.
```
———————————————————————————————————— Thread #3 infomation continues here.
```
54.  LOG FILE ENTRIES:
55.  (offset = 0x700, size = 63, max = 32, hi = 7)
56.  LOG FILE #1:
57.  (#  1) DISK$WR3:[V7ROOT.DB_RDBMS5]ORA_LOG1.RDO
58.  Thread 1 redo log links: forward=2 backward=0
59.  siz=0x3e8 seq=0x3c5 hws=0x1 bsz=512 nab=0xffffffff flg=0x8
60.  Archive links: fwrd=0 back=5 Prev scn: 1f4.912955e5
61.  Low scn: 1f4.912955e7 04/15/94 17:52:56
62.  Next scn: ffff.ffffffff 04/15/94 17:52:47
63.  LOG FILE #2:
64.  (#  2) DISK$WR3:[V7ROOT.DB_RDBMS5]ORA_LOG2.RDO
65.  Thread 1 redo log links: forward=0 backward=1
66.  siz=0x3e8 seq=0x3c4 hws=0x2 bsz=512 nab=0x2 flg=0x1
67.  Archive links: fwrd=0 back=0 Prev scn: 1f4.01068bb6
68.  Low scn: 1f4.912955e5 04/15/94 17:52:47
69.  Next scn: 1f4.912955e7 04/15/94 17:52:56
70.  LOG FILE #3.
```
———————————————————————————————— Log file#3 to log file#7 information continues here.
```
71.  DB FILE ENTRIES:
72.  (offset = 0xee0, size = 107, max = 32, hi = 8)
73.  DATA FILE #1:
74.  (#  3) DISK$WR3:[V7ROOT.DB_RDBMS5]ORA_SYSTEM.DBS
75.  size=5120 bsize=2048 status=xf head=3 tail=3 dup=1
76.  Checkpoint cnt:888 scn: 1f4.912955e8 stop scn: ffff.ffffffff 04/14/94 23:16:33
77.  Creation Checkpointed at scn: 0.00000003 01/08/93 11:30:50
78.  thread:1 rba:(1.3.10)
79.  enabled threads:01000000 00000000 00000000 00000000 00000000 00000000 00000000
80.  Offline scn: 0.00000000
81.  Online Checkpointed at scn: 0.00000000 01/01/88 00:00:00
82.  thread:0 rba:(0.0.0)
83.  enabled threads:00000000 00000000 00000000 00000000 00000000 00000000 00000000
84.  DATA FILE #2:
85.  (#  4) DISK$WR3:[V7ROOT.DB_RDBMS5]ORA_SYSTEM2.DBS
86.  size=512 bsize=2048 status=xf head=4 tail=4 dup=1
87.  Checkpoint cnt:836 scn: 1f4.912955e8 stop scn: ffff.ffffffff 04/14/94 23:16:33
88.  Creation Checkpointed at scn: 80.000bc80f 01/19/93 12:52:55
89.  thread:1 rba:(27.250.192)
90.  enabled threads:01000000 00000000 00000000 00000000 00000000 00000000 00000000
91.  Offline scn: 0.00000000
92.  Online Checkpointed at scn: 0.00000000 01/01/88 00:00:00
93.  thread:0 rba:(0.0.0)
94.  enabled threads:00000000 00000000 00000000 00000000 00000000 00000000 00000000
95.  DATA FILE #3:
96.  (#  5) DISK$WR3:[V7ROOT.DB_RDBMS5]USERS1.DBS
97.  size=5120 bsize=2048 status=xe head=5 tail=5 dup=1
```

**FIGURE 6-3.**    *Partial dump of control file on Oracle7 release 7.1.2* (continued)

```
 98.  Checkpoint cnt:69 scn: 1f4.912955da stop scn: ffff.ffffffff 04/14/94 23:30:37
 99.  Creation Checkpointed at scn: 1f4.01068793 01/04/94 11:58:38
100.  thread:2 rba:(68.25e.186)
101.  enabled  threads:01100000 00000000 00000000 00000000 00000000 00000000 00000000
102.  Offline scn: 1f4.912955af
103.  Online Checkpointed at scn: 1f4.912955ba 04/14/94 23:32:08
104.  thread:1 rba:(3c3.19c.14)
105.  enabled  threads:01110000 00000000 00000000 00000000 00000000 00000000 00000000
106.  DATA FILE #4:
107.  (#  8) DISK$WR3:[V7ROOT.DB_RDBMS5]TEST1.DBS
108.  size=1024 bsize=2048 status=x80 head=8 tail=8 dup=1
```
————————————————————————————————— Data file #4 information continues here.
```
109.  DATA FILE #5:
110.  (#  9) DISK$WR3:[V7ROOT.DB_RDBMS5]ORA_SYSTEM3.DBS
111.  size=5120 bsize=2048 status=xf head=9 tail=9 dup=1
```
————————————————————————————————— Data file #5 information continues here.
```
112.  DATA FILE #6:
113.  (# 11) DISK$WR3:[V7ROOT.DB_RDBMS5]TEST.DBS
114.  size=5 bsize=2048 status=x10 head=11 tail=11 dup=1
```
————————————————————————————————— Data file #6 information continues here.
```
115.  DATA FILE #7:
116.  (# 14) DISK$WR3:[V7ROOT.DB_RDBMS5]TEST2.DBS
117.  size=5 bsize=2048 status=x80 head=14 tail=14 dup=1
```
————————————————————————————————— Data file #7 information continues here.
```
118.  DATA FILE #8:
119.  (# 15) DISK$WR3:[V7ROOT.DB_RDBMS5]TEST3.DBS
120.  size=10 bsize=2048 status=x86 head=15 tail=15 dup=1
```
————————————————————————————————— Data file #8 information continues here.
```
121.  LOG FILE HISTORY ENTRIES:
122.  (offset = 0x8060, size = 24, max = 1600, hi = 1134)
123.  Earliest log history:
124.  Record 1: Thread=1 Seq#=1 Link=1
125.  Low scn: 0.00000001 01/08/93 11:30:25 Next scn: 0.00000076
126.  Latest log history:
127.  Record 1134: Thread=1 Seq#=964 Link=1133
128.  Low scn: 1f4.912955e5 04/15/94 17:52:47 Next scn: 1f4.912955e7
129.  *** END OF DUMP ***
```

**FIGURE 6-3.**  *Partial dump of control file on Oracle7 release 7.1.2 (continued)*

file. *File size* is the physical size of the control file in blocks. 280 is the decimal value and 118 is its hex representation. Note that this doesn't include the file header block. So 281 * block size gives the size of the control file in bytes. The block size is given on the next line as 512 bytes, which is the same as the operating system block size. Oracle defines file types for control files, log files, and database files. Line 23 indicates that the control file type is 1 and the file number is zero.

After the generic file header, the control file dump is divided into 5 sections:

- Database entry
- Redo thread entries
- Log file entries
- Data file entries
- Log file history entries

The *database entry* portion of the control file gives information regarding the database. Lines 24 through 36 of Figure 6-3 contain data structures that belong to the database entry. Let's examine some of the important data structures.

Line 25 gives the *offset* in hexadecimal bytes. This is the offset where the database entry starts in the control file, and *size* is the size of the database entry in bytes.

Line 29 is of importance to DBAs. These structures are normally updated after doing incomplete recovery. If *count* is a nonzero value, then *Resetlogs SCN* gives the SCN value at which the database was open with the RESETLOGS option. We have learned in Chapter 5 that Oracle will not allow the DBA to apply redo to this database that was created before the *resetlogs SCN*. This is why the DBA must take a backup of the database after starting it up with the RESETLOGS option.

On line 31, *#Data files* gives the number of data files that belong to the database, whether offline or online. The files that are dropped from the database (using the **drop tablespace** command) are not counted. In this database, there are a total of eight data files, of which three files are offline.

Line 33 gives information regarding the total number of threads that are enabled and open. If *#open* is greater than one, this indicates that this database is running with the parallel server option. Note that this database is accessed by only one instance but two more threads have been created ( *#enabled=3)*. The instance that started the database has one thread open. The other two threads are enabled but not open.

Line 35 shows that this database can have a maximum of two log file members per group. The parameter MAXLOGMEMBERS is specified during the creation time of the database. Note that the maximum number of data file members is one. At this time Oracle doesn't support mirroring of data files. This is reserved for future use.

Line 36 gives the last updated entry in the circular log history table that resides in the control file. Any redo with a start SCN below the *force SCN* will be forced to archive out. The force SCN is the SCN before which all log files are archived out.

*Redo thread entries* is the second part of the control file dump, which starts at line 37. On line 38, *max* indicates the maximum number of redo threads that can be enabled and *hi* gives the number of threads currently enabled. Since three threads are enabled, information of thread 1 follows from lines 39 through 45; information of thread 2 from lines 46 through 52, and so on.

The *status* on line 39 indicates that this thread is *publicly enabled and open*. Note that the status of thread 1 is different from that of thread 2 (line 39 versus line 46). This is because thread 2 is publicly enabled but not open.

Line 40 gives some important information regarding the log file groups of thread 1. *#logs* indicates the number of log file groups that thread 1 has, and the *current* log file group that the LGWR process is writing to is log #1. This log file has a log sequence number of 0x3c5 (hex), as indicated on line 40. The SCN at which thread 1 is enabled is given, followed by the time stamp on line 41. Similarly, the next line gives the time stamp at which this thread was opened.

The third part of Figure 6-3 gives the *log file entries* information for each log file group of all the threads. As indicated on line 55, (hi = 7), there are a total of seven log file groups. The full path name of the first log file is given on line 57.

The next two lines indicate that this log file belongs to thread 1 and the size of the log file is 0x3e8 (hex). The sequence number of this log file is 0x3c5 (hex) and the log file, similar to the control file, has a block size of 512 bytes. The structure *nab* is the next available block in the log file that the LGWR process can write to. If this log file is the current log file that the LGWR process is writing to, then this value is set to infinity as shown on line 59. When a log switch happens, a low SCN is allocated to the new log file, which is the same as the high SCN of the log file that it just filled. The high SCN of a current log is infinite. The low SCN and next SCN on lines 61 and 62 are the low and high SCN values of the log file.

The fourth part of Figure 6-3 gives the *data file entries* information for each data file starting at line 71. Line 72 indicates, similar to the log file entries, that there are eight data files in this database. The full path name of the data file is given. When you select from the V$DATAFILE view, this is where it gets the information. The *status* indicates that this file belongs to the system tablespace.

On line 76, the checkpoint counter has a value 888. This is the number of times a checkpoint was done on this file. This counter keeps incrementing every time a checkpoint is done on this file, even when the data file is in hot backup mode. The *stop SCN* is the SCN after which no recovery is required for this file. Note that this value will be set only when the database is shut down normally. While the database is open, this value is set to infinity.

Oracle7 introduced a new **alter database create datafile** command. This command allows a DBA to create and recover a new data file when the original file is lost. So Oracle keeps track of the SCN value from which recovery needs to be applied after creating such a file. On line 77 is the creation checkpoint SCN, meaning that this was the SCN when this file was created. When a file is taken offline (by taking the tablespace offline), the SCN at which the file is taken offline is recorded as the *offline SCN* in the control file. This is shown on lines 80 and 102.

The offline SCN on line 80 corresponds to that of the system data file, and thus has a zero value since system data files can never be taken offline. Line 102 shows the offline SCN at which USER1.DBS is taken offline.

Similarly, when a tablespace is put in hot backup mode by using the **alter tablespace begin backup** command, a checkpoint is done on all the data files that belong to this tablespace. This is recorded as the *online checkpointed at SCN* as shown on lines 81 and 103. This information is recorded for every data file.

It is interesting to observe the status set for different data files. Note that the data files ORA_SYSTEM.DBS, ORA_SYSTEM2.DBS, and ORA_SYSTEM3.DBS belong to the SYSTEM tablespace. Every other data file belongs to its own tablespace, which has the same name as its data file. Before taking the control file dump, the following was done:

- Tablespace TEST was taken offline immediate

- Tablespaces TEST1 and TEST2 were taken offline normal

- Tablespace TEST3 was put in READ ONLY mode (available from release 7.1)

- Tablespace USER1 was put in HOT BACKUP mode

Now observe the status of each data file given in Figure 6-3.

The last portion of Figure 6-3 gives the information regarding *log file history entries*. The control file dump, even when set to level 10, doesn't dump the complete log history table. There is a special event to dump the log history entries, which we discussed in the previous section. If the database is open, selecting from the V$LOG_HISTORY table would give all the entries. Line 122 indicates that a total of 1600 log history entries can be stored in the control file, of which 1134 records are created. Note that this is a circular table. The first and last records from this table are given when the control file is dumped. Line 124 gives the log sequence number and the thread number of the first entry. The next line gives the low and high SCNs that are recorded in this log file. Similar information is given for the latest entry of the log file history table.

# Redo Log File Dump

In this section, we will examine the file dump of a redo log file header. To diagnose some of the data corruptions, it is often necessary for Oracle Worldwide Support analysts to take a look at the contents of the redo log file as well. The **alter system** command to dump the contents (redo information) of a redo log file is introduced.

### File Header
Figure 6-4 gives the output of a redo log file header dump. Note that the **alter system** command dumps the header information to the trace file for every online log file.

```
SQLDBA> alter session set events 'immediate trace name redohdr level 10';
1.   Dump file C:\ORACLE7\RDBMS70\trace\ORA07655.TRC
2.   Tue Nov 29 07:00:28 1994
3.   ORACLE V7.0.16.6.0 - Beta vsnsta=1
4.   vsnsql=7 vsnxtr=3
5.   MS-WINDOWS Version 3.10
6.   Tue Nov 29 07:00:28 1994

7.   *** SESSION ID:(6.3)

8.   DUMP OF LOG FILES: 2 logs in database

9.   LOG FILE #1:
10.  (#  2) C:\ORACLE7\DBS\wdblog1.log
11.  Thread 1 redo log links: forward=2 backward=0
12.  siz=0x190 seq=0x6 hws=0xd bsz=512 nab=0xffffffff flg=0x8
13.  Archive links: fwrd=0 back=0 Prev scn: 0.0000194e
14.  Low scn: 0.0000195f 11/24/94 09:22:29
15.  Next scn: ffff.ffffffff 11/24/94 09:21:46
16.  FILE HEADER:
17.  Software vsn=117507584=7010600, Compatibility Vsn= 117489664= 700c000
18.  Db Id=1082323460=4082f204, Db Name='ORACLE'
19.  Control Seq=386=182, File size=400=190
20.  File Number=1, Blksiz=512, File Type=2
21.  descrip:"Thread 0001, Seq# 0000000006, SCN 0x00000000195f-0xffffffffffff"
22.  thread:1 nab:0xffffffff seq:0x6 hws:0xd eot:1 dis:0
23.  reset logs count:0xd06f592 scn: 0.000018aa
24.  Low scn: 0.0000195f 11/24/94 09:22:29
25.  Next scn: ffff.ffffffff 11/24/94 09:21:46
26.  Enabled scn: 0.000018aa 10/19/94 15:04:50
27.  Thread closed scn: 0.00001999 11/27/94 09:20:25

28.  LOG FILE #2:
29.  (#  1) C:\ORACLE7\DBS\wdblog2.log
30.  Thread 1 redo log links: forward=0 backward=1
31.  siz=0x190 seq=0x5 hws=0x7 bsz=512 nab=0x12 flg=0x1
32.  Archive links: fwrd=0 back=0 Prev scn: 0.0000193f
33.  Low scn: 0.0000194e 11/24/94 09:21:46
34.  Next scn: 0.0000195f 11/24/94 09:22:29
35.  FILE HEADER:
36.  Software vsn=117507584=7010600, Compatibility Vsn= 117489664= 700c000
37.  Db Id=1082323460=4082f204, Db Name='ORACLE'
38.  Control Seq=386=182, File size=400=190
39.  File Number=2, Blksiz=512, File Type=2
40.  descrip:"Thread 0001, Seq# 0000000005, SCN 0x00000000194e-0x00000000195f"
41.  thread:1 nab:0x12 seq:0x5 hws:0x7 eot:0 dis:0
42.  reset logs count:0xd06f592 scn: 0.000018aa
43.  Low scn: 0.0000194e 11/24/94 09:21:46
44.  Next scn: 0.0000195f 11/24/94 09:22:29
45.  Enabled scn: 0.000018aa 10/19/94 15:04:50
46.  Thread closed scn: 0.0000194e 11/24/94 09:21:46
```

**FIGURE 6-4.** *Dump of redo log file header*

Most of the data structures in Figure 6-4 should be familiar to the readers by now. Lines 1 through 7 give the header of the trace file. Line 8 indicates that this is a log file header dump. There are two log groups in this database. With Oracle7, when the log file or data file header is dumped, the trace file contains not only the header information of the requested file but also its corresponding entries from the control file. In Figure 6-4, lines 9 through 15 are taken from the *log file entries* portion of the control file for this log group. Lines 16 through 20 give the *generic file header* stored in the log file. The information in lines 21 through 27 is derived from the log file header. In other words, the data structures given between lines 9 through 15 and 21 through 27 should be identical.

Line 21 gives the most important information that a DBA needs. It indicates that this log group belongs to thread 1, has a log sequence number of 6, a low SCN of 0x195f, and next SCN of infinity, indicating that this is the current online log that the LGWR process is writing to. The same information is repeated for log file group 2. Note that the high SCN of log file #2 (line 40) is the same as the low SCN of log file #1.

## Dumping Redo

The **alter system** command can be used to dump the contents of a redo log file into your session's trace file. The command can be issued when the database is in a *nomount, mount,* or *open* state. The records from an online or offline log file can be dumped. A redo log file that belongs to a different database on the same operating system can be dumped to trace as well. This is very useful, as many times Oracle Worldwide Support asks the customer to send the complete log file and dumps the contents of it in house. The complete syntax of this command is given below:

```
ALTER SYSTEM DUMP LOGFILE 'filename' option option...;
option  =  rba min seqno . blockno ¦
           rba max seqno . blockno ¦
           dba min fileno . blockno ¦
           dba max fileno . blockno ¦
           time min value ¦
           time max value ¦
           layer value ¦
           opcode value
```

Note that the statement is not an **alter session** statement but an **alter system** statement. If no options are specified, this statement dumps the entire contents (redo records) of a log file (online or archive) to trace. The *filename* is the name of the log file to be dumped and should be specified in single quotes. The *rba* is the address of the redo information. If a minimum and maximum value of rba is specified, Oracle dumps only the redo records specified between the addresses to the trace file. Alternatively, if the min and max values of a *dba* (data block address) are specified, Oracle dumps all the changes (redo) for that range of data blocks to trace. Specifying a time range would dump the redo created within that time frame. *Layer* and *opcode* should be specified to dump a particular type of redo, for example, all commit records or end hot backup redo records. The values for the opcode, layer, dba, or rba will be supplied by the Oracle Worldwide Support analyst when needed. The following example illustrates the use of this command.

```
SQLDBA> alter system switch logfile;
Statement processed.
SQLDBA> update backup set c2 = 'phy_backup';
2 rows processed.
SQLDBA> commit;
Statement processed.
SQLDBA> select * from backup;
C1        C2
----      ----
1         phy_backup
2         phy_backup
2 rows selected.
SQLDBA> archive log list
Database log mode              NOARCHIVELOG
Automatic archival             ENABLED
Archive destination            C:\ORACLE7\RDBMS70\ARCHIVE
Oldest online log sequence 8
Current log sequence           9
SQLDBA> alter system dump logfile 'C:\ORACLE7\DBS\wdblog2.log';
Statement processed.
SQLDBA> exit
SQL*DBA complete.
```

In the above example, we have opened a new log file by switching logs. An update statement has modified two rows and then the transaction is committed. The **archive log list** command shows that the online redo log file with sequence number 9 contains the change made to the table, *backup*. From views V$LOG and V$LOGFILE, the name of the redo log file can be found. The **alter system** statement dumps this online log file. Figure 6-5 shows the output of the trace file created by the **alter system** command.

# Data File Dump

Data file dumps are very similar to log file dumps. Data file headers can be dumped to a trace file using the **alter session** command. All data file header

```
Dump file C:\ORACLE7\RDBMS70\trace\ORA06471.TRC
Wed Nov 30 07:12:49 1994
ORACLE V7.0.16.6.0 - Beta vsnsta=1
vsnsql=7 vsnxtr=3
MS-WINDOWS Version 3.10
Wed Nov 30 07:12:49 1994


*** SESSION ID:(6.3)

DUMP OF REDO FROM FILE 'C:\ORACLE7\DBS\wdblog2.log'
Opcodes *.*
DBA's: 00000000 thru ffffffff
RBA's: 0x000000:0x00000000:0x0000 thru 0xffffffff:0xffffffff:0xffff
SCN's scn: 0.00000000 thru scn: ffff.ffffffff
Times: creation thru eternity

FILE HEADER:
    Software vsn=117507584=7010600, Compatibility Vsn= 117489664= 700c000
    Db Id=1082323460=4082f204, Db Name='ORACLE'
    Control Seq=397=18d, File size=400=190
    File Number=2, Blksiz=512, File Type=2
descrip:"Thread 0001, Seq# 0000000009, SCN 0x0000000019be-0xffffffffffff"
thread:1 nab:0xffffffff seq:0x9 eot:1 dis:0
reset logs count:0xd06f592 Reset scn: 0.000018aa
Low scn: 0.000019be 11/30/94 07:10:30
Next scn: ffff.ffffffff 11/30/94 07:01:46

REDO RECORD - Thread:1 RBA:0x000009:0x00000002:0x0010 LEN:0x0131 VLD:0x09
NEW MARK SCN scn: 0.000019bf 11/30/94 07:11:34
CHANGE #0 CLASS:15 DBA:0x03000016 INC:0x00001001 SEQ:0x00000a61 OPCODE 5.2
ktudh redo: slt:11 sqn:0x21 flg:0x12 siz:126 fbi: 0uba: 300009d.12.08
CHANGE #1 CLASS:16 DBA:0x0300009d INC:0x00010025 SEQ:0x00000008 OPCODE 5.1
ktudb redo: siz:126 spc:1106 flg:0x12 seq:18 rec:8 xid: 04.0b.21
CHANGE #2 CLASS:1 DBA:0x020000da INC:0x00000065 SEQ:0x00000006 OPCODE 11.5
KTB Redo, op: F  xid: 04.0b.21  uba: 300009d.12.08
code=URP  xtype=XA  bdba=020000da
    hdba=020000d9
itli=1  ispac=0  maxfr=1177
flag=0x2c  lock=1  ckix=0  tabn=0
slot=0  ncol=2  nnew=1  size=0
col 1=[10] Dump of memory from 817a6640 to 817a664a
817A6640 5F796870 6B636162 00067075

REDO RECORD - Thread:1 RBA:0x000009:0x00000002:0x0141 LEN:0x0023 VLD:0x01
CONTINUE SCN scn: 0.000019bf 11/30/94 07:11:34
```

**FIGURE 6-5.** *Dump of redo log file*

```
CHANGE #0 CLASS:1 DBA:0x020000da INC:0x00000065 SEQ:0x00000007 OPCODE 4.1
Block cleanout record, scn: 0.000019bf, entries follow...

REDO RECORD - Thread:1 RBA:0x000009:0x00000002:0x0164 LEN:0x00cd VLD:0x01
CONTINUE SCN scn: 0.000019bf 11/30/94 07:11:34
CHANGE #0 CLASS:16 DBA:0x0300009d INC:0x00010025 SEQ:0x00000009 OPCODE 5.1
ktudb redo: siz:86 spc:978 flg:0x22 seq:18 rec:9 xid: 04.0b.21
CHANGE #1 CLASS:1 DBA:0x020000da INC:0x00000065 SEQ:0x00000008 OPCODE 11.5
KTB Redo, op: C  uba: 300009d.12.09
code=URP  xtype=XA  bdba=020000da
    hdba=020000d9
itli=1  ispac=0  maxfr=1177
flag=0x2c  lock=1  ckix=128  tabn=0
slot=1  ncol=2  nnew=1  size=0
col 1=[10] Dump of memory from 817a6638 to 817a6642
817A6620 5F796870 6B636162
817A6640 01057075

REDO RECORD - Thread:1 RBA:0x000009:0x00000003:0x0041 LEN:0x0045 VLD:0x03
COMMIT SCN scn: 0.000019c0 11/30/94 07:11:37
CHANGE #0 CLASS:15 DBA:0x03000016 INC:0x00001001 SEQ:0x00000a62 OPCODE 5.4
ktucm redo: slt:11 sqn:33 srt:0 sta:9 flg:2ktucf redo: uba: 300009d.12.09 ext:33 spc:890
fbi:0

REDO RECORD - Thread:1 RBA:0x000009:0x00000004:0x0010 LEN:0x002b VLD:0x01
CONTINUE SCN scn: 0.000019c0 11/30/94 07:11:44
CHANGE #0 CLASS:1 DBA:0x020000da INC:0x00000065 SEQ:0x00000009 OPCODE 4.1
Block cleanout record, scn: 0.000019c0, entries follow...
itli: 1  flg: 2  scn: 0.19c0
END OF REDO DUMP
```

**FIGURE 6-5.** *Dump of redo log file* (continued*)*

information will be dumped to the trace file. In this section, a dump of a data file header is shown. Then a brief description of a data block dump follows.

## File Header

Figure 6-6 shows a partial dump of data file headers. The lines are numbered to reference the data structures in the discussion to follow.

Similar to the log file header dump, the dump of a data file header also dumps the control file entry for that data file. This information is derived from the *data file entry* portion of the control file. Information derived from the control file is shown between lines 10 and 19. Information between lines 25 and 31 is derived from the data file header. The *checkpointed at SCN* in the file header (line 29) should match the *SCN* in the control file (line 12). Similarly, the checkpoint counter (indicated as *chkpt cnt* on line 28) in the data file header should match the counter in the control file (indicated as *checkpoint cnt* on line 12). If an old data file is restored

```
1.   Dump file C:\ORACLE7\RDBMS70\trace\ORA07655.TRC
2.   Tue Nov 29 07:01:09 1994
3.   ORACLE V7.0.16.6.0 - Beta vsnsta=1
4.   vsnsql=7 vsnxtr=3
5.   MS-WINDOWS Version 3.10
6.   Tue Nov 29 07:01:09 1994

7.   *** SESSION ID:(6.5)

8.   DUMP OF DATA FILES: 4 files in database

9.   DATA FILE #1:
10.  (#  6) C:\ORACLE7\DBS\wdbsys.ora
11.  size=4096 bsize=2048 status=xf head=6 tail=6 dup=1
12.  Checkpoint cnt:136 scn: 0.0000199a stop scn: ffff.ffffffff 11/27/94 09:20:25
13   Creation Checkpointed at scn: 0.00000003 07/04/94 19:54:13
14.  thread:0 rba:(0.0.0)
15.  enabled  threads:  00000000 00000000 00000000 00000000 00000000 00000000 00000000
16.  Offline scn: 0.00000000
17.  Online Checkpointed at scn: 0.00000000 01/01/88 00:00:00
18.  thread:0 rba:(0.0.0)
19.  enabled  threads:  00000000 00000000 00000000 00000000 00000000 00000000 00000000
20   FILE HEADER:
21.  Software vsn=117507584=7010600, Compatibility Vsn= 117485568= 700b000
22.  Db Id=1082323460=4082f204, Db Name='ORACLE'
23.  Control Seq=386=182, File size=4096=1000
24.  File Number=1, Blksiz=2048, File Type=3
25.  Creation    at    scn: 0.00000003 07/04/94 19:54:13
26.  Backup taken at scn: 0.00000000 01/01/88 00:00:00 thread:0
27.  reset logs count:0xd06f592 scn: 0.000018aa recovered at 11/24/94 09:21:45
28.  status:0x104 root dba:0x01000179 chkpt cnt: 136 ctl cnt:135
29.  Checkpointed at scn: 0.0000199a 11/29/94 06:51:54
30.  thread:1 rba:(6.5d.10)
31.  enabled  threads:  01000000 00000000 00000000 00000000 00000000 00000000 00000000

32.  DATA FILE #2: ——————————————————  same information repeats for data files 2,3, and 4
```

**FIGURE 6-6.**   *Partial dump of data file header*

before starting up the database, this is how Oracle knows that media recovery for that file is required.

## Block Dump

While diagnosing block corruptions, it's common to examine the data, index, and rollback segment blocks. The **alter session** command can be used to take block dumps of such segments. Calculating the address of the data block is operating system–dependent because the number of bits representing the file number and block number are different for different operating systems. Oracle Worldwide

Support analysts usually give the address in decimal form to DBAs when a block dump is required. The following example illustrates using the **alter session** command to take a block dump.

Let's assume that a table called BACKUP has two rows. We are interested in dumping the data block of this table. The contents of the table are as follows:

```
SQLDBA> select * from backup;
C1        C2
----      ----
1         log_backup
2         phy_backup
2 rows selected.
SQLDBA> alter session set events 'immediate trace name blockdump
level 33554650';
Statement processed.
```

The above **alter session** command will dump the data block to a trace file. Figure 6-7 gives the output of the trace.

# Oracle Errors and Resolution

This section is divided into two parts. The first part focuses on common errors that a DBA encounters on a day-to-day basis in the areas of space management and general database administration. These common errors, their background, resolution, and some proactive measures are discussed. Oracle internal errors are uncommon yet severe, and may cause down production database or applications. Such internal errors are usually due to various data structure corruptions caused by hardware and software failures. Such problems are categorized and diagnostic actions to DBAs are suggested. Next, a few examples are provided to illustrate how to deal with block corruptions.

## Common Oracle Errors

A user approaches the DBA and tells him that he can't add rows to his table because Oracle is giving some error. This is a very common scenario, and one of the less stressful situations compared to some others that DBAs face. In this section, we discuss some of the typical problems that DBAs face on a day-to-day basis, such as space management issues with tables and indexes. Errors due to memory fragmentation problems with shared pool area, problems with snapshots, and finally rollback segment management are discussed in this section. Problem resolution or workarounds are suggested where applicable.

```
Dump file C:\ORACLE7\RDBMS70\trace\ORA12447.TRC
Wed Nov 30 10:08:58 1994
ORACLE V7.0.16.6.0 - Beta vsnsta=1
vsnsql=7 vsnxtr=3
MS-WINDOWS Version 3.10
Wed Nov 30 10:08:58 1994

*** SESSION ID:(6.1)
buffer dba: 20000DA inc: 65 seq: 10 ver: 1 type: 6=trans data
Block header dump: dba: 20000da
Object id on Block? Y
seg/obj: 35d  csc: 00.19d1  itc: 1  flg: O  typ: 1 - DATA
fsl: 0  fnx: 0
itl 01:  xid: 01.18.21  uba: 1000734.28.04  flg: C--- lkc: 0  scn: 0.19d1
data_block_dump
===============
tsiz: 0x7b8
hsiz: 0x16
pbl=81ac04a4
bdba: 020000da
flag=---------
ntab=1
nrow=2
frre=-1
fsbo=0x16
fseo=0x796
avsp=0x780
tosp=0x780
0xe:pti[0]  nrow=2  offs=0
0x12:pri[0] offs=0x7a7
0x14:pri[1] offs=0x796
block_row_dump:
tab 0, row 0, @0x7a7
tl=17 fb: --H-FL-- lb: 0x0 cc: 2
col 0: [2]
c1 02
col 1: [10]
6c 6f 67 5f 62 61 63 6b 75 70
tab 0, row 1, @0x796
tl=17 fb: --H-FL-- lb: 0x0 cc: 2
col 0: [2]
c1 03
col 1: [10]
70 68 79 5f 62 61 63 6b 75 70
end_of_block_dump
```

**FIGURE 6-7.**  *Data block dump*

## ORA-1545

When we see a rollback segment with NEEDS RECOVERY status, it means precisely that the rollback segment needs to be recovered. Here is some useful information on the issue and how to work around it.

In Chapter 5, we have learned that on instance startup, Oracle performs crash recovery. This leaves the database in a state in which the roll forward is complete and there is no more redo to be applied. Then the rollback segments are scanned to roll back all the uncommitted or active transactions that are detected by looking at the transaction table of the rollback segments. If undo can be applied to all the uncommitted transactions, the rollback will be successful and complete. If Oracle cannot, for any reason, apply the undo, then the rollback segment is not recovered completely and will be put in the NEEDS RECOVERY state. The best way to detect this is to set the diagnostic events 10013 and 10015 as discussed earlier in this chapter. When these events are set, the transaction table is dumped to the trace file for all the rollback segments both before and after recovery. For rollback segments that are completely recovered, there will be a dump for both—that is, before and after recovery of the rollback segment. But for irrecoverable rollback segments, there will be a *before image* dump with a stack trace. By scanning the transaction table before recovery, you should see active transaction entries. In the trace file, there will also be an Oracle error, ORA-1135, somewhere after the transaction table dump. The error indicates that a particular data file is offline, and looks something like the following:

```
ORA-01135 file name accessed for DML/query is off-line
```

This indicates that there is a data file that is offline and undo needs to be applied to this file. If the INIT.ORA file specifies a rollback segment to be acquired for the instance, which is marked as NEEDS RECOVERY, you will get the ORA-1545 error, which says

```
ORA-01545 rollback segment #'name' was not available
```

Unfortunately, the message doesn't say why it is unavailable. By simply taking the rollback segment name off of the ROLLBACK_SEGMENTS parameter list in INIT.ORA, you should be able to start up the database if that's the only segment that needs recovery. The DBA might find that there is more than one rollback segment in NEEDS RECOVERY state, but this gets you over the problem temporarily. The important question you might ask is, *why can't undo be applied while rolling back?* The most probable reason is that either the DBA has taken a tablespace offline using the *immediate* option, or has made a file offline before opening the database, while mounted. This problem can be permanently resolved in one of two ways:

- Bring the tablespace online so that the online command will cause the undo to be applied and change the status of the rollback segment.

- Drop the tablespace so that the drop command will trash the undo, as it is no longer required. Obviously, this action can be taken only if the tablespace can be rebuilt.

Either of the above actions can be taken while the database is open. If neither can be used, then bringing the database up without the rollback segments specified in the INIT.ORA and leaving the database open for a while (maybe 30 minutes) will change the rollback segment's status from NEEDS RECOVERY to AVAILABLE. This undercover job is done by SMON, which, among other things, looks at the rollback segments and copies the unapplied undo to *saveundo* (a deferred rollback segment). The DBA needs to make sure that there is sufficient free space in the system tablespace for this to happen. The save undo will stay there until the tablespace in question is available again. If the system rollback segment has a transaction that is active, and can't be rolled back because of a tablespace being offline, then the DBA needs to go back to a backup. Needless to say, this should be a rare case and possible only if this database contains a single rollback segment.

### ORA-1547
The ORA-1547 error message simply says that there is no more space to allocate in a specific tablespace. In release 7.1, the error message has been changed to indicate that space cannot be allocated to a specific object in the database. The ORA-1547 error message (only available in Oracle7.0) has been replaced with the following error messages in release 7.1:

| | |
|---|---|
| ORA-1652 | No more space is available to allocate to a temporary segment |
| ORA-1653 | No more space available to allocate to a table |
| ORA-1654 | No more space available to allocate to an index |
| ORA-1655 | No more space available to allocate to a cluster |

Some new concepts in space management have been introduced in release 7.2 that will reduce the administrative overhead while doing space management. One of these is the concept of dynamically resizing data files. Without adding a data file, the DBA can manually extend a file to add more space or shrink a file to reclaim the free space in the database. Appendix A discusses the new features introduced in versions 7.1 and 7.2.

**NOTE**
In this section we assume that the DBA is using Oracle 7.0.

The ORA-1547 error is possibly the most common Oracle error message a DBA would see. You need to understand under what circumstances it arises and the options you have to resolve the error. In Chapter 2, you have learned that Oracle uses the logical *tablespace* unit; however, the physical aspect of the tablespace unit is the data file. The data file, which is created physically on disk, is where all objects within that tablespace reside. In order to add space to the tablespace, you must add a data file. When the ORA-1547 error arises, the problem is due to lack of space in a particular tablespace. The error message gives two parameters: SIZE, which tells the DBA how many Oracle blocks the system was not able to find, and TABLESPACE, which tells the user where the space is needed. Oracle will always try to allocate contiguous space. Although the tablespace may have enough free space, if it is not contiguous, the error will still occur.

In order to see the free space available for a particular tablespace (say, USERS), you must use the view SYS.DBA_FREE_SPACE. Within this view, each record represents one fragment of free space. For example:

```
SQL> SELECT FILE_ID, BLOCK_ID, BLOCKS, BYTES FROM
2 > SYS.DBA_FREE_SPACE WHERE TABLESPACE_NAME='users';
```

| FILE_ID | BLOCK_ID | BLOCKS | BYTES |
|---------|----------|--------|---------|
| 4 | 2 | 20 | 40960 |
| 4 | 1465 | 72 | 147456 |
| 4 | 22 | 25 | 51200 |
| 4 | 147 | 1318 | 2699264 |

4 rows selected.

This query tells you that there are four chunks of free space within the tablespace USERS and each of their sizes, in Oracle blocks and bytes. The above query, however, doesn't properly display the contiguous chunks of free space. If you alter the query a bit by adding an order by clause, the output will be easy to read.

```
SQL> SELECT FILE_ID, BLOCK_ID, BLOCKS, BYTES FROM
2 > DBA_FREE_SPACE WHERE TABLESPACE_NAME='users'
3 > ORDER BY BLOCK_ID;
```

| FILE_ID | BLOCK_ID | BLOCKS | BYTES |
|---------|----------|--------|---------|
| 4 | 2 | 20 | 40960 |
| 4 | 22 | 25 | 51200 |
| 4 | 147 | 1318 | 2699264 |
| 4 | 1465 | 72 | 147456 |

4 rows selected.

You can see that there are really two chunks of contiguous space instead of four. If you carefully examine the output, you see that at block #2, there are 20 blocks of free space. The next chunk of free space starts with block #22, which would make those two chunks contiguous. The same thing applies to block #147. When you add the number of blocks at that location, you see that they end at block 1464, which is adjacent to the next chunk of space.

The information in this view is very important to understand, and this is the area where version 6 differs from Oracle7. Under version 6, the database will coalesce the free space, but only on an as-needed basis. Under Oracle7, the SMON background process wakes up every 5 minutes and coalesces the free space. We have seen in the *setting trace events* section that the DBA can set events to coalesce space immediately.

Using the same example from above, if you try and create a table of 1,325 Oracle blocks (or 2,650K), the free space is coalesced:

```
SQL> CREATE TABLE bulletin (y NUMBER) STORAGE (INITIAL 2650K)
2 > TABLESPACE users;

Table created.

SQL> SELECT FILE_ID, BLOCK_ID, BLOCKS, BYTES FROM
2 > DBA_FREE_SPACE WHERE TABLESPACE_NAME='users'
3 > ORDER BY BLOCK_ID;

FILE_ID   BLOCK_ID   BLOCKS   BYTES
-------   --------   ------   -----
4         2          45       92160
4         1472       65       133120

2 rows selected.
```

In addition, it is important to understand how the space algorithm works internal to Oracle. The RDBMS initially tries to find an exact sized extent. If this doesn't exist, it will then break up an extent of a larger size. Finally, if it still is not able to find space, it will coalesce. Note that dropping the object, has no effect on coalescing. Consider the following example:

```
SQL> DROP TABLE bulletin;

Table dropped.

SQL> SELECT FILE_ID, BLOCK_ID, BLOCKS, BYTES FROM
2 > DBA_FREE_SPACE WHERE TABLESPACE_NAME='users'
3 > ORDER BY BLOCK_ID;
```

```
FILE_ID   BLOCK_ID   BLOCKS   BYTES
-------   --------   ------   -----
4         2          45       92160
4         147        1325     2713600
4         1472       65       133120
```

3 rows selected.

A simpler approach is simply to see what is the biggest chunk of free space you have, and see if it is smaller than the size the error is giving. This is the only approach needed for Oracle7.

Perform the following query:

```
SELECT MAX(BLOCKS) FROM SYS.DBA_FREE_SPACE WHERE TABLESPACE_NAME='name';
```

This will return one record that shows the biggest chunk of space free in the tablespace in question. This number will be lower than the one returned by the error. If you wish to compare the contiguous space with total space, perform the following query:

```
SELECT SUM(BLOCKS) FROM SYS.DBA_FREE_SPACE WHERE TABLESPACE_NAME='name';
```

This also returns one record. This value can be compared to the above to see how much of the total space is contiguous. Note that if there is no space in a tablespace, no records will be retrieved from the SYS.DBA_FREE_SPACE view.

Sometimes a user might try to do an insert into one tablespace and get an error on another tablespace. To understand this, let's examine the objects that can grow in the database.

**Data Dictionary**   The ORA-1547 error will occur if the data dictionary objects need to extend but there is not enough space in the system tablespace for them to do so. This situation presents itself with the ORA-604 error before the ORA-1547 error. For example, if creating a table forces the dictionary table **tab$** to extend and if the SYSTEM tablespace doesn't have enough space, the create table will receive the ORA-604 error followed by the ORA-1547 error.

**Tables and Indexes**   The ORA-1547 error will occur if additional space is needed to satisfy an insert or update of an object. If this error arises on the creation of an index or table, the specified storage or tablespace default storage parameters need to be investigated.

**Rollback Segments**    If the error occurs with a rollback segment, the ORA-1562 error will always precede the ORA-1547 error. The ORA-1562 error indicates that it couldn't extend the rollback segment and the reason is the ORA-1547 error (not enough space). The ORA-1562 error message is given below:

```
ORA-1562 failed to extend rollback segment (id = num)
```

**NOTE**
The ORA-1562 error has been replaced by the ORA-1650 error in release 7.1.

**Temporary Tables**    Temporary tables are created by the Oracle kernel to do a sort on behalf of the user. A user can tell that he or she is running out of space for a temporary table, based on the operation he or she is performing (such as creating an index, doing a query with an ORDER BY clause, or a lengthy *join* statement). In this case, the temporary tablespace of the user needs to be found using the following query:

```
SELECT TEMPORARY_TABLESPACE FROM SYS.DBA_USERS WHERE USERNAME = 'username';
```

If the space being used seems excessive, you may want to investigate the default storage for the temporary tablespace, as it is possible that the defaults are too large. To see the default storage, perform the following query:

```
SELECT INITIAL_EXTENT, NEXT_EXTENT, MIN_EXTENTS, PCT_INCREASE FROM
SYS.DBA_TABLESPACES WHERE TABLESPACE_NAME='name';
```

The default storage of the temporary (or any) tablespace can be altered using the following SQL command:

```
ALTER TABLESPACE name DEFAULT STORAGE (INITIAL xxx NEXT yyy);
```

Rather than add space to the temporary tablespace, you may opt to alter the user so that he or she uses a tablespace you know has more free space. If you wish to change the temporary tablespace for the user, issue the following command:

```
ALTER USER username TEMPORARY TABLESPACE new_tablespace_name;
```

Space can be added to a tablespace using the **alter tablespace** command. This statement will create a database file on disk, and add the file to the tablespace. The **alter tablespace** statement can be performed on any tablespace (including system) without shutting down the database or taking the tablespace offline. Immediately following the completion of the statement, the space is available for the DBA. Once a data file is added, it cannot be deleted, short of dropping the tablespace.

While adding a data file to a tablespace, a DBA might accidentally add a bigger file than needed. In such cases, some DBAs tend to shut the database down, mount it, and use the **alter database** command to take the file offline and then open the database. Then they drop the data file they just added. This is a very dangerous operation. It will work as long as Oracle doesn't allocate any space from this data file. Note that even if the file is taken offline, Oracle will still try to allocate space to it as the free space is seen by Oracle in the **fet$** table. So the only solution to such problems is to export the data in that tablespace, drop the tablespace, re-create the tablespace with the right file sizes, and finally import the data back. A data file can be added to the tablespace using the following command:

```
ALTER TABLESPACE tablespace_name ADD DATAFILE 'filename' SIZE size_of_file;
```

To get an idea of the naming conventions, or locations for existing files, perform the following query:

```
SELECT FILE_NAME FROM SYS.DBA_DATA_FILES WHERE TABLESPACE_NAME='name';
```

Often, users receive the ORA-1547 error while running an import. Some of the common reasons are discussed here.

### Compress Option
Exporting with COMPRESS=Y modifies the *initial extent* storage parameter to be equal to the space that the table has allocated at the time of export. If a user tries to import specific tables into an existing database, the import often fails because it cannot find contiguous space. Consider the scenario where a table is spread across 4 extents of 10MB each. When this table is exported with COMPRESS=Y, the *initial extent* for this table is now 40MB. The user drops the table, then tries to import. The RDBMS cannot find 40MB of contiguous space, which raises an ORA-1547 error. Although the table existed in the tablespace, import can no longer re-create it.

To work around this problem, without adding space to the tablespace, the DBA can do one of the following:

- Export the table and specify COMPRESS=N. This preserves the table's original storage parameters.

- Precreate the table with specific storage parameters before importing.

- Truncate the table before importing the data rather than dropping it.

### Creating Indexes
If the import fails when creating the indexes, you need to modify your temporary tablespace. The solution is to create enough space for the

RDBMS to do the sorting for the index. One workaround is to pre-create the table and index before importing. This should only be used if it is not possible to add the space, even for a short period of time. This method also has a grave effect on the import's performance because every time a row is inserted, the index tree needs to be traversed to insert the key. If you are using SQL*LOADER to load data, a better workaround is to pre-create the index with the *nosort* option. Then you need to pre-sort the data at the OS level before loading it into the table.

**Rollback Segments**     By default, the import utility commits at the end of each table; therefore, it is very likely your rollback segments will run out of space. To work around this problem, without adding space to the rollback segment tablespace, you can specify the COMMIT=Y option on import. This overrides the default and commits at the end of each *buffer* (also an import parameter), rather than at the end of the table. This will impact performance, because every commit forces the LGWR process to write the commit record to the log file on disk, hence doing more I/O.

### ORA-1555

There are various reasons why users can get the ORA-1555 error. The most common reason is that the rollback segments are too small, but there are other reasons as well. The following discussion gives a complete summary of all the situations that would cause the ORA-1555 error and how to resolve them. In order to understand the discussion, you need to be familiar with some of the internal mechanisms of Oracle, so a brief explanation about read consistency and block cleanouts is given.

Oracle always enforces statement-level read consistency. This guarantees that the data returned by a single query is consistent with respect to the time when the query began. Therefore, a query never sees the data changes made by transactions that commit during the course of execution of the query.

We have learned in Chapter 5 that an SCN can be defined as the state of the database at any given point in time. To produce read consistency, Oracle marks the current SCN as the query enters the execution phase. The query can only see the snapshot of the records as of that SCN. Oracle uses rollback segments to reconstruct the read-consistent snapshot of the data. Whenever a transaction makes any changes, a snapshot of the record before the changes were made is copied to a rollback segment and the data block header is marked appropriately with the address of the rollback segment block where the changes are recorded. The data block also maintains the SCN of the last committed change to the block. As data blocks are read on behalf of the query, only blocks with lower SCN than the query SCN will be read. If a block has uncommitted changes of other transactions, or changed data with more recent SCN, then the data is reconstructed using the saved snapshot from the rollback segments. In some rare situations, if the RDBMS is not able to reconstruct the snapshot for a long-running query, the query results in the ORA-1555 error.

A rollback segment maintains the snapshot of the changed data as long as the transaction is still active (commit or rollback has not been issued). Once a transaction is committed, the RDBMS marks it with the current SCN and the space used by the snapshot becomes available for reuse. Therefore, the ORA-1555 error will result if the query is looking for a snapshot that is so old that the rollback segment doesn't contain it due to wrap around or overwrite.

There are four main reasons why the ORA-1555 error occurs.

**Few and Small Rollback Segments**    If a database has many concurrent transactions changing data and committing very often, then the chances of reusing the space used by a committed transaction is higher. A long-running query then may not be able to reconstruct the snapshot due to wrap around and overwrite in rollback segments. Larger rollback segments in this case will reduce the chance of reusing the committed transaction slots.

**Corrupted Rollback Segments**    Corrupted rollback segments can cause this error as well. If the rollback segment is corrupted and cannot be read, then a statement needing to reconstruct a before image snapshot will result in this error.

**Fetch-Across Commits**    A fetch-across commit is a situation in which a query opens a cursor, loops through fetching, changes data, and then commits the records on the same table. For example, suppose a cursor was opened at an SCN value of 10. The execution SCN of the query is then marked as SCN=10. Every fetch by that cursor now needs to get the read-consistent data from SCN=10. Let's assume that the user program fetches $x$ number of records, changes them, and then commits them with an SCN value of 20. If a later fetch happens to retrieve a record that is in one of the previously committed blocks, then the fetch will see that the SCN value is 20. Since the fetch has to get the snapshot from SCN=10, read consistency needs to be performed on the data using the rollback segment. If it cannot roll back to SCN 10, the ORA-1555 error occurs. Committing less often in this case will result in larger rollback segments and *reduce* the probability of getting the error.

**Fetch Across Commits with Delayed Block Cleanout**    When a data or index block is modified in the database and the transaction is committed, Oracle does a fast commit by marking the transaction as committed in the rollback segment header, but does not clean the locks in the data blocks that were modified. The next transaction that does a select on the modified blocks will do the actual cleanout of the block. This is known as a *delayed block cleanout*.

Now let's take the same example as with fetch across commits, but instead of assuming one table, let's assume that there are two tables that the transaction uses—in other words, the cursor is opened, and then in a loop, fetches from one table and changes records in another, and commits. Even though the records are getting committed in another table, it could still cause the ORA-1555 error because cleanout has not been done on the table from which the records are being fetched. This is possible because some other transaction has modified this table before we did the select. For this case, a full table scan before opening and fetching through the cursor will help.

Note that *fetch-across commits*, as explained in the last two cases, are not supported by ANSI SQL standards. According to the standard, a cursor is invalidated when a commit is performed and should be closed and reopened before fetching again. Though not ANSI SQL standard, Oracle, unlike some other database vendors, allows users to do fetch-across commits but users should be aware that this might result in the ORA-1555 error.

### ORA-1594

The most probable cause of the ORA-1594 error is small extent sizes. Shrinking of extents is started when a request is made for an undo block and the kernel detects that the current extent of the rollback segment is reaching the end of its free space. If several extents are to be freed, this can generate substantial undo, which may eventually wrap into the extent that is being freed up. This will cause the ORA-1594 error to occur. Having a smaller number of larger extents is a good way of dealing with this problem.

### ORA-4031

Fragmentation of shared pool memory area is a common problem that application programmers and DBAs often face, and the ORA-4031 error is commonly a result of such fragmentation. Here, we will discuss some of the workarounds that are available today and future enhancements that are under consideration.

Imagine the SHARED_POOL being similar to a tablespace. While you may get the ORA-1547 error when you cannot get sufficient contiguous free space in the tablespace, you will get the ORA-4031 error when you cannot get contiguous free space in the SHARED_POOL (SGA). Application programmers usually get this error while attempting to load a big package or while executing a very large procedure and there is not sufficient contiguous free memory available in the SHARED_POOL. This may be due to fragmentation of the shared pool memory or insufficient memory in the shared pool.

If it is due to fragmentation, one needs to flush the shared pool and/or break up the package or procedure into smaller blocks. If the shared pool is badly fragmented, even using small packages or procedures can result in this error.

Flushing the shared pool might not help all the time because it will not flush the PINNED buffers that are being changed at that time.

If it is due to insufficient memory, SHARED_POOL_SIZE should be increased from the default value, which is 3.5MB. Increasing the SHARED_POOL might not be a viable solution in some shops that have high availability requirements, because you allocate the size of the SHARED_POOL during startup time, and increasing the SHARED_POOL means shutting down and restarting the database. Unfortunately, this size is fixed and cannot be extended on the fly.

Current workarounds include the following:

■ Utilize the **dbms_shared_pool** package, available with Oracle versions 7.0.13 and higher. This package allows users to display the sizes of objects in the shared pool and mark them for PINNING (discussed in Chapter 2) in the SGA in order to reduce memory fragmentation. The DBA must grant to user SYS the EXECUTE privilege on the package in order to keep the package in the shared pool. Procedures are run under the schema of the owner; therefore, if user SYS does not have EXECUTE privileges on the package, SYS will get an error stating that the object doesn't exist.

■ Increase the SHARED_POOL_SIZE as the current default tends to be a low estimate when utilizing the *procedural option.*

There are plans in the future to change the functionality to reduce the occurrence of this problem. At the current time, Oracle needs one contiguous chunk of memory to process a given package or procedure. In future releases of Oracle, the PL/SQL code will be modified such that it will request a certain amount of memory and will accept several smaller contiguous chunks for the same package or procedure, thereby reducing the probability of this error.

At times, ORA-4031 can be very annoying to application programmers and DBAs. However, with the help of the **dbms_shared_pool** package, and careful planning and administration, the DBA can eliminate this error for good.

## ORA-12004
You need to understand the concepts of *snapshots* and *procedures* before you read this section. Please refer to the *Oracle7 Server Application Developer's Guide* for details on snapshots and procedures. This section gives some debugging information on snapshots. Most of the snapshot problems can be approached this way.

An ORA-12004 occurs when you try to do a *fast refresh* and the attempt fails because Oracle could not use the snapshot log. For example, assume that the procedure **dbms_snapshot.set_up** is executed (remotely) at the master site. One query in the procedure is

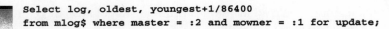

```
Select log, oldest, youngest+1/86400
from mlog$ where master = :2 and mowner = :1 for update;
```

This procedure retrieves the log name and updates the timestamps in the snapshot log. If the update fails, if you are not able to get the log name, or if any other error occurs, then this procedure does not return a log name and the ORA-12004 error is signaled.

Consider the scenario where the procedure **dbms_snapshot.get_log_age** is executed (again, remotely at the master site). This procedure returns a date defined by

```
Select oldest into oldest from sys.mlog$ where mowner = mow and master = mas;
```

This date (call it *log_date*) is then compared to the date of this snapshot's most recent refresh (call it *snap_date*). *snap_date* is given by the snaptime column in the **snap$** base data dictionary table. If *snap_date* is earlier than *log_date*, then the ORA-12004 error is signaled.

To summarize, there are two possible causes for the ORA-12004 error. Either you were unable to retrieve the name of the log file (from **dbms_snapshot.set_up**), or the log is out of date, possibly because the snapshot log has been purged (snapshot logs can be purged manually using **dbms_snapshot.purge_log**; Oracle also purges the log automatically after refreshes, but the automatic purge shouldn't age out any other snapshots).

To debug this problem, you can run **dbms_snapshot.set_up** by hand. The name of the log table is an out variable. So consider the following procedure:

```
create table foo (a varchar(30));

declare
owner varchar(30);
master varchar(30);
log varchar(30);
snapshot date;
snaptime date;
begin
    snapshot := SYSDATE;
    snaptime := SYSDATE;
    owner := 'SCOTT';
    master := 'EMP';
    dbms_snapshot.set_updblink(owner, master, log, snapshot, snaptime);
    insert into foo(a) values (log);
end;
```

After executing this, the log name for the master table should be in *foo*. This can be verified as follows:

```
SQLDBA> select * from foo;
A
--------------------
MLOG$_EMP
1 row selected.
```

As a side effect, this procedure will cause the master site (and mlog$ and snapshot logs) to believe that a snapshot has occurred, and will result in future refreshes, possibly returning the ORA-12004 error for out-of-date reasons. So be prepared to do full refreshes on your snapshots after running this test.

If **dbms_snapshot.set_up** appears to be running correctly, then you can attempt to figure out why your log tables are outdated using the above queries.

## Oracle Internal Errors

Internal to Oracle Worldwide Support, all high-priority problems reported by customers are divided into seven categories. Most of the time, these problems are kernel related. However, some major functionality not working in an application could potentially stop a production or development workshop, resulting in a high-priority problem as well. These kinds of problems need to be diagnosed as soon as possible and some initial diagnostics can be taken by DBAs. This section gives information on Oracle internal errors, such as the ORA-600 error. Next, an overview of the various categories of priority 1/priority 2 problems and the standard diagnostics a DBA can collect before calling Worldwide Support are discussed. Last, some examples illustrate how to deal with memory or block corruptions.

### ORA-600

As discussed earlier in this chapter, the main purpose of trace files is to record information when error conditions occur. All errors that are signaled by Oracle have a code associated with them. While some common errors are displayed onscreen to the users, some fatal or internal errors are recorded in the alert file in addition to creating a trace file. For example, the ORA-1578 error means that a block has been corrupted. All of the *ORA-* errors are documented either in the *Oracle7 Server Messages and Codes Manual* or the *Oracle Installation and User's Guide* for a specific platform. There is a special Oracle error code that has meaning only to Oracle Worldwide Support and development. The ORA-600 error is signaled when a sanity check fails within the Oracle code. To illustrate what is meant by a sanity check, examine the following pseudo-code:

```
/* Pseudo-code to get file# F, block# B from the database */
```

```
get(F,B)
Begin
    If (F > MAX_NUMBER_OF_FILES)
        signal ("ORA 600 [2858] [F]");
        exit ( )
    endif;
    ......
end
```

In this code segment, the *if* statement tests for the validity of the file number requested. If the file number requested is out of range for possible file numbers, the program will signal the error and exit. Note that this is not the complete meaning of the actual ORA-600 [2858] error, but an illustration of a sanity check.

The first argument in the ORA-600 error is used as a tag for the location in the code where the error is signaled. Each first argument is unique to one section of the code. The second through fifth arguments are used to give additional information such as the file number in the previous example.

The ORA-600 error message informs Oracle Worldwide Support where the error occurred in the code, but doesn't indicate what the RDBMS was doing when it entered the routine containing the error. The *stack trace dumps* help to determine what was happening at the time the error occurred. The *stack trace* is a dump of the execution stack of a process. It contains the names of all active routines and the values of the arguments passed to those routines. Stack traces are read from the bottom up, with the top routine usually being the routine that prints out the stack trace. The arguments on the stack trace of an Oracle process are usually not very helpful, since they are mostly address pointers and not the values of actual data structures. But the routine names help Oracle Worldwide Support determine what type of activity led up to this error. For example, it can be determined that a corrupted block was found during the act of building a consistent read block if the routine that builds consistent read blocks is on the stack.

The dump of a stack trace is done by making a call to the operating system that Oracle is currently running on. This causes the appearances of stack traces to look different from one platform to another. On UNIX platforms, the dump of the stack trace will include the routine names, whereas on VMS the stack trace is dumped with the routine names encrypted as addresses in the code. To make the stack trace readable, the DBA should format the trace file using the TRCFMT command on the machine on which the trace file is created. This will convert the addresses to routine names and will be in a human-readable format.

The ORA-600 error is often followed by state dumps in the trace files. There are two types of state dumps, *system state* and *process state*. A system state will give information about objects currently held by the Oracle RDBMS. A process state dump will show objects held by a particular process. These dumps are usually large in size and difficult to decipher. But one of the key pieces of the information contained in these dumps is the blocks held by each process. When a process hits an error condition, it is often due to some information it has extracted from a block it is holding. If we know the blocks held by the errant process, it is easier to track down the source of the problem. By using the data block addresses in the system or process state dump, we can see what objects are encountering the signaled errors. If more information is required, Oracle Worldwide Support will request that the DBA dump more information concerning a block, or a process state, or system state, depending on the error (the syntax for dumping the system state and the process state are discussed earlier in this chapter).

## Categories of Priority 1/Priority 2 Problems and Diagnostic Actions

Following are the various categories of problems that could impact the availability of the database or question the data integrity of the database. This is followed by a description and the diagnostic actions that a DBA needs to take before calling Oracle Worldwide Support. Note that it might be necessary to take some of the actions with the help of an Oracle Worldwide Support analyst.

- Data corruptions
- Logical corruptions
- System hangs
- Performance problems
- System crashes
- Critical functionality not available
- Memory corruptions

**Data Corruptions**    *Data corruptions* include all block format corruptions, invalid index entries, and corruptions of meta-data (e.g., the data dictionary). An example is a user getting the ORA-600 [3339] error on a system data file when selecting from a table. There could be various reasons why data corruptions occur. For example, it could be the hardware vendor's operating system problem with clustered disks. Standard or typical diagnostic actions for these kinds of problems include

- Collecting trace files (and formatting them where applicable) if the corruption is reported as an internal error.
- Dumping the redo logs corresponding to the time of corruption. If you are not sure how many log files to dump, saving all the redo log files and contacting Oracle Worldwide Support is suggested.

■ Asking the system manager for complete hardware diagnostics to be carried out if there is a reason to suspect vendor OS problem.

■ Where appropriate, determining if the problem is generic or port specific.

**NOTE**
Some of these actions might be appropriate for Oracle Worldwide Support analysts as well.

**Logical Corruptions**      *Logical corruptions* refer to the case where the data (either as stored or as returned by a query) is incorrect, although it isn't necessary that an error is returned externally. Typical examples of a logical corruption would be phantom rows in a table after updating a column to null, or a query returning different results when using different types of optimizer. Logical corruptions are very dangerous as they are difficult to detect. Standard diagnostic actions to DBAs include

■ Trying to create a reproducible test case.

■ Collecting trace files (and formatting them where applicable) if the corruption is reported as an internal error (e.g., ORA-600 [13004]).

■ When appropriate, determining if the problem is generic or port specific

**System Hangs**      *System hangs* can be defined as users unable to log on to the database or to execute operations. System hangs could also mean that the database hangs on open after media or crash recovery. For example, a process holding a latch on a crucial data structure and spinning might cause a system hang. Standard diagnostic actions during system hangs are

■ In the case of a hang on database open, set events and diagnose at which stage of recovery the database is stuck, and dump the diagnostic information (e.g., the header of the undo segment if spinning while doing transaction recovery ). In the case of a system hang, take the system state dumps at appropriate intervals, either using a tool such as ORADBX or by using the **alter session** command. Monitor CPU and I/O activity of background and foreground processes.

■ When appropriate, determine if the problem is generic or port specific.

■ If reproducible, create a test case.

■ If reproducible only at your site with reasonable frequency, set up a modem for Oracle Worldwide Support personnel to dial in and monitor.

**Performance Problems**     *Performance problems* can be classified into two kinds. General cases of deterioration in response time or batch completion times is one. The other is performance degradation on increase in concurrent activity. These kinds of problems are generally time consuming and require patience. Poor response times can sometimes be due to waits for library cache pins. Standard diagnostic actions include

- Documenting performance degradation in terms of specific indicators such as response time, batch completion time, number of concurrent logins supported, efficiency of shared pool management, and so on.

- Providing a reproducible test case, if possible, or documenting in detail the environment and factors leading to poor performance. For example, in the case where reproducibility depends on concurrency in a production environment, it is appropriate to document circumstances surrounding degradation, such as number of logins, average memory usage, typical functionality invoked, I/O activity, and dynamic statistics on Oracle activity.

- Setting up a modem for Oracle Worldwide Support personnel to dial in and monitor if the problem is reproducible only at your site with reasonable frequency.

- When appropriate, determining if the problem is generic or port specific.

**System Crashes**     *System crashes* include cases where the database crashes, usually due to one of the background processes dying. These kinds of problems are not common; but if the database crashes, DBAs should take the following diagnostics.

- Check the alert file to see if any ORA-600 errors have occurred, and if so, get the trace files and format them if necessary.

- Find out what the users were doing at the time of the crash or any applications running at that time. If a specific application is isolated, try reproducing the problem by running the application on a test machine.

- When appropriate, determine if the problem is generic or port specific.

**Critical Functionality Not Available**     *Critical functionality not available* refers to all situations where functionality or vital features that rely on a production application become unavailable, typically due to a bug in the database software or any third-party software that runs on top of Oracle. Some examples that fall under this category include cases where Oracle utilities core dump or the applications error out. In some cases, a function not available might affect the availability of the database indirectly. For example, consider a case in which a database is being recovered from a full database export and import from multiple tapes doesn't work correctly, thereby preventing a database rebuild of a production database. Again, the standard diagnostics in this case include

- Collecting trace files and dumping relevant redo log files depending on the error (under Oracle Worldwide Support guidance) and documenting the circumstances leading up to the error.

- Providing a reproducible test case if possible.

- Providing detailed information such as utilities used, storage structures accessed, DDL/DML performed, and procedures or packages executed during the time the error occurred is necessary if providing a reproducible test case is not possible.

- When appropriate, determining if the problem is generic or port specific.

**Memory Corruptions**    *Memory corruptions* include internal errors signaling memory leaks, corruptions of memory data structures, and cache corruptions. Diagnostic actions include

- Collecting a trace file if the error produces one.

- Providing a reproducible test case if possible, or documenting circumstances that caused the error, such as the following:

  - Details of OCI or the Oracle tool/utility or the pre-compiler used in application

  - Operating system tools or third-party tools used in conjunction with the application

  - Triggers fired by application

  - Packages or procedures executed.

## Resolving Block Corruptions

Data corruption can occur for numerous reasons, and in most cases it goes undetected at the time the corruption occurs. It is only later, when that piece of information is needed, that the corruption is detected. The Oracle RDBMS keeps its information, including data, in block format. The Oracle data block can be (and in many cases is) composed of several operating system blocks. For instance, if the Oracle block size is 2048 bytes and the operating system block size is 512 bytes, then the Oracle block is composed of 4 operating system blocks. The INIT.ORA parameter DB_BLOCK_SIZE will indicate the current Oracle block size.

Each block of an Oracle data file is formatted with a fixed header that contains information about the particular block. This information provides a means to ensure the integrity for each block and, in turn, the entire Oracle database. One component of the fixed header of a data block is the *data block address.* This structure is a 32-bit integer that stores the file number of an Oracle database and the Oracle block number offset relative to the beginning of the file. Whenever there is a problem with the data block address while reading a block from disk to cache, Oracle will signal an internal error along with two internal arguments. The error message will look something like the following:

```
ORA-00600 [3339] [arg1] [arg2] [] [] [] []
ORA-1578: Data block corrupted in file # x block # y
```

The first argument (arg1) is the data block address that Oracle found in the data block just read from disk. The second argument (arg2) is the data block address that Oracle expects to find in that data block. If they are different, then the ORA-600 error is displayed, as shown above. This error is typically caused by some form of operating system or hardware malfunction.

Oracle uses standard C system function calls to read/write blocks from all the files it maintains. This would include system calls such as lseek( ), read( ), readv( ), write( ) writev( ). Once the block is read, it is mapped to shared memory (the SGA) by the operating system. Oracle then does sanity checks on the block to ensure the integrity of the fixed header. The data block address check is the first check Oracle makes on the fixed header.

In some cases, arg1 is displayed as 0 while arg2 is a 32-bit number. This means that the data block address component for the block just read is 0. Usually, this is because a portion of the Oracle block has been zeroed out. Typically, the first operating system block piece of an Oracle block is zeroed out when there is a soft error on disk and the operating system attempted to repair its block. In addition, disk repairing utilities will also cause this zeroing out affect. One known Oracle software bug specific to UNIX platforms is caused by running multiple database writers (INIT.ORA parameter DB_WRITERS > 1) and was addressed in versions 6.0.33.2 and higher. Note that the ORA-1578 error message does not necessarily accompany the ORA-600 error.

In other cases, both arguments of the ORA-600 error display large numbers. This implies that the data block address in the physical block on disk is incorrect. There are various reasons why this could happen.

One reason why this can happen is if the block is corrupted in memory and is written to disk. This situation is quite rare. In most cases it is caused by memory faults that go undetected. If the DBA suspects that there may be memory problems with the system, he or she should enable further sanity block checking by placing the event codes 10210 and 10211 in the INIT.ORA file. The syntax is given in the "Setting Trace Events" section of this chapter. However, when these events are set, and if the DBWR process detects a corrupted block in cache prior to writing it to disk, it will signal the ORA-600 [3398] error and will *crash* the instance. The block in question is thus never written to disk, thereby preventing the database from corruptions. Various arguments including the data block address are passed to the ORA-600 [3398] error. The DBA should simply restart the instance and contact Oracle Worldwide Support with the trace files.

A second reason is that blocks are sometimes written into the wrong places in the data file. This is called *write blocks out of sequence*. In this case, both data block addresses given in the arguments are valid. This typically happens when the operating system's I/O mechanism fails to write the block in the proper locations that Oracle requests via the lseek( ) system call. Some hardware/operating system vendors support *large files* or *large file systems*. These can contain physical files as large as 4.2 gigabytes. This is larger than what can be represented by a 32-bit, unsigned number. Oracle doesn't support files larger than 2 gigabytes. Hence, the operating system must translate the *offset* transparent to the application (i.e. Oracle). On such configurations, even smaller Oracle data files suffer corruptions caused by blocks being written out of sequence because the lseek( ) system call did not translate the correct location.

A third cause is I/O error. In this case, both of the data block addresses are valid but the data block address in argument 1 of the error (arg1) is from the previous block read into the SGA prior to this read request. The calls that Oracle makes to lseek( ) and read( ) are checked for return error codes. In addition, Oracle checks to see if the number of bytes read by the read( ) system call is a multiple of BLOCK SIZE bytes. If these checks appear to be successful, Oracle assumes that the direct read succeeded. Upon sanity checking, the data block address is incorrect and the database operation request fails due to the fact that I/O read really never took place. In this case, the data block address that Oracle reads is really the address of another block in the database.

The fourth reason you may get the ORA-600 error with valid data block addresses for both its arguments is because of reading a wrong block from the same disk drive. Typically, this is caused by a very busy disk. In some cases, the block read is off by one block and can range into several hundreds of blocks. Note that the data block addresses of both the arguments are valid. Since this occurs when the disk is very busy and under high load conditions, ensuring that the disk drive has the current EPROM release helps. No doubt, there could be other reasons why block corruptions happen. The above four reasons are from my personal experience.

Note that in the third and fourth cases above, the database will not be corrupted and the operation can be tried again with success. However, if a data block does get corrupted, a DBA should know how to retrieve data from that table. Retrieving data from a corrupt table can be done in different ways. The following example illustrates how data can be retrieved from a corrupt table using index scans.

```
Select distinct(key) from corrupt_table
where key > (lowest value for the key)
and substr(rowid,1,8) = corrupt_block_id
order by 1;
```

This method can be used only if the corrupt table has an index. The first step involves selecting all the distinct key values that are in the corrupted block. Note that since we cannot do a full table scan, the key values will be selected from the index leaf block. The following query will give the key values that belong to the corrupt block.

Note that *key* is the name of the column on which the index is created and *corrupt_table* is the name of the corrupted table. *Corrupt_block_id* is the actual hexadecimal value that identifies the corrupt block. When the corrupt block is first detected by the Oracle process or a user process, the ORA-1578 error message is displayed. As part of the error message, the block number of the corrupted block is given. This is the value that *corrupt_block_id* should be equated to. The above query will be fully satisfied by an index scan since both *rowid* and *key* are in the index. Note that in the **where** clause, the predicate *key* > (*lowest value for the key*) is a dummy clause that forces Oracle to do an index scan.

The second step involves selecting all the data from the table before the *lowest key value* in the corrupted block and after the *highest key value* in the corrupted block and putting that into a new table. This can be done by the following query:

```
Create new_table as select * from corrupt_table
where key > (lowest value for the key)
and key NOT IN (key list)
```

The *key list* is the list of key values that we derived from the previous select statement.

For non-unique indexes this method may cause some data loss if the duplicates are located in blocks that are not corrupted, but this can be managed to some extent by using descending index scans. For example, if key value 100 has four occurrences and one of them has a rowid pointing to the bad block, and if the other three keys in the index leaf block are *after* this bad key, then these three keys can be retrieved using the following query:

```
Select /*+ use descending scan on index */ *
from corrupt_table where key = 'duplicate key' and
rownum < 4;
```

Finding the number of occurrences of a key should not be a problem because we can still use index scans to count the occurrences of the key. The first query in this example will give the distinct keys that are in the block. Do a **count** on each one of them. If more than one key is pointing to the bad block, this can be solved by doing the above query iteratively, changing the rownum until the query succeeds. Now in the above example, if the occurrences are mixed, then both ascending and descending scans may have to be used in the *trial and error* fashion. For keys that reside between the bad blocks in the index page, there seems to be no other way short of dumping some blocks. In this case, the DBA is suggested to contact Oracle Worldwide Support.

# CHAPTER 7

# Case Studies of
# Backup and Recovery

**Y**our Honor, we have proof that the defendant was at the murder scene the
night of July 8th, and we can show it to you right now." The attorney started
opening the packet. There was absolute silence in the court room.

Beep...beep....beep...beep.....

Shaken by the annoying sound of the beeper, I came back to reality from
watching the TV and picked up the phone to call Henry.

"Henry, what's up?"

"Hi Rama! We have the customer on the line. The disk controller failed and
they lost their data files. They have a backup from last week. They don't want to
lose any data and they can't be down for more than three hours. They want to
know what is the best and fastest way to recover. Can you assist?"

If you don't want to be in a situation like this Oracle customer is, you should read this chapter very carefully. In this chapter, we discuss some of the case studies of backup and recovery that are based on different kinds of failures that have occurred in real life at customer sites and recovery procedures that Oracle Worldwide Support has recommended. Each case study has several sections and is presented in the following format:

- *Scenario:* The scenario section presents the kinds of backups taken at the site, their frequency, and other background information, including the version of the database.

- *Problem:* This section describes the kind of failure that occurred or the situation the DBA is facing while operating the database.

- *Solution:* This section gives all possible alternatives to recover the database for the specified failure.

- *Test:* In this section, the recommended solution is tested on the Oracle database. For this purpose, a 7.2 database is used on a UNIX operating system. The machine's name is *cosmos*. For some cases, a 7.1 database is used to demonstrate the difference in functionality between releases 7.1 and 7.2. For some simple and obvious cases, the test section is skipped.

- *Observation:* Here we summarize the situation and the important points to learn from the test that we have performed earlier.

We start with some of the simple cases and study more difficult cases as we go along.

# Case 1: NOARCHIVELOG Mode and Recovery ✓

The purpose of this case study is to show the ramifications of operating the database in NOARCHIVELOG mode. There are some risks involved in operating in this mode and this case study should make them clear.

### Scenario

John uses an Oracle database to maintain the inventory of his grocery store. Once every week, he runs a batch job to insert, update, and delete data in his database. He uses a stand-alone UNIX machine running Oracle7 release 7.1. John starts the database up in the morning at 8 A.M., shuts it down at 5 P.M. and operates the database all day in NOARCHIVELOG mode. He takes an offline (cold) backup of the database once a week, on every Sunday, by copying all the data files, log files, and control files to tape.

## Problem

On a Wednesday morning, John realized that he had lost a data file that contained all the user data. He tried to start up the database using the **startup open** command and got the following error:

```
ORA-01157: cannot identify data file 4 - file not found
ORA-01110: data file 4: '/home/orahome/data/7.1/users01.dbf'
```

He realized that he had accidentally deleted one of the data files while trying to free up some space on the disk.

## Solution

One solution in this case is to restore the complete database from the recent offline backup taken on Sunday, and start up the database.

**NOTE**
You will lose the data entered Monday and Tuesday.

Follow these steps:

1. Take a backup of all the current data files, online log files, and control files. This is a precautionary step, in case your backup data files are bad.

2. Delete all the control files, data files, and online log files.

3. Restore all the control files, data files, and online log files from Sunday's offline backup.

4. Start up the database using the **startup open** command.

## Observation

When the database is operating in NOARCHIVELOG mode, the changes made to the database are not archived to the archive log files. So in this case, after John restores the database, it is current as of Sunday. All the changes he made to the database from Monday through Wednesday are lost and he needs to re-enter the data. If the data file that is lost doesn't contain any data (e.g., a data file belonging to the TEMPORARY tablespace), you can start the database by taking the data file offline and rebuilding the tablespace. This is discussed in the next case study. In addition to the offline backup taken once a week, if John takes a full database export every week and an incremental export every night, a second solution can be considered here, as follows:

1. Back up all data files, control files, and redo log files as a precautionary measure.

2. Delete all database files, re-create the database, and import the data using the *complete* and *incremental export* backups. The database will now be current as of Tuesday night.

# Case 2: Dropping Data Files in
# NOARCHIVELOG Mode

Even when you are operating the database in NOARCHIVELOG mode, depending on the type of data file that is lost, it might be possible to survive a media failure without any data loss. This case study tells you how you can do this. However, operating the database in NOARCHIVELOG mode is not recommended if you don't want to lose your data when a media failure occurs.

### Scenario
Consider the same scenario as in Case 1.

### Problem
The disk crashed and one of the data files was lost. In this case, the data file belonged to the TEMPORARY tablespace.

### Solution
In Chapter 2, we have learned that the TEMPORARY tablespace is used by Oracle to do the intermediate work while executing certain commands that require sorting of data. For example, creating an index of certain SQL commands that include ORDER BY or GROUP BY clauses would require Oracle to store the sorted data in the data file that belongs to the TEMPORARY tablespace. No user tables or indexes should be stored in this data file, so it is okay to drop this data file and start up the database. To drop the data file, you need to use the **alter database datafile** *'filename'* **offline drop** command. Note that after opening the database, the tablespace is online but the data file is offline. Any other data files that belong to this tablespace are online and can be used. However, Oracle recommends re-creating the tablespace. There is a specific reason for this and it will be discussed later in Case 9.

## Test

Let's perform a test by setting the database in the ARCHIVELOG mode, switching log files, and shutting down the database using the *abort* option. To simulate the loss of the data file, we will delete **temp.dbf** at the OS level and then try to take the data file offline while the database is mounted.

```
cosmos% sqldba lmode=y                              Connects to SQL*DBA.

SQL*DBA: Release 7.2.1.0.0 - Beta on Sat Feb  4 18:42:01 1995
Copyright (c) Oracle Corporation 1979, 1994.  All rights reserved.
Oracle7 Server Release 7.2.1.0.0 - Beta Release
With the distributed and parallel query options
PL/SQL Release 2.2.1.0.0 - Beta

SQLDBA> connect internal                     Logs you on to the database.
Connected.
SQLDBA> startup mount                         Starts the background processes and mounts the
ORACLE instance started.                      database.
Database mounted.
SQLDBA> archive log list                      Gives information of the mode the database is
Database log mode          ARCHIVELOG         operating in. Also gives sequence numbers of online
Automatic archival         ENABLED            redo log files.
Archive destination        /home/orahome/product/7.2.1/dbs/arch
Oldest online log sequence    59
Next log sequence to archive  61
Current log sequence          61

SQLDBA> alter database noarchivelog;          Switches the database from ARCHIVELOG mode
Statement processed.                          to NOARCHIVELOG mode.
SQLDBA> alter database open;                   Opens the database.
Statement processed.
SQLDBA> alter system switch logfile;          LGWR switches the current log file. This does
Statement processed.                          an implicit checkpoint.
SQLDBA> alter system switch logfile;
Statement processed.


SQLDBA> shutdown abort                         Abnormally terminates the database. Used here to
ORACLE instance shut down.                     simulate a database crash.
SQLDBA> host
cosmos% rm /home/orahome/data/721/temp.dbf    Deleting the datafile to simulate a loss.
cosmos% exit
SQLDBA> startup mount
ORACLE instance started.
Database mounted.
SQLDBA> alter database open;                   Opens the database.
ORA-01157: cannot identify data file 6 - file not found
ORA-01110: data file 6: '/home/orahome/data/721/temp.dbf'
SQLDBA> alter database datafile '/home/orahome/data/721/temp.dbf' offline;
ORA-01145: offline immediate disallowed unless media recovery enabled
```

Takes the datafile offline by updating
the control file. Used when running in
ARCHIVELOG mode.

```
SQLDBA> alter database archivelog;
ORA-00265: Instance recovery required, cannot set ARCHIVELOG mode
SQLDBA> alter database datafile '/home/orahome/data/721/temp.dbf' offline drop;
Statement processed.
SQLDBA> alter database open;
Statement processed.
SQLDBA> drop tablespace temp including contents;
Statement processed.
SQLDBA> create tablespace temp datafile '/home/orahome/data/721/temp.dbf' size 1m;
statement processed.
```

Same as the previous 'offline' command but used when operating in NOARCHIVELOG mode.

## Observation

Note that first we tried to take the data file offline using the following command:

```
SQLDBA> alter database datafile '/home/orahome/data/721/temp.dbf' offline;
```

This failed because in Oracle7, this command can be used only if the database is operating in ARCHIVELOG mode. Since the error indicates this, we tried to put the database in ARCHIVELOG mode. This failed because the database needs to be shut down cleanly before we can change the mode of the database. Since we shut the database with the abort option, until crash recovery is performed, Oracle will not allow us to put the database in ARCHIVELOG mode. However, we can't start up the database unless we have recovered the lost data file; so the only option is to take the data file offline by issuing the **alter database datafile .... offline drop** command. This command would bypass the check to see if the database is in ARCHIVELOG mode or not. Once we took the data file offline, the database opened fine. Note that we have to re-create the tablespace as shown in the test by dropping and re-creating the TEMP tablespace. You might ask the question: why can't we just add another data file and keep using the database? Why do we need to re-create the tablespace? These questions will be answered in Case 9.

Note that this procedure can be used even if a data file that belongs to the USER tablespace or INDEX tablespace is lost. However, since the tablespace needs to be re-created, you need to make sure that you have the data to re-create the tablespace. If it is a USER tablespace, you need to re-create all the tables and insert data manually. Alternatively, you can restore the backup database onto a test machine and export the data of the USER tablespace and import it into the production database. If it is the INDEX tablespace, you can just re-create the indexes.

# ✓ Case 3: Loss of a System Data File

There are only limited recovery options that you have if some of the crucial data files such as the SYSTEM data files are lost. A solid backup procedure is the only way out of such disasters. This case study shows how to recover your database when the data file belonging to the SYSTEM tablespace is lost.

## Scenario
Moe is the DBA of a real-time call-tracking system. He uses Oracle7 release 7.1 of the database on a VAX/VMS system and takes an online backup of the database every night. (Note that online backups can be performed only if the database is running in ARCHIVELOG mode). The total database size is 5Gb and the real-time call tracking system is a heavy OLTP (Online Transaction Processing) system, primarily with the maximum activity between 9 A.M. and 9 P.M. every day. At 9 P.M., a batch job runs a command procedure that puts the tablespaces in *hot backup* mode, takes the backup of all the data files to tape at the operating system level, and then issues the **alter tablespace end backup** command in SQLDBA.

## Problem
One afternoon a disk crashed, losing the SYSTEM data file residing on the disk. As this happened at peak processing time, Moe had to keep the down time to a minimum and open the database as soon as possible. He wanted to start the database first and then restore the data file that was lost, so he took the system data file offline. When he tried to open the database, he got the following error:

```
ORA-01147: SYSTEM tablespace file 1 is offline

ORA-01110: data file 1: 'DISK$WR3:[RDBMSPT.ORACLE.DATA]SYSTEM.DBS'
```

## Solution
A data file can be taken offline and the database started up, with the exception of the data files belonging to the SYSTEM tablespace. In this case, the data file that was lost belongs to the SYSTEM tablespace. The only solution here is to restore the SYSTEM data file from the previous night's online backup, and then perform database recovery. Note that if the disk crash has damaged several data files, then all the damaged data files need to be restored from the online backup. The database needs to be mounted and the **recover database** command issued before the database can be opened.

## Observation
In this case, it took Moe approximately 45 minutes to bring the database to normal operation. This included the time to restore the SYSTEM data file from tape to disk and roll forward the data file. The restore took approximately 43 minutes and the roll forward took only 2 minutes. One way to reduce the MTTR (mean time to recover) is by maintaining a backup copy of all the database files on disk, thereby reducing the time to restore the data file from backup. Another option is to use the operating system's disk mirroring option. In future releases of Oracle, multiplexing of the data files will be supported, which will help to reduce the MTTR if properly used.

One very important point to note in this scenario is the backup scheme Moe uses. The batch job puts all the tablespaces in hot backup mode and then takes an OS backup of all the data files. This is not the recommended procedure. Oracle Worldwide Support suggests doing hot backup of one tablespace at a time.

# Case 4: Loss of a Non-SYSTEM Data File Without Rollback Segments

As a DBA, you have a lot of options when you lose a non-SYSTEM data file that doesn't contain rollback segments. This case study gives you three recovery methods that you can use, and discusses the advantages and disadvantages of each method.

### Scenario
Use the scenario for Case 3 again.

### Problem
Let's assume that instead of a SYSTEM data file, a non-SYSTEM data file is lost due to the disk crash. We also assume that this data file doesn't contain any rollback segments. Recovery of a data file that contains rollback segments is discussed in Case 5.

### Solution
When a non-SYSTEM data file is lost, there are three methods by which the data file can be recovered. First, as discussed in Case 2, the **recover database** command can be used. This requires the database to be mounted but not open, which means offline recovery needs to be performed. The second method is to use the **recover datafile** command. Here, the data file needs to be offline but the database can be open or mounted. The third method is to use the **recover tablespace** command, which requires the tablespace to be offline and the database to be open. We will test all the above three methods in the next section.

### Test
The machine (called *cosmos*) contains an Oracle7 release 7.2 database. In the first part of the test, let's create a table and insert data into the table. Then, let's simulate the loss of a non-SYSTEM data file by deleting the data file at the operating system level and shutting down the database. Next, all three methods recommended in the solution are tested. The user input is in bold letters.

```
cosmos% sqldba lmode=y

SQL*DBA: Release 7.2.1.0.0 - Beta on Fri Feb  3 22:43:28 1995
Copyright (c) Oracle Corporation 1979, 1994.  All rights reserved.
Oracle7 Server Release 7.2.1.0.0 - Beta Release
With the distributed and parallel query options
PL/SQL Release 2.2.1.0.0 - Beta

SQLDBA> connect internal
Connected.
SQLDBA>  create table case4(c1 number) tablespace users;
Statement processed.
SQLDBA> insert into case4 values (3);    Inserts a record into table CASE 4.
1 row processed.
SQLDBA> insert into case4 values (3);    Inserts a second record into CASE 4.
1 row processed.
SQLDBA> commit;                          Transaction committed.
Statement processed.
SQLDBA> alter system switch logfile;
Statement processed.
SQLDBA> host
cosmos% rm /home/orahome/data/721/users01.dbf    Simulates loss of datafile.
cosmos% exit
SQLDBA> shutdown abort
ORACLE instance shut down.                          Restore from backup.
SQLDBA> host
cosmos% cp /home/orahome/backup/users01.dbf /home/orahome/data/721
cosmos% exit                                                    Oracle
SQLDBA> startup open                                    recognizes that
ORACLE instance started.                                  the datafile is
Database mounted.                                          from backup
ORA-01113: file 4 needs media recovery                   and asks for
ORA-01110: data file 4: '/home/orahome/data/721/users01.dbf'  recovery.
Attempting to dismount database........Database dismounted.
Attempting to shutdown instance........ORACLE instance shut down.
```

**Method 1: Database Recovery**   Now let's test the first method in recovering this database, by using the **recover database** command.

```
SQLDBA> startup mount
ORACLE instance started.
Database mounted.                                    Media recovery performed on the
                                                     database. Any file needing media
                                                     recovery will be recovered.
SQLDBA> recover database
ORA-00279: Change 6232 generated at 02/03/95 08:45:58 needed for thread 1
ORA-00289: Suggestion : /home/orahome/product/7.2.1/dbs/arch1_50.dbf
ORA-00280: Change 6232 for thread 1 is in sequence #50
Specify log: {<RET>=suggested | filename | AUTO | FROM logsource | CANCEL}
enter                                                Hit return to apply the suggested log.
Applying suggested logfile...
Log applied.
ORA-00279: Change 6269 generated at 02/03/95 19:46:32 needed for thread 1
ORA-00289: Suggestion : /home/orahome/product/7.2.1/dbs/arch1_51.dbf
ORA-00280: Change 6269 for thread 1 is in sequence #51
ORA-00278: Logfile '/home/orahome/product/7.2.1/dbs/arch1_50.dbf' no longer needed
for this recovery
Specify log: {<RET>=suggested | filename | AUTO | FROM logsource | CANCEL}
auto                                                 Type "auto" if you want automatic
Applying suggested logfile...                        recovery enabled.
Log applied.
ORA-00279: Change 6276 generated at 02/03/95 19:49:31 needed for thread 1
ORA-00289: Suggestion : /home/orahome/product/7.2.1/dbs/arch1_52.dbf
ORA-00280: Change 6276 for thread 1 is in sequence #52
ORA-00278: Logfile '/home/orahome/product/7.2.1/dbs/arch1_51.dbf' no longer needed
for this recovery

Applying suggested logfile...
Log applied.
Media recovery complete.

SQLDBA> alter database open;                          Opens database after recovery.
Statement processed.
SQLDBA> select * from case4;                          Verify that recovery worked. Check to
C1                                                   see if the two rows originally inserted
--                                                   are there.
3
3
2 rows selected.
```

## Method 2: Data File Recovery

This method involves taking the data file offline and opening the database before issuing the **recover datafile** command.

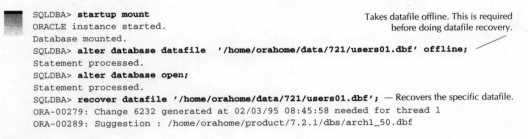

```
SQLDBA> startup mount                                 Takes datafile offline. This is required
ORACLE instance started.                             before doing datafile recovery.
Database mounted.
SQLDBA> alter database datafile '/home/orahome/data/721/users01.dbf' offline;
Statement processed.
SQLDBA> alter database open;
Statement processed.
SQLDBA> recover datafile '/home/orahome/data/721/users01.dbf'; — Recovers the specific datafile.
ORA-00279: Change 6232 generated at 02/03/95 08:45:58 needed for thread 1
ORA-00289: Suggestion : /home/orahome/product/7.2.1/dbs/arch1_50.dbf
```

```
ORA-00280: Change 6232 for thread 1 is in sequence #50
Specify log: {<RET>=suggested ¦ filename ¦ AUTO ¦ FROM logsource ¦ CANCEL}
auto
Applying suggested logfile...
Log applied.
ORA-00279: Change 6269 generated at 02/03/95 19:46:32 needed for thread 1
ORA-00289: Suggestion : /home/orahome/product/7.2.1/dbs/arch1_51.dbf
ORA-00280: Change 6269 for thread 1 is in sequence #51
ORA-00278: Logfile '/home/orahome/product/7.2.1/dbs/arch1_50.dbf' no longer needed
for this recovery
Applying suggested logfile...
Log applied.
ORA-00279: Change 6276 generated at 02/03/95 19:49:31 needed for thread 1
ORA-00289: Suggestion : /home/orahome/product/7.2.1/dbs/arch1_52.dbf
ORA-00280: Change 6276 for thread 1 is in sequence #52
ORA-00278: Logfile '/home/orahome/product/7.2.1/dbs/arch1_51.dbf' no longer needed
for this recovery
Applying suggested logfile...
Log applied.
Media recovery complete.
```

Brings the datafile online after recovery.

```
SQLDBA> alter database datafile '/home/orahome/data/721/users01.dbf' online;
Statement processed.
SQLDBA> select * from case4;
C1
—
3
3
2 rows selected.
```

Verify that recovery worked.

## Method 3: Tablespace Recovery

```
SQLDBA> startup mount
ORACLE instance started.
Database mounted.

SQLDBA> alter database datafile '/home/orahome/data/721/users01.dbf' offline;
Statement processed.
SQLDBA> alter database open;
Statement processed.
SQLDBA> alter tablespace users offline;
Statement processed.
SQLDBA> recover tablespace users;
ORA-00279: Change 6232 generated at 02/03/95 08:45:58 needed for thread 1
ORA-00289: Suggestion : /home/orahome/product/7.2.1/dbs/arch1_50.dbf
ORA-00280: Change 6232 for thread 1 is in sequence #50
Specify log: {<RET>=suggested ¦ filename ¦ AUTO ¦ FROM logsource ¦ CANCEL}
auto
Applying suggested logfile...
Log applied.
ORA-00279: Change 6269 generated at 02/03/95 19:46:32 needed for thread 1
ORA-00289: Suggestion : /home/orahome/product/7.2.1/dbs/arch1_51.dbf
ORA-00280: Change 6269 for thread 1 is in sequence #51
```

Opens database.

Takes tablespace USERS offline before recovery.

Recovers all datafiles that belong to tablespace USERS.

```
ORA-00278: Logfile '/home/orahome/product/7.2.1/dbs/arch1_50.dbf' no longer needed
for this recovery
Applying suggested logfile...
Log applied.
ORA-00279: Change 6276 generated at 02/03/95 19:49:31 needed for thread 1
ORA-00289: Suggestion : /home/orahome/product/7.2.1/dbs/arch1_52.dbf
ORA-00280: Change 6276 for thread 1 is in sequence #52
ORA-00278: Logfile '/home/orahome/product/7.2.1/dbs/arch1_51.dbf' no longer needed
for this recovery
Applying suggested logfile...
Log applied.
Media recovery complete.
```

```
SQLDBA> select * from case4;                              See if you can access data when
C1                                                        tablespace is offline.
```

```
ORA-00376: file 4 cannot be read at this time
ORA-01110: data file 4: '/home/orahome/data/721/users01.dbf'
```

```
SQLDBA> alter tablespace users online;                   Bring tablespace online.
Statement processed.
```

```
SQLDBA> select * from case4;                              Verify that tablespace recovery worked.
C1
3
3
2 rows selected.
```

## Observation

There are a few important points to note in these tests. In method 1, note that when Oracle requested archive log **arch1_50.dbf**, we pressed the ENTER key, and this applied only the suggested log file. When Oracle asked for the second log, we entered **auto**, which turned *auto recovery* on. This means Oracle will automatically apply the log files if it can find them in the archive destination. If you are doing complete recovery and have to apply a lot of log files, it's easy for you to use auto recovery. Also, in method 1, we have done database recovery, which requires the database to be mounted but not open (offline recovery).

Methods 2 and 3 show how to do online recovery. Note that the database is open before doing recovery. However, the data file to be recovered was offline during recovery. While doing tablespace recovery, all files belonging to the tablespace should be offline. In method 3, after recovery, the SELECT statement failed because the data file was still offline. Once the tablespace was brought online, the SELECT statement succeeded.

So which method should you use? To determine that, you need to ask yourself: How many log files do I need to apply, and can I afford to keep the database down for that long? If you can, then use method 1, where the database is not open during recovery. However, if you have to open the database so that users can use other parts of the database, then you have to do online recovery by choosing method 2 or method 3.

How do you determine when to use data file recovery versus tablespace recovery? In this case study, the tablespace has only one data file, so it doesn't make a difference whether you use method 2 or 3. However, if you have a number of data files that belong to a tablespace and one of them is lost, you might want to do data file recovery (method 2) because you can keep the other data files of the tablespace available to the users. Note that if an application tries to read data from the offline data file, it will fail.

If most of the data files that belong to a tablespace are lost, using data file and tablespace recovery have their own advantages. For example, if a tablespace has 20 data files and all of them are lost, by using data file recovery, you can parallelize recovery but you need to issue the recovery command 20 times. Even if you recover multiple data files in one command, you still have to type the full path name of each data file. On the other hand, if you decide to do tablespace recovery, you have to issue the recovery command just once. Note that release 7.1 provides parallel recovery. Appendix A gives details on parallel recovery.

An alternative method to recover a lost non-SYSTEM data file is to use the **alter database create datafile** command. This method will be discussed in Case 12.

## Case 5: Loss of a Non-SYSTEM Data File with Rollback Segments

If a non-SYSTEM data file that is lost contains rollback segments, recovery needs to be performed with care. You should understand the ramifications of recovering from such disasters, especially if you decide to do online recovery. This case study gives you some helpful hints while trying to recover non-SYSTEM data files that contain rollback segments.

### Scenario

Anita is a DBA in a banking firm. She administers an Oracle7 release 7.2 database on a UNIX server. She stores all the user data in the USERS tablespace, index data in the INDEXES tablespaces, and all the rollback segments in the RBS tablespace. In addition, she has other tablespaces to store data for various banking applications. Since the database operates 24 hours a day, 7 days a week, she has an automated procedure to take online backups every night. In addition, she takes an export once a month of all the important tables in the database.

### Problem

On Monday morning, due to a media failure, all the data files that belong to the rollback segments tablespace RBS were lost. It was the beginning of the week and a lot of applications needed to be run against the database, so she decided to do online recovery. Once she took the data files offline and opened the database, she tried to select from a user table and got the Oracle error:

```
ORA-00376: file 2 cannot be read at this time
```

File 2 happens to be one of the data files that belongs to the rollback segment tablespace.

## Solution

If the data file that is lost belongs to a rollback segment tablespace, recovery could be tricky. Since Anita decided to do online recovery, she did the right thing by taking all the data files offline that were lost during the media failure. This means that all the rollback segments that belong to the data file need to be recovered. However, while recovery is being performed, no rows that are involved in an active transaction that points to the rollback segments can be accessed. Until you recover the data files that contain the rollback segments, you need to create some temporary rollback segments to process the new applications. The following test will make the process of recovering the data files that contain rollback segments clear.

## Test

In this test, to simulate the loss of data files, we will shut the database down with the *abort* option and delete the data files at the OS level.

```
cosmos% sqldba lmode=y

SQL*DBA: Release 7.2.1.0.0 - Beta on Sat Feb  4 18:42:01 1995
Copyright (c) Oracle Corporation 1979, 1994.  All rights reserved.
Oracle7 Server Release 7.2.1.0.0 - Beta Release
With the distributed and parallel query options
PL/SQL Release 2.2.1.0.0 - Beta

SQLDBA> connect internal
SQLDBA> create table case5 (c1 number) tablespace users;
SQLDBA> select * from case5;
C1
--
0 rows selected.
SQLDBA> commit;
Statement processed.
SQLDBA> set transaction use rollback segment r01;    — Use rollback segment r01
Statement processed.                                    for the next transaction.
```

```
SQLDBA> insert into case5 values(5);
1 row processed.
SQLDBA> shutdown abort
ORACLE instance shut down.
SQLDBA> host
cosmos% rm /home/orahome/data/721/rbs01.dbf      — Simulate loss of datafile that
                                                    contains rollback segments.
cosmos% exit
```

Before we start recovery, there is a very important step that needs
to be performed here. The INIT.ORA file needs to be modified and the
ROLLBACK_SEGMENTS parameter needs to be commented out. If this is not
done, while opening up the database, Oracle will not be able to find the rollback
segments and you can't open the database.

```
SQLDBA> startup mount
ORACLE instance started.
Database mounted.
SQLDBA> alter database datafile '/home/orahome/data/721/rbs01.dbf' offline;
Statement processed.
SQLDBA> alter database open;
Statement processed.
SQLDBA> select * from case5;  ─────────────      Cannot read table case5 since Oracle
C1                                               doesn't know if transaction was committed
ORA-00376: file 2 cannot be read at this time    or rolled back.
ORA-01110: data file 2: '/home/orahome/data/721/rbs01.dbf'
SQLDBA> select segment_name, status from dba_rollback_segs;
SEGMENT_NAME   STATUS
------------   ------
SYSTEM         ONLINE
R01            NEEDS RECOVERY
R02            NEEDS RECOVERY
R03            NEEDS RECOVERY
R04            NEEDS RECOVERY
5 rows selected.                                        Restore datafile from backup.
SQLDBA> host                                                                 /
cosmos% cp /home/orahome/backup/rbs01.dbf /home/orahome/data/721/rbs01.dbf
cosmos% exit                                     Recover all datafiles that belong to
SQLDBA> recover tablespace rbs;  ─────────       tablespace 'rbs.'
ORA-00279: Change 6393 generated at 02/04/95 17:36:02 needed for thread 1
ORA-00289: Suggestion : /home/orahome/product/7.2.1/dbs/arch1_61.dbf
ORA-00280: Change 6393 for thread 1 is in sequence #61
Specify log: {<RET>=suggested | filename | AUTO | FROM logsource | CANCEL}

Applying suggested logfile...
Log applied.
ORA-00279: Change 6423 generated at 02/06/95 14:37:23 needed for thread 1
ORA-00289: Suggestion : /home/orahome/product/7.2.1/dbs/arch1_62.dbf
```

```
ORA-00280: Change 6423 for thread 1 is in sequence #62
ORA-00278: Logfile '/home/orahome/product/7.2.1/dbs/arch1_61.dbf' no
longer needed for this recovery
Specify log: {<RET>=suggested ¦ filename ¦ AUTO ¦ FROM logsource ¦ CANCEL}

Applying suggested logfile...
Log applied.
Media recovery complete.
SQLDBA> alter tablespace rbs online;        ──────────  Brings tablespace online.
Statement processed.
SQLDBA> select * from case5;        ────────────────  Worked! Since the transaction is rolled
C1                                                     back and you see no data.
--
0 rows selected.                                       Rollback segments
SQLDBA> select segment_name, status from dba_rollback_segs;  ── are in 'Needs
SEGMENT_NAME    STATUS                                 Recovery' state.
-----------     ------                                 Need to bring
                                                       them online.
SYSTEM          ONLINE
R01             NEEDS RECOVERY
R02             NEEDS RECOVERY
R03             NEEDS RECOVERY
R04             NEEDS RECOVERY
5 rows selected.

SQLDBA> alter rollback segment r01 online;      ──── Brings rollback segment 'r01' online.
Statement processed.
SQLDBA> alter rollback segment r02 online;
Statement processed.
SQLDBA> alter rollback segment r03 online;
Statement processed.
SQLDBA> alter rollback segment r04 online;
Statement processed.
```

## Observation

In the above test we first created a table and inserted a row into it. Before we committed the transaction, we shut down the database with the *abort* option. This means that the rollback segment's transaction table will now show that the transaction is active. Also, note that before we inserted the data, we made sure that the transaction uses rollback segment R01, which resides in the data file that belongs to the rollback segment tablespace. The **set transaction use rollback...** command is used for this purpose.

Now, after the database is open, the **select * from case5** command tried to read the data block. Oracle cannot read the block because recovery has finished the roll forward but not the roll back of uncommitted transactions. That means that Oracle cannot determine if the row we have inserted is committed or rolled back. This is because we have taken the data files that contain the rollback segments offline.

Note that the rollback segments show that they are in NEEDS RECOVERY state. Once we have finished tablespace recovery, the rollback segments are still in NEEDS RECOVERY. However, since recovery has rolled back the uncommitted transactions, we can select from the table **case5**. At this point we need to bring all the rollback segments online using the **alter rollback segment** command.

An alternative way to do recovery in this scenario is to do data file recovery. Case 4 discusses the advantages and disadvantages of using data file recovery and tablespace recovery.

# Case 6: Loss of an Unarchived Online Log File

Any online log file that hasn't been archived yet by the ARCH process is called an *unarchived online log file.* Losing these files can cause data loss if you don't multiplex the online logs. This case study gives you information on how to recover from such failures.

### Scenario
Sara works in a software company as a DBA to administer a small development database on a UNIX machine. She created a 500MB database with Oracle7 release 7.2. She decided to mirror the control files but not the online log files, so she created the database with three log groups with one member each. Her backup strategy includes taking online backups twice a week and a full database export once a week.

### Problem
A power surge caused the database to crash and also caused a media failure, losing all the online log files. All the data files and the current control files are intact.

### Solution
Although the data files are OK after the crash, these files cannot be used because crash recovery cannot be performed (since all online log files are lost). Forcing the database open in a situation like this may cause database inconsistency. If any of the unarchived log files are lost, crash recovery cannot be performed and, instead, media recovery needs to be performed. In this case, all the data files need to be restored from an online (or offline) full backup and rolled forward until the last available archived log file is applied. Since this is *incomplete recovery,* tablespace or data file recovery is not possible. The only option is to use the **recover database** command.

## Test

This test simulates the loss of online log files by shutting down the database with the *abort* option and deleting all the online log files. The backup data files are restored and the current control file is used to do incomplete recovery.

```
SQLDBA> shutdown abort
ORACLE instance shut down.
SQLDBA> exit
SQL*DBA complete.
cosmos% rm /home/orahome/data/721/*.log ————————————   Simulates loss of online log files.
cosmos% cp /home/orahome/backup/*.dbf /home/orahome/data/721 — Restore all datafiles
cosmos% sqldba lmode=y                                          from backup.

SQL*DBA: Release 7.2.1.0.0 - Beta on Fri Feb  3 23:21:38 1995
Copyright (c) Oracle Corporation 1979, 1994.  All rights reserved.
Oracle7 Server Release 7.2.1.0.0 - Beta Release
With the distributed and parallel query options
PL/SQL Release 2.2.1.0.0 - Beta


SQLDBA> connect internal
Connected.
SQLDBA> startup mount
ORACLE instance started.
Database mounted.
SQLDBA> recover database until cancel; ———————————   Perform incomplete recovery.


ORA-00279: Change 6232 generated at 02/03/95 08:45:58 needed for thread 1
ORA-00289: Suggestion : /home/orahome/product/7.2.1/dbs/arch1_50.dbf
ORA-00280: Change 6232 for thread 1 is in sequence #50
Specify log: {<RET>=suggested ¦ filename ¦ AUTO ¦ FROM logsource ¦ CANCEL}
enter
Applying suggested logfile...
Log applied.
ORA-00279: Change 6269 generated at 02/03/95 19:46:32 needed for thread 1
ORA-00289: Suggestion : /home/orahome/product/7.2.1/dbs/arch1_51.dbf
ORA-00280: Change 6269 for thread 1 is in sequence #51
ORA-00278: Logfile '/home/orahome/product/7.2.1/dbs/arch1_50.dbf' no longer needed
for this recovery
Specify log: {<RET>=suggested ¦ filename ¦ AUTO ¦ FROM logsource ¦ CANCEL}
enter
Applying suggested logfile...
Log applied.
```

.........(Log files 52 through 55 are applied)

Oracle is asking to apply this log file, which is the one that was lost.

```
ORA-00279: Change 6310 generated at 02/03/95 22:55:43 needed for thread 1
ORA-00289: Suggestion : /home/orahome/product/7.2.1/dbs/arch1_56.dbf
ORA-00280: Change 6310 for thread 1 is in sequence #56
ORA-00278: Logfile '/home/orahome/product/7.2.1/dbs/arch1_55.dbf' no longer needed
for this recovery
Specify log: {<RET>=suggested ¦ filename ¦ AUTO ¦ FROM logsource ¦ CANCEL}
cancel ————————————————————————————————————————————————   Stop recovery.
Media recovery cancelled.
```

```
SQLDBA> alter database open resetlogs;    ──────────      Open database with 'resetlogs' option.
Statement processed.
SQLDBA> shutdown
Database closed.
Database dismounted.
ORACLE instance shut down.
SQLDBA> exit
SQL*DBA complete.
cosmos% ls ─────────────────────────────────      Online logs are automatically created by
control01.ctl   rbs01.dbf    redo03.log    test1.dbf      Oracle as part of database open. This is
control02.ctl   redo01.log   system01.dbf  tools01.dbf    required for normal operation of the database.
control03.ctl   redo02.log   temp.dbf      users01.dbf
```

## Observation

Note that all the data files need to be restored from the backup before applying recovery. The **recover database until cancel** command lets you apply the log files one at a time, and you can cancel when the last archive log file is applied. Alternatively, **recover database until change** or **recover database until time** commands can be used if you want to roll forward to a specific SCN or time. After recovery, the **ls** command on the UNIX operating system shows the database files in the directory. Note that Oracle has created the online log files **redo01.log**, **redo02.log**, and **redo03.log** automatically when the database was opened with the RESETLOGS option.

The best way to protect the database from losing the online log files is to mirror them. We have learned in Chapter 2 that each log group can have multiple members and each member should be placed on a different disk drive mounted under a separate disk controller. Multiplexing the log files is strongly recommended by Oracle Corporation.

# Case 7: Database Crash During HOT Backups

While taking online backups, if the database crashes, recovery would have been unnecessarily complicated until release 7.2. This case study is presented to illustrate the new functionality introduced in 7.2 with which a data file can be put in end backup mode when the database is not open. The mean time to recover (MTTR) will improve drastically as there is no recovery that needs to be done.

## Scenario

Kevin is one of the DBAs of a Fortune 500 financial company, and maintains one of the company's most crucial databases. A UNIX machine is used to store a 500-gigabyte database using Oracle7 release 7.2. The database operates 24 hours a day, 7 days a week, with 200 to 250 concurrent users on the system at any one given time. There are 250 tablespaces and the backup procedure involves keeping the tablespaces in hot backup mode and taking an online backup. Each log file is

10MB. Between issuing the **begin backup** and **end backup** commands, Oracle generates about 50 archive log files.

## Problem

On Friday afternoon, while taking hot backups, the machine crashed, bringing the database down. As this is a mission-critical workshop, Kevin needed to bring the database up as fast as possible. Once the machine was booted, he tried to start the database and Oracle asked for media recovery starting from log file sequence number 2300. The current online log file had sequence number 2335, which meant that about 35 log files needed to be applied before the database could be open. Realizing that this would require a significant amount of database down time, Kevin nervously reached for the phone to call Oracle Worldwide Support.

## Solution

Oracle7 release 7.2 introduces a wonderful new functionality that gives the DBAs the ability to end the backups of data files that are in hot backup mode by using the command

```
alter database datafile 'file_name' end backup;
```
Changes the file status from backup mode to nobackup mode.

However, in the case of release 7.1, you still need to apply recovery when the database crashes while taking online backups. You may wonder what happens if the data file is replaced with a backup data file before issuing the above command. The next section will perform this test.

## Test

This test puts the tablespace TEST in begin backup mode. After taking the backup of the data file at the OS level, data is inserted into the table that resides in the tablespace TEST. Then the database is shut down with the *abort* option to simulate the database crash.

```
cosmos% sqldba lmode=y

SQL*DBA: Release 7.2.1.0.0 - Beta on Sat Feb  4 15:58:49 1995
Copyright (c) Oracle Corporation 1979, 1994.  All rights reserved.
Oracle7 Server Release 7.2.1.0.0 - Beta Release
With the distributed and parallel query options
PL/SQL Release 2.2.1.0.0 - Beta

SQLDBA> connect internal
Connected.
SQLDBA> startup
ORACLE instance started.
Database mounted.
```

```
Database opened.

Total System Global Area          4481448 bytes
    Fixed Size                      47152 bytes
    Variable Size                 4016504 bytes
    Database Buffers               409600 bytes
    Redo Buffers                     8192 bytes

SQLDBA> archive log list
Database log mode                 ARCHIVELOG
Automatic archival                ENABLED
Archive destination               /home/orahome/product/7.2.1/dbs/arch
Oldest online log sequence        53
Next log sequence to archive      55
Current log sequence              55

SQLDBA> alter tablespace test begin backup;        ── Puts all datafiles of this tablespace in 'hot
Statement processed.                                  backup' mode.
SQLDBA> host
cosmos% cp /home/orahome/data/721/test1.dbf /home/orahome/backup/hot
cosmos% exit                                              ──── Take datafile backup
SQLDBA> create table case7 (c1 number) tablespace test;        at OS level.
Statement processed.
SQLDBA> insert into case7 values(7);
Statement processed.
SQLDBA> commit;
Statement processed.
SQLDBA> alter system switch logfile;
Statement processed.
SQLDBA> shutdown abort
ORACLE instance shut down.
```

Now we will perform two tests. The first test involves attempting to open the database with the current data file, **test01.dbf**. The second test involves replacing the current data file **test01.dbf** with the backup version of this file and trying to fool Oracle into thinking that it's the current file.

## Test 1: Using the Current Data File

```
SQLDBA> startup mount
ORACLE instance started.
Database mounted.
SQLDBA> alter database open;
ORA-01113: file 5 needs media recovery
ORA-01110: data file 5: '/home/orahome/data/721/test1.dbf'
SQLDBA> alter database datafile '/home/orahome/data/721/test1.dbf' end backup;
Statement processed.
```

```
SQLDBA> alter database open;
Statement processed.
```

## Test 2: Using the Backup Data File

```
cosmos% rm /home/orahome/data/721/test1.dbf          ———————  Remove current datafile.
cosmos% cp /home/orahome/backup/hot/test1.dbf /home/orahome/data/721 —  Replace current datafile
SQLDBA> startup mount                                                   with backup datafile to
ORACLE instance started.                                                see if Oracle can
Database mounted.                                                       recognize it.
SQLDBA> alter database open;
ORA-01113: file 5 needs media recovery                         ⌐ Oracle tells you that the file is from
ORA-01110: data file 5: '/home/orahome/data/721/test1.dbf'     ⌐ backup, thus needs recovery.
SQLDBA> alter database datafile '/home/orahome/data/721/test1.dbf' end backup;
ORA-01235: END BACKUP failed for 1 file(s) and succeeded for 0     ⌐ Oracle distinquishes
ORA-01122: database file 5 failed verification check                 between a current
ORA-01110: data file 5: '/home/orahome/data/721/test1.dbf'           datafile and a
ORA-01208: data file is an old version - not accessing current version ⌐ backup datafile.

SQLDBA> recover database   ——————————————————————  Recovers the datafile.
Media recovery complete.
SQLDBA> alter database open;  ——————————————————  Now, open the database.
Statement processed.
SQLDBA> exit
SQL*DBA complete.
```

## Observation

Note that when a tablespace is in hot backup mode, only some data structures in the data file header (or headers, if multiple data files exist for that tablespace) are updated, while the others are frozen. However, the contents of the file are current. For example, if an update is done on a table in this data file, the update is not blocked. But when a checkpoint is done, the *checkpointed at SCN* value is not written to the file header. This means that if a crash occurs during a hot backup, Oracle really needs to update only the file header and not the contents of the data file while opening the database. Issuing the **alter database datafile filename end backup** command does exactly that.

In the second test that we performed, we tried to replace the data file with a backup copy. Oracle can distinguish between a current data file in hot backup mode and a restored copy of the data file by comparing the checkpoint counters in the file header and the control file. So, to summarize, you should not replace the data file since the file contents are perfectly fine and all you need to do is just mount the database and end the backup before opening the database.

Note that the error that we received while trying to open the database for the first time after the crash is not very helpful—it just indicates that media recovery is required for a specific file(s) but doesn't tell us why. If you want to know if any data files are in hot backup mode, select from the V$BACKUP view. This view will give you the status of all the files. If the status says ACTIVE, then the file is in hot backup mode. For example:

```
SQLDBA> select file#, status from v$backup;
FILE#          STATUS
-----          ------
1              ACTIVE
2              NOT ACTIVE
3              NOT ACTIVE
4              NOT ACTIVE
4 rows selected.
```

# Case 8: Recovery with a Backup Control File

While using a backup control file, recovery can be tricky. You should always try to do recovery with the current control file if possible; the second best option would be to create a new control file. Using the backup control file should be the last option to use as the database needs to be started up with the RESETLOGS option. This case study gives a clear explanation of why this is true, and the precautions you should take after starting up the database.

### Scenario
Jane uses Oracle7 release 7.1 for Windows on her PC for her home business. She maintains a small 20MB database and takes regular cold backups. Her backup procedure involves shutting down the database and copying the data files, log files, and control file to floppy disks. She maintains only one copy of the control file and doesn't mirror the control file because she thinks mirroring the control file doesn't make sense since she has only one hard disk.

### Problem
Jane accidentally deleted her control file. Since she didn't have a copy of the control file, she copied the backup control file and tried to start up the database. While opening the database, Oracle complained that an old control file was being used.

### Solution
In this case, Jane has two options. Since all her data files and online log files are safe, she can create a new control file using the **create controlfile** command, perform recovery if required, and start up the database. Alternatively, she can use the backup control file. If you use a backup control file, you need to perform media recovery. Also, Oracle will force you to use the *using backup controlfile* option. Once recovery is done, you must start up the database with the RESETLOGS

option, and have to take a complete backup of your database. For this reason, it's a better idea to use the first solution in this case.

## Test

```
cosomos% sqldba lmode=y


SQL*DBA: Release 7.2.1.00 - Beta on Sat Feb 4 18:26:23 1995
Copyright (c) Oracle Corporation 1979, 1994. All rights reserved.
Oracle7 Server Release 7.2.1.0.0 - Beta Release
With the distributed and parallel query options
PL/SQL Release 2.2.1.0.0 - Beta

SQLDBA> connect internal
Connected.
SQLDBA> startup open
ORACLE instance started.
Database mounted.
Database opened.
Total System Global Area       4480888 bytes
    Fixed Size              47152 bytes
    Variable Size         4015944 bytes
    Database Buffers       409600 bytes
    Redo Buffers             8192 bytes

SQLDBA> select name, status, enabled from v$datafile;

NAME                                   STATUS      EBABLED
----                                   ------      -------
/home/orahome/data/721/system01.dbf    SYSTEM      READ WRITE
/home/orahome/data/721/rbs01.dbf       ONLINE      READ WRITE
/home/orahome/data/721/tools01.dbf     ONLINE      READ WRITE
/home/orahome/data/721/users01.dbf     ONLINE      READ WRITE
/home/orahome/data/721/test1.dbf       ONLINE      READ ONLY
/home/orahome/data/721/temp.dbf        ONLINE      READ WRITE
6 rows selected.

SQLDBA> create table case8 (c1 number) tablespace users;
Statement processed.
SQLDBA> insert into case8 values (8);
1 row processed.
SQLDBA> commit;
Statement processed.
SQLDBA> alter system switch logfile;
Statement processed.
SQLDBA> alter system switch logfile;
Statement processed.
SQLDBA> alter system switch logfile;
Statement processed.
SQLDBA> shutdown abort
ORACLE instance shut down.
```

```
SQLDBA> host
cosmos% cp /home/orahome/backup/control01.ctl /home/orahome/data/721        ——— Restores backup
cosmos% exit                                                                     control file.
SQLDBA> startup mount
ORACLE instance started.
Database mounted.
SQLDBA> alter database open;        ————————————————        Try to open database
ORA-01122: database file 1 failed verification check                    ┐ Indication that you
ORA-01110: data file 1: '/home/orahome/data/721/system01.dbf'          │ are using an old
ORA-01207: file is more recent than control file - old control file   ─┘ control file.


SQLDBA> recover database
ORA-00283: Recovery session canceled due to errors                      ┐ Try to recover the
ORA-01122: database file 1 failed verification check                    │ database. Oracle
ORA-01110: data file 1: '/home/orahome/data/721/system01.dbf'          │ responds you have
ORA-01207: file is more recent than control file - old control file   ─┘ to use correct syntax.


SQLDBA> recover database using backup controlfile;
ORA-00283: Recovery session canceled due to errors                      ┐ Read-only
ORA-01233: file 5 is read only - cannot recover using backup controlfile│ tablespaces
ORA-01110: data file 5: '/home/orahome/data/721/test1.dbf'            ─┘ should be
                                                                          offline first.

SQLDBA> alter database datafile '/home/orahome/data/721/test1.dbf' offline; ———
Statement processed.
                                                  Take read-only datafile online. at the end

SQLDBA> recover database using backup controlfile;  ——————— Recover database.
ORA-00279: Change 6428 generated at 02/04/95 18:28:50 needed for thread 1
ORA-00289: Suggestion : /home/orahome/product/7.2.1/dbs/arch1_64.dbf
ORA-00280: Change 6428 for thread 1 is in sequence #64
Specify log: {<RET>=suggested | filename | AUTO | FROM logsource | CANCEL}
/home/orahome/data/721/redo01.log
Applying logfile...
Log applied.
Media recovery complete.
                                               ——— Try opening database without the
                                                   RESETLOGS option.
SQLDBA> alter database open;  ———
ORA-01589: must use RESETLOGS or NORESETLOGS option for database open
SQLDBA> alter database open noresetlogs;
ORA-01588: must use RESETLOGS option for database open
SQLDBA> alter database open resetlogs;  ————————   This is the only way you can open the
Statement processed.                               database often doing recovery with a
                                                   backup control file.
SQLDBA> archive log list
Database log mode             ARCHIVELOG
Automatic archival            ENABLED
Archive destination           /home/orahome/product/7.2.1/dbs/arch
Oldest online log sequence    1
Next log sequence to archive  1
Current log sequence          1


SQLDBA> select name, status, enabled from v$datafile;
NAME                                       STATUS        EBABLED
----                                       ------        -------
/home/orahome/data/721/system01.dbf        SYSTEM        READ WRITE
```

```
/home/orahome/data/721/rbs01.dbf          ONLINE       READ WRITE
/home/orahome/data/721/tools01.dbf        ONLINE       READ WRITE
/home/orahome/data/721/users01.dbf        ONLINE       READ WRITE
/home/orahome/data/721/test1.dbf          OFFLINE      READ ONLY
/home/orahome/data/721/temp.dbf           ONLINE       READ WRITE
6 rows selected.
SQLDBA> alter tablespace test online;
Statement processed.
SQLDBA> select * from case8;
c1
--
6
1 rows selected.
```

Remember to bring the read-only datafile back online by making the tablespace online.

## Observation

When you use a backup control file, you must use the *using backup controlfile* option. Oracle will not allow you to do recovery without this option. Also, after finishing media recovery, you must start up the database with the RESETLOGS option. The error message that you receive while trying to open the database is not very clear since it says that you have to open the database with either the RESETLOGS or the NORESETLOGS option. However, if you try to open the database with the NORESETLOGS option, Oracle tells you that you should open the database with the RESETLOGS option. The reason you have to start the database with the RESETLOGS option, if you use a backup control file, is that Oracle needs to update certain data structures in the backup control file before opening the database, and this is done during RESETLOGS. After the database is open, you should *immediately* take a full online or offline backup of the database because you cannot restore any of the data files from before RESETLOGS and try to roll forward through a RESETLOGS, as described in Case 11.

Another important point to note is that if the backup control file indicates that the status of a data file is READ-ONLY, you should take the file offline before recovery and the tablespace online after startup. This is because read-only data files will not have any changes to be applied, hence no recovery is required.

Last but not least, even when you have only one disk, it is advisable to mirror control files, as it might help you with some failures, such as accidentally deleting a control file.

# Case 9: Space Management in Release 7.1

This case study discusses more about space management than backup and recovery. However, it is presented here due to the fact that many DBAs make the mistake of deleting data files without rebuilding the tablespace. The ramifications of this could be severe. Case 10 discusses an alternative solution to this problem.

## Scenario

Matt, the DBA of a financial firm, administers a 100-gigabyte database on an IBM mainframe running Oracle7 release 7.1. Matt operates the database in ARCHIVELOG mode. Every night, the system manager takes an operating system backup of the system. As part of this backup, all Oracle database files are copied from DASD to tape. The Oracle database is shut down before the backups are taken. In addition, Matt takes a full database export once every three months and incremental exports once a month.

## Problem

One day, while doing space management, Matt added a small data file to a tablespace, then decided that he really needed more space. He didn't want to add another data file, but instead decided to replace the smaller data file with a new, bigger data file. Since a data file cannot be dropped, he merely took the new data file offline and added a larger data file to the same tablespace. He deleted the data file at the OS level, assuming that Oracle would never need the file since he hadn't added any data to it, and also because it was offline. Shortly after he started running an application, he got the following error during an insert operation:

```
ORA-00376: file 6 cannot be read at this time
```

He found out that the data file Oracle is referring to (file 6) is the same data file that he had taken offline and deleted earlier.

## Solution

When you take a data file offline and open the database, you have to apply one of the following three methods:

1. Restore the data file that was taken offline from a backup and do data file recovery.

2. If no backups exist, create the data file using the **alter database create datafile** command and then recover it.

3. Rebuild the tablespace.

To apply method 1, you need to have a backup of the data file from an online or offline backup, and you need to have all the archived and online log files to recover the file. To use method 2, you need to have all the redo log files that are generated from the time the data file was originally created. In addition, the current control file or a backup control file that recognizes the offline data file should be used. Even if one of the archived log files is missing, methods 1 and 2 cannot be performed and the only option is to use method 3, which involves dropping the tablespace to which the offline data file belongs, and re-create it.

With Oracle7 releases 7.2 and higher, there is no need to take the data file offline if you want to modify the size of the data file. There is a new RESIZE option that can be used to modify the size of the data file. Case 10 discusses this option.

### Test

Note that this test is performed on an Oracle7 database running release 7.1.4. The tablespace in question is called ROTEST and it contains two data files. With the database open, one of two files is taken offline. Then data is inserted into the ROTEST tablespace until Oracle tries to allocate space from the data file that is taken offline.

```
SQLDBA> connect internal                                                    Take datafile offline.
Statement processed
SQLDBA> alter database datafile '/mcsc2/orahome/data/PROD/rotest.dbf' offline;
Statement processed.
SQLDBA> select tablespace_name, status from dba_tablespaces;    Tablsespace that the offline file
TABLESPACE_NAME        STATUS                                   belongs to is still online.
---------------        ------
SYSTEM                 ONLINE
RBS                    ONLINE
TEMP                   ONLINE
TOOLS                  ONLINE
USERS                  ONLINE
ROTEST                 ONLINE

SQL> select name, status from v$datafile;          Control file marks the offlined file as in
NAME                                       STATUS   'RECOVER' status.
----                                       ------
/mcsc2/orahome/data/PROD/system01.dbf      SYSTEM
/mcsc2/orahome/data/PROD/rbs01.dbf         ONLINE
/mcsc2/orahome/data/PROD/temp01.dbf        ONLINE
/mcsc2/orahome/data/PROD/tools01.dbf       ONLINE
/mcsc2/orahome/data/PROD/users01.dbf       ONLINE
/mcsc2/orahome/data/PROD/rotest.dbf        RECOVER
/mcsc2/orahome/data/PROD/rotest2.dbf       ONLINE

SQLDBA> insert into rotab3 select * from scott.dept;    Oracle needs more space, so is trying
ORA-00376: file 6 cannot be read at this time           to allocate space in offlined file.
ORA-01110: data file 6: '/mcsc2/orahome/data/PROD/rotest.dbf'
SQL> select * from fet$ where ts#= 5;
TS#      FILE#      BLOCK#     LENGTH
---      ----       ------     ------
5        6          17         1008

SQLDBA> alter tablespace rotest add datafile '/mcsc2/orahome/data/PROD/rotest3.dbf'
size 50k;                                               More space added to tablespace.
Statement processed.
SQLDBA> select * from fet$ where ts#=5;
TS#      FILE#      BLOCK#     LENGTH
---      -----      ------     ------
5        6          17         1008
5        8          2          24
```

```
SQLDBA> insert into rotab3 select * from scott.dept
ORA-00376: file 6 cannot be read at this time                    ┐ Oracle still tries to allocate
ORA-01110: data file 6: '/mcsc2/orahome/data/PROD/rotest.dbf'    │ space in the offline file.
SQLDBA> create table rotab4 (c1 number) tablespace rotest;       ┘
ORA-00376: file 6 cannot be read at this time
ORA-01110: data file 6: '/mcsc2/orahome/data/PROD/rotest.dbf'


SQLDBA> alter database datafile '/mcsc2/orahome/data/PROD/rotest.dbf' online;
ORA-01113: file 6 needs media recovery                    ──── Try to bring the datafile online.
ORA-01110: data file 6: '/mcsc2/orahome/data/PROD/rotest.dbf'
SQLDBA> recover tablespace rotest; ───────────────── Recover tablespace.
ORA-00283: Recovery session canceled due to errors               ┐ Oracle tells you to do
ORA-01124: cannot recover data file 7 - file is in use or recovery│ datafile recovery, not
ORA-01110: data file 7: '/mcsc2/orahome/data/PROD/rotest2.dbf'   ┘ tablespace recovery.
SQLDBA> recover datafile '/mcsc2/orahome/data/PROD/rotest.dbf'; ── Do datafile
ORA-00279: Change 11852 generated at 09/14/94 12:22:45 needed for thread 1    recovery.
ORA-00289: Suggestion : /mcsc2/orahome/admin/PROD/arch/arch.log1_13.dbf
ORA-00280: Change 11852 for thread 1 is in sequence #13
Specify log: {<RET>=suggested | filename | AUTO | FROM logsource | CANCEL}


Applying suggested logfile...
Log applied.
Media recovery complete. ───────────────────── Recovery worked.         Bring
SQLDBA> alter database datafile '/mcsc2/orahome/data/PROD/rotest.dbf' online; ─ datafile
Statement processed.                                                           online.
SQLDBA> insert into rotab3 select * from scott.dept where rownum <2; ── Now Oracle can
1 row processed.                                                        allocate space from
                                                                       datafile.
```

## Observation

When a data file is taken offline, the file cannot be written to or read by Oracle. The control file indicates that the file is offline. However, while doing space management, Oracle will look at the base data dictionary table **fet$** (free extents table, discussed in Chapter 2) to figure out how much free space is available in the database. Even when the data file is taken offline, its free space can be seen from this table since this file is still part of the database. Even though a new datafile was added to ROTEST, the space in it could not be used because the space search algorithm scans **fet$** sequentially from top to bottom. File 6 will be selected even though it is offline because the code module responsible for scanning **fet$** has no knowledge of the file's status. An error is only generated when another code module is called to allocate blocks from the extent in file 6, so the newly added space in file 8 is effectively unusable.

The only way to reliably remove files from a tablespace is to re-create it with fewer component files and use export/import to rebuild the data. Offlining the unwanted files (or OFFLINE DROP when running in NOARCHIVELOG mode) will allow access to data in the remaining files; but when space allocation is required, the scenario outlined above could easily occur—making it necessary to re-create the tablespace.

# Case 10: Resizing Data Files in Release 7.2

Release 7.2 introduces the concept of *resizing* data files to help DBAs reduce administrative time. This case study shows you how to use this feature.

## Scenario

Consider the same scenario as in Case 9.

## Problem

Consider the same problem as in Case 9.

## Solution

Data file sizes can grow dynamically in Oracle7 release 7.2. The RESIZE option can be used to manually change the size of a data file or the AUTO EXTEND option can be used to allow the files do grow dynamically when more space is required. An upper boundary can be set for the file size. For more information on this feature, refer to Appendix A.

## Test

```
cosmos% sqldba lmode=y
SQL*DBA: Release 7.2.1.0.0 - Beta on Tue Feb  7 10:13:15 1995
Copyright (c) Oracle Corporation 1979, 1994.  All rights reserved.
Oracle7 Server Release 7.2.1.0.0 - Beta Release
With the distributed and parallel query options
PL/SQL Release 2.2.1.0.0 - Beta


SQLDBA> connect internal
Connected.
SQLDBA> startup mount
ORACLE instance started.
Database mounted.
SQLDBA> archive log list
Database log mode            ARCHIVELOG
Automatic archival           ENABLED
Archive destination          /home/orahome/product/7.2.1/dbs/arch
Oldest online log sequence   59
Next log sequence to archive 61
Current log sequence         61

SQLDBA> alter database open;
Statement processed.
SQLDBA> select file#, blocks, ts# from file$;
```

```
FILE#      BLOCKS     TS#
-----      ------     ---
1          5120       0
2          1536       1
3          512        2
4          512        3
5          512        4
6          512        5
6 rows selected.
SQLDBA> alter tablespace users add datafile '/home/orahome/data/721/users02.dbf'
size 40k;
Statement processed.
SQLDBA> select file#, blocks, ts# from file$;
FILE#      BLOCKS     TS#
-----      ------     ---
1          5120       0
2          1536       1
3          512        2
4          512        3
5          512        4
6          512        5
7          20         3
7 rows selected.

SQLDBA> host
cosmos% ls -l /home/orahome/data/721/users02.dbf
-rw-r----   1 oracle7    dba          43008 Feb  7 10:20
/home/orahome/data/721/users02.dbf
cosmos% exit
cosmos%
SQLDBA> alter database datafile '/home/orahome/data/721/users02.dbf' resize 1m;
Statement processed.
SQLDBA> select file#, blocks, ts# from file$;
FILE#      BLOCKS     TS#
-----      ------     ---
1          5120       0
2          1536       1
3          512        2
4          512        3
5          512        4
6          512        5
7          512        3
7 rows selected.
SQLDBA> host
cosmos% ls -l /home/orahome/data/721/users02.dbf
-rw-r----   1 oracle7    dba        1050624 Feb  7 10:23
/home/orahome/data/721/users02.dbf
```

Check the datafile size at OS level.

Resize the file to 1MB.

Now the datafile at OS level is bigger in size (approx. 1MB).

## Observation

Note that the data file's size is increased from 40Kb to 1MB. The size of the data file is updated in the base data dictionary table **file$**. The actual physical size is also changed at the OS level as shown by the **ls** command. When the data file size is changed, a redo record is written to the log file. In the future, if this data file is lost due to a media failure, the backup of the data file should be restored and recovery applied as usual. Note that recovery would change the size of the data file as well. When the RESIZE option is used and the file size is changed, it is not necessary for you to take a backup of the data file.

# Case 11: Recovery Through RESETLOGS

Using the RESETLOGS option to open a database should be the last option for DBAs; but if it is inevitable, you should understand the ramifications of doing so. This case study illustrates the steps that you need to take before and after using this option to open the database.

### Scenario

Bob works as a DBA in a telecommunications company. He maintains an Oracle7 database in the human resources department. The database is installed on a UNIX server. Bob takes regular cold backups of the database. His backup procedure involves shutting down the database, making a disk-to-disk copy of the database files, and starting up the database. Then he copies all the database files from the backup disk to tape.

### Problem

Figure 7-1 shows the time line and various events that occurred in a sequential order. The log sequence numbers at various times are pointed out as well.

At point A, Bob has taken a cold backup of the database and opened the database for normal operation. At point B, a media failure occurred and he lost all the online log files. Since Bob doesn't multiplex the online logs, he had to do incomplete recovery. So Bob restored the database as of point A and recovered the database using the **recover database until cancel** command. He applied recovery until the last archive log file and started up the database with the RESETLOGS option at point B. As shown in Figure 7-1, the *current log sequence number* was reset to 1 again at point B.

After a few days (at point C), another media failure occurred and Bob lost data file 5. All the online log files and the control files were intact, so Bob restored the backup data file for file 5 from point A and tried to do recovery. Oracle complained that data file 5 is from a point before B. Bob tried to restore the backup control file and recover the database. This time Oracle complained that file 1 is from a point after B. Not knowing what was going on, Bob decided to restore all the data files and the control file from the cold backup (from point A) and tried to do recovery again. Recovery went fine until point B, but he couldn't go past point B since Oracle didn't recognize the log files after point B. If Bob couldn't recover up to point C, he would lose all the data that he had inserted from point B to point C.

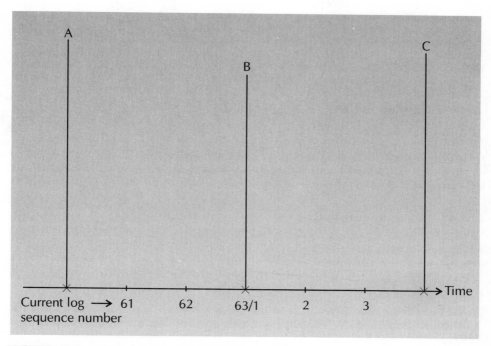

**FIGURE 7-1.**    *Database events at various points in time*

## Solution

It's absolutely necessary to take a backup of the database after the database is started with the RESETLOGS option. In the above scenario, Bob should have taken a cold backup at point B. Since he hasn't done so, Bob now has only the following two options:

1. At point C, take the data file 5 offline, open the database and export all the data from the tablespace (all objects in file 5 will be inaccessible), drop and re-create the tablespace, and import all the data taken from the export. Then shut the database down and take a cold backup. This way, Bob will lose all the data that was ever entered in file 5.

2. Restore all data files and the control file from the offline backup (point A) and roll forward up to point B. Then start up the database with the RESETLOGS option. This way, Bob will have all the data as of point B, but the data inserted between points B and C will be lost. After startup, shut down the database and take a full database backup.

The following test will simulate the above scenario.

## Test
Since this test is a bit complicated, we will comment after every important step of the test.

```
cosmos% sqldba lmode=y
SQL*DBA: Release 7.2.1.0.0 - Beta on Tue Feb  7 10:33:45 1995
Copyright (c) Oracle Corporation 1979, 1994.  All rights reserved.
Oracle7 Server Release 7.2.1.0.0 - Beta Release
With the distributed and parallel query options
PL/SQL Release 2.2.1.0.0 - Beta

SQLDBA> connect internal
Connected.
SQLDBA> startup
ORACLE instance started.
Database mounted.
Database opened.
Total System Global Area        4480888 bytes
   Fixed Size              47152 bytes
   Variable Size          015944 bytes
   Database Buffers       409600 bytes
   Redo Buffers             8192 bytes
SQLDBA> create table case11 (c1 number) tablespace users;
Statement processed.
```

The above **create** statement is created in the current online log file, which has sequence number 61. Next, switch the log file and make the current log sequence number 62. An insert will be done so the redo for the insert will be in log sequence number 62. Another switch will change the current log sequence number to 63. Note that at this point, we have the archive log files for log sequence numbers 61 and 62.

```
SQLDBA> alter system switch logfile;   61
Statement processed.
SQLDBA> insert into case11 values (11);
1 row processed.
SQLDBA> commit;
Statement processed.
SQLDBA> alter system switch logfile;   62
Statement processed.
SQLDBA> shutdown
Database closed.
```

```
Database dismounted.
ORACLE instance shut down.
SQLDBA> startup mount
ORACLE instance started.
Database mounted.

SQLDBA> archive log list
Database log mode              ARCHIVELOG
Automatic archival             ENABLED
Archive destination            /home/orahome/product/7.2.1/dbs/arch
Oldest online log sequence     61
Next log sequence to archive   63
Current log sequence           63
```

```
SQLDBA> recover database until cancel;  ——————  Perform incomplete recovery.
Media recovery complete.
SQLDBA> alter database open resetlogs;
Statement processed.
SQLDBA> archive log list;
Database log mode              ARCHIVELOG
Automatic archival             ENABLED
Archive destination            /home/orahome/product/7.2.1/dbs/arch
Oldest online log sequence     0
Next log sequence to archive   1
Current log sequence           1
```

```
SQLDBA> insert into case11 values(11);
1 row processed.
SQLDBA> commit;
Statement processed.
SQLDBA> alter system switch logfile;
Statement processed.
```

Note that the second row is inserted into table **case11** and the redo for this insert is in log sequence number 1.

```
SQLDBA> shutdown
Database closed.
Database dismounted.
ORACLE instance shut down.
SQLDBA> host
cosmos% rm /home/orahome/data/721/users01.dbf  —— Simulate loss of datafile.    Recover
cosmos% cp /home/orahome/backup/users01.dbf /home/orahome/data/721  ——  datafile
cosmos% exit                                                              from
cosmos%                                                                   backup.
SQLDBA> startup mount
ORACLE instance started.
Database mounted.
```

```
SQLDBA> recover database
ORA-00283: Recovery session canceled due to errors
ORA-01190: control file or data file 4 is from before the last RESETLOGS
ORA-01110: data file 4: '/home/orahome/data/721/users01.dbf'
```

Oracle tells you that datafile is from before RESETLOGS.

The above recovery statement failed because the control file and all data files are from a point after the RESETLOGS was done, except for the **users01.dbf** file, which was restored from the backup. So Oracle is complaining that file 4 is from before point B of Figure 7-1.

```
SQLDBA> shutdown
ORA-01109: database not open
Database dismounted.
ORACLE instance shut down.
SQLDBA> host
cosmos% cp /home/orahome/backup/control01.ctl /home/orahome/data/721
cosmos% exit
cosmos%
SQLDBA> startup mount
ORACLE instance started.
Database mounted.
SQLDBA> recover database using backup controlfile;  ——— Try recovery.
ORA-00283: Recovery session canceled due to errors
ORA-01190: control file or data file 1 is from before the last RESETLOGS
ORA-01110: data file 1: '/home/orahome/data/721/system01.dbf'
```

Restore control file from backup.

The above recovery statement failed because we have restored a backup of the control file and data file **users01.dbf**, but all other data files are from after point B of Figure 7-1. Oracle is complaining that file 1 is after point B. If, for example, you replace file 1 with the backup data file, then it will complain about file 2 not being from the backup, and so on. This means that all the data files and control files need to be from the backup. So now let's restore all the data files from backup and see what happens.

```
SQLDBA> shutdown
ORA-01109: database not open
Database dismounted.
ORACLE instance shut down.
SQLDBA> host
cosmos% cp /home/orahome/backup/*.* /home/orahome/data/721
cosmos% exit
cosmos%

SQLDBA> startup mount
ORACLE instance started.
Database mounted.
SQLDBA> archive log list
```

Restore all datafiles from backup.

```
Database log mode                ARCHIVELOG
Automatic archival               ENABLED
Archive destination              /home/orahome/product/7.2.1/dbs/arch
Oldest online log sequence       59
Next log sequence to archive     61
Current log sequence             61
```

```
SQLDBA> recover database using backup controlfile;
ORA-00283: Recovery session canceled due to errors
ORA-01233: file 5 is read only - cannot recover using backup controlfile
ORA-01110: data file 5: '/home/orahome/data/721/test1.dbf'
```

The above recovery failed for a different reason this time. The backup control file shows the status of file 5 as read-only. Recall that while doing media recovery, we cannot have any read-only data files online. So let's take this data file offline.

```
SQLDBA> alter database datafile '/home/orahome/data/721/test1.dbf' offline;
Statement processed.
```

```
                                                          Recover database. Trying to do
SQLDBA> recover database using backup controlfile; ────── complete recovery.
ORA-00279: Change 6406 generated at 02/04/95 17:36:35 needed for thread 1
ORA-00289: Suggestion : /home/orahome/product/7.2.1/dbs/arch1_61.dbf
ORA-00280: Change 6406 for thread 1 is in sequence #61
Specify log: {<RET>=suggested ¦ filename ¦ AUTO ¦ FROM logsource ¦ CANCEL}

Applying suggested logfile...
Log applied.
ORA-00279: Change 6422 generated at 02/07/95 10:34:53 needed for thread 1
ORA-00289: Suggestion : /home/orahome/product/7.2.1/dbs/arch1_62.dbf
ORA-00280: Change 6422 for thread 1 is in sequence #62
ORA-00278: Logfile '/home/orahome/product/7.2.1/dbs/arch1_61.dbf' no longer needed
for this recovery
Specify log: {<RET>=suggested ¦ filename ¦ AUTO ¦ FROM logsource ¦ CANCEL}

Applying suggested logfile...
Log applied.
ORA-00279: Change 6425 generated at 02/07/95 10:35:26 needed for thread 1
ORA-00289: Suggestion : /home/orahome/product/7.2.1/dbs/arch1_63.dbf
ORA-00280: Change 6425 for thread 1 is in sequence #63
ORA-00278: Logfile '/home/orahome/product/7.2.1/dbs/arch1_62.dbf' no longer needed
for this recovery
Specify log: {<RET>=suggested ¦ filename ¦ AUTO ¦ FROM logsource ¦ CANCEL}
/home/orahome/product/7.2.1/dbs/arch1_1.dbf ──────
Applying logfile...                                     Can't recognize past
ORA-00310: archived log contains sequence 1; sequence 63 required  the RESETLOGS.
ORA-00334: archived log: '/home/orahome/product/7.2.1/dbs/arch1_1.dbf'
Specify log: {<RET>=suggested ¦ filename ¦ AUTO ¦ FROM logsource ¦ CANCEL}
cancel ───────────────────────────────────────────────── Stop recovery.
Media recovery cancelled.
```

Note that in the above recovery procedure, we have applied log sequence numbers 61 and 62. At this point, RESETLOGS was done so the next log sequence number that is available to us is log sequence number 1. When we applied this log Oracle didn't recognize it since it was looking for log sequence number 63. This proves that we cannot cross this point (at which RESETLOGS was done), so we try to stop recovery here and open the database.

```
SQLDBA> alter database open resetlogs; ─────
ORA-01113: file 1 needs media recovery
ORA-01110: data file 1: '/home/orahome/data/721/system01.dbf'
```
Can't open since you did incomplete recovery without issuing the proper recovery command.

Note we cannot open the database because we are doing complete recovery. We started doing recovery by issuing the **recover database** command so Oracle will open the database only if all the redo for the thread is applied. Since we don't have all the redo for the thread, we should do incomplete recovery by issuing the command **recover database.... until cancel**. So let's try doing recovery again with the right recovery options.

Recover database and allow incomplete recovery.

```
SQLDBA> recover database using backup controlfile until cancel; ───
ORA-00279: Change 6425 generated at 02/07/95 10:35:26 needed for thread 1
ORA-00289: Suggestion : /home/orahome/product/7.2.1/dbs/arch1_63.dbf
ORA-00280: Change 6425 for thread 1 is in sequence #63
Specify log: {<RET>=suggested | filename | AUTO | FROM logsource | CANCEL}
cancel
Media recovery cancelled.
SQLDBA> alter database open resetlogs; ─────────
Statement processed.
```
Open database after incomplete recovery.

Note that when we tried to do recovery again, Oracle didn't request the changes starting all the way from log sequence number 61, but asked for the latest log sequence number, which is 63. This shows that when you stop and start media recovery again, Oracle continues from where you left off.

```
SQLDBA> select * from case11; ─────────
C1
--
11
1 row selected.
```
Proof that you can't recover 'through' RESETLOGS. Can't see the second row!

Since we recovered only until point B and didn't cross this point, the second row that we inserted into this table was lost. So the **select** statement shows only one row in the table, which is expected.

## Observation

There are some very important points to note from this test:

- If RESETLOGS is done at a point in time, you cannot restore the backup of the database from before the RESETLOGS and recover through the RESETLOGS point. This means that any time the database is opened with the RESETLOGS option, you should take another backup immediately.

- If you want to do incomplete recovery, you should use the **until cancel** option in the **recover database** command.

- If you are using a backup control file, all the read-only data files should be offline. In addition, the **using backup controlfile** option should be used with the **recover database** command.

# Case 12: Creating Data Files

It is comforting to have the option of creating a data file when you lose one, but there are ramifications of doing so. This case study gives you an idea when, why, and how to use this option.

## Scenario

Tom is the DBA of a pharmaceutical company. He administers a 20-gigabyte database on a VAX/VMS system running Oracle7 release 7.1. His backup procedure includes taking a hot backup of the database once a week. Every Sunday night he submits a batch job that puts the tablespaces in *hot backup* mode, one at a time. The data files are then copied to multiple tk50 tapes.

## Problem

Monday afternoon, while running an application, Tom got an Oracle error saying that there is no more space in a specified tablespace. He then added a data file to that tablespace. Since the application does a lot of DML (Data Manipulation Language) operations and modifies a lot of tables, he decided to wait until the application finished so that he could take a backup of the data file he just added. Friday morning, a media failure occurred and Tom lost the new data file he had added on Monday. He then realized that he forgot to take a backup of the data file on Monday. He could take the file offline and start up the database, but he would lose a lot of data that the application had inserted into that data file. Tom could restore from the backup and roll forward, but this wouldn't work because the backup didn't have the new data file he added on Monday.

## Solution

This is a perfect scenario for re-creating the data file. To re-create the data file, Tom needs the current control file or a backup control file that recognizes the new data file that was added on Monday. Next, all the archive log files and online log files need to be available. All Tom needs to do is mount the database and issue the **alter database create datafile** command to re-create the data file. Once the file is created, he needs to apply the redo (i.e., roll forward) from the time the file was created to the present time. The following test illustrates this scenario.

## Test

```
cosmos% sqldba lmode=y
SQL*DBA: Release 7.2.1.0.0 - Beta on Tue Feb  7 12:03:46 1995
Copyright (c) Oracle Corporation 1979, 1994.  All rights reserved.
Oracle7 Server Release 7.2.1.0.0 - Beta Release
With the distributed and parallel query options
PL/SQL Release 2.2.1.0.0 - Beta

SQLDBA> connect internal
Connected.
SQLDBA> startup open
ORACLE instance started.
Database mounted.
Database opened.
Total System Global Area        4480888 bytes
    Fixed Size            47152 bytes
    Variable Size       4015944 bytes
    Database Buffers      09600 bytes
    Redo Buffers           8192 bytes
```

```
SQLDBA> alter tablespace users add datafile '/home/orahome/data/721/users02.dbf'
size 40k;                                                    Adds a datafile to tablespace USERS.
Statement processed.
SQLDBA> alter system switch logfile;
Statement processed.
SQLDBA> alter system switch logfile;
Statement processed.
SQLDBA> alter system switch logfile;
Statement processed.
SQLDBA> shutdown
Database closed.
Database dismounted.
ORACLE instance shut down.

SQLDBA> host                                                 Simulate loss of datafile. No backup for
cosmos% rm /home/orahome/data/721/users02.dbf                this datafile available.
```

```
cosmos% exit
cosmos%
SQLDBA> startup mount
ORACLE instance started.
Database mounted.
```
```
SQLDBA> alter database create datafile '/home/orahome/data/721/users02.dbf';
Statement processed.
```
— Creates the datafile.
```
SQLDBA> recover datafile '/home/orahome/data/721/users02.dbf'
```
— Recovers the datafile.
```
ORA-00279: Change 6420 generated at 02/07/95 11:00:51 needed for thread 1
ORA-00289: Suggestion : /home/orahome/product/7.2.1/dbs/arch1_62.dbf
ORA-00280: Change 6420 for thread 1 is in sequence #62
Specify log: {<RET>=suggested | filename | AUTO | FROM logsource | CANCEL}

Applying suggested logfile...
Log applied.
Media recovery complete.
SQLDBA> alter database open;
Statement processed. ─────────────────────── Works!
SQLDBA> host
cosmos% ls -l /home/orahome/data/721/users02.dbf
-rw-r-----   1 oracle7  dba         43008 Feb  7 13:09
/home/orahome/data/721/users02.dbf
```

## Observation

The **alter database create datafile** command expects the use of a control file that has the file entry for the data file to be re-created. It is therefore important to have one of the following:

**1.** The current control file

**2.** The backup control file that has the file entry for the data file to be re-created—this means you should take a backup of the control file immediately after a schema change.

Also, note in the above test that the **alter database create datafile** command actually creates the data file for you at the OS level and the **recover datafile** command reads the changes from the redo log file and applies them to the datablocks.

# Case 13: System Clock Change and Point-in-Time Recovery

This case study is probably the toughest one to understand. Point-in-time recovery is a type of incomplete recovery. To complicate matters, if this kind of recovery is done after the system clock is changed, you can run into problems. If you take a full online or offline backup of your database after you change the system clock, you will never face the situation discussed in this case study.

## Scenario

Richard is the DBA of an Oracle7 database at a blood bank. He administers a 10-gigabyte database on a UNIX machine. The database contains 10 tablespaces and the backup procedure involves taking an online backup once every week on Sunday. Richard doesn't take any logical backups of the database.

## Problem

Wednesday morning at 1:58 A.M., one of the users accidentally dropped a very important table. He didn't have an export backup of the table. The user called Richard and requested that his table be restored from the backup. Since the user was inserting a lot of data into the table before he dropped it, he wanted the table to be recovered as close as possible to 1:58 A.M. Richard decided to do time-based recovery from the most recent online backup, with the intention of halting recovery at 1.55 A.M. To further complicate the issue, the system clock was moved back an hour at 2 A.M. (from 2 A.M. to 1 A.M.) on Wednesday morning (see Figure 7-2). Richard was unable to get close to the drop time, so he had to stop recovery an hour before the table was dropped. The user lost more than an hour's worth of data.

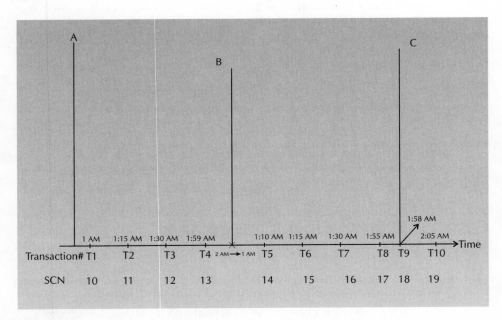

**FIGURE 7-2.** *Database events at various points in time*

## Solution

At point A, the online backup of the database was taken. At point B, the system clock was changed from 2 A.M. to 1 A.M. At point C, the user accidentally dropped his table. The transaction numbers, the SCN allocated to the transaction, and the timestamps when the transactions have committed are shown between points A and B, as well as B and C. For example, transaction T1 committed at time 1 A.M. and an SCN = 10 is allocated to it. Transaction T9 with SCN = 18, committed at 1:58 A.M. (at point C), which dropped the user's table. Since the table was dropped at point C (in Figure 7-2), Richard wanted to roll forward up to T8 and stop.

The only solution here is to restore the online backups from point A and roll forward up to transaction T4. The reason for this is that when point-in-time recovery is performed, Oracle uses SCNs to do recovery. However, to determine which SCN to roll forward to, it looks at the time stamps in the redo records. In this scenario, if recovery is to stop before 1:58 A.M. (point C in Figure 7-2, where the table is dropped), you would issue the following command:

```
recover database until time 'yyyy-mm-dd:01:58:00';
```

This command rolls forward the database and stops before 1:58 A.M. Since the redo log files are scanned sequentially, looking at the time line in Figure 7-2, Oracle will read the redo generated by T4; and since its time stamp is greater than 1:58 A.M., it stops after applying the changes made by T3. For example, if you change the time in the recovery statement to 2:00 A.M., looking again at Figure 7-2, you can see that all transactions have a timestamp less than 2 A.M., except T10. That means Oracle will apply all changes to the database made by transactions up to T9. But that doesn't help since transaction T9 has dropped the table.

Note that in this case, if you do complete recovery all transactions will be applied. However, if you decide to do point-in-time recovery, you might not be able to roll forward to a point that lies between points B and C of Figure 7-2. This depends on the activity in the database. For example, in Figure 7-2, if we didn't have any transactions between points A and B, then it's quite possible to roll forward to a point that lies between points B and C. So it is important to note that you should take a backup of the database after changing the system clock if you ever intend to use the backup and do point-in-time recovery.

## Test

We will perform two tests here. The first test demonstrates how to do a simple point-in-time recovery. The second test involves changing the system clock in addition to doing point-in-time recovery. After every important step, some explanation is given.

### Test1: Simple Point-in-Time Recovery
Table **timer** has two columns. The first column (column A) gives the record number, and the second column (column B) gives the timestamp at which the record was inserted.

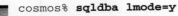

```
cosmos% sqldba lmode=y
SQL*DBA: Release 7.2.1.0.0 - Beta on Tue Feb  7 12:03:46 1995
Copyright (c) Oracle Corporation 1979, 1994.  All rights reserved.
Oracle7 Server Release 7.2.1.0.0 - Beta Release
With the distributed and parallel query options
PL/SQL Release 2.2.1.0.0 - Beta

SQLDBA> connect internal
Connected
SQLDBA> select a, to_char(b, 'hh24:mi:ss') time from timer;
A       TIME
--      ----
1       17:48:59
2       17:50:36
3       17:51:07
4       17:52:00
5       17:53:05
6       17:54:45
7       17:56:37
7 rows selected.
```

Now the database is shut down with the *normal* option and we restored the backup data files that were taken at 17:45. The current control file and redo log files are used for recovery.

```
SQLDBA> connect internal
Connected.
SQLDBA> startup mount
ORACLE instance started.
Database mounted.
SQLDBA> recover database until time '1994-09-15:17:55:00';
Media recovery complete.
SQLDBA> alter database open resetlogs;
Statement processed.
SQLDBA> select a, to_char(b, 'hh24:mi:ss') time from timer;
A       TIME
--      ----
1       17:48:59
2       17:50:36
```

Apply recovery up to time 17:55:00.

Before 17:55:00 only six rows inserted.

```
3          17:51:07
4          17:52:00
5          17:53:05
6          17:54:45
6 rows selected.
```

## Test2: System Clock Change and Point-in-Time Recovery   Table **timer**
has three columns. The first column gives the record number, the second column
gives the timestamp at which an operation happened, and the third column gives
the name of the operation that was done at that time.

```
SQL> select a, to_char(b, 'HH24:MI:SS') time, c from timer;
A      TIME              C
--     --------          ----------
1      15:49:02          Switched Logs
2      15:51:51          Insert
3      15:55:38          Insert
4      15:57:29          Switched Logs
5      16:00:31          Insert
6      16:02:03          Insert
7      16:04:44          Switched Logs
8      15:04:34          Time Switch
9      15:07:27          Insert
10     15:09:35          Switched Logs
11     16:05:38          Time Change
12     15:05:25          Time Change
13     15:08:14          Switched Logs
13 rows selected.
SQLDBA> connect internal
Connected.
SQLDBA> startup mount
ORACLE instance started.
Database mounted.
SQLDBA> archive log list;
Database log mode              ARCHIVELOG
Automatic archival             ENABLED
Archive destination            /mcsc2/orahome/admin/PROD/arch/arch.log
Oldest online log sequence     7
Next log sequence to archive   9
Current log sequence           9
```
                                          Recover up to 16:05. Only 10 rows
                                          should be recovered in the table.
```
SQLDBA> recover database until time '1994-09-16:16:05:00';
ORA-00279: Change 13388 generated at 09/16/94 14:26:25 needed for thread 1
ORA-00289: Suggestion : /mcsc2/orahome/admin/PROD/arch/arch.log1_3.dbf
ORA-00280: Change 13388 for thread 1 is in sequence #3
Specify log: {<RET>=suggested | filename | AUTO | FROM logsource | CANCEL}

Applying suggested logfile...
Log applied.
ORA-00279: Change 13427 generated at 09/16/94 15:46:33 needed for thread 1
ORA-00289: Suggestion : /mcsc2/orahome/admin/PROD/arch/arch.log1_4.dbf
```

```
ORA-00280: Change 13427 for thread 1 is in sequence #4
ORA-00278: Logfile '/mcsc2/orahome/admin/PROD/arch/arch.log1_3.dbf' no longer needed
for this recovery
Specify log: {<RET>=suggested | filename | AUTO | FROM logsource | CANCEL}

Applying suggested logfile...
Log applied.
ORA-00279: Change 13446 generated at 09/16/94 15:48:55 needed for thread 1
ORA-00289: Suggestion : /mcsc2/orahome/admin/PROD/arch/arch.log1_5.dbf
ORA-00280: Change 13446 for thread 1 is in sequence #5
ORA-00278: Logfile '/mcsc2/orahome/admin/PROD/arch/arch.log1_4.dbf' no longer needed
for this recovery
Specify log: {<RET>=suggested | filename | AUTO | FROM logsource | CANCEL}

Applying suggested logfile...
Log applied.
ORA-00279: Change 13451 generated at 09/16/94 15:57:13 needed for thread 1
ORA-00289: Suggestion : /mcsc2/orahome/admin/PROD/arch/arch.log1_6.dbf
ORA-00280: Change 13451 for thread 1 is in sequence #6
ORA-00278: Logfile '/mcsc2/orahome/admin/PROD/arch/arch.log1_5.dbf' no longer needed
for this recovery
Specify log: {<RET>=suggested | filename | AUTO | FROM logsource | CANCEL}

Applying suggested logfile...
Log applied.
Media recovery complete. ——————————————————  Incomplete recovery is finished.

SQLDBA> alter database open;
ORA-01589: must use RESETLOGS or NORESETLOGS option for database open
SQLDBA> alter database open resetlogs;
Statement processed.

SQL> select a, to_char(b, 'HH24:MI:SS') time, c from timer; — Works!
A       TIME                 C
--      --------             ----------
1       15:49:02             Switched Logs
2       15:51:51             Insert
3       15:55:38             Insert
4       15:57:29             Switched Logs
5       16:00:31             Insert
6       16:02:03             Insert
7       16:04:44             Switched Logs
8       15:04:34             Time Switch
9       15:07:27             Insert
10      15:09:35             Switched Logs
10 rows selected.
```

## Observation

Test 1 is straightforward. Point-in-time recovery was done up to 17:55. Since record 7 was inserted after this time, recovery is done only up to record 6. The **select** statement shows that there are six records in the table after recovery.

In test 2, we have moved the system clock back twice. Once from 16:04 to 15:04 and again after an hour later, from 16:05 to 15:05. Point-in-time recovery was done until 16:05:00. Note that record 7 shows that a log switch happened at 16:04:44, which is less than 16:05:00. After that the time stamp goes back to 15:04. The first record that has a time stamp greater than or equal to 16:05:00 is record 11. So recovery has rolled forward through the first system clock change but stopped at record 10. Therefore, the **select** statement shows that ten records exist in the table. In the above example, if we had done point-in-time recovery until 16:04:00, we would have recovered only the first 6 records.

# Case 14: Offline Tablespaces and Media Recovery

As a DBA, you need to be careful when you do media recovery. Sometimes you might finish doing recovery, but when you start the database up, you may realize to your surprise, that roll forward did not happen to some of the data files. This case study gives you a scenario in which this could happen and how to prevent it.

### Scenario

Nancy administers a large database of 150 gigabytes at a factory. She uses Oracle7 release 7.2 on a UNIX server and takes weekly offline backups of the database. She triple mirrors her disk drives, and once a week she shuts the database down, unlinks one of the mirrors, and starts up the database. At this point the database is double mirrored. She then uses tape drives to copy the database files onto the tape. She also keeps a copy of the database on a separate set of disk drives. Once the copying is done, she connects the third mirror to the double mirror. Nancy runs the database in ARCHIVELOG mode. Every day, about 100 archived log files are generated. An automated process copies the archived log files to tape at regular intervals, and one week's worth of archived log files are kept online on disk. The control files and online log files are multiplexed.

### Problem

On Sunday, an offline backup of the database was taken. Nancy observed that the current log sequence number was 100. Thursday morning, one of the tablespaces (TS1) was taken offline and the current log sequence number at that time was 450. On Thursday afternoon, due to a disk controller problem, some of the data files were lost. The current log sequence number at the time of the failure was 500.

Nancy decided to delete all the data files, restore data files from the offline backup from Sunday, and roll forward. She restored all the data files from the cold backup, and used the current control file to do database recovery. Nancy issued the **recover database** command and applied around 400 archived log files. Since all the archived log files were in the archive destination, Nancy issued the **auto** command and Oracle automatically applied all 400 archived log files. The recovery took about 13 hours and Nancy could finally bring the database to normal operation.

Once the database was open, she decided to bring tablespace TS1 online. Oracle asked for recovery for all the data files that belong to tablespace TS1. Nancy expected Oracle to ask for recovery starting at log sequence number 450, since that's when the tablespace was taken offline. However, when she issued the **recover tablespace** command, she realized that Oracle asked for recovery starting from log sequence number 100, all the way from when the backup was taken. Worrying that this would take another 13 hours, Nancy picked up the phone to call Oracle Worldwide Support.

## Solution
Note that when a control file indicates that a data file is offline, that data file will not be recovered during database recovery. Since Nancy used the current control file, which shows that all the data files that belong to tablespace TS1 are offline, recovery did not recover any of the data files that belong to that tablespace. Since all the files were restored from backup, tablespace recovery for TS1 asked for recovery starting from the offline backup.

In this scenario, Nancy has to apply all the archived log files again to make the data files that belong to tablespace TS1 current. However, recovery will be shorter than 13 hours this time since all the changes are already applied to the data blocks except for the changes that belong to tablespace TS1. Also, since tablespace TS1 was taken offline at log sequence number 450, there will not be any redo that needs to be applied between log sequence numbers 450 and 500. The exact time to recover depends on the amount of changes that need to be applied to TS1. In this case, it took Nancy 2 hours to roll forward the second time.

A better recovery solution in a situation like this is to do the following:

1. Restore all data files from the cold backup (or selected data files, depending on which data files are lost).

2. Mount the database and select from the V$DATAFILE view to see if any of the data files are offline.

3. If any data files are offline, bring them online.

4. Recover the database using the **recover database** option and open the database.

5. Bring the tablespace online.

## Test
The following test simulates the above scenario. We first start up the database, take a tablespace offline, and shut the database down using the *abort* option. We then delete all the data files and restore the data files from a cold backup.

```
cosmos% sqldba lmode=y
SQL*DBA: Release 7.2.1.0.0 - Beta on Sun Feb 12 16:16:04 1995
Copyright (c) Oracle Corporation 1979, 1994.  All rights reserved.
Oracle7 Server Release 7.2.1.0.0 - Beta Release
With the distributed and parallel query options
PL/SQL Release 2.2.1.0.0 - Beta

SQLDBA> connect internal
Connected.
SQLDBA> startup open
ORACLE instance started.
Database mounted.
Database opened.
Total System Global Area      4480888 bytes
   Fixed Size           47152 bytes
   Variable Size        15944 bytes
   Database Buffers     409600 bytes
   Redo Buffers         8192 bytes

SQLDBA> archive log list
Database log mode              ARCHIVELOG
Automatic archival             ENABLED
Archive destination            /home/orahome/product/7.2.1/dbs/arch
Oldest online log sequence     60
Next log sequence to archive   62
Current log sequence           62

SQLDBA> alter system switch logfile;
Statement processed.
SQLDBA> alter system switch logfile;
Statement processed.
SQLDBA> alter tablespace USERS offline;
Statement processed.
SQLDBA> alter system switch logfile;
Statement processed.
SQLDBA> archive log list
Database log mode              ARCHIVELOG
Automatic archival             ENABLED
Archive destination            /home/orahome/product/7.2.1/dbs/arch
Oldest online log sequence     63
Next log sequence to archive   65
Current log sequence           65
SQLDBA> shutdown abort
ORACLE instance shut down.

SQLDBA> host
cosmos% rm /home/orahome/data/721/*.dbf       ———— Simulates loss of all datafiles.
cosmos% cp /home/orahome/backup/*.dbf /home/orahome/data/721
cosmos% exit                                  Restores all datafiles from backup.
cosmos%
```

Next, we present two recovery methods. The first method is the recovery procedure used by Nancy in this example. The second recovery method is a better way of doing recovery, and is recommended by Oracle since the log file(s) need to be applied only once.

## Recovery Method 1

```
SQLDBA> startup mount
ORACLE instance started.
Database mounted.

SQLDBA> recover database
ORA-00279: Change 6420 generated at 02/07/95 11:00:51 needed for thread 1
ORA-00289: Suggestion : /home/orahome/product/7.2.1/dbs/arch1_62.dbf
ORA-00280: Change 6420 for thread 1 is in sequence #62
Specify log: {<RET>=suggested | filename | AUTO | FROM logsource | CANCEL}

Applying suggested logfile...
Log applied.
Media recovery complete.

SQLDBA> alter database open;
Statement processed.
SQLDBA> alter tablespace users online;
ORA-01113: file 4 needs media recovery
ORA-01110: data file 4: '/home/orahome/data/721/users01.dbf'
SQLDBA> recover tablespace users
ORA-00279: Change 6420 generated at 02/07/95 11:00:51 needed for thread 1
ORA-00289: Suggestion : /home/orahome/product/7.2.1/dbs/arch1_62.dbf
ORA-00280: Change 6420 for thread 1 is in sequence #62
Specify log: {<RET>=suggested | filename | AUTO | FROM logsource | CANCEL}

Applying suggested logfile...
Log applied.
Media recovery complete.
SQLDBA> alter tablespace users online;
Statement processed.
```

## Recovery Method 2

```
SQLDBA> startup mount
ORACLE instance started.
Database mounted.
SQLDBA> select * from v$datafile;

SQLDBA> select name,  status,  enabled from v$datafile;
NAME                                 STATUS    ENABLED
-----------------------------------  ------    -------
/home/orahome/data/721/system01.dbf  SYSTEM    READ WRITE
```

```
/home/orahome/data/721/rbs01.dbf        ONLINE      READ WRITE
/home/orahome/data/721/tools01.dbf      ONLINE      READ WRITE
/home/orahome/data/721/users01.dbf      OFFLINE     DISABLED
/home/orahome/data/721/test1.dbf        ONLINE      READ WRITE
/home/orahome/data/721/temp.dbf         ONLINE      READ WRITE
6 rows selected.

SQLDBA> alter database datafile '/home/orahome/data/721/users01.dbf' online;
Statement processed.
SQLDBA> recover database
ORA-00279: Change 6420 generated at 02/07/95 11:00:51 needed for thread 1
ORA-00289: Suggestion : /home/orahome/product/7.2.1/dbs/arch1_62.dbf
ORA-00280: Change 6420 for thread 1 is in sequence #62
Specify log: {<RET>=suggested ¦ filename ¦ AUTO ¦ FROM logsource ¦ CANCEL}

Applying suggested logfile...
Log applied.
Media recovery complete.
```

```
SQLDBA> select name, status, enabled from v$datafile;   Datafile is online.
NAME                              STATUS      ENABLED
--------------------------------  ------      -------
/home/orahome/data/721/system01.dbf  SYSTEM   READ WRITE
/home/orahome/data/721/rbs01.dbf     ONLINE   READ WRITE
/home/orahome/data/721/tools01.dbf   ONLINE   READ WRITE
/home/orahome/data/721/users01.dbf   ONLINE   DISABLED
/home/orahome/data/721/test1.dbf     ONLINE   READ WRITE
/home/orahome/data/721/temp.dbf      ONLINE   READ WRITE
6 rows selected.
```

```
SQLDBA> alter database open;
Statement processed.
SQLDBA> select tablespace_name, status from dba_tablespaces; — Tablespace is offline.
TABLESPACE_NAME    STATUS
---------------    ------
SYSTEM             ONLINE
RBS                ONLINE
TOOLS              ONLINE
USERS              OFFLINE
TEST               ONLINE
TEMP               ONLINE
6 rows selected.
```
                                                    Trying to create a table when
                                                    tablespace is offline and datafile is
```
SQLDBA> create table case14 (c1 number) tablespace users; — online doesn't work.
ORA-01542: tablespace 'USERS' is offline, cannot allocate space in it
SQLDBA> alter tablespace users online; ————————  Take Tablespace online.
Statement processed.
SQLDBA> create table case14 (c1 number) tablespace users; — Try to create table again and
Statement processed.                                        it works!
SQLDBA> exit
SQL*DBA complete.
```

## Observation

Note that in method 2 in the above test, once the database is opened, the tablespace USERS is offline but its underlying data file is online. This is because we have taken the data file online while the database is mounted. However, Oracle has no knowledge of the status of the tablespace when the database is not open. This is because *tablespace* is a logical entity, as we have discussed in Chapter 2.

In this scenario, a slight variation to method 2 would be to use the backup control file. Then the data file doesn't need to be brought online, since the backup control file would indicate that all data files are online. However, the disadvantage of doing recovery with a backup control file is that once recovery is done, you must open the database with the RESETLOGS option, which means a cold backup needs to be taken immediately.

# Case 15: Read-Only Tablespaces and Recovery

If you are using read-only tablespaces, there are some special considerations while doing media recovery. This case study is dedicated to doing testing on media recovery while using read-only tablespaces. We will present three scenarios and will perform a total of six tests. We will test these scenarios using the current control file and repeat them using the backup control file.

## Scenario

Figure 7-3 gives the three scenarios in which read-only tablespaces are used. In all three scenarios, point A denotes the time when a cold backup (or a hot backup) of the database is taken. Also, at point A, Figure 7-3 shows whether the tablespace in question is in read-only or read-write mode at the time the cold backups are taken. Point B is where the tablespace is changed from read-only mode to read-write mode or vice versa, depending on the scenario. Point C indicates a media failure where all the data files are lost. In all cases we restore the data files from point A and perform media recovery. We test the three scenarios, first with the current control file, and then with a backup control file. Note that if we are using the current control file, this is the control file at Point C in Figure 7-3. If using a backup control file, the asterisk (*) in Figure 7-3 indicates the point at which the backup of the control file is taken.

## Test

Following are the six tests that we will perform:

1. Tablespace is in read-only mode at backup and also before the failure occurred, and media recovery is done with the current control file.

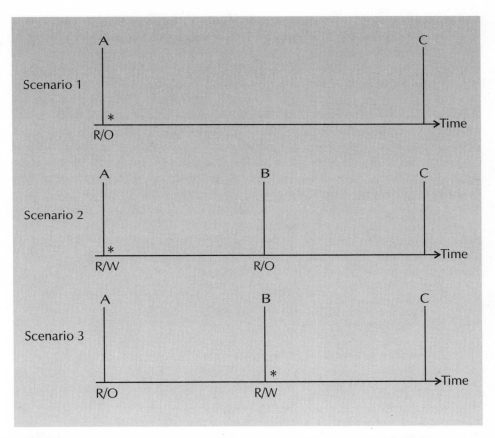

**FIGURE 7-3.** *Three different scenarios for read-only and read-write tablespaces*

**2.** Tablespace is in read-write mode at backup, but is changed to read-only mode before the failure occurred; and media recovery is done with the current control file.

**3.** Tablespace is in read-only mode at backup, but is changed to read-write mode before the failure occurred; and media recovery is done with the current control file.

**4.** Tablespace is in read-only mode at backup and also before the failure occurred, and media recovery is done with the backup control file.

**5.** Tablespace is in read-write mode at backup, but is changed to read-only mode before the failure occurred; and media recovery is done with the backup control file.

**6.** Tablespace is in read-only mode at backup, but is changed to read-write mode before the failure occurred; and media recovery is done with the backup control file.

Note that tests 1 to 3 are identical to tests 4 to 6, except the first three use the current control file and the second three tests use the backup control file.

## Test 1

```
SQLDBA> startup
ORACLE instance started.
Database mounted.
Database opened.
Total System Global Area        4480888 bytes
            Fixed Size            47152 bytes
         Variable Size          4015944 bytes
      Database Buffers           409600 bytes
          Redo Buffers             8192 bytes

SQLDBA> select name, enabled from v$datafile;
NAME                                    ENABLED
--------------------------------        -------
/home/orahome/data/721/system01.dbf     READ WRITE
/home/orahome/data/721/rbs01.dbf        READ WRITE
/home/orahome/data/721/tools01.dbf      READ WRITE
/home/orahome/data/721/users01.dbf      READ ONLY
/home/orahome/data/721/test1.dbf        READ WRITE
/home/orahome/data/721/temp.dbf         READ WRITE
6 rows selected.

SQLDBA> alter system switch logfile;
Statement processed.
SQLDBA> alter system switch logfile;
Statement processed.
SQLDBA> alter system switch logfile;
Statement processed.

SQLDBA> shutdown abort
ORACLE instance shut down.
SQLDBA> host
cosmos% rm /home/orahome/data/721/*.dbf
cosmos% cp /home/orahome/backup/*.dbf /home/orahome/data/721
```

```
cosmos% exit
SQLDBA> startup mount
ORACLE instance started.
Database mounted.
SQLDBA> recover database
ORA-00279: Change 6420 generated at 02/07/95 11:00:51 needed for thread 1
ORA-00289: Suggestion : /home/orahome/product/7.2.1/dbs/arch1_62.dbf
ORA-00280: Change 6420 for thread 1 is in sequence #62
Specify log: {<RET>=suggested ¦ filename ¦ AUTO ¦ FROM logsource ¦ CANCEL}

Applying suggested logfile...
Log applied.
Media recovery complete.
SQLDBA> alter database open;
Statement processed.
SQLDBA> select name, enabled from v$datafile;
NAME                                 ENABLED
--------------------------------     -------
/home/orahome/data/721/system01.dbf  READ WRITE
/home/orahome/data/721/rbs01.dbf     READ WRITE
/home/orahome/data/721/tools01.dbf   READ WRITE
/home/orahome/data/721/users01.dbf   READ ONLY
/home/orahome/data/721/test1.dbf     READ WRITE
/home/orahome/data/721/temp.dbf      READ WRITE
6 rows selected.
```

## Test 2

```
SQLDBA> startup
ORACLE instance started.
Database mounted.
Database opened.
Total System Global Area       4480888 bytes
            Fixed Size           47152 bytes
         Variable Size         4015944 bytes
      Database Buffers          409600 bytes
          Redo Buffers            8192 bytes
```

```
SQLDBA> select name, enabled from v$datafile;    All datafiles in read-write mode.
NAME                                 ENABLED
--------------------------------     -------
/home/orahome/data/721/system01.dbf  READ WRITE
/home/orahome/data/721/rbs01.dbf     READ WRITE
/home/orahome/data/721/tools01.dbf   READ WRITE
/home/orahome/data/721/users01.dbf   READ WRITE
/home/orahome/data/721/test1.dbf     READ WRITE
/home/orahome/data/721/temp.dbf      READ WRITE
```

```
6 rows selected.

SQLDBA> alter system switch logfile;
Statement processed.
SQLDBA> alter system switch logfile;
Statement processed.
SQLDBA> alter tablespace USERS read only;        Make USERS read-only.
Statement processed.
SQLDBA> alter system switch logfile;
Statement processed.


SQLDBA> shutdown abort
ORACLE instance shut down.
SQLDBA> host
cosmos% rm /home/orahome/data/721/*.dbf
cosmos% cp /home/orahome/backup/*.dbf /home/orahome/data/721
cosmos% exit
SQLDBA> startup mount
ORACLE instance started.
Database mounted.
SQLDBA> recover database
ORA-00279: Change 6507 generated at 02/12/95 18:33:31 needed for thread 1
ORA-00289: Suggestion : /home/orahome/product/7.2.1/dbs/arch1_70.dbf
ORA-00280: Change 6507 for thread 1 is in sequence #70
Specify log: {<RET>=suggested ¦ filename ¦ AUTO ¦ FROM logsource ¦ CANCEL}

Applying suggested logfile...
Log applied.
Media recovery complete.
SQLDBA> alter database open;
Statement processed.
SQLDBA> select name, enabled from v$datafile;
NAME                                  ENABLED
---------------------------------     -------
/home/orahome/data/721/system01.dbf   READ WRITE
/home/orahome/data/721/rbs01.dbf      READ WRITE
/home/orahome/data/721/tools01.dbf    READ WRITE
/home/orahome/data/721/users01.dbf    READ ONLY
/home/orahome/data/721/test1.dbf      READ WRITE
/home/orahome/data/721/temp.dbf       READ WRITE
6 rows selected.
```

Restore datafile from backup. File is in read-write mode at backup.

File is in read-only mode after recovery. It works!

## Test 3

```
SQLDBA> startup
ORACLE instance started.
Database mounted.
```

```
Database opened.
Total System Global Area         4480888 bytes
            Fixed Size            47152 bytes
          Variable Size         4015944 bytes
        Database Buffers         409600 bytes
            Redo Buffers           8192 bytes
```

SQLDBA> **select name, enabled from v$datafile;** ──────  users01.dbf is in read-only mode.

```
NAME                                ENABLED
--------------------------------    -------
/home/orahome/data/721/system01.dbf   READ WRITE
/home/orahome/data/721/rbs01.dbf      READ WRITE
/home/orahome/data/721/tools01.dbf    READ WRITE
/home/orahome/data/721/users01.dbf    READ ONLY
/home/orahome/data/721/test1.dbf      READ WRITE
/home/orahome/data/721/temp.dbf       READ WRITE
6 rows selected.
```

SQLDBA> **alter system switch logfile;**
Statement processed.
SQLDBA> **alter system switch logfile;**
Statement processed.
SQLDBA> **alter tablespace USERS read write;** ──    Make USERS read-write.
Statement processed.
SQLDBA> **alter system switch logfile;**
Statement processed.

SQLDBA> **shutdown abort**
ORACLE instance shut down.
SQLDBA> **host**
cosmos% **rm /home/orahome/data/721/*.dbf** ─ Simulate loss of datafile.    Restore datafile
cosmos% **cp /home/orahome/backup/*.dbf /home/orahome/data/721**─ from backup. File is
cosmos% **exit**                                                    in read-only mode.
SQLDBA> **startup mount**
ORACLE instance started.
Database mounted.
SQLDBA> **recover database**
ORA-00279: Change 6551 generated at 02/12/95 18:39:37 needed for thread 1
ORA-00289: Suggestion : /home/orahome/product/7.2.1/dbs/arch1_72.dbf
ORA-00280: Change 6551 for thread 1 is in sequence #72
Specify log: {<RET>=suggested ¦ filename ¦ AUTO ¦ FROM logsource ¦ CANCEL}

Applying suggested logfile...
Log applied.
Media recovery complete.
SQLDBA> alter database open;
Statement processed.
SQLDBA> **select name, enabled from v$datafile;** ─  After recovery, datafile is in read-write
                                                    mode. It Works!
```
```

```
NAME                                       ENABLED
--------------------------------           -------
/home/orahome/data/721/system01.dbf        READ WRITE
/home/orahome/data/721/rbs01.dbf           READ WRITE
/home/orahome/data/721/tools01.dbf         READ WRITE
/home/orahome/data/721/users01.dbf         READ WRITE
/home/orahome/data/721/test1.dbf           READ WRITE
/home/orahome/data/721/temp.dbf            READ WRITE
6 rows selected.
```

## Test 4

```
SQLDBA> select name, enabled from v$datafile;  ──────  Datafile users01.dbf is in
NAME                                       ENABLED         read-only mode.
--------------------------------           -------
/home/orahome/data/721/system01.dbf        READ WRITE
/home/orahome/data/721/rbs01.dbf           READ WRITE
/home/orahome/data/721/tools01.dbf         READ WRITE
/home/orahome/data/721/users01.dbf         READ ONLY
/home/orahome/data/721/test1.dbf           READ WRITE
/home/orahome/data/721/temp.dbf            READ WRITE
6 rows selected.

SQLDBA> alter system switch logfile;
Statement processed.
SQLDBA> alter system switch logfile;
Statement processed.
SQLDBA> shutdown abort
ORACLE instance shut down.
SQLDBA> host
cosmos% rm /home/orahome/data/721/*.dbf    ──────────  Simulate loss of datafile.
cosmos% rm /home/orahome/data/721/*.ctl    ──────────  Simulate loss of current control file.
cosmos% cp /home/orahome/backup/*.dbf /home/orahome/data/721─ Restore datafile from backup.
cosmos% cp /home/orahome/backup/*.ctl /home/orahome/data/721─ Restore backup control file.
cosmos% exit
SQLDBA> startup mount
ORACLE instance started.
Database mounted.

SQLDBA> recover database using backup controlfile;
ORA-00283: Recovery session canceled due to errors                ┐ Oracle
ORA-01233: file 4 is read only - cannot recover using backup controlfile │ can't recover
ORA-01110: data file 4: '/home/orahome/data/721/users01.dbf'      ┘ read-only files.
                                                                    Take files
SQLDBA> alter database datafile '/home/orahome/data/721/users01.dbf' offline; ── offline.
Statement processed.
SQLDBA> recover database using backup controlfile;
ORA-00279: Change 6522 generated at 02/12/95 18:34:54 needed for thread 1
ORA-00289: Suggestion : /home/orahome/product/7.2.1/dbs/arch1_70.dbf
ORA-00280: Change 6522 for thread 1 is in sequence #70
Specify log: {<RET>=suggested ¦ filename ¦ AUTO ¦ FROM logsource ¦ CANCEL}
```

```
Applying suggested logfile...
Log applied.
ORA-00279: Change 6539 generated at 02/13/95 16:19:08 needed for thread 1
ORA-00289: Suggestion : /home/orahome/product/7.2.1/dbs/arch1_71.dbf
ORA-00280: Change 6539 for thread 1 is in sequence #71
ORA-00278: Logfile '/home/orahome/product/7.2.1/dbs/arch1_70.dbf' no longer needed
for this recovery
Specify log: {<RET>=suggested ¦ filename ¦ AUTO ¦ FROM logsource ¦ CANCEL}

Applying suggested logfile...
Log applied.
ORA-00279: Change 6542 generated at 02/13/95 16:19:38 needed for thread 1
ORA-00289: Suggestion : /home/orahome/product/7.2.1/dbs/arch1_72.dbf ── Asking log sequence number
ORA-00280: Change 6542 for thread 1 is in sequence #72              72, which is an online log file.
ORA-00278: Logfile '/home/orahome/product/7.2.1/dbs/arch1_71.dbf' no longer needed
for this recovery
Specify log: {<RET>=suggested ¦ filename ¦ AUTO ¦ FROM logsource ¦ CANCEL}
/home/orahome/data/721/redo03.log ────────────  Apply one of the online logs.
Applying logfile...
Log applied.
Media recovery complete. ──────────────────  Successful recovery!

SQLDBA> alter database open resetlogs;
Statement processed.
SQLDBA> alter tablespace users online; ─────────  Bring read-only tablespace online.
Statement processed.
SQLDBA> select name, enabled from v$datafile; ─────  Verify it works!
NAME                                  ENABLED
------------------------------        -------
/home/orahome/data/721/system01.dbf   READ WRITE
/home/orahome/data/721/rbs01.dbf      READ WRITE
/home/orahome/data/721/tools01.dbf    READ WRITE
/home/orahome/data/721/users01.dbf    READ ONLY
/home/orahome/data/721/test1.dbf      READ WRITE
/home/orahome/data/721/temp.dbf       READ WRITE
6 rows selected.
```

## Test 5

```
SQLDBA> archive log list
Database log mode              ARCHIVELOG
Automatic archival             ENABLED
Archive destination            /home/orahome/product/7.2.1/dbs/arch
Oldest online log sequence     69
Next log sequence to archive   71
Current log sequence           71

SQLDBA> select name, enabled from v$datafile; ─────  All files in read-write mode.
NAME                                  ENABLED
------------------------------        -------
/home/orahome/data/721/system01.dbf   READ WRITE
/home/orahome/data/721/rbs01.dbf      READ WRITE
/home/orahome/data/721/tools01.dbf    READ WRITE
```

```
/home/orahome/data/721/users01.dbf     READ WRITE
/home/orahome/data/721/test1.dbf        READ WRITE
/home/orahome/data/721/temp.dbf         READ WRITE
6 rows selected.

SQLDBA> create table test_5 (c1 number) tablespace users;
Statement processed.
SQLDBA> insert into test_5 values(5);
1 row processed.
SQLDBA> commit;
Statement processed.

SQLDBA> alter system switch logfile;
Statement processed.
SQLDBA> alter tablespace USERS read only;
Statement processed.
SQLDBA> archive log list
Database log mode                 ARCHIVELOG
Automatic archival                ENABLED
Archive destination               /home/orahome/product/7.2.1/dbs/arch
Oldest online log sequence        70
Next log sequence to archive      72
Current log sequence              72

SQLDBA> alter database backup controlfile to '/home/orahome/data/721/ro_control.ctl';
Statement processed.
SQLDBA> alter system switch logfile;
Statement processed.
SQLDBA> shutdown abort
ORACLE instance shut down.
SQLDBA> host
cosmos% rm /home/orahome/data/721/*.dbf
cosmos% rm /home/orahome/data/721/*.ctl
cosmos% cp /home/orahome/backup/*.dbf /home/orahome/data/721
cosmos% cp /home/orahome/backup/*.ctl /home/orahome/data/721
cosmos% exit

SQLDBA> startup mount
ORACLE instance started.
Database mounted.
SQLDBA> recover database using backup controlfile;
ORA-00279: Change 6539 generated at 02/13/95 17:02:34 needed for thread 1
ORA-00289: Suggestion : /home/orahome/product/7.2.1/dbs/arch1_71.dbf
ORA-00280: Change 6539 for thread 1 is in sequence #71
Specify log: {<RET>=suggested ¦ filename ¦ AUTO ¦ FROM logsource ¦ CANCEL}


Applying suggested logfile...
Log applied.
ORA-00279: Change 6562 generated at 02/13/95 17:05:37 needed for thread 1
ORA-00289: Suggestion : /home/orahome/product/7.2.1/dbs/arch1_72.dbf
ORA-00280: Change 6562 for thread 1 is in sequence #72
ORA-00278: Logfile '/home/orahome/product/7.2.1/dbs/arch1_71.dbf' no longer needed
for this recovery
Specify log: {<RET>=suggested ¦ filename ¦ AUTO ¦ FROM logsource ¦ CANCEL}
```

Set tablespace USERS to read-only mode.

Take backup of control file as a precautionary measure.

Simulate loss of data file.
Simulate loss of current control file.
Recover datafile from backup.
Recover control file from backup.

Recover database.

```
Applying suggested logfile...
Log applied.
ORA-00279: Change 6566 generated at 02/13/95 17:07:27 needed for thread 1
ORA-00289: Suggestion : /home/orahome/product/7.2.1/dbs/arch1_73.dbf
ORA-00280: Change 6566 for thread 1 is in sequence #73
ORA-00278: Logfile '/home/orahome/product/7.2.1/dbs/arch1_72.dbf' no longer needed
for this recovery
Specify log: {<RET>=suggested | filename | AUTO | FROM logsource | CANCEL}
/home/orahome/data/721/redo01.log
Applying logfile...
Log applied.
Media recovery complete. ─────────────────      Recovery complete!

SQLDBA> select name, enabled from v$datafile; ───   Check status of datafiles from the control
NAME                                ENABLED            file. USERS01.dbf is not read-only yet.
--------------------------------    -------
/home/orahome/data/721/system01.dbf    READ WRITE
/home/orahome/data/721/rbs01.dbf       READ WRITE
/home/orahome/data/721/tools01.dbf     READ WRITE
/home/orahome/data/721/users01.dbf     READ WRITE
/home/orahome/data/721/test1.dbf       READ WRITE
/home/orahome/data/721/temp.dbf        READ WRITE
6 rows selected.

SQLDBA> alter database open resetlogs; ─────────   Open database.
Statement processed.
SQLDBA> select * from test_5;
C1
--
5
1 row selected.
SQLDBA> select name, enabled from v$datafile; ───   Now file is read-only. It worked!
NAME                                ENABLED
--------------------------------    -------
/home/orahome/data/721/system01.dbf    READ WRITE
/home/orahome/data/721/rbs01.dbf       READ WRITE
/home/orahome/data/721/tools01.dbf     READ WRITE
/home/orahome/data/721/users01.dbf     READ ONLY
/home/orahome/data/721/test1.dbf       READ WRITE
/home/orahome/data/721/temp.dbf        READ WRITE
6 rows selected.
```

# Test 6

```
SQLDBA> archive log list
Database log mode              ARCHIVELOG
Automatic archival             ENABLED
Archive destination            /home/orahome/product/7.2.1/dbs/arch
Oldest online log sequence     68
Next log sequence to archive   70
Current log sequence           70
```

```
SQLDBA> select name, enabled from v$datafile;                    File USERS01.dbf is in read-only mode.
NAME                               ENABLED
--------------------------------   -------
/home/orahome/data/721/system01.dbf    READ WRITE
/home/orahome/data/721/rbs01.dbf       READ WRITE
/home/orahome/data/721/tools01.dbf     READ WRITE
/home/orahome/data/721/users01.dbf     READ ONLY
/home/orahome/data/721/test1.dbf       READ WRITE
/home/orahome/data/721/temp.dbf        READ WRITE
6 rows selected.
SQLDBA> alter system switch logfile;
Statement processed.
SQLDBA> alter tablespace users read write;                       Change datafile to read-write mode.
Statement processed.
SQLDBA> alter database backup controlfile to '/home/orahome/data/721/rw_control.ctl';
Statement processed.
```

Backup the control file. This is ABSOLUTELY necessary and very important.

```
SQLDBA> create table test_6 (c1 number);
Statement processed.
SQLDBA> insert into test_6 values (6);
1 row processed.
SQLDBA> commit;
Statement processed.
SQLDBA> alter system switch logfile;
Statement processed.
SQLDBA> archive log list
Database log mode                  ARCHIVELOG
Automatic archival                 ENABLED
Archive destination                /home/orahome/product/7.2.1/dbs/arch
Oldest online log sequence         70
Next log sequence to archive       72
Current log sequence               72


SQLDBA> shutdown abort
ORACLE instance shut down.
SQLDBA> host
cosmos% rm /home/orahome/data/721/*.dbf       Simulate datafile     Restore datafile and
cosmos% rm /home/orahome/data/721/*.ctl       and control file loss. control file from backup.
cosmos% cp /home/orahome/backup/*.dbf /home/orahome/data/721
cosmos% mv /home/orahome/data/721/rw_control.ctl /home/orahome/data/721/control01.ctl
cosmos% exit


SQLDBA> startup mount
ORACLE instance started.
Database mounted.
SQLDBA> recover database using backup controlfile;               Recover database.
ORA-00279: Change 6507 generated at 02/12/95 18:33:31 needed for thread 1
ORA-00289: Suggestion : /home/orahome/product/7.2.1/dbs/arch1_70.dbf
ORA-00280: Change 6507 for thread 1 is in sequence #70
Specify log: {<RET>=suggested | filename | AUTO | FROM logsource | CANCEL}

Applying suggested logfile...
Log applied.
ORA-00279: Change 6532 generated at 02/13/95 16:48:01 needed for thread 1
```

```
ORA-00289: Suggestion : /home/orahome/product/7.2.1/dbs/arch1_71.dbf
ORA-00280: Change 6532 for thread 1 is in sequence #71
ORA-00278: Logfile '/home/orahome/product/7.2.1/dbs/arch1_70.dbf' no longer needed
for this recovery
Specify log: {<RET>=suggested ¦ filename ¦ AUTO ¦ FROM logsource ¦ CANCEL}

Applying suggested logfile...
Log applied.
ORA-00279: Change 6545 generated at 02/13/95 16:50:06 needed for thread 1
ORA-00289: Suggestion : /home/orahome/product/7.2.1/dbs/arch1_72.dbf
ORA-00280: Change 6545 for thread 1 is in sequence #72
ORA-00278: Logfile '/home/orahome/product/7.2.1/dbs/arch1_71.dbf' no longer needed
for this recovery
Specify log: {<RET>=suggested ¦ filename ¦ AUTO ¦ FROM logsource ¦ CANCEL}
```
**/home/orahome/data/721/redo03.log**
```
Applying logfile...
Log applied.
Media recovery complete.  ──────────────────────  Recovery complete!

SQLDBA> select name, enabled from v$datafile;  ──────  It works!
NAME                                ENABLED
--------------------------------    -------
/home/orahome/data/721/system01.dbf   READ WRITE
/home/orahome/data/721/rbs01.dbf      READ WRITE
/home/orahome/data/721/tools01.dbf    READ WRITE
/home/orahome/data/721/users01.dbf    READ WRITE
/home/orahome/data/721/test1.dbf      READ WRITE
/home/orahome/data/721/temp.dbf       READ WRITE
6 rows selected.

SQLDBA> alter database open resetlogs;
Statement processed.
SQLDBA> select * from test_6;
C1
--
6
1 row selected.
```

## Observation

Test 1 shows that while doing media recovery with one of the data files in
read-only mode, Oracle does recovery as it normally would. In this case, all the
data files are taken from point A (see scenario 1 of Figure 7-3) and the current
control file used. However, in test 4 we performed the same test, but used the
backup control file from point A as well. When you use a backup control file, you
have to start up the database with the RESETLOGS option. Any read-only files
should be offline, otherwise the RESETLOGS option has to write to read-only files.
For this reason, when you use the backup control file, Oracle asks you to take the
read-only data files offline. Note that the read-only tablespace can be brought
online again once we open the database with the RESETLOGS option. It is very
important to note that Oracle will allow you to read no files from before a

RESETLOGS was done, with the exception of read-only tablespaces and any tablespaces that are taken offline with the *normal* option.

For test 2, we did media recovery by restoring the data files from point A and using the current control files. After the recovery is done and the database opened, tablespace USERS is in read-only mode. Test 5 is identical to test 2, except a backup of the control file from point A is used. If you use a backup control file from point B in this case, recovery won't work because you have to take the USER's data files offline. This is because the control file from point B will identify the USER's data files as read-only. So we need to have a backup copy of the control file that recognizes the files as being in read-write mode from point A.

In test 3, as opposed to test 2, some of the restored data files from point A have a read-only status. If the current control file is used, you don't need to worry about the recovery since it doesn't matter if there are any data files with read-only status. However, as shown in test 6, when a backup control file is used, it cannot be from point A but has to be from point B (or anywhere between points B and C). The reason for this is that if you use the backup control file from point A, the control file identifies the USER's data files as being in read-only mode, so you have to take them offline. If the data files are taken offline, the changes made to the data files between points B and C are not applied as part of recovery.

To summarize the above tests, you need to note the following points:

1. If you are using the current control file, crash recovery or media recovery with a read-only data file is no different from a read-write file. There is nothing special you need to do. Oracle will recognize the files and do the appropriate recovery automatically.

2. If the data file is in read-only mode and doesn't change to read-write during media recovery, the file should be offline during recovery if you are using a backup control file. You should bring the tablespace online after recovery.

3. If you are doing media recovery and if any data files switch between read-only and read-write mode during recovery, you should use the current control file if available. If you don't have a current control file, then use a backup control file that recognizes the files in read-write mode. If you don't have a backup control file, then create a new control file using the **create controlfile** command.

4. From the above three points, it should be clear that you *should* take a backup of the control file every time you switch a tablespace from read-only mode to read-write mode, and vice versa.

# Case 16: Problem Solving with Standby Databases

The purpose of this case study is to show solutions to commonly encountered problems when using the standby database feature with Oracle7 Release 7.3. In this case study we discuss four common problem areas. Under each problem area, we will discuss some of the common *symptoms* and the suggested *solutions*.

## Different Operating System Configurations on Standby and Primary Databases

If different configurations are used for the primary and standby databases, then problems may occur at the standby database. Using different operating systems usually does not work because of different storage formats.

**Symptoms:**    Cannot start or mount the standby database, or, initialization parameters are reported as invalid.

**Solution:**    Problems caused by different configurations will usually show up when the standby database is started. Errors reporting that *initialization parameters are not recognized* usually indicate that the parameters are not supported by Oracle on that platform. Whenever problems are encountered when starting or mounting the standby database, check that the versions of the operating system and Oracle software match those at the primary. If errors are reported when the standby database is mounted, then check that all controlfiles are present and current.

## Activating

When the primary database fails, you need to activate the standby database.

**Symptoms:**    Cannot open the standby database.

```
alter database open;
*
ORA-01666: controlfile is for a standby database
```

**Solution:**    An easy mistake through force of habit. To activate the standby database, use the **ALTER DATABASE ACTIVATE STANDBY DATABASE** command.

## Controlfiles

Because the standby database has a different control file than the primary, it's easy to run into some common problems with control files.

**Symptoms:** Control file rejected at startup.

```
alter database mount standby database;
*
ORA-01665: controlfile is not a standby controlfile
```

**Solution:** The most common problem when starting a standby database is attempting to use the wrong controlfile. For example, the primary controlfile was copied to the standby site instead of the standby controlfile. Use a controlfile created with the **ALTER DATABASE CREATE STANDBY CONTROLFILE** command.

**Symptoms:** Controlfile not found at startup.

```
alter database mount standby database;
*
ORA-00205: error in identifying control file
'/ds1/oracle/7.3.1/dbs/ctl1stby.ctl'
ORA-07360: sfifi: stat error, unable to obtain information about file.
SEQUENT DYNIX/ptx Error: 2: No such file or directory
```

**Solution:** Ensure that a standby control file is available. If necessary you can copy and rename the control files to match those specified in the standby initialization file.

## Application of Archive Log Files

During maintenance of the standby database, if the primary database continues to run but an archive is lost before application at the standby database, then the standby database cannot be made concurrent with the primary; that is, the standby database must be rebuilt.

**Symptoms:** Recovery process rejects an archive log file as invalid.

```
ORA-00279: Change 7799 generated at 09/13/95 16:46:06 needed for thread 1
ORA-00289: Suggestion : /ds1/oracle/7.3.1/dbs/arch/arch1_42.dbf
ORA-00280: Change 7799 for thread 1 is in sequence #42
ORA-00308: cannot open archived log /ds1/arch/arch1_42.dbf
ORA-07366: sfifi: invalid file, file does not have valid header block
```

**Solution:** The above error occurs because the physical structure of the file is not recognized. Check that the file was transferred correctly. This error can occur if **ftp** was used to transfer the file, but the *binary* option was not used. Another possibility is that the file format is incompatible with the standby operating system. Check that the same operating system and version is operating at the primary.

**Symptoms:**    Recovery process cannot find an archive.

```
ORA-00279: Change 7176 generated at 09/13/95 16:46:06 needed for thread 1
ORA-00289: Suggestion : /ds1/oracle/7.3.1./dbs/arch/arch1_41.dbf
ORA-00280: Change 7176 for thread 1 is in sequence #41
Specify log: {<RET>=suggested \ filename | AUTO | CANCEL}

ORA-00308: cannot open archived log /ds1/arch/arch_41.dbf
ORA-07360: sfifi: stat error, unable to obtain information about file
SEQUENT DYNIX/ptx Error: 2: No such file or directory
```

**Solution:**    Usually, the needed archive log file was not transferred to the standby database.

If you use an automatic mechanism to transfer and apply archives, then check that the automatic transfer script is running, and that the network and primary database are working properly. If so, ensure the needed archive log file is transferred to continue with automatic propagation and archive application.

If you are manually applying archives, then ensure that the archive log file is transferred and type AUTO to continue.

If you cannot obtain the needed archive log file because the primary has failed, then you must consider activating the standby database to make it the primary database.

**Symptoms:**    When manually applying archive log files, the recovery process rejects an archive log file.

```
ORA-00279: Change 8087 generated at 09/13/95 16:46:06 needed for thread 1
ORA-00289: Suggestion : /ds1/oracle/7.3.1./dbs/arch/arch1_57.dbf
ORA-00280: Change 8087 for thread 1 is in sequence #57
Specify log: {<RET>=suggested \ filename | AUTO | CANCEL}
/ds1/logs/log2st73.dbf
ORA-00310: archived log contains sequence 56; sequence 57 required
ORA-00334: archived log: '/ds1/logs/log2st73.dbf'
```

**Solution:**    Find the needed archive log file and type AUTO to continue. Ensure that the needed archive log file was transferred correctly. If a **copy** command was used to transfer the archive across a network, check that the filename is correct for the needed archive log file.

**Symptoms:**    Recovery process rejects archive log file as corrupted.

```
ORA-00279: Change 7799 generated at 09/13/95 16:46:06 needed for thread 1
ORA-00289: Suggestion : /ds1/oracle/7.3.1/dbs/arch/arch1_42.dbf
ORA-00280: Change 7799 for thread 1 is in sequence #42
Specify log: {<RET>=suggested | filename | AUTO | CANCEL}


ORA-00283: Recovery session canceled due to errors
ORA-00333: redo log read error block 2 count 256
```

**Solution:**    Assuming that the correct file was transferred, then it is possible that the file became corrupt because of the transfer mechanism. Check that the file transfer mechanism is not inappropriately converting the file to the wrong format. Ensure that the transfer is not occurring when the archive log files are being created. Re-obtain the completed archive log file from the primary database and restart recovery at the standby database.

**Symptoms:**    Data file is not found.

```
ORA-00279: change 22130 generated at 09/13/95 06:46:01 needed for thread 1
ORA-00289: Suggestion : /ds1/oracle/7.3.1/arch/arch1_71.dbf
ORA-00280: Change 22130 for thread 1 is in sequence #71
Specify log: {<RET>=suggested | filename | AUTO | FROM logsource| CANCEL
...
ORA-00283: Recovery session canceled due to errors
ORA-01670: new datafile 8 needed for standby database recovery
```

**Solution:**    This problem occurs when a datafile was added to the primary and not previously created at the standby database. The problem can be fixed at the standby database by creating the datafile and restarting recovery. Note that the recovery process only detects the problem after it has updated the standby controlfile, which now has all relevant information needed for the missing datafile. Thus, the V$DATAFILE can be used to obtain the missing datafile name, as follows.

**SELECT NAME FROM V$DATAFILE WHERE FILE#** = *filenumber;*

This command can be issued while the standby database is mounted. You don't need to activate the database. Use the *filenumber* shown in the ORA-1670, which in the above example is 8. Thereafter, you create the datafile using the ALTER DATABASE CREATE DATAFILE command, but *without* the size option. The size information is available in the standby controlfile.

# Summary

The above case studies should give you an idea of the kinds of failures that happen in the real world and how you should recover with no data loss. Here are some points you should remember while designing backup procedures or recovering a database from a failure:

- Always mirror control files.

- Always multiplex online redo log files and keep a copy on different disk drives mounted under different controllers.

- Try to take online or offline backups (or both) at frequent intervals, depending on your business needs. Automate all backup procedures. Keep a copy of all database files on tape as well as an online copy, if possible.

- Try to take logical backups of your database whenever you can. If it's a very big database, try taking exports of the important tables at least, if possible.

- Copy the archive log files to tape very frequently in addition to keeping a copy on disk. Mirror the disk that has the archived log files at the OS level.

- At least once every 3 months (or whenever appropriate) use a test machine to restore from a backup. Simulate various failures and try restoring the database.

- If the schema of the database changes (adding or dropping data files) always take a backup of the new data file(s) that you add and also a backup of the control file IMMEDIATELY. Also, update your automated backup procedures to include the new data file(s) that you added to the database.

- When a failure occurs, always check to see if you can do complete recovery. If not, then perform incomplete recovery. Always remember that you will lose data when you do incomplete recovery.

- Always check to see if you can do online recovery. If not, then perform offline recovery.

- Make sure that all the appropriate data files are online before attempting recovery. The view V$DATAFILE will help you get this information.

- Always try to use the current control file while trying to do recovery, if possible. If the current control file is not available, try creating a new control file. Use the backup control file as the last option, as you have to start up the database with RESETLOGS option.

- If you start the database with the RESETLOGS option, IMMEDIATELY plan for an offline or an online backup.

- Before calling Oracle Worldwide Support, make sure you gather all the diagnostics, as described in Chapter 6.

- Most importantly, be prepared for disasters. Don't think you will never see a failure. Every DBA will experience a database failure. It's just a matter of when.... Good Luck.

# APPENDIX A

# New Features
# of Oracle7 Releases
# 7.1, 7.2, and 7.3

This appendix lists all the references in this book to new features of Oracle7 in Releases 7.1, 7.2, and 7.3. Most of the major new features are listed without going into much detail. However, some of the database administration enhancements that affect backup and recovery are discussed in detail. If you are using Oracle7 Release 7.1, 7.2 or 7.3, some of these features are very useful to you as a DBA in administering the database. Some of the enhancements mentioned in this chapter are beyond the scope of this book. For detailed information, you should refer to the latest *Oracle7 Server Administrator's Guide*.

# New Features of Release 7.1

Some of the main features introduced or enhanced in release 7.1 are

- The Server Manager
- Symmetric replication
- Consistent snapshot refresh
- SQL and PL/SQL enhancements
- Read-only tablespaces
- Parallel recovery
- Parallel query option
- Dynamic SQL

To enable the new features introduced in release 7.1, the INIT.ORA parameter COMPATIBLE should be set to 7.1.0. A brief description of these new features is given below. For details, refer to the *Oracle7 Documentation Addendum for Release 7.1.*

## Server Manager

The Server Manager is the new Oracle administration tool with a graphical user interface (GUI). The Server Manager allows you to monitor and control the Oracle database easily. All of the common administrative tasks that are done through SQL*DBA can be executed using the menus of the Server Manager's graphical user interface. Alternatively, commands can by typed into the SQL Worksheet of the Server Manager and executed.

## Symmetric Replication

Symmetric replication allows multiple updatable copies of data at different sites in a distributed environment. For example, let's assume that three machines (say A, B, and C) are connected by a network. Each machine has an Oracle database and the same data is maintained in each database. If data is changed in the database residing on machine A, this change needs to be propagated to the databases on machines B and C. Similarly, changes made at B will be propagated to A and C, and so on. Symmetric replication allows you to replicate data, *n* ways.

A problem might arise, however, if the same data is modified at two different locations at the same time. For example, if the value of column X is changed to 20 at database A and changed to 30 at database B, we have created a conflict. Symmetric replication supplies automatic conflict-resolution routines. You might want to use one or more of these routines if you are using row-level replication. In addition to using the supplied conflict-resolution routines, you can create your own conflict-resolution functions as long as you adhere to the rules set by Oracle.

## Consistent Snapshot Refresh

Release 7.1 allows you to create a *snapshot group*. The snapshot group contains a collection of snapshots (for a discussion of snapshots, refer to the *Oracle7 Server Concepts Manual*). If two snapshots have a parent-child relationship, they should be placed under the same snapshot group. Oracle allows you to update all the snapshots in the snapshot group to the same point in time. This allows you to preserve the parent-child relationship between snapshots.

## SQL and PL/SQL Enhancements

Some additions have been made to the SQL syntax to make reading the SQL code easier. You can now use the AS keyword to define column/expression aliases in release 7.1. The defined alias can be used in an ORDER BY clause:

```
SELECT ename, empno AS id FROM emp ORDER BY id;
```

This really doesn't add any new functionality but makes it easy to read the SQL code.
    Release 7.1 also allows user-defined PL/SQL functions to be used in SQL statement expressions. This increases the productivity of users and efficiency of the queries. For example, the PL/SQL functions can be called from the following:

- The select list of the SELECT statement
- The *condition* of the WHERE and HAVING clauses
- The CONNECT BY, START WITH, ORDER BY, and GROUP BY clauses
- The VALUES clause of the INSERT command
- The SET clause of the UPDATE command

Release 7.1 allows multiple triggers of the same type to be defined on a single table. This increases flexibility in applications. For example, user applications can use AFTER ROW triggers on tables that maintain snapshot logs.

## Read-Only Tablespaces

Some applications, such as data warehousing, contain large static tables that don't change after initial insertion of data. These tables are used for query only. Since the data never changes, it doesn't make sense to perform a backup of these tables too often. Release 7.1 allows the DBA to set a tablespace in *read-only* mode after the objects are created in the tablespace. When the tablespace is set to read-only mode, all the files belonging to the tablespace are set to read-only mode as well, and can be moved to a read-only device if desired. The files belonging to the read-only tablespace will not be updated by Oracle so static data can be stored in the read-only tablespaces, thereby avoiding the need for backup and recovery of such tablespaces.

To set a tablespace to read-only mode, the following conditions should be met:

- There should be no active transactions in the database.
- The tablespace should contain no rollback segments.
- The tablespace must be online.
- The tablespace must not be in hot backup mode.
- The INIT.ORA parameter COMPATIBLE should be set to 7.1.0 or greater.

When a tablespace is set to read-only mode, the control file is updated to indicate this change for all the files that belong to the tablespace. Read-only tablespaces can be taken online or offline just like any other tablespaces. If you wish to modify data in a read-only tablespace, you need to bring the tablespace to *read-write mode.* If the tablespace is residing on a read-only device (e.g., an optical disk), the files should first be relocated to a writable device. Once the tablespace is set to read-write mode, backups should be performed on the tablespace again. The following examples show how to set a tablespace to read-only mode and read-write mode.

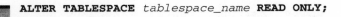

**ALTER TABLESPACE** *tablespace_name* **READ ONLY;**

**ALTER TABLESPACE** *tablespace_name* **READ WRITE;**

When an Oracle instance crashes, Oracle performs either instance or crash recovery. Normally, crash/instance recovery ignores read-only data files as there will be no changes (redo) to be applied to the read-only data files. If read-only data files are restored from a backup taken when they were in read-write mode, media recovery needs to be applied. Media recovery can recover read-only data files from their backups (even if the backup files are in read-write or read-only mode) as long as all the redo belonging to the data files is available and the current control file is used during media recovery.

If a backup control file is used to do media recovery, and if the data file is in read-only mode, an ORA-1233 error will occur. If recovery is not required for the read-only file, it should be taken offline first, before doing media recovery. However, if recovery is required for this file because at some point during roll forward the file might be in read-write mode, an appropriate backup of the control file, which indicates that the data file is in read-write mode, should be used. Alternatively, a new control file can be created before doing media recovery. The new control file should have only the read-write files in *online* status and the read-only files should be in *offline* status.

## Parallel Recovery

*Mean time to recover* (MTTR) is a key factor while running mission-critical databases or very large databases (VLDB) with high availability requirements. While Oracle7 doesn't fully exploit the system resources such as CPU, memory, and I/O on symmetric multiprocessor (SMP) and massively parallel processor (MPP) systems, release 7.1 provides the ability to do database recovery using multiple threads. The INIT.ORA parameter RECOVERY_PARALLELISM determines the number of parallel processes to use for any recovery operation. If you are using parallel server configuration, the total number of recovery processes is divided among the available instances. While issuing the **recover database**, **recover tablespace**, or **recover datafile** commands, the **parallel** option can be specified. For example,

```
RECOVER DATABASE PARALLEL DEGREE 5 INSTANCES 2;
```

specifies that there should be five recovery processes applying redo entries to data files on each instance. We have also specified that there are two instances that should use parallel recovery. This means that the total number of recovery processes used will be ten.

The process that issues the **recover** command is a *dedicated process* (or *coordinator process*) that starts *slave* processes. The dedicated process reads the redo entries from the redo log files and forwards the change vectors to the slave processes. The slave processes read the data blocks into the cache and apply the changes. Data blocks are split between slave processes, and Oracle makes sure that changes to a particular data block are always sent to the same slave process. This ensures that all changes to a data block are applied in SCN order.

Using synchronous I/O, benchmarking figures show that parallel recovery could be up to nine times faster compared to non-parallel recovery. Using asynchronous I/O, the improvement is less significant (about two times faster). In both cases, a large number of processes were used while benchmarking. On operating systems that don't support asynchronous I/O, it's reasonable to have four to six parallel recovery processes per CPU. On operating systems that do support asynchronous I/O, a relatively small degree of parallelism is sufficient.

# Parallel Query Option

Today, we have massively parallel processor (MPP) machines such as nCUBE that allow parallel processing. We also have symmetric multiprocessor (SMP) machines such as IBM 3090, Pyramid Niles, Sequent, and VAX/VMS 6600. These machines share memory and/or disks (clusters). Parallel hardware requires software that can exploit multiple CPUs, multiple disks, and high bandwidth data transfer. Oracle release 7.1 introduces the *parallel query option*, which includes the following features:

- Parallel data query
- Parallel index creation
- Parallel data loading

The performance of bulk operations like queries, index creation, and data loading can be improved with parallel processing on multiple CPUs. The performance gain has been found to be almost linearly scaleable. The parallel query option is useful for data-intensive operations associated with VLDB or DSS (Decision Support Systems) applications.

## Parallel Data Query

Parallel data query (PDQ) uses the operator model of parallelism and supports both inter-operator and intra-operator parallelism. Parallelism is achieved by creating and managing *slave* processes or *query servers* and coordinating the execution through a single process called the *query coordinator*. The query coordinator breaks down the execution functions into parallel pieces and then integrates the partial results produced by the slave processes. The slave processes are called upon during execution of the SQL statement and not during the parsing of the statement. The number of slave processes determines the *degree of parallelism* for a query. The query coordinator uses information such as the hints of a query, the table's definition, and INIT.ORA parameters to decide how to parallelize a statement and how many slave processes to use. The following is a list of operators that can be parallelized:

- Table Scan
- Nested Loops Join and Sort Merge Join

- Union All
- Group By and Order By
- Distinct
- Union, Intersect, and Minus

The degree of parallelism can be set by using a hint in the SQL statement, using the PARALLEL option in the **create table/cluster** command, or using the PARALLEL option in the **alter table/cluster** command. For complete syntax, refer to *Oracle7 Server Documentation Addendum Release 7.1*. The following examples show different ways to set the degree of parallelism:

```
SELECT  /* + FULL(table_name) PARALLEL (table_name 5) */ column FROM table_name;

CREATE TABLE table_name(column_name type) PARALLEL (DEGREE 5 INSTANCES 2);

ALTER TABLE table_name PARALLEL (DEGREE 4);
```

In the above examples, HINT is used in the **select** statement to specify that the degree of parallelism is 5. The *table_name* is the name of the table you want to specify. The second example shows how to specify the degree of parallelism while creating the table. The last example shows how to modify the degree of parallelism for an existing table by using the **alter table** command.

## Parallel Index Creation

While building indexes on large tables that are a few gigabytes in size, it takes a lot of time to create indexes. This could impact performance and affect the applications. While running DSS applications it might be necessary to create indexes frequently. Serial index builds don't exploit the system resources. Release 7.1 allows building indexes in parallel by multiple processes. *Parallel create index* uses the same process management and communication mechanisms used with *parallel data query*. One set of query processes scans the table to obtain the rowids and column values for the column to be indexed. The other set of processes then performs the sort of index entries and passes the values to the query coordinator. The query coordinator builds the B*-tree index using the sorted lists.

Parallelism can be specified by users while creating the index in the **create index** command. If parallelism is not specified while creating the index, it defaults to the parallelism associated with the table. For example,

```
CREATE INDEX index_name ON table_name (column_name) PARALLEL (DEGREE 4);
```

### Parallel Data Loading

Parallel data loading allows multiple SQL*Loader processes to load into the same table concurrently. Parallelizing direct path loads enables effective utilization of I/O resources as well as CPU. Each parallel loader session acquires a shared lock on the table. Separate extents are acquired by each session to load data into. At the end of the load, all extents are merged and allocated to the segment. Any unused blocks in the last extent of each segment are returned to the database as free space. Each session will input data from its input file to a specific data file. For example, the following command should be typed at the O/S prompt to invoke a SQL*Loader session.

```
SQLLOAD USERID=SCOTT/TIGER CONTROL=LOAD1.CTL DIRECT=TRUE PARALLEL=TRUE
```

## Dynamic SQL

The DBMS_SQL package allows the use of dynamic SQL in stored procedures and anonymous PL/SQL blocks. Both DDL and DML statements can be parsed with DBMS_SQL, allowing objects to be created or dropped from within a PL/SQL procedure. This is not possible in 7.0.

# New Features of Release 7.2

The features of release 7.2 can be categorized into the following areas:

- Database administration enhancements
- Application development enhancements
- Miscellaneous

The enhancements in each of the categories are described in this section.

# Database Administration Enhancements

*Parallel Create Table as Select* is a new feature that lets you copy tables in the database. The *unrecoverable* and *parallel* components let you copy the tables faster with multiple concurrent processes. Also, the space management tasks for DBAs are made simple by allowing the data files to grow dynamically. Some of the recovery procedures are automated, reducing the administrative work for the DBA.

## Parallel Create Table as Select

The *Parallel Create Table as Select* feature is designed to improve management of DSS-type applications in data warehousing environments. Both the process of table population and the populating subquery are executed in parallel. In release 7.1, however, only the subquery was parallelizable. For clustered tables the population is still serial though. Redo logging can be turned off by using the UNRECOVERABLE option for **create table as select** and **create index** operations with observed performance gains of up to 30 percent. Undo is never logged for these operations. For clustered tables both undo and redo are always logged. Consider the following example:

```
CREATE TABLE emp_sal (empno, comm CHECK (comm < 2000), sal NOT NULL)
UNRECOVERABLE
PARALLEL (DEGREE 3)
AS SELECT empno, comm, sal FROM emp;
```

This example creates the table *emp_sal* by copying the data from the *emp* table. The full table scan on the *emp* table, the population of the *emp_sal* table, and the enforcement of the NOT NULL and CHECK constraints on the *emp_sal* table are all performed as parallel operations. The UNRECOVERABLE option turns off redo logging for the new table or for any indexes that are created on the table as a result of enabling constraints specified in the **create table as select** command. If the RECOVERABLE/UNRECOVERABLE option is omitted, Oracle takes the default value based on these criteria: If the database is operating in the ARCHIVELOG mode, the default value would be RECOVERABLE; otherwise, the default would be UNRECOVERABLE. The **create index** command works the same way as the **create table as select** command with the same options.

If a table is created using the **create table as select** command with the UNRECOVERABLE option, then the DBA should take a backup of the new table by using the export utility. If the data files are lost after an index or table creation, the DBA should restore the data files from a backup and perform media recovery. Media recovery will recover all the objects except for the ones created with the UNRECOVERABLE option. During recovery Oracle marks these objects as *logically corrupt*. If you try to access these objects after recovery, the ORA-1578 error will occur. The unrecoverable objects should be dropped and re-created. If a table is created with the UNRECOVERABLE option and an index is created on that table with the RECOVERABLE option, then media recovery would logically corrupt the table but not the index. However, the index points to corrupt blocks (since the table blocks are corrupted). In this case, the index needs to be dropped and re-created as well, after the table is recreated.

### Resizable Datafiles

This feature reduces the amount of DBA intervention required by space management issues. With Oracle7 release 7.1 or earlier, Oracle errors such as the ORA-1547 and ORA-1625 are common problems when you run out of space. With the new *resizable data files* feature, data files can be dynamically extended without altering or recreating the tablespace. This operation can be performed automatically with predetermined increments up to a maximum size (or the OS maximum). Similarly, unused space in data files can be reclaimed on demand. Consider the following examples:

```
ALTER DATABASE DATAFILE 'filename' 50M;

ALTER DATABASE DATAFILE 'filename' AUTOEXTEND OFF;

ALTER DATABASE DATAFILE 'filename' AUTOEXTEND ON NEXT 100K MAXSIZE 250M;
```

The first example manually increases or decreases the data file size to 50MB. The file will reduce in size only if there is free space available. The second example terminates automatic expansion of the data file. The last example turns on automatic expansion for the data file. The size is incremented in chunks of 100K. If the space needed for the new extent is greater than 100K, then the required size is added. The file extends until it reaches 250MB.

The data file resizing can also be specified in the **create database**, **create tablespace**, and **alter tablespace** commands. The new data dictionary table **filext$** stores information about data files that have automatic expansion turned on.

### Backup and Recovery Enhancements

The new *checksum* feature allows early detection of database corruptions through the new INIT.ORA parameters LOG_BLOCK_CHECKSUM and DB_BLOCK_CHECKSUM. If the parameter LOG_BLOCK_CHECKSUM is set to TRUE, Oracle allows redo block corruptions to be detected earlier during archiving or recovery. If all members of the log file have invalid checksums, archiving will hang. Note that you should set the COMPATIBLE parameter in INIT.ORA to 7.2.0 or higher if using this checksum. When the DB_BLOCK_CHECKSUM parameter is enabled, Oracle calculates the checksum of each data block (when read into cache from disk for the first time) and stores it in the data block header. The next time the data block is read, the checksum is validated to detect corrupt data blocks. The checksum is a measure of the state of the entire block. The DB_BLOCK_CHECKSUM parameter existed with a different name in previous releases of Oracle7 and was not documented. These parameters should be turned on when suggested by Oracle Worldwide Support.

The next important functionality change is related to online backups. In previous releases of Oracle7, if the database crashes while performing online backups, media recovery is required during the next startup. Depending on the size of log files and the activity that was happening during the crash, the next startup could take a long time. With release 7.2, the command

**alter database datafile** '*filename*' **end backup;**

can be issued while the database is mounted and not open. This command allows online backup to be ended without performing media recovery. This command *must not* be used on files restored from an online backup, because in some cases, it is not possible for Oracle to distinguish between a restored file and a file that was in *online backup* mode when the database crashed. In such cases, using this parameter to bring up the database may cause database inconsistency and logical corruptions.

Another new feature is the **alter database clear log file** command. This command allows a corrupted log file to be cleared without resetting the log file.

# Application Development Enhancements

Important features have been added to PL/SQL in release 7.2. Some of them are discussed briefly here. For details, refer to *Oracle7 Server New Features and Options for Release 7.2*.

### PL/SQL Wrapper
The PL/SQL wrapper wraps (encrypts) package, package body, function, procedure, and trigger creation statements in SQL code, providing protection of application code. All other SQL statements are left intact, though comments (REM) outside a package or subprogram are deleted.

### Cursor Variables
Cursor variables allow a stored procedure to return the results of multirow queries to a client as cursor variables, from which individual rows can be fetched.

### Non-Blocking OCI
Non-blocking OCI allows client applications to return immediately from a server call, and then it polls the server to check whether the pending call finished. This is particularly useful in GUI and real-time applications.

### New Packages
The DBMS.SYSTEM package will allow a user to turn on SQL tracing for another session. The DBMS.INFORMATION package can be used to supply information

about the application to the RDBMS. This will give more meaning to the MODULE and ACTION fields in V$SESSION.

## Miscellaneous Features

Some of the miscellaneous features are related to network security, national language support, and hash clusters.

### NLSRTL 3.1
The new NLSRTL release 3.1 contains the following features:

- Run-time loadable NLS data
- Additional NLS environment variables
- Calendar systems
- Support for Arabic/Hebrew display character sets

### Network Security
Some key enhancements in network security are

- Secure external authentication
- Proxy authentication for remote login
- Authorization using network roles

### Hash Clusters
Release 7.2 allows user-specified hash functions to reduce collisions since no single hash function works well with a range of inputs. The hash function is stored in the base data dictionary table **cdef**$.

## New Features of Release 7.3

Some of the new features and enhancements of Release 7.3 are:

- Fast Transaction Rollback
- New Media Recovery Views

■ Thread Recovery Changes

■ Hot Standby Databases

For detailed information, you should refer to the *Oracle7 Server Administrator's Guide.*

# Fast Transaction Rollback (7.3)

Recalling from Chapter 5, (refer to "Recovery Methods" section) recovery is done in two parts. The first part is *roll forward*, which involves applying redo records to the corresponding data blocks through the cache, also known as cache recovery. The second part of recovery is *roll back* or *transaction recovery*, where active or uncommitted transactions are rolled back. After these two parts of the recovery is performed, the database is opened by Oracle for users to access.

Oracle7 release 7.3 uses the new *fast transaction rollback* feature for providing higher availability of the database and also to improve performance of transaction recovery. Higher availability is achieved by opening the database after cache recovery and before transaction recovery is performed. This is also known as *fast warmstart*. Performance of transaction recovery is improved by recovering multiple uncommitted transactions in parallel.

How does this work? This feature is relevant only when opening a database after a crash occurs. When the database is opened, Oracle performs cache recovery and rolls forward the database. Then the database is generally available for users. Full transaction recovery will occur after the database is opened. New transactions that do not touch the *active transaction* blocks are processed. Active transactions that need recovery are marked as *dead* for later recovery. Rollback segments that contain these active transactions are marked *partially available*. Rows locked by the failed transactions are not immediately available. TX locks are released after transaction has been recovered or rolled back.

In the past (before release 7.3), only PMON used to perform transaction recovery by serially performing *complete recovery* on transactions. Now PMON as well as foreground processes perform parallel recovery. PMON loops over the base data dictionary table **undo$** to find transactions that are marked dead or non-distributed and does *partial recovery* of transactions by applying a small number of redo records per transaction across all the rollback segments. This prevents short uncommitted transactions from backing up against long uncommitted transactions. This means PMON makes multiple passes over all the transactions that need recovery and applies certain amount of undo per pass. In addition to PMON, if a foreground process hits a row locked by a *need-to-be-recovered* transaction, then the foreground process recovers the transaction completely by itself. It also does partial recovery on the rest of the rollback segment.

## New Media Recovery Views

Some new x$views and v$views are added in release 7.3 to monitor media recovery. These views can be accessed after the recovery session is started. The views reside in the PGA and are destroyed when the recovery session is terminated.

### V$RECOVERY_FILE_STATUS

> FILENUM
> FILENAME
> STATUS

The status of the file can be "*In Recovery*", "*Current*" or "*Not recovered*". *In recovery* indicates that the file is being recovered. *Current* means the file needs no media recovery. *Not recovered* means the file is not being recovered because it is offline and **recover database** command was issued. Note that **recover database** command will recover only online datafiles. The offline datafiles will have a *Not recovered* status at that time. You should query for files with status='NOT RECOVERED' during recovery especially before opening the database with the RESETLOGS option.

### V$RECOVERY_STATUS

> REASON
> RECOVERY_CHECKPOINT
> THREAD
> SEQUENCE_NEEDED
> SCN_NEEDED
> TIME_NEEDED
> PREVIOUS_LOG_NAME
> PREVIOUS_LOG_STATUS

While all the columns are self explanatory, the *reason* column gives you the reason why recovery is returning control to the user at this point and can have the following values:

> NEED LOG—a new log name is needed
> LOG REUSED—an online log was overwritten and the archive copy is needed
> THREAD DISABLED—this thread was disabled at this point

After completion of recovery, the view **v$recovery_status** should have zero rows.

# Thread/Instance Recovery Changes

In an Oracle Parallel Server environment, during roll forward stage of thread/instance recovery, some internal changes have been made to improve performance.

# Standby Databases

Oracle7 Release 7.3 introduces a disaster recovery feature called the *Standby Database* or *Hot Standby Databases*. This new feature provides higher availability and is especially useful during catastrophic failures of the production database such as fire and earthquake which usually cause loss of entire machine.

This feature involves maintaining a duplicate, identical database called the standby database. This database is mounted and is in recovery mode. The archive log files generated at the production or *primary* site are transferred and applied to the standby database. When the primary database fails, the standby database is *activated* and the users are switched from the primary database to the standby database. For complete details on planning, implementation and maintenance of standby databases, refer to the "Disaster Recovery" section in Chapter 5.

# Index

## A

# U

# V

# W

# Oracle Education℠
# Is Your Source...

...for the most comprehensive selection of quality training available for Oracle products and related IT technologies.

**Instructor-Led Training:** In-depth knowledge, hands-on experience and personal guidance from expert instructors

**Oracle Learning Architecture:** Internet-based training providing immediate access to interactive, hands-on training straight from the Web

**The Oracle Channel:** Live, interactive training broadcast via satellite, ideal for expert-level technical drilldowns or broad overviews

**Organizational Change Management:** Maximizing your technology investment with organizational assessment, change management plans and total learning solutions

**Media-Based Training:** A variety of structured, self-paced courses deliverable to any desktop in your organization

Oracle Education works closely with Oracle software developers to provide you with the most **up-to-date and cost-effective training options** as new products are released. For more information, call **1.800.633.0575** for your copy of the *Oracle Education Americas Schedule and Catalog.*

## Call us today at
## 1.800.633.0575
or 301.657.7819 from outside the U.S.

You can also learn more about our offerings by visiting Oracle Education on the Web at **http://www.oracle.com** or by calling EASI InfoFax at **1.800.405.6336.**

ORACLE®
Enabling the Information Age™

# FUTURE CLASSICS FRO[M]

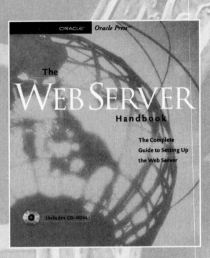

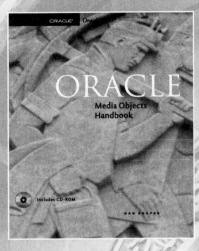

## THE WEB SERVER HANDBOOK

by Cynthia Chin-Lee and Comet

**Learn how to set up and maintain a dynamic and effective Web site with this comprehensive guide that focuses on Oracle's new Web solutions.**

ISBN: 0-07-882215-7
Price: $39.95 U.S.A.
Includes One CD-ROM

## ORACLE MEDIA OBJECTS HANDBOOK

by Dan Shafer

**The power, flexibility, and ease of Oracle Media Objects (the cross-platform multimedia authoring tools) are within your reach with this definitive handbook.**

ISBN: 0-07-882214-9
Price: $39.95 U.S.A.
Includes One CD-ROM

## ORACLE DEVELOPER'S GUIDE

by David McClanahan

**Loaded with code for common tasks, developers will find all the information they need to create applications and build a fast, powerful, and secure Oracle database.**

ISBN: 0-07-882087-1
Price: $34.95 U.S.A.

## ORACLE: THE COMPLETE REFERENCE

**Third Edition**

by George Koch and Kevin Loney

ISBN: 0-07-882097-9
Price: $34.95 U.S.A.

## ORACLE DBA HANDBOOK

by Kevin Loney

ISBN: 0-07-881182-1
Price: $34.95 U.S.A.

## ORACLE: A BEGINNER'S GUIDE

by Michael Abbey and Michael J. Corey

ISBN: 0-07-882122-3
Price: $29.95 U.S.A.

## TUNING ORAC[LE]

by Michael J. Corey, Michael Abbey, and Daniel J. Dechichio, Jr

ISBN: 0-07-881181-3
Price: $29.95 U.S.A.

# The Books to Use When There

Save Time and Get

the Information You

Need with this Critically

Acclaimed Series from

Osborne/McGraw-Hill.

**The Internet
for Busy People**
by Christian Crumlish
$22.95 USA
ISBN: 0-07-882108-8

**Windows 95
for Busy People**
by Ron Mansfield
$22.95 USA
ISBN: 0-07-882110-X

**Word for Windows 95
for Busy People**
by Christian Crumlish
$22.95 USA
ISBN: 0-07-882109-6

**Excel for Windows 95
for Busy People**
by Ron Mansfield
$22.95 USA
ISBN: 0-07-882111-8